Comparative Legal Aid Systems and India

This book provides an in-depth analysis of the functioning and challenges of the legal aid system in India. The legal aid system was set up to promote the interests of the economically weaker sections of society that did not have equitable access to judicial systems. However, the system has been largely unsuccessful in delivering justice.

Drawing on empirical data from 18 states and 36 districts in India, the book highlights the institutional setbacks that plague the legal aid system and urges us to take cognizance of the hindrances faced by the beneficiaries in availing of these services. It acknowledges the gaps that exist in the governance of the legal aid system in India at the grassroots level and suggests approaches and ways to address these roadblocks to deliver free, swift, and economical access to justice to the poor legal aid beneficiaries.

An important critical study of the commitment and competence of legal aid counsels in India, this volume will be an essential read for scholars and researchers of law, Indian law, constitutional law, political science, comparative law, law and gender, and social work.

Jeet Singh Mann, Teacher of Legal Education and Research, National Law University Delhi, India.

Comparative Legal Aid Systems and India

Jeet Singh Mann

Routledge
Taylor & Francis Group
LONDON AND NEW YORK

Cover image: © Highdog / Getty Images

First published 2023
by Routledge
4 Park Square, Milton Park, Abingdon, Oxon OX14 4RN

and by Routledge
605 Third Avenue, New York, NY 10158

Routledge is an imprint of the Taylor & Francis Group, an informa business

British Library Cataloguing-in-Publication Data
A catalogue record for this book is available from the British Library

Library of Congress Cataloging-in-Publication Data
A catalog record for this book has been requested

ISBN: 978-0-367-70338-7 (hbk)
ISBN: 978-0-367-74527-1 (pbk)
ISBN: 978-1-003-15832-5 (ebk)

DOI: 10.4324/9781003158325

Typeset in Sabon
by Apex CoVantage, LLC

Contents

Tables

Figures

Foreword

Justice to all is an unfinished agenda of legal education.

– *Srikrishna Deva Rao*

Law as a powerful instrument of social change played a crucial role in ameliorating the conditions of poor and marginalized communities in India. Access to justice is one such ameliorative function of catering justice to the unmet legal needs of citizens. It is also a constitutional right and a perambulatory promise. Indeed, legal aid is the constitutional duty of putting the power of law in the hands of the people.

The Gujarat Legal Aid Committee in 1971 memorably observed that "the ignorance and illiteracy of law of poor leads to helplessness and further impoverishment." The Committee further observed that if poor people are educated in their rights and obligations, it will serve three important ends. *First*, it would save them from legal troubles arising from ignorance. *Second*, it would enable them to seek legal advice in time, which would avoid further legal difficulties and prevent litigation. *Third*, it would generate power among the poor because knowledge is power. *Last*, it would make them self-reliant.

The two path-breaking reports of legal aid, *Processual Justice to People* (1973) and *National Judicare – Equal Justice – Social Justice* (1978), have inspired the emergence of the access to justice movement in India. They advocated the principle of equal justice that requires access to legal advice and assistance as a duty and responsibility of the state in the case of indigent people.

The actual emergence of legal aid activism in the early eighties was spearheaded by the pioneering work of the four judges of the Indian Supreme Court, Justices *P. N. Bhagawathi, V. R. Krishna Iyer, O. Chinnappa Reddy, and D. A. Desai.* The social action litigation, the Indian brand of public interest litigation, brought new themes and issues before the courts. The Supreme Court also invented new tools, methods, and mechanisms to sustain the development of the legal aid movement in India. *Prof. Upendra Baxi* succinctly pointed out that "the social action litigation expanded the regime of rights converting the Supreme Court of India into a permanent Constituent Assembly of India, sculpting the nature and future of rights movement."

Legal aid is a fundamental human right and integral to the right to life and personal liberty. It flows from the golden quadrangle of Articles 14, 21, 22, and 39A of the Indian Constitution. Even though legal aid and support have been a declared aspiration of the Indian Constitution, it was given a statutory footing only in 1987 with the passing of the National Legal Services Authority Act (NALSA). A comprehensive legal aid law, NALSA ensured that opportunities to secure justice are not denied to any citizen because of economic or other disabilities. Legal aid schemes were offered across states through legal aid boards, societies, and law departments after that.

Another significant effort of NALSA was introducing the paralegal volunteers (PLVs) in 2009 under the Legal Services Authorities (LSA) Act. Through this initiative, institutionalized paralegal services brought legal aid much closer to the people. The community paralegals will be better positioned to ensure justice for people and build synergies between law, society, and people.

Docket Exclusion

We hear about the crippling pendency of cases from all over India, but we rarely hear about denying the meaningful access of marginalized people to the legal system. We keep hearing that *docket explosion* is a problem, but we rarely seriously address *docket exclusion.*

This present book analyzes numerous impediments impacting the successful flow of legal aid services in India. The book presents the field experiences from the grassroots secured through empirical research. It underlines the issues faced by major stakeholders of the legal aid system ("LSA") in India. Further, the comparative study underscores the gaps and deficiencies pointed out by the legal aid beneficiaries, including women, judicial officers, regulators, and legal aid counsels. This book analyzes the legal aid practices around the globe, with a special focus on legal aid beneficiaries under the LSA Act, 1987. It provides an overall picture of the current state of the legal aid system in India.

Legal aid includes legal advice, assistance, representation, and education and creating enabling mechanisms for alternate dispute resolution to develop and maintain a just and fair legal system. Through its legal aid services system (LASS), the National Legal Services Authority provides legal aid in various forms to specified beneficiaries. The legal aid counsels (LACs) play a pivotal role in providing legal aid services. LACs are undoubtedly the most important agency in delivering access to justice to the beneficiaries. The real question is how far the LAS facilitates the needs of the poor and ensure adequate protection of their rights.

In several cases, the Supreme Court of India emphasized that providing legal aid is a constitutional obligation to the poor prisoners at all levels of the legal process beginning from their first production before the magistrate. *Hussainara Khatoon (AIR 1979 SC 1369)*, *Sunil Batra (AIR 1978 SC 1675)*, *Khatri [1981) 1 SCC 635]*, and *Re-Inhuman Conditions in 1382 Prisons [W P (C) NO. 406/2013]* emphasized the issues of legal aid to the needy and release of under-trials in the light of overcrowding of prisons in the different states of India. They also called for the establishment and proper functioning of under-trial review committees throughout the country. The book also reiterates the importance of effective prison legal aid, which may reduce prison overcrowding and the detention rate at the pretrial stage.

Justice to All

Justice to all is the spirit behind the legal aid movement in India, spanning over five decades. It advocates using the power of law to make the world a fair and just place for people to live in. The present book provides some answers to improve the overall quality of legal aid while expanding the services for the poor.

There is a massive "justice gap" between the massive demand for legal services for the poor and the inadequate resources of trained lawyers. Most of the Indian population are poor and illiterate and have inadequate access to legal services. The services of lawyers are costly, and the process of justice is prolonged. The litigation through the formal legal process is unable to serve the legal needs of the people. The impoverished communities need new kinds of legal education, new lawyering styles, and delivery of legal services. Legal education has to develop a new brand of clinical lawyers and community paralegals to serve the people who are excluded from the formal justice system.

It is true that the challenge of the justice gap cannot be solved simply with more lawyers, judges, and courthouses. Practicing law for people requires new tools, methods, and strategies of experiential learning by innovative clinical learning methods in partnership with the judiciary, legal professionals, and legal support groups in community settings.

Mauro Cappelletti identified three waves of access to the justice movement: *first*, the delivery of legal services to the poor; *second*, extending legal representation to diffuse interests; and *third*, a community dispute resolution system. I would like to add the *fourth* wave: legal empowerment, combining all three waves.

A paradigm shift and thinking are necessary to ensure quality and competent legal aid. The Indian National Education Policy, 2020, also underscores the broader access to justice and timely delivery of justice.

I appreciate my colleague, *Dr. Jeet Singh Mann*, and his team for undertaking this remarkable research study highlighting the key concerns affecting the free flow of legal aid services. I recommend this book to the legal aid fraternity to better understand its institution's intricate and practical realities in securing access to legal aid services both in letter and spirit.

In conclusion, access to justice for the poor is still a distant dream. Sustainable development goals provide another occasion to initiate massive education for the poor and the have-nots. The road to access to justice is always an unfinished agenda of the social justice mission of legal education.

Prof. Srikrishna Deva Rao
Vice Chancellor
National Law University Delhi
November 15, 2021

Preface

Nations across the globe offer legal aid services as a fundamental right of every citizen. To provide these services, governments created institutions through various instruments and apparatuses of legal aid services. Apart from government institutions, the judiciary is proactive, protective, and vocal in promoting free legal aid services for poor and needy people. One of the principal objectives of legal aid institutions is that they are entrusted to provide timely access to justice for society's lower strata. However, providing free legal aid services and the governance aspect of the legal aid services have always been an issue. Furthermore, the legal aid counsels' services have been an area of contention among the beneficiaries who avail of these free legal aid services.

This book is based on empirical research/study that primarily focuses on the level of commitment and competence of legal aid counsels (LACs) in India. It also emphasizes the beneficiaries' impediments while availing of the free legal aid services in India. This empirical study's scope extends across six zones in India, covering 36 districts in 18 states from the North, South, East, West, Central, and North East Zones of India. To collect accurate and representative data, the stratified sampling method was employed.

The book first delves into India's advent of the LAS and explains various instruments through which beneficiaries receive free legal aid services in India. It then focuses on the international aspect of free legal aid and offers a brief overview of the legal aid framework in various regions of the world. The other half elaborates upon the responses collected, collated, and analyzed from all the five stakeholders, including beneficiaries of legal aid, legal aid counsels, judicial officers, and regulators involved in governing and delivering the legal aid to beneficiaries at the district level.

These responses are answers to structured and unstructured questions asked from all the five stakeholders during the book's research. The questionnaires were broadly based on the parameters of commitment and competence of LACs and the factors liable for diminishing the trust of a potential beneficiary over the free legal services. Also, the questionnaires were distributed to the stakeholder's centers to evaluate and mark the level of proficiency skills of LACs for delivering the legal aid services in their respective districts.

Based on the feedback received from all the stakeholders, this book highlights that India's LAS is suffering from institutional setbacks and that there are hindrances faced by the beneficiaries in availing of legal aid services provided by the LACs. Thus, this book acknowledges the gaps existing in the governance of the LAS in India at the grassroots level, then suggests and recommends approaches and ways to address these roadblocks to deliver free, swift, and economical access to justice for the poor and needy legal aid beneficiaries in India.

The author would like to acknowledge the generous support from the Indian Council of Social Science Research (ICSSR), which has sponsored the research project titled *An Empirical Study to Examine the Impact of the Legal Aid Services by the Legal Aid Counsels on the Quality of the Legal Aid System in India*, 2017–19.

It also becomes essential to recognize the contributions made by skilled professionals during this research assignment. This research would not have been possible without the support and reassurance of judicial officers, regulators, LACs, and legal aid beneficiaries. The researcher is also grateful to the National Legal Services Authority (NALSA) for supporting the research team's accomplishments in collecting primary data from beneficiaries, LACs, and regulators.

The author also acknowledges the support and efforts of the team of research staff: Satyam Malaviya (research associate), for supervising field investigators in the districts; collecting, collating, and analyzing the data; and assisting with the writing of the book, and Pooja Tiwari (research assistant), for assisting with the editing. Finally, the book is also indebted to Prof. Srikrishna Deva Rao, vice chancellor of NLU Delhi, for supporting and relieving the author from all academic assignments during the book's said research. The author also acknowledges and is thankful for the efforts of various professionals who have directly or indirectly assisted and supported in the completion of the final research for the book.

Jeet Singh Mann
Teacher of Legal Education and Research
7 April 2021

Abbreviations

ADJ	additional/assistant district and sessions judge
AIR	All India Reporter
BLAS	Bombay Legal Aid Society
BPL	below poverty line
CAW	crimes against women
CHRI	Commonwealth Human Rights Initiative
CILAS	Committee for Implementing Legal Aid Schemes
CrPC	Code of Criminal Procedure, 1973
CSD	Council for Social Development
DLSA	District Legal Services Authority
FLAS	free legal aid service
FTC	fast track court
GoI	Government of India
HP	Himachal Pradesh
HC	high court
Hon'ble	Honorable
IBM	International Business Machines
ICSSR	Indian Council of Social Science Research
LAC	legal aid counsel
LAS	legal aid system
LASA	Legal Aid Services Authority
LASS	legal aid services system
LSA	Legal Services Authority
LSAA	Legal Services Authorities Act, 1987
MACT	Motor Accidents Claims Tribunal
NALSA	National Legal Services Authority
NGOs	non-governmental organizations
NLU	National Law University
Ors.	Others
PLP	private legal practitioner
PLV	paralegal volunteer
Prof.	Professor
RTI	right to information

SC	scheduled caste
SC	Supreme Court
SCC	Supreme Court cases
SCLSC	Supreme Court Legal Services Committee
SLSA	State Legal Services Authority
SPSS	Statistical Package for the Social Sciences
ST	scheduled tribe
UK	United Kingdom
USA	United States of America
UP	Uttar Pradesh
UDHR	Universal Declaration of Human Rights
v.	versus

1 Legal Aid System in India

1.1. Introduction

In India, the legal aid services for poor and needy people were institutionalized in November 1995. It received recognition as a fundamental right under Article 21[1] and as a directive principle of state policy under Article 39-A of the Constitution of India. Further, it is enshrined in various international and national legal instruments that promote social, economic, and political justice and access to justice for the deprived and underprivileged. For instance, the International Covenant on Civil and Political Rights, 1966, specifies under Article 14, para. 3 (d), that every individual should be entitled, *inter alia*,

> to be tried in his presence, and to defend himself in person or through legal assistance of his choosing; to be informed if he does not have legal assistance, of this right; and to have legal assistance assigned to him in any case where the interests of justice so require, and without payment by him in any such case if he does not have sufficient means to pay for it.

The Government of India (hereinafter referred to as "GoI") has been assigning significant resources for providing legal aid services in partnership with the state governments. Nonetheless, the ground reality portrays a substandard narrative of the legal aid system ("LAS") in India. It has been found that under the legal aid services, beneficiaries fail to trust the second-rate quality of the services offered by the legal aid counsels ("LACs"). This lack of faith stems from several factors that have even been acknowledged and pointed out by the Indian Supreme Court in a catena of cases. These include a lack of proper amenities and a lack of infrastructure for the justice delivery system under LAS. Although services offered by LACs are free of cost, people do not opt for them. Instead, they often opt for the services offered by private legal practitioners ("PLPs"). The preference given to paid services over free services raises many questions about the services offered by LACs. This empirical study is an attempt to assess the efficiency of LACs in India. The study assesses LACs based on their commitment and competence in dealing

DOI: 10.4324/9781003158325-1

with cases under free legal aid. The assertion for empirical research traces its base because LACs are comparatively less committed to the mandate of free legal aid.

Moreover, LACs are relatively incompetent in comparison to PLPs. This study examines the efficiency of empaneled LACs in India. The primary objective of this research is to recognize the deficiencies in the legal aid services that are provided by LACs and submit a viable solution to enhance the quality and efficiency of legal aid services in India. To achieve the stated objective of the research, competence, and commitment of LACs are two independent variables that ought to be analyzed.

1.2. An Outline of the Legal Aid System in India

The introduction and expansion of free legal aid services ("FLAS") are closely associated with a welfare state's ideals. The LAS intends to provide free legal services in civil and criminal matters to the society's poor and marginalized sections.[2] One can understand legal services as availing of a lawyer for the conduct of a case or a legal proceeding.

Traditionally, legal aid services have played an important role in guaranteeing people's economic, social, and cultural rights. They have helped in ensuring social security, social care, health care, fair employment law, and protection against discrimination.[3] As the rise of classic welfare states was underway worldwide, citizens and their respective states assumed a collective social responsibility to offer legal aid to those who were unable to avail of any legal assistance for themselves. The idea behind this was to enforce economic, social, and cultural rights through policies rather than individual legal action. Therefore, the formulation and enactment of laws to support these ideas became a widespread phenomenon. Legal aid schemes became a part of one such system. The establishment of these schemes was initially based on the state's responsibility to assist those engaged in legal disputes related to family law and divorce. It later stretched to cover every aspect of social life.

Consequently, the legal aid service schemes endeavored to fulfill the constitutional commitment in letter and spirit. They also seek to ensure that access to justice is equally available to the historically oppressed and weaker strata of the society. The state is obligated to see that the LAS promotes justice based on equality and equal opportunity for every citizen. It should provide free legal services to those who are unable to access justice because society's economic, social, and political structures act as constraints for them.[4]

In the realm of legislative policies and administration of justice, *social justice* as a key concept is a very modern term. Today, equality has become the very pulse of social movements and political organizations around the world. It is the basis of all modern systems of jurisprudence and the administration of justice.

The First Law Commission of India recognized this very aspect and stated, "Unless some provision is made for assisting the poor man for the payment of court fees and lawyer's fees and other incidental costs of litigation, he is denied equality in the opportunity to seek justice."[5] Hence, providing legal aid to indigent litigants becomes a question of fundamental character for any welfare state.

The preamble of the Constitution of India lays down what it seeks to achieve for the Indian citizens – social, economic, and political justice. Logical interpretation and implementation of the Constitution's provisions are the need of the hour so that legal justice is available for poor, indigent, weaker, helpless, and vulnerable sections of society.[6]

1.2.1. Evolution of Legal Aid Services in India

The history of legal aid in India dates back to the Vedic period as legal or social aid elements are mentioned in the Rig Veda. The quotient of social and cultural values of Indian society was high and harmonious in those times. According to Smritis, the objective of kingship was the enforcement of *dharma*. The administration of justice was one of the essential functions of the king. For instance, "a bona fide plaintiff could institute suits without payment of any court fees."[7] Although, then, there wasn't any separate institution or concept of legal aid, the village and community panchayats' justice reached even the poorest.

Further, an adequate formulation of the judicial system took place during the Mughal era. It is a well-documented fact in *Fiqu-e-Firoz-Shahi* that under Shah Jahan's reign, government *vakils* (advocates) were engaged to defend civil suits. Additionally, during the reign of Aurangzeb, the practices of appointing state lawyers known as *vakil-e-sarkar* or *vakil-e-sharai* to assist indigent litigants and give them free legal advice were popular.[8]

The concept of legal aid for the poor in India finds its roots in numerous conferences of law ministers and law commissions since 1952. Before this, in the pre-independence phase, there was only the Bombay Legal Aid Society ("BLAS"), which came into existence in 1924.[9] The main aim of BLAS was to make justice accessible to the poor. The credit for bringing GoI's attention towards the Rushcliffe Committee's recommendations goes to civil society.

Inspired by BLAS's suggestion, the Government of Bombay formulated a committee under Justice N. H. Bhagwati's chairmanship. For a person to be eligible for legal aid, the committee recommended a prima facie case test and (II) means test. Later, a legal aid scheme that focused on three-tier institutional structures was suggested by the Trevor Harris Committee in West Bengal to deliver free legal services.[10] Under the scheme, the court fee and process fee were waived off for the assisted party, and the legal aid fund was to bear such expenses.

In the year 1970, the Government of Gujarat appointed Justice P. N. Bhagwati as the Legal Aid Committee chairman. This committee's task was to propose various means to assist and provide free legal services to society's poor section. Additionally, Justice P. N. Bhagwati also presided over the State Legal Aid Committee's chairmanship to manage the pilot project of free legal aid and advice in Gujarat. This pilot project illuminated the path of India's current legal aid program, including installing legal aid camps in rural areas, working with NGOs, and establishing legal aid clinics.[11]

The principle of equal justice and free legal aid was stressed in the 14th Law Commission of India. The Law Commission report states that "if laws do not provide for equality of opportunity to seek justice to all segments of society, they have no protective value and unless some arrangement is made for providing a poor man the means to pay Court fees, advocates fees and other incidental costs of litigation, he is denied an opportunity to seek justice."[12]

In May 1973, under Justice V. Krishna Iyer as the chairperson, a committee conducted sample surveys and presented its findings in a report titled "Processionals Justice to Poor." The report deals with poverty and access to justice. It outlines the significance of an extensive LAS in India to let the law reach the people rather than compelling people to reach the law. It also notes the need for a constitutional basis for legal aid. It states that "legal aid is an integral part of the legal system, not a matter of charity or confined to the four walls of the court building."[13]

Later in 1977, a committee under the chairmanship of Justice P. N. Bhagwati and Justice Krishna Iyer recognized – in the report titled "National Juridicare Equal Justice and Social Justice" – that a lawyer's services play a vital role in access to justice.[14] It acknowledged that the current legal service structure reflected western ideas and that it failed to address the poor people's issues in terms of their legal problems. The committee admitted that programs like legal aid were aimed at transforming the socioeconomic structure of the society. It also highlighted that legal aid service program "must be framed in the light of socio-economic conditions prevailing in the country" and "the traditional legal service program, which is essentially court or litigation-oriented, cannot meet the specific needs and the peculiar problems of the poor in our country." The committee also drafted a legislation based on recommendations and named it Social Action Litigation.

In 1980, Justice P. N. Bhagwati supervised a national-level committee known as Committee for Implementing Legal Aid Schemes ("CILAS"), which was tasked with monitoring legal aid activities throughout the country. CILAS introduced *Lok Adalats* to India's legal justice system and provided a complementary forum to the litigants for conciliatory settlement of their disputes.[15] These developments led to the enactment of the Legal Services Authorities (LSA) Act, 1987, which provided a statutory base for legal aid programs across the country. The act made legal aid the very heart of access to justice. Since then, many delivery models, as discussed later in this chapter, have been in practice to address the legal-aid-related concerns of society's most vulnerable stratum.

1.2.2. *Sources of Constitutional Paradigm for Legal Aid Services in India*

In 1976, India's Constitution included the aspect of free legal aid under the 42nd Amendment Act. It amended Article 39A and aimed at providing free legal aid. Article 39A, Equal Justice and Free Legal Aid, after the amendment, reads that

> the State shall secure that the operation of the legal system promotes justice, based on an equal opportunity, and shall provide free legal aid, by suitable legislation or schemes or in any other way, to ensure that opportunities for securing justice are not denied to any citizen because of economic or other disabilities.

Apart from the previously mentioned constitutional provisions, the spectrum of legal aid services expands through various statutes that have explicitly acknowledged the right to legal aid. A few of these important statutes are the LSA Act, 1987; Order XXXIII of the Code of Civil Procedure, 1908; Section 304 of the Code of Criminal Procedure, 1973; the Scheduled Castes and the Scheduled Tribes (Prevention of Atrocities) Act, 1989; the National Legal Services Authority (Free and Competent Legal Services) Regulations, 2010; and the National Legal Services Authority (Legal Aid Clinics) Regulations, 2011. These enactments demonstrate that various legal instruments that strive to ensure FLAS are available within the Indian legislative and executive domain.

1.2.2.1. *The Code of Criminal Procedure, 1973*

Section 304 of the Code of Criminal Procedure entitles every accused person to receive legal services by a legal practitioner at the state's expense. The statute emphasizes that the state must be compliant with the provision during the pendency of cases before the court of session. It further gives the state the discretion to extend the section's application to any class of trial before other courts. The decision delivered by any court will be deemed invalid or null or void if the provisions under the section are not followed or are violated.[16]

The Supreme Court of India has reiterated the same in numerous landmark judgments. In *Khatri and Ors. (II) v. State of Bihar*,[17] the Supreme Court, while examining the nature and scope of Section 304, observes that

> the State is under a constitutional mandate to provide free legal aid to an accused person who is unable to secure legal services on account of the indigent and whatever is necessary for his purpose has to be done by the State. The State may have its financial constraints and their priority in the expenditure the law does not empower any Government

> to deprive its citizens of constitutional rights on a plea of poverty. Moreover, this constitutional obligation to provide free legal services to an indigent accused does not arise only when the trial commences but also attaches when the accused is for the first time produced before the magistrate. It is elementary that the jeopardy to his personal liberty arises as soon as a person is arrested and produced before a magistrate, for it is at that stage that he gets the first opportunity to apply for bail and obtain his release as to resist remand to police or jail custody. That is the stage at which an accused person needs competent legal advice, representation, and no procedure can be said to be reasonable, fair, and just, which denies legal advice and representation to him at this stage. We must, therefore, hold that the State is under a constitutional obligation to provide free legal services to an indigent accused not only at the stage of trial but also at the stage when he is first produced before the magistrate as also when he is remanded from time to time.[18]

1.2.2.2. *The Code of Civil Procedure, 1908*

In the domain of civil cases, a provision for legal aid comes in the form of Order XXXIII of the Code of Civil Procedure, 1908. It allows any indigent person to carry out legal proceedings before civil courts without paying the court fee.[19] It further enables the civil court to assign a legal practitioner for any such person who is incapable of doing so.[20]

1.2.2.3. *The Legal Services Authorities Act, 1987*

The LSA Act, 1987, aims to incorporate the essence laid in Article 39A of the Constitution of India.[21] It established a pan-India network that provides free and fair legal services to the disadvantaged sections of society. The act made the state guarantee a legal system that endorses justice based on equal opportunity for every individual and where the constitutional principles are fulfilled in letter and spirit. It structured legal services authorities across the country so that they are able to provide professional legal services of the empaneled lawyers to society's weaker strata free of cost. The idea behind the act is to make social justice available to people whose access to judicial bodies and administrative tribunals gets hindered due to social, legal, and financial difficulties. Under the act, FLAS is offered at all levels of the Indian judicial system – including the Supreme Court, high courts, subordinate courts, and tribunals.

Upon reading Section 12 and Section 13 of the act, it can be noted that certain categories of persons are eligible to avail of legal aid services. Per Section 2(1)(aaa), "court" means "a civil, criminal or revenue court and includes any tribunal or any other authority constituted under any law for the time being in force, to exercise judicial or quasi-judicial functions." The term "legal services" is defined under Section 2(1)I as including "the rendering of any service in the conduct of any case or other legal proceeding before any court or other authority or tribunal and the giving of advice on any legal matter."

The LSA Act, 1987, also formulates various statutory bodies that play a key role in administering the LAS in India. It established the National Legal Services Authority ("NALSA"), which oversees and monitors the operational aspects of India's legal aid programs. The act also established the Supreme Court Legal Services Committee ("SCLSC") for the Supreme Court, the High Court Legal Services Committee ("HCLSC") in every high court, the District Legal Services Committee ("DLSC") at the district level, and *Taluka* Legal Services Committee ("TLSC") to administer and manage legal aid services at their respective level.[22]

1.2.2.4. National Legal Services Authority

The National Legal Services Authority ("NALSA") is constituted under Chapter 2, Section 3 of the LSA Act, 1987. NALSA is a national-level statutory body that exercises powers and functions assigned to it by the LSA Act. As the apex and central body of India's legal aid domain, it lays down the policies and principles to frame economic and effective legal aid schemes. The authority is also responsible for organizing legal aid camps, encouraging dispute settlement through alternative methods, undertaking social justice litigation, disbursing funds and grants to the State Legal Services Authorities ("SLSA"), and so on. It is also tasked with promoting legal literacy in universities, law colleges, and legal aid clinics.

1.2.2.5. Supreme Court Legal Services Committee

The LSA Act, 1987, established the Supreme Court Legal Services Committee ("SCLSC"). The legal aid covers the cost of preparing the matter. It also covers the advocate's fees for preparation and argumentation in the case. To avail of benefits, a beneficiary is required to apply to the committee with all the case-related documents. They are also supposed to establish their eligibility for receiving legal aid. The SCLSC also covers legal aid services for individuals coming from the middle-income group administered by the Supreme Court Middle Income Group Society.

1.2.2.6. State Legal Services Authority

The LSA Act, 1987, makes it mandatory to have a State Legal Services Authority ("SLSA") in every state. The SLSA administers the policies and schemes of NALSA at the state level. It manages various District Legal Services Authorities ("DLSAs") within its jurisdiction and organizes *Lok Adalats* apart from providing FLAS. SLSAs are headed by the chief justices of respective high courts in every state, while a serving or retired judge of the high court serves as the executive chairperson of the SLSA.

1.2.2.7. District Legal Services Authority

At the district level, the District Legal Services Authority ("DLSA") holds the command to administer legal aid services schemes and policies. The chairperson of the DLSA is the district judge of the respective district court.

1.2.2.8. Taluka *Legal Services Committee*

To further the cause of access to justice and penetrate legal aid to the grassroots level, the LSA Act, 1987, under Sections 11-A and 11-B, focuses explicitly on the role of the *Taluka* Legal Services Committee ("TLSC"). The working mechanism of TLSC consists of their respective state rules and regulations in the administration of legal aid. TLSCs are often headed by a senior civil judge who is also the ex officio chairperson of the committee.

1.2.3. The National Legal Services Authority (Free and Competent Legal Services) Regulations, 2010

1.2.3.1. FLAS and Eligible Persons

Section 12 of the LSA Act, 1987, lays down who all are entitled to avail of FLAS.[23] The individuals from weaker sections of the society, including those belonging to vulnerable groups, such as scheduled castes, scheduled tribes, women, and children, are covered under the act.[24] Besides, it also covers workers in an industrial setup and persons in custody.[25] The legal aid services may also be granted in cases of great public importance or in other special cases that deserve legal aid services.[26]

In terms of setting the income limit for individuals eligible for free legal aid, Section 12 (h) follows a ceiling limit, the upper limit, which varies from every state. Other than these, in cases before the Supreme Court, a person will be entitled to free legal aid only if they are in receipt of an annual income that is less than INR five lakhs.[27]

The NALSA (Free and Competent Legal Services) Regulations, 2010,[28] provide the regulations that govern the structure of free legal services in India. Under Regulation 5, if a person provides and submits a self-attested proof and self-certification that they belong to the category of entitled persons as laid down in Section 12 of the LSA Act, 1987, at the time of applying to a competent authority, then the applicant qualifies for free legal services.[29] If an individual is incapable of applying with self-attested proofs because they are either disabled or illiterate, then the designated SLSA, DLSA, or TLSC is obligated to make a filling arrangement on behalf of the applicant.[30]

1.2.3.2. The Extent of FLAS

A potential beneficiary can get the benefits of FLAS. These services expand from the disbursement of process fees, court fees, and various other charges incurred while drafting or preparing for legal proceedings by the designated panel lawyer.[31] Additionally, the executive chairperson of the legal institution may maintain a separate group of senior lawyers, retired judicial officers, councilors, and so on to facilitate FLAS beneficiaries by drafting and conveying.[32] The scope of free legal services also covers the cost incurred in supplying the certified judgment copies and maintaining other legal proceedings papers.[33]

However, the scope of FLAS does not cover offenses related to the cases falling in the domain of defamation, contempt of court, economic offenses, and offenses described as against the Protection of Civil Rights Act, 1955, and the Immoral Traffic (Prevention) Act, 1956.[34] The free legal services can be withdrawn if any discrepancy is found in the applicants' eligibility criteria.[35] The benefits availed of under LSA Act, 1987, and NALSA Regulations, 2010, can also be axed if there is a change in the financial status of a beneficiary or the beneficiary is not cooperating with the Legal Aid Committee while availing of the free legal services. Further, the free legal services can no longer be availed of in case a beneficiary is deceased.[36]

1.2.3.3. Selection and Appointment of the Panel Lawyers

To take up the cases under the LSA Act, 1987, by providing free legal services, legal institutions empanel a group of lawyers to either advise or represent beneficiaries during litigation. It is desirable that these panels comprise panel lawyers having varied interests and expertise in different branches of legal practice.

Usually, in actual practice, applicants for empanelment as panel lawyers are required to have experience in dealing with criminal cases for not less than three years if they are seeking empanelment at any magisterial court and around five years of experience in dealing with criminal cases if they are seeking empanelment at a sessions court.

For instance, the monitoring committee often seeks applicants who have at least two years of experience in civil courts before a civil judge (ARC, ACJ, SCJ, guardianship courts) and at least five years of practice if an applicant is seeking empanelment at the level of civil courts before ADJs, Labor, MACT, and so on. In order to be empaneled for undertaking family court cases, an applicant must have at least five years' experience in matrimonial cases related to litigation.

Similarly, for empanelment in tribunals (Central Administrative Tribunal, Armed Forces Tribunal, National and State Consumer Disputes Redressal Commission, National Green Tribunal, etc.), applicants should have at least five years' work experience before these tribunals or in the same area. These panels are usually constituted for a three-year cycle, and the list of empaneled lawyers is revised after every cycle.

1.2.3.3.1. CRITERION FOR LACS TO BE EMPANELED AT HIGH COURT LEGAL SERVICES COMMITTEE

To be empaneled in the High Court Legal Services Committee ("HCLSCs") in various states, an advocate is expected to hold a certain degree of experience. This includes at least five years of standing at the bar of that particular high court for matters before a single bench and at least seven years of standing and practice in matters before the division bench.

1.2.3.3.2. QUALIFICATION FOR EMPANELMENT ON THE JAIL VISITING PANEL

If an advocate wants to be inducted as a jail visiting advocate, they must usually have at least three years of experience in litigation at the high court to be eligible for empanelment in the jail visiting panel. The applicant should also have significant experience in handling criminal cases before the high court and must be well-versed with rules for drafting petitions and appeals at the high court.

1.2.3.4. Procedure for the Appointment of LACs

Legal services institutions, such as DLSA, SLSA, HCLSC, and SCLSC, invite applications for legal practitioners working under their respective jurisdictions for empanelment as panel lawyers.[37] The applicants have to submit their eligibility-related documents and particularly point out their respective types of cases that they are well-versed with and that they may prefer after empanelment.[38]

The applications received are scrutinized by either the executive chairman or the chairman of the legal services institution. The scrutinization is conducted with the consultation of an attorney general for the Supreme Court, an advocate general for the high court, a district attorney or government pleader for various districts and their *talukas*, and the presidents of respective bar associations at every level.[39] Additionally, the executive chairperson of the legal services institution can empanel any legal practitioner without any such procedure.[40] After selecting the required strength of panel lawyers, the DLSAs and TLSCs must get approval from the executive chair of the SLSA.[41] Legal services institutions may maintain separate panels based on the types of cases, such as criminal law, civil law, constitutional law, juvenile justice, labor law, and environmental law.[42] The reconstitution of the panel takes place every third year after new panel lawyers have been inducted.[43] The legal services institutions may withdraw any case from a panel lawyer during any stage of the proceedings.[44] Similarly, panel lawyers may also withdraw from the cases assigned to them after stating a proper reason for withdrawal to the member secretary or secretary, and they may be relieved after a proper order.

1.2.3.5. Payment of Honorarium to Panel Lawyers

The panel lawyers are paid honorarium as mentioned in their respective schedule of the fee approved under the state regulations.[45] The SLSA and DLSA carry out periodic revisions in the schedule of fees based on a panel lawyer's services and other considerations.[46] The panel lawyers are entitled to receive their honorarium as soon as they submit the report of completion of proceedings.[47] Further, panel lawyers also receive financial assistance in selective legal aid cases based on additional expenditures, like summoning the witnesses or documentation expenses for obtaining certified copies.[48]

1.2.3.6. The Front Office's Accountability in the LAS of India

The legal services institution maintains a front office in which a retainer lawyer and a paralegal sit during office hours.[49] These front offices serve as the single window for potential legal aid beneficiaries to receive FLAS or information about their legal aid cases.[50] The front office also receives the application for legal aid services from the beneficiaries.

1.2.3.7. Accountability of LACs: Monitoring

To ensure and maintain the panel lawyers' accountability, legal services institutions have a monitoring committee to monitor free legal services' activities and operations and enhance the cause of various legal aid schemes in India.[51] The monitoring committee is mandatory at every level of the judicial system in India. In the case of the Supreme Court, the committee consists of a senior advocate or an advocate with at least 15 years of experience and a renowned academician or an advocate-on-record with more than ten years of experience, both nominated by the chairperson, the secretary, and a legal consultant from SCLSC.[52] Similarly, at the high court level, the monitoring committee consists of a nominated senior advocate or an advocate with at least 15 years and the secretary of HCLSC.[53] Likewise, at the state or district level, the monitoring committee consists of a member secretary or secretary of either the SLSA or DLSA, one serving judicial officer from the state's higher judicial services, and one retired judicial officer or an advocate of 15 years' standing.[54]

The monitoring committee maintains the record of every court-based legal aid case provided to applicants at their respective legal services institutions.[55] The committee further assists the institution in terms of planning various training programs for panel lawyers.[56] The committee maintains a day-to-day register to monitor the progress of legal aid cases in terms of their success or failure.[57] The register is scrutinized every month by the chairperson or secretary of the legal services institutions for any fault or discrepancies.[58] The committee meets at least once a fortnight.[59]

The committee prepares a twice a month report about its assessment for every legal aid case and submits it to the executive chairperson of their respective legal services institutions.[60] The report includes the performances of panel lawyers and retainers.[61] The legal services institutions send a copy of these bimonthly reports to their respective central authorities to evaluate legal aid schemes' quality.[62]

1.2.4. Preventive and Strategic Legal Services Schemes

NALSA has also introduced issue-centric schemes. These new schemes, also known as preventive and strategic legal services schemes, specifically focus on aiding and uplifting people who face socioeconomic stigmas or are disadvantaged in any other way.

1.2.4.1. NALSA (Legal Services to Disaster Victims Through Legal Services Authorities) Scheme, 2010

Section 12€ of the LSA Act, 1987, makes the victims of disasters (natural or otherwise) eligible for FLAS. Based on this, the scheme delves into strategic intervention at the time of disaster to safeguard the right of access to justice for the victims of any disaster.

The scheme helps in minimizing the impact of disasters and provides an avenue to recover from their adverse effects. The scope of strategic intervention ranges from ensuring immediate help to governmental and nongovernmental agencies to counseling the victims who have been subjected to psychological shock. This scheme's fundamental objective is to provide legal services to the victims of unwanted circumstances (ethnic violence, caste atrocities, flood, drought, earthquakes, industrial disasters, etc.).

1.2.4.2. NALSA (Victims of Trafficking and Commercial Sexual Exploitation) Scheme, 2015

This scheme emerges from Section 4 (b) of the LSA Act, 1987, which focuses on the "Central Authority [NALSA here] to frame the most effective and economic scheme" for making legal services available to every beneficiary eligible under the act. It can be understood that victims of commercial sexual exploitation, those who were either wtrafficked and forced into sex work or voluntarily took it up, are highly marginalized and vulnerable groups of society. The scheme focuses on delivering free legal services and addressing the concerns of victims of trafficking at every stage – be it prevention, rescue, and/or rehabilitation. The role of SLSAs/DLSAs is to bridge the gap between the respective institutions and the victim and sensitize all departments and institutions on trafficking. It is important to note that this scheme is also applicable to transgender people.

1.2.4.3. NALSA (Legal Services to the Workers in the Unorganized Sector) Scheme, 2015

The unorganized sector in India is at the core of the economy as it employs a very significant majority of the total workforce. The most distinct feature of this sector is its lack of compliance with most of the labor laws. Since unorganized workers lack collective bargaining power, this scheme aims to institutionalize essential legal services for all unorganized workers.

The scheme also aims to make workers engaged in the unorganized sector aware of the statutory provisions regarding their legal rights. Under the scheme, legal services institutions identify the categories and number of unorganized workers. Further, the scheme also provides instruments for the SLSA to formulate special cells. These special cells comprise one panel lawyer specializing in labor laws. It is important to note that under this scheme, the special cells will provide legal assistance and legal aid by way of legal representation before any court as required by the unorganized workers.

1.2.4.4. NALSA (Child-Friendly Legal Services to Children and Their Protection) Scheme, 2015

This scheme emerges from Section 12(c) of the LSA Act, 1987, which states that a child is eligible for FLAS. The fundamental objective of this scheme is to outline the rights and benefits of children. The scheme strives to ensure legal representation for the children in need of care and protection. The scheme also aims to create an environment of juvenile justice where children's rights are valued and respected. The scheme mandates SLSAs and DLSAs to organize awareness programs to educate the public and all the stakeholders in the legal aid services on child rights and their protection, on protection services that are available, and about relevant schemes at all levels.

1.2.4.5. NALSA (Legal Services to the Mentally Ill and Mentally Disabled Persons) Scheme, 2015

Section 12 of the LSA Act, 1987, provides FLAS to all the disabled as defined in clause (i) of Section 2 of the Persons with Disabilities (Equal Opportunities, Protection of Rights and Full Participation) Act, 1995. This scheme focuses on and covers persons with disabilities because they are either sidelined by the authorities or face marginalization in some other way. The objective behind this scheme is the removal of stigmatization of the specially abled in the LAS. It guides the legal services institutions to understand the human rights and aspirations of disabled persons. The scheme also directs the legal services institutions to promote respect for the mentally disabled persons' inherent dignity and independence. The scheme aims at preventing mentally disabled persons' exploitation and abuse and seeks to protect them from any form of discrimination.

1.2.4.6. NALSA (Effective Implementation of Poverty Alleviation Schemes) Scheme, 2015

The preamble of the LSA Act, 1987, underlines that legal services authorities are supposed to focus on the weaker sections of the society and emphasizes that access to justice shall not be denied to any citizen based on economic or other disabilities. This scheme deals with the problems of widespread poverty and related difficulties in accessing legal institutions. The scheme defines poverty as a multidimensional experience and does not limit it to the issues of income. This scheme's primary objective is to ensure access to fundamental rights and benefits for socially or economically weaker sections of society. The scheme aims to strengthen legal aid services at national, state, district, and *taluka* levels for marginalized sections of society. The scheme encourages the promotion and organization of awareness programs for panel lawyers, paralegal volunteers ("PLVs"), and officers about poverty alleviation schemes to enhance their skill set that may eventually help them in developing a more profound sense of engagement with poor people. The scheme further obliges the state authorities to hold meetings every six months to review this scheme's functioning and effectiveness.

1.2.4.7. NALSA (Protection and Enforcement of Tribal Rights) Scheme, 2015

NALSA launched this scheme intending to improve the conditions of tribal people from the perspective of their access to justice. The scheme focuses on facilitating access to justice on every possible front, such as access to rights, legal aid, and benefits. NALSA's principal motive for this scheme is to assure that the constitutional guarantee of justice – social, economic, and political – is truly experienced by the country's tribal population. The scheme guarantees to keep a tab on various constitutional and legal rights of tribal people, such as the Fifth and Sixth Schedules of the Constitution; the Scheduled Tribes and Other Traditional Forest Dwellers (Recognition of Forest Rights) Act, 2006 ("FRA"); and the Scheduled Castes and Scheduled Tribes (Prevention of Atrocities) Act, 1989. This scheme ensures that violation of the legal rights of tribal peoples does not take place. The scheme directs the SLSAs to take initiatives related to litigation where an exclusive panel of lawyers drawn from the tribal communities should be in the panel. The scheme further obligates the DLSAs to identify tribal populations in the districts and educate them about their legal and fundamental rights.

1.2.4.8. *NALSA (Legal Services to the Victims of Drug Abuse and the Eradication of the Drug Menace) Scheme, 2015*

The recent and tremendous rise of drug trafficking and drug abuse among youth, children, and adolescents in India has become a significant issue. Although many state agencies and NGOs are working in the field to eradicate drug abuse, there is a lack of coordination between them. Focusing upon this very issue, the 13th All India Meet of State Legal Services Authorities in Ranchi passed a resolution to include drug abuse and trafficking as a significant area of concern for all the legal services institutions. This scheme's principal objective is to spread awareness among the masses about the legal provisions, policies, and schemes in respect of narcotic drugs and psychotropic substances. The SLSA, under this scheme, is supposed to formulate ten-member special cell units in all the *talukas*, *mandals*, and subdivisions in the state. The scheme also mandates that these special cell units visit the rehabilitation and de-addiction centers at least once a month.

1.2.4.9. *NALSA (Legal Services to Senior Citizens) Scheme, 2016*

Senior citizens face innumerable challenges in social, physical, mental, and economic terms, which are unique to their peculiar circumstances. Further, the level of crime against senior citizens is also an indication of the urgent requirement for legal services and related institutional structures to fit their needs. Taking these factors into consideration, NALSA formulated this scheme in 2016. This scheme's primary objective is to strengthen the LAS to represent senior citizens at the national, state, district, and *taluka* levels. The scheme aims to ensure that the authorities and institutions, such as tribunals and the appellate tribunals under the Maintenance and Welfare of Parents and Senior Citizens Act, 2007, and old age homes for senior citizens have been established and are properly functioning. To achieve these objectives, the schemes mandate SLSAs to set up legal services clinics at every tribunal and appellate tribunal to assist the senior citizens with well-trained PLVs.

1.2.4.10. *NALSA (Legal Services to Victims of Acid Attack) Scheme, 2016*

The number of acid attacks in India has alarmed the citizenry in the recent past few years. Not only are they the most pernicious form of violence resorted to, but they also tend to be gender-specific. Therefore, NALSA came forward with this scheme in 2016 with the intention of strengthening legal aid for victims of acid attacks so that they may avail of the benefits of various legal provisions and compensation schemes. The scheme's mandate is to ensure that every acid attack victim gets access to medical facilities and rehabilitation services. To ensure the objectives mentioned earlier, the scheme mandates SLSAs and DLSAs to make sure that acid attack victims do not face any delay in procedural wrangles and that interim compensation is timely awarded. It further mandates that DLSAs shall depute enough PLVs for the implementation of this scheme. The scheme also stresses making PLVs an interface between the acid attack victims and legal services institutions. Further, the scheme mandates that SLSAs set up legal services cells at hospitals with specialized facilities to treat acid attack victims.

Therefore, we can see that NALSA has expanded the scope of legal aid for issues-based and victim-centric schemes. These schemes support the legal framework of already existing laws and policies under the LSA Act, 1987.

1.2.5. Judiciary as the Promoter of Legal Aid Services

The idea of free legal services in India has been a rudimentary edifice in providing access to justice to the marginalized and deprived sections of society. In delivering the very mandate of the LSA Act, 1987, the Supreme Court of India has been instrumental in endorsing and guarding FLAS for the society's poor and marginalized sections. The Apex Court has laid down critical guidelines in various landmark judgments for the establishment of a free LAS. For instance, the Supreme Court flagged the issue of free legal aid for the first time in *Janardan Reddy and Ors. V. State of Hyderabad* and *Ors.*[63] To ensure the idea of a fair trial. Although the court did not comprehensively deal with free legal aid, it passed a reference by holding the view that the absence of legal aid should not vitiate a trial. The judiciary's further interventions to deliver the mandate of free legal services in letter and spirit have been discussed.

In an array of verdicts, the Supreme Court has laid down that free legal aid is a fundamental right under Article 21. It also recognized that it is explicitly mentioned as a directive principle of state policy under Article 39A of the Constitution. For example, in *Hussainara Khatoon v. State of Bihar*,[64] Justice P. N. Bhagwati observed that

> free legal service is an inalienable element of reasonable, fair and just procedure for without it a person suffering from economic or other disabilities would be deprived of the opportunity for securing justice. The right to free legal services is, therefore, clearly an essential ingredient of reasonable, fair and just procedure for a person accused of an offence and it must be held implicit in the guarantee of Article 21.

Justice Krishna Iyer strongly promoted the mandate of free legal aid and protection for the weaker sections of the society in *Madhav Hayawadanrao Hoskot v. State of Maharashtra*.[65] He opined that

> if a prisoner sentenced to imprisonment, is virtually unable to exercise his constitutional and statutory right of appeal, inclusive of special leave to appeal, for want of legal assistance, it is implicit in the Court under

> Article 142, read with Articles 21, and 39A of the Constitution, the power to assign counsel for such imprisoned individual for doing complete justice. . . . The inference is inevitable that this is a State's duty and not government's charity.

He stressed providing a reasonable remuneration to lawyers involved in providing FLAS. Further, Justice Krishna Iyer was also of the belief that the court may judge the situation whether it is necessary (or not) to provide free legal aid for the ends of justice.

Another such instance where the judiciary reinforced the idea of free legal aid was in *Tara Singh v. State of Punjab*,[66] where the Apex Court opined upon the statutory provisions giving an accused the right to a lawyer, which is a privilege given to an accused and his/her duty to ask for a lawyer, if he/she wants to engage one, or get his/her relatives to engage one. Similarly, in 1986, in the case of *Sukdas v. Union Territory of Arunachal Pradesh*,[67] Justice P. N. Bhagwati, while referring to *Hussainara Khatoon*'s[68] judgment, observed that more than 70% of the Indian masses living in rural parts are illiterate and impoverished. Further, even literate people are not aware of their rights and entitlements under the law.

Justice Bhagwati pointed out that the absence of legal awareness among the masses is responsible for their deception, exploitation, and deprivation of legal rights and benefits. It is this ignorance and poverty that makes approaching the lawyers – in case of legal issues – difficult, which in turn magnifies their trouble. The Constitutional Bench of the Supreme Court held that the right to free legal service is a must for a reasonable, fair, and just legal procedure.

The Honorable Supreme Court has been proactive in advocating the use of legal aid to ensure a fair trial. The landmark judgment of *Sunil Batra v. Delhi Administration*[69] has categorically laid down that legal aid should be made available to prisoners to seek justice and, if necessary, to challenge the decision in court in cases where they are too poor or unable to secure legal help on their own. Ensuring a fair trial is certainly one of the fundamental principles of natural justice.

The Apex Court has also enshrined the legal aid to females in general and women prisoners. In *Sheela Barse v. State of Maharashtra*,[70] the issue of custodial violence against women prisoners and detainees in the state of Maharashtra came up. This case highlighted many issues related to women prisoners and the inadequacy of measures taken by the government. The Apex Court gave directions to the police to follow the procedure by informing the nearest legal services institution as and when an individual is taken in custody or arrested. Further, if the arrestee is willing to avail of and accept free legal services at the state's expense, the concerned legal services institution should make the necessary arrangement.

Besides, the judiciary has also been proactive in keeping a check on the LSA Act's functioning through regularly questioning the level of competence and commitment shown by various stakeholders under the edifice of FLAS. For instance, in *Asmaniya Bai v. State of Madhya Pradesh*,[71] the high court questioned the LAC's cross-examination skills. The high court stated that trial court's judges are obligated to ensure that a poor litigant gets legal aid and that they get it through competent LACs.

In the case of *Sunil Damodar Gaikwad v. State of Maharashtra*,[72] the Bombay High Court observed that the trial court should have appointed an LAC with sufficient experience. Further, the Allahabad High Court in *Ram Awadh v. State of Uttar Pradesh*[73] also pointed out the LAC's lack of competence in representing the accused under FLAS. An analysis of these judgments shows that the judiciary has been at the forefront whenever it anticipates that quality legal aid is not granted to the poor beneficiary.

In *Ramchandra Nivrutti Mulak v. State of Maharashtra*,[74] the Bombay High Court reiterated that free legal aid is a beneficiary's fundamental right. It was also noted that the empanelment of incompetent lawyers for FLAS when they are not even conversant with the Criminal Procedure or Evidence Act would not serve the cause of legal aid assistance.

The judiciary also noted that the state could not discharge itself with the burden of free legal aid by merely fixing some fees, but it must ensure that competent lawyers should be empaneled.

In another instance, the Gujarat High Court, in the judgment of *State of Gujarat v. Manjuben D/O. Kasturbhai*,[75] categorically noted that the legal aid provided to the beneficiaries is just for the namesake and considered the services a farce. The court opined that legal aid is not a platform for young lawyers to get trained and gain experience. The high court questioned the competence of empaneled lawyers since they were incompetent even to cross-examine. The high court went ahead and stated that "the presence of counsel on record means effective, genuine and faithful presence and not a mere farcical, sham or a virtual presence that is illusory, if not fraudulent."

Furthermore, the courts, at times, have also observed and remarked upon the level of commitment shown by the LACs. In the case of *Bal Bahadur v. Customs Air Custom Officer IGI Airport*[76] before the High Court of Delhi, it was highlighted that the LAC appointed for the beneficiary was absent from performing their mandated task and was incompetent and inexperienced. In another case, *Sudhakar Tiwari v. State*,[77] the High Court of Delhi observed that the LAC appointed for the accused remained absent on days of the trial proceedings because of which the LAC failed to cross-examine for defense.

The Apex Court, in the judgment of *Imtiyaz Ramzan Khan v. State of Maharashtra*,[78] directed all the legal aid services authorities and committees to facilitate videoconferencing between the counsel and any accused lodged in jail. The Apex Court ordered the initiation of this process due to empaneled lawyers' incapacities for having a dialogue with their respective beneficiaries. Similarly, Tihar Jail also adopted a videoconferencing facility for providing legal aid.[79]

It was believed that jail visiting advocates and LACs of under-trials are restrained from visiting a beneficiary in jail, perhaps due to their occupancy in their other private cases. The videoconferencing method has made empaneled lawyers accessible to the beneficiaries of legal aid.

In the year 2019, the Supreme Court of India, during the final hearing of *Joydeep Mukharjee v. State of West Bengal & Others*,[80] lashed out at the LACs because of their lack of seriousness, as demonstrated by them in assisting the poor beneficiaries. The Supreme Court warned those LACs that they would be removed from the group of empaneled lawyers who did not appear for the cases of their respective beneficiaries.[81] Taking note of all these cases, it can be safely concluded that the lack of commitment demonstrated by LACs during the course of the trial is under the notice of the Honorable Supreme Court and high courts.

The judiciary's proactive approach demonstrates that it has always been the patron of FLAS in India. Legal aid is not a charity but an obligation of the state and the right of every citizen, as has also been reiterated by the Supreme Court of India in various judgments.

1.2.6. The Scheme of the Book

This study is a conscious and systematic effort to bring out in black and white the experience gained in the field. In this book, the offices of DLSAs, the jail premises, and the court premises were visited in order to assess the quality and competence of the LACs engaged by the DLSAs in their respective districts. The study highlights the issues faced by major stakeholders of the LAS in India.

The book is divided into eight chapters. The second chapter deals with legal aid practices around the globe with a special focus on geographical reasons. The third chapter focuses on legal aid beneficiaries under the LSA Act, 1987, and examines the empirical survey data. It focuses on the responses received from the beneficiaries regarding the competence and commitment of LACs in their respective district. The analysis is categorized according to different zones and states. The fourth chapter delves into the responses from women who are entitled to FLAS but instead opted for PLPs' paid services. The fifth chapter covers regulators' or DLSA secretaries' perspectives on the practice of FLAS in their DLSA and analyzes their feedback.

The sixth chapter captures the views of judicial officers in civil and criminal courts from the six zones. It strives to bring the perspective of judicial officers or judges as they see the institution of the LAS in India. The seventh chapter focuses on LACs' views on the provisions of FLAS. It brings out the complex reality that LACs face daily in providing free legal aid to their respective beneficiaries. The final chapter inspects the research hypotheses based on the feedback from the stakeholders and on other important field observations.

Notes

1 Hussainara Khatoon & Ors. v. Home Secretary, State of Bihar, Govt. of Bihar, Patna, (1980) SCC (1) 81
2 *FAQ*, National Legal Services Authority (NALSA), available at https://nalsa.gov.in/content/faq last seen on 7/02/2019
3 Regan, Francis, *The transformation of legal aid: comparative and historical studies*, Oxford University Press, pp. 89–90 (1990)
4 *Free Legal Aid*, Lawyers Club, available at www.lawyersclubindia.com/articles/Free-Legal-Aid-5166.asp#.UWpqLLVaZSg/last seen on 27/02/2019
5 First Law Commission of India, 14th Report, *Reform on Judicial Administration,* Volume-1, Chapter-27, Legal Aid (1958), available at http://lawcommissionofindia.nic.in/1-50/Report14Vol1.pdf, last seen on 27/02/2019
6 Dr Singh, J. S., Right to legal aid, A human right perspective, *Nyaya Deep*, 8(3), 74 (2007), *See also* N. R. Madhava Menon, Dr. A. C. Pal and Mrs. Rupa Mehta, Social justice and the indian legal system, *Civil and Military Law Journal*, 41 (2005)
7 Gustav Oppert, *Sukranitisara (Sanskrit)*, Madras 182 Ssukra IV.5, p. 228 (1885)
8 231 Report of Expert Committee on Legal Aid, *Processual Justice To The People*, May 43, (1973) available at http://reports.mca.gov.in/Reports/15-Iyer%20committee%20report%20of%20the%20expert%20committee%20in%20legal%20aid,%201973.pdf, last seen on 08/02/2019
9 Supra 5, at 221
10 Supra 6
11 Supra 8, at 32–33
12 Supra 5
13 Report of Expert Committee on Legal Aid, Processual *Justice To The People*, May 43 (1973) available at http://reports.mca.gov.in/Reports/15-Iyer%20committee%20report%20of%20the%20expert%20committee%20in%20legal%20aid,%201973.pdf last seen on 08/02/2019
14 Report on National Juridicare: *Equal Justice- Social Just*ice, Government of India, (1977)
15 *NALSA Introduction and History*, NALSA available at https://nalsa.gov.in/about-us last seen on 08/02/2019
16 S. 304, The Code of Criminal Procedure, 1973: "Legal aid to accused at state expense in certain cases: (1) where, in a trial before the Court of Session, the accused is not represented by a pleader, and where it appears to the court that the accused has not sufficient means to engage a pleader, the court shall assign a pleader for his defence at the expense of the state. (2) The High Court may, with the previous approval of the state government make rule providing for – (a) the mode of selecting pleaders for defence under sub-section (2); (b) the facilities to be allowed to such pleaders by the courts; (c) the fee payable to such pleaders by the government, and generally, for carrying out the purposes of sub-section (1). (3) The state government may, by notification, direct that, as from such date as may be specified in the notification, the provisions of sub-sections (1) and (2) shall apply in relation to any class of trials before other courts in the state as they apply in relation to trials before the courts of session."
17 (1981) 1 SCC 635
18 *Ibid.*
19 Order XXXIII Rule 17, The Code of Civil Procedure, 1908.
20 Rule 9A, The Code of Civil Procedure, 1908: "Court to assign a pleader to an unrepresented indigent person (1) where a person, who is permitted to sue as an indigent person, is not represented by a pleader, the court may, if the circumstances of the case so require, assign a pleader to him. (2) the high court may,

with the previous approval of the state government, make rules providing for – (a) the mode of selecting pleaders to be assigned under sub-rule (1); (b) the facilities to be provided to such pleaders by the court; (c) any other matter which is required to be or may be provided by the rules for giving effect to the provisions of sub-rule (1)."

21 Act No. 39 of 1987; w.e.f. October 11, 1987

22 Supra note 10

23 S. 12, Legal Services Authorities Act, 1987

24 S. 2(2), Disabilities (Equal Opportunities, Protection of Right and Full Participation) Act, 1995

25 Section 2(2) Immoral Traffic (Prevention) Act, 1956, or in a juvenile home under the meaning of S. 2 (J) of the Juvenile Justice Act, 1986, or in a psychiatric hospital or psychiatric nursing home under the S. 2 (2) of the Mental Health Act, 1987

26 Regulation 15, The SCLSC Regulations, 1996

27 *Eligibility*, Who are Entitled to Free Legal Services, available at https://nalsa.gov.in/services/legal-aid/eligibility, last seen 22/08/2020

28 S. 29 LSA, 1987 (39 of 1987) and applicable to all legal services authorities established under the LSA, https://nalsa.gov.in/acts-rules/regulations/national-legal-services-authority-free-and-competent-legal-services-regulations-2010, last seen 22/08/2020

29 Regulation 5, Proof of Entitlement of Free Legal Services, NALSA (Free and Competent Legal Services), 2010

30 S. 13, Legal Services Authorities Act, 1987: "Entitlement to legal services (1) persons who satisfy or any of the criteria specified in section 12 shall be entitled to receive legal services provided that the concerned authority is satisfied that such person has a prima-facie case to prosecute or to defend. Requests received through e-mails and interactive on-line facility may be considered free legal services after verification of the identity of the applicant and on ensuring that he or she owns the authorship of the grievances projected. Persons who satisfy any of the criteria shall be entitled to receive legal services. However, the concerned authority should be satisfied that such person has a prim facie case to prosecute or to defend. A person as to satisfy the requisite limit of income or other conditions, as specified in the Act should make an affidavit. Subsequently the appropriate authority has the discretion to confirm on the aid. (2) An affidavit made by a person as to his income may be regarded as sufficient for making him eligible to the entitlement of legal services under this act unless the concerned authority has reason to disbelieve such affidavit."

31 Regulation 13, NALSA (Free and Competent Legal Services) Regulations, 2010

32 Regulation 9, NALSA (Free and Competent Legal Services) Regulations, 2010

33 Regulation 13, SCLSC Regulations, 1996, similar provisions are also available under the DLSA Regulation, 2002 and NALSA (Free and Competent Legal Services) Regulations, 2010

34 *Ibid.*

35 *Ibid.*

36 Regulation 18, SCLSC Regulations, 1996: "Legal service shall not be withdrawn without giving due notice thereof to the aided person or to his legal representatives in the event of his death, to show causes as to why the legal service should not be withdrawn. Where the legal services are withdrawn on the grounds set out above, the Committee shall be entitled to recover from the aided person the amount of legal service granted to him."

37 Regulation 8(1) Selection of Legal Practitioner as Panel Lawyers, NALSA (Free and Competent Legal Services) Regulations, 2010

38 *Ibid.*
39 Regulation 8 (2)
40 *Ibid.*
41 Regulation 8 (4)
42 Regulation 8 (7)
43 Regulation 8 (13)
44 *Ibid.*
45 Regulation 14, (1) Payment of Fee to Panel Lawyers, NALSA (Free and Competent Legal Services) Regulations, 2010
46 Regulation 14 (2), NALSA (Free and Competent Legal Services) Regulations, 2010
47 Regulation 14(3), NALSA (Free and Competent Legal Services) Regulations, 2010
48 Regulation 13(1), Financial Assistance, NALSA (Free and Competent Legal Services) Regulations, 2010
49 Regulation 4(1), Legal Services Institution to have Front Office, NALSA (Free and Competent Legal Services) Regulations, 2010
50 Regulation 4(1A), NALSA (Free and Competent Legal Services) Regulations, 2010
51 Regulation 10 (1), NALSA (Free and Competent Legal Services) Regulations, 2010
52 Regulation 10(2)(i)
53 Regulation 10(3), NALSA (Free and Competent Legal Services) Regulations, 2010
54 Regulation 10(4)
55 Regulation 11(1), Procedure of the Monitoring and Mentoring Committee
56 Regulation 11(3)
57 Regulation 11(4)
58 *Ibid.*
59 Regulation 11(9)
60 Regulation 12(1), Monitoring and Mentoring Committee to Submit Bi-Monthly Reports
61 *Ibid.*
62 Regulation 16, Evaluation of the Legal Aid Cases by National Legal Services Authority and State Legal Services Authorities
63 Janardan Reddy and Ors. v. State of Hyderabad and Ors, (1951) SC 217
64 Hussainara Khatoon v. State of Bihar, (1979) SC 1369
65 Madhav Hayawadanrao Hoskot v. State of Maharashtra, (1987) SC 1548
66 Tara Singh v. State of Punjab, (1951) SC 411
67 Sukdas v. Union Territory of Arunachal Pradesh (1986) 4 SCC 401
68 Supra 64
69 Sunil Batra v. Delhi Administration, (1980) SC 1579
70 Sheela Barse v. State of Maharashtra AIR 1983 SC 378
71 Asmaniya Bai v. State of M.P 2000 (3) MPLJ 272
72 Sunil Damodar Gaikwad v. State of Maharashtra Criminal Appeal (2014) 1 SCC 129
73 Ram Awadh v. State of Uttar Pradesh (1998) SCC OnLine All 1234
74 Ramchandra Nivrutti Mulak v. State of Maharashtra (2015) 14 Supreme Court Cases 327
75 State of Gujarat v. Manjuben D/O. Kasturbhai Criminal Confirmation Case No. 1 of 2018
76 Bal Bahadur v. Customs Air Custom Officer IGI Airport (2009) SCC OnLine Del 718

77 Sudhakar Tiwari v. State (2012) SCC OnLine Del 195
78 Imtiyaz Ramzan Khan v. State of Maharashtra 2018 (9) SCC 160
79 Abhishek Saran, *Legal aid a video call away for Tihar inmates*, Hindustan Times, available at www.hindustantimes.com/delhi-news/legal-a-video-call-away-for-tihar-inmates/story-agXkNrae2QNf36BuMEzxBL.html, last seen on 17/04/2019
80 Joydeep Mukharjee v. State of West Bengal & Others (2011) SC 1169
81 Times of India, *"Sack lawyers who don't show up for poor clients,"* available at https://timesofindia.indiatimes.com/india/Sack-lawyers-who-dont-show-up-for-poor-clients/articleshow/6548354.CMs, last seen on 17/04/2019

2 Legal Aid Practices Across the Globe

2.1. Introduction

Almost every democratic country provides free legal assistance in criminal cases and in civil cases. The advent of this aspect of social justice can be traced to the end of the First World War. In 1924, the International Committee of Legal Aid was formulated, and justice for the poor and needy was given utmost priority by the committee. The committee submitted its report to the League of Nations in 1927 after surveying the instruments of free legal services in countries across the globe.[1]

In the modern-day context of various nation-states, the earliest institutionalization of the legal aid movement can be traced back to 1851, when France passed the law on legal aid (assistance judiciaries). This formed the basis of France's current legal aid system ("LAS").[2] Similarly, in the United States of America ("USA"), civil legal assistance came into existence in 1876 with the founding of the Legal Aid Society of New York.[3] In the United Kingdom ("UK"), the development of the LAS dates back to 1944, when the Rushcliffe Committee came into existence to enquire into the facilities, as they prevailed then, for providing legal advice to the poor in England and Wales.[4] It also made recommendations on the legality and need for legal assistance to a person.

The Universal Declaration of Human Rights ("UDHR"), 1948, sought to establish that universal peace is possible only if social justice is ensured for every human being. The declaration signified that legal protection aid for each individual is a principal instrument of access to justice. The concept of social and economic justice finds its reference in the preamble of the UDHR. Articles 7, 8, and 10 of the UDHR envision the prospects of legal aid from the perspective of human rights. Briefly put, UDHR, in certain ways, connect legal aid as the instrument to protect the dignity of humans. Another convention of great importance is the European Convention of Human Rights, 1950, which was signed in Rome on November 4, 1950. It came into force in 1953. Article 6(3)I of the convention states,

> Everyone charged with a criminal offence has the following minimum rights: to defend himself in person or through legal assistance of his own

DOI: 10.4324/9781003158325-2

choosing or, if he has no sufficient means to pay for legal assistance, to be given it free when the interests of justice so require.[5]

In the year 1965, the need for free legal services in the form of aid was recognized at the Third United Nations Congress on the Prevention of Crime and Treatment of Offenders ("UNCPCTO").[6] The conference discussed free legal assistance for accused, convicted, and arrested persons.[7]

The right to legal assistance of an individual who is incapable of getting legal assistance due to their financial condition is acknowledged by Article 14(3)(d) of the International Convention of Civil and Political Rights ("ICCPR"), 1966.[8]

The legal assistance by a counsel and sponsored by the state as an undeniable right for every individual is also recognized under Article 8(2)€ of the American Convention on Human Rights, 1969. Besides, the convention guarantees all individuals equality before the law and grants them the protection of the law without any discrimination.[9]

The Convention on International Access to Justice, in its Article 1, ensures that any individual – regardless of their nationality – is eligible for legal aid in proceedings related to civil and commercial matters.[10]

Even the African Charter on the Rights and Welfare of the Child, 1990, under its Article 17(2)I(iii), mandates that legal assistance must be ensured to every child who is accused in order to defend himself/herself.[11] Similarly, migrant workers are also eligible for legal assistance at the state's expense if they lack the proper financial means to pay under Article 18(3)(d) of the International Convention on the Protection of the Rights of All Migrant Workers and Members of Their Families, 1999.[12]

Principle 18 of the Protection of Persons with Mental Illness and the Improvement of Mental Health Care, 1991, acknowledges free legal services for mentally ill individuals. It emphasizes that patients are eligible to appoint and select their legal representative, and if they fail to appoint, the liability lies on the State to appoint or provide a legal counsel without any payment.[13]

Chapter 6 of the Charter of Fundamental Rights of the European Union, 2000, provides for the right to an effective remedy and fair trial in Article 47 and the right of defense and presumption of innocence in Article 48. The first part of Article 47 states that anyone whose rights guaranteed by the European Union have been violated shall be entitled to a remedy before the court of law or a relevant tribunal. It has been stated that everyone shall have the possibility of being advised, defended, and represented. It further states that legal aid *shall* be made available to those who lack sufficient resources. The usage of the word "shall" emphasize the obligation cast upon the State.

Legal aid services have been acknowledged and promoted as fundamental rights by various international instruments, conventions, and agreements worldwide. These international instruments have structurally transformed the municipal legislation on the aspects of legal services. Free legal assistance has become the norm in various states for the individuals who belong to the society's economically and socially lower strata. The welfare and regulatory state has now taken over the responsibility to provide free legal assistance at the public exchequer's expense in order to ensure access to justice. The following section touches upon the aspects of legal aid established and practiced in various regions across the globe, adhering to the various international conventions, codes, and instruments discussed earlier.

2.2. Comparative Perspective of Legal Aid in Different Regions of the World

Before delving into the responses received from various stakeholders in the empirical study, it is essential to briefly understand the legal aid framework as practiced in different parts of the world as it will give a sense of where India's LAS stands. This section informs us, in brief, about the LAS framework in countries in different geographical regions, such as South Asia, East Asia, Europe, the Americas, and Africa. It provides a comparative overview of the legal aid framework based on whether a country has a constitutional mandate for legal aid services or a dedicated statute to provide legal aid services, the eligibility criteria for a beneficiary, the process of getting these services, the administration and governance of the scheme and the terms on which LACs are engaged to provide FLAS.

2.2.1. South Asia

2.2.1.1. Nepal

A) BRIEF

The Constitution of Nepal recognizes

1. the right to consult a legal practitioner of choice and to be defended by such a practitioner upon arrest and
2. an indigent party's right to free legal aid as a fundamental right of all Nepalese citizens.

Thus, Articles 20(2) and 20(10) of the Nepalese Constitution identify free legal aid under rights related to justice.

The Legal Aid Act, 2054 (1997), lays out the framework of legal aid in Nepal. The act came into existence to manage legal aid. Section 6 of the act deals with a Central Legal Aid Committee's constitution, functions, duties, and powers.[14] Section 12 mandates that the Central Legal Aid Committee has the power to frame necessary rules to implement the act's objective.[15] Thus, Legal Aid Rules, 2055 (1998), formulated by the Central Legal Aid Committee, provide the roadmap for delivering legal aid in Nepal.

B) ELIGIBILITY OF ENTITLEMENT

The persons entitled to free legal aid in Nepal should have an annual income of less than 40,000[16] and should be either children, women, persons with physical or mental disabilities, internally displaced persons, or ethnic or religious minorities. Legal Aid Rules, 2055 (1998), is the principal document referred by the committee to decide whether a person is eligible for free legal aid or not. Rule 6 (2) denies any entitlement of free legal aid to a party that is convicted in cases under the Espionage Act, 2018 (1962); the Human Trafficking (Control) Act, 2043; and Ancient Monuments Preservation Act, 2013, which have punishment under Chapter on Rape of the General Code; Prevention of Corruption Act, 2017; Commission for the Investigation and Abuse of Authority Act, 2048; the Revenue Leakages Control Act, 2052; Drug (Control) Act, 2033; and other cases as prescribed by the Central Committee.[17]

C) PROCESS FOR AVAILING OF BENEFITS

Chapter 2, Rule 3 of the Legal Aid Rules, 2055 (1998), describes the process for availing of the benefits of free legal aid. A Nepalese citizen, in order to get free legal aid, needs to apply to the Legal Aid Committee with a recommendation from either the chairperson or member or secretary of the Village Development Committee or, in the case of municipality, by the concerned ward's chairperson. The Legal Aid Committee member examines the application and puts it forward to the Legal Aid Committee for approval. The Legal Aid Committee has 45 days to make its decision from the date of application whether an applicant will get free legal aid or not.

D) GOVERNANCE OF THE SCHEME – REGULATIONS AND FUNDING

The Central Legal Aid Committee ("C-LAC") is responsible for implementing a legal aid scheme in Nepal. Per Section 6 of the Legal Aid Act, 2054 (1997), the committee comprises five members. The law and justice minister is the chair of the committee, and the secretary of the Nepal Bar Association is the member secretary of the committee. The other three members are the chairperson of the Nepal Bar Council, the president of the Nepal Bar Association, and one legal expert nominated by the committee. The membership tenure in the committee is for three years.

It is the C-LAC that supervises and governs the performances of District Legal Aid Committees ("D-LACs"). C-LAC is also responsible for funding legal aid and providing a grant to every D-LAC. The C-LAC can also make a panel of lawyers to represent indigent persons at the Supreme Court.

The D-LACs function in every district of Nepal and come under the C-LAC. They comprise a chairperson, member secretary, and members.[18] The chairperson of a D-LAC is either a government attorney where the appellate court is located or a district court government advocate where such an appellate court is not located. The president of the superior bar unit among the Bar Association units in the district and two lawyers nominated by the district committee serve as members of the D-LAC. The D-LAC member secretary is the superior bar unit secretary among the Bar Association units located in that district.

The C-LAC receives funds from the Government of Nepal to carry out activities related to legal aid in Nepal. Money received as grants, aid, and subscription from an individual, associations, or institutions also contribute to Nepal's legal aid scheme's funding. The C-LAC and D-LACs keep an account of the income and expenditure of these funds.

E) TERMS AND CONDITIONS OF ENGAGING LACS

The C-LAC, in the case of the Supreme Court, and D-LACs, in the case of the district courts, prepare the list of LACs or panel lawyers for empanelment. D-LAC may also list lawyers from other districts as panel lawyers in their list of empaneled lawyers. D-LACs determine the remuneration of lawyers at the district level, and the C-LAC determines the remuneration for panel lawyers at Supreme Court. Section 5 of the Legal Aid Act, 2054 (1997), deals with the remuneration aspects of LACs or empaneled lawyers. However, there exists no such slab for the remuneration of panel lawyers. The C-LAC and D-LACs have the power to remove or exclude any empaneled lawyer from the list. Further, if any panel lawyer performs carelessly or shows negligence in providing legal aid, the Legal Aid Committee has the power to recommend the Bar Council take action against the concerned panel lawyer.[19]

2.2.1.2. *People's Republic of Bangladesh*

A) BRIEF

The Constitution of Bangladesh, in Article 27, guarantees all citizens equality before the law and entitles them to equal protection of the law. Further, Article 31 ensures that every person has the right to enjoy the law's protection and to be treated in accordance with the law. So providing legal aid to every litigant incapable of seeking justice on their own became the mandate guaranteed by Bangladesh's Constitution. The legal framework that provides free legal aid to every citizen or non-citizen rests on the Legal Aid Services Act, 2000; Legal Aid Services Principles, 2014; and Legal Aid Services Regulation, 2015. Section 3 of the Legal Aid Services Act, 2000, established the National Legal Aid Services Organization ("NLASO") for carrying out the services related to FLAS in Bangladesh.[20] The functions and administration of affairs of NLASO vest in the National Governing Board.

B) ELIGIBILITY OF ENTITLEMENT

The Legal Aid Services Act, 2000, focuses on providing legal aid for litigants who cannot seek justice for financial reasons, helplessness, and various socioeconomic conditions. The Legal Aid Services Rules, 2014, delves into the criteria for a person to be eligible for FLAS. Under Rule 2 of the Legal Aid Services Rules, 2014, a person whose annual income is less than Tk. 150,000 for legal aid in Supreme Court and lower than Tk. 100,000 for Legal Aid in any other court is eligible for free legal aid in Bangladesh. The eligibility criteria also cover physically challenged persons and jobless persons. Subsection 2 of the same rule enlists any child, victim of human trafficking, child or woman victim of abuse (physical, mental, or sexual), homeless person, person belonging to minor races or ethnic sets, victim of family violence, victim of acid burning, or disabled person as the eligible beneficiaries for free legal aid under Legal Aid Services Act, 2000.

C) PROCESS FOR AVAILING OF BENEFITS

The process of availing of the services under free legal aid requires an entitled person to apply to Supreme Court Committee, a district committee, or a special committee.[21] Further, the Legal Aid Services Act, 2000, ensures that if any committee rejects the application for free legal aid, the applicant may appeal to the National Board for reconsideration. The applicant must submit an appeal for reconsideration within 60 days from their application's rejection date.

D) GOVERNANCE OF THE SCHEME – REGULATIONS AND FUNDING

The governance of legal aid services in Bangladesh rests upon the NLASO. To discharge its duties and functions, it has a National Governing Board. The minister at the Ministry of Law, Justice, and Parliamentary Affairs is the board's chairman. The other board members are two members of Parliament, the attorney-general of Bangladesh, the secretary of the Ministry of Home Affairs and Social Welfare, and so on. The director heads the NLASO and acts as the member secretary for the board. One of the primary duties of NLASO is to set up the criteria for determining the eligibility of beneficiaries for free legal aid who are incapable of seeking justice on their own. The organization is also responsible for expanding, upgrading, and promoting legal aid programs in Bangladesh. It also supervises and controls the Supreme Court Committee's, the district committees', and the special committees' activities.

The Supreme Court of Bangladesh constitutes the Supreme Court Committee for Legal Aid Services. The chief justice nominates a judge of the high court division as the chairman of the committee. The chair is responsible for the overall administrative responsibilities for implementing Legal Aid programs administered by the Supreme Court.[22]

At the district level, the Legal Aid Services Act, 2000, established a district committee of the organization.[23] The district and sessions judge is the chair of a district committee. The district committee is responsible for providing legal aid for the beneficiaries per the determined criteria. The committee decides the types and terms of legal aid for an applicant or beneficiary of legal aid.

The government funds the entire structure of the Legal Aid Framework in Bangladesh. The board receives the funds in the form of grants made by governments and local authorities and money received from foreign organizations. The board then allocates the funds to various district committees in Bangladesh. Similarly, the Supreme Court Committee and special committees receive funds from the board or any foreign organization.

E) TERMS AND CONDITIONS OF ENGAGING LACS

The panel lawyers for providing the legal aid to the entitled beneficiaries are engaged differently by the respective committees at the Supreme Court, district, and special levels per Section 15 of the Legal Aid Services Act, 2000. The Supreme Court Committee requires that panel lawyers have at least five years of practice at the Supreme Court. Similarly, at the district committee level, the committee selects panel lawyers having at least five years of experience in the district court. Moreover, a special committee also selects panel lawyers from the group of lawyers who have at least five years of experience in the labor court or outpost court to provide legal services to beneficiaries.

The panel lawyers in Bangladesh have a distinct feature of women's representation. In Section 15, Subsection 3 mandates that at least one-third of each panel made under the committee must represent women lawyers if found eligible. The Legal Aid Services Act, 2000, also takes into consideration the litigant's choice in appointing a panel lawyer to their case.

2.2.1.3. Sri Lanka

A) BRIEF

The Constitution of the Democratic Socialist Republic of Sri Lanka promises equality before the law and equal protection of the law to every person in Sri Lanka.[24] Further, under Article 13 (3), the Constitution also guarantees the right "to be heard, in person or by an attorney-at-law, at a fair trial by a competent court." The Government of Sri Lanka provides free legal aid under Legal Aid Act No. 27 of 1978.[25] The Law Commission, established in 1978, administers free legal aid in Sri Lanka.

B) ELIGIBILITY OF ENTITLEMENT

The Legal Aid Act guarantees legal assistance to every "deserving person" who passes the means test. Per the Legal Aid Commission of Sri

Lanka, any person or individuals receiving a monthly income of Rs. 25,000 or less is eligible for the benefits under the Legal Aid Act.[26] The *Grama Niladhari* verifies the income status of an individual applicant. Additionally, applicants having a monthly income of less than Rs. 6,000 are also eligible for lawyer assistance.[27] Apart from this, in maintenance cases, women seeking maintenance for themselves and for their children can also be legal aid beneficiaries regardless of their income or financial status.[28]

C) PROCESS FOR AVAILING OF BENEFITS

The legal aid applicants may contact any branch of the Legal Aid Commission by post or over the telephone.[29] The eligible beneficiaries can submit an application form issued by the Legal Aid Commission to the divisional Secretariat and certify their monthly income from *Grama Niladhari*. After the applications qualify for the means test, the director receives notifications on individual applicants' problems and decides whether legal assistance is needed.[30] Legal aid beneficiaries receive a registration number and a card upon receiving the benefits of legal assistance.[31]

D) GOVERNANCE OF THE SCHEME – REGULATIONS AND FUNDING

The Legal Aid Commission of Sri Lanka is responsible for administrating legal aid in the country. It came into existence in 1978 through the Legal Aid Act.[32] The commission is responsible for establishing regional and district committees throughout Sri Lanka and promoting legal aid research.[33] The commission has nine members, of which the minister appoints three members and the Bar Council of Sri Lanka nominates six remaining members.[34] The appointed members hold their offices for three years. The chairman of the commission is appointed for a period of one year, and he/she should be an attorney of not less than five years' standing at the bar.[35] The Legal Aid Act also established a legal aid fund that manages the commission's financial needs.[36] The Government of Sri Lanka provides grants to the commission. Certain funds from its consolidated funds are subjected to approval by the Sri Lankan Parliament.[37] The Legal Aid Commission functions with over 120 permanent legal officers and over 1,000 panel lawyers from the regional bar associations.[38]

E) TERMS AND CONDITIONS OF ENGAGING LACS

There is no such special provision in the Legal Aid Act of Sri Lanka that defines the terms of engagement of LACs. However, the commission offers membership to register for panel lawyers. The essential eligibility criteria to be a panel lawyer for the commission is that a lawyer should be registered as an attorney-at-law.

2.2.2. *East Asia*

2.2.2.1. *China*

A) BRIEF

The People's Republic of China ("PRC") guarantees equal access to justice to its citizens under Article 33 of its Constitution. It states that all citizens are equal before the law.[39] The right to legal aid came to be first recognized through the establishment of the National Legal Aid Center by the Ministry of Justice. It is the Ministry of Justice that administers the legal aid scheme in the PRC. The Ministry of Justice provides legal aid to the beneficiaries through instruments prescribed in the Criminal Procedure Law of the PRC,[40] the Lawyers Law of the PRC,[41] and the Legal Aid Regulations 2003 ("Regulations").[42] The state-funded legal aid is available at the national, regional, and local levels.

B) ELIGIBILITY OF ENTITLEMENT

Article 1 of the Regulations guarantees access to legal services to citizens with financial difficulties. Further, Chapter 2, Article 10 mandates that citizens facing economic difficulties may apply for legal aid to a legal aid agency by requesting for advocating different purposes and activities as laid down.

Under Article 11 of the Regulations, citizens can also apply for legal aid from a legal aid agency under criminal proceedings if the criminal suspect has not hired a lawyer due to financial difficulties even after the first interrogation or if the victim and their legally designated representative or their close relatives in the public prosecution case have not appointed a prosecution agent due to financial difficulties. Further, the Regulations also has provisions for legal aid for blind, dumb, or deaf people and for minors.

C) PROCESS FOR AVAILING OF BENEFITS

There exist different provisions for availing of the benefits of legal aid in the PRC. The person eligible for legal aid under Article 10 of the Regulations can submit their application to the legal aid agency based on the cause of their legal issue. For instance, if a beneficiary requests state compensation, they must apply to a legal aid agency where the compensation obligation agency is located. In cases where the beneficiary requests social insurance benefits or minimum living security benefits, the application needs to be submitted to the local legal aid agency. Similarly, persons covered under Article 11 of the Regulations should apply to the legal aid agency where the local court hearing is taking place. In terms of a detained criminal suspect's application, Article 15 of the Regulations obligates the detention center to transfer the application to a legal aid agency within 24 hours. Citizens must submit their valid identity cards, proof of economic difficulties, and case material related to legal aid applied for, along with their applications.

After submission of a legal aid application, the legal aid agency conducts a review of the applications received and decides upon the various applicants' types of legal assistance. In case of rejection of the application, the legal aid agency binds to notify the applicant with the reasons for not getting legal aid. Article 19 gives a window to apply to the Judicial Administrative Department in case the applicant disagrees with the local legal aid agency's decision of rejection. Such applicants may apply for reconsideration within a period of five days from the date of rejection to avail of the benefits of legal assistance.

D) GOVERNANCE OF THE SCHEME – REGULATIONS AND FUNDING

In the PRC, the Judicial Administrative Department of the State Council supervises and administers issues related to legal aid.[43] Similarly, the Judicial Administrative Department at the local and county level manages and supervises the legal aid work in their respective areas. Under the central government's supervision, the judicial administrative departments in municipalities, cities, and counties established legal aid agencies to carry out day-to-day legal aid to beneficiaries.[44] The All-China Lawyers Association and local lawyers' associations also assist with legal aid work at the national, regional, and local levels.

E) TERMS AND CONDITIONS OF ENGAGING LACS

Article 42 of the Lawyers Law of the People's Republic of China (2017 Revision) obligates every lawyer and law firm to perform their share of legal aid obligations in accordance with state regulations. The legal aid agency appoints a panel lawyer to provide services to a legal aid beneficiary.[45] In terms of cases in the People's Court, the legal aid agency provides a list of contractors to the court three days before the court session. The panel lawyers get a subsidized remuneration for their services after they have submitted all the closing documents related to the legal aid case. The local judicial administrative department and financial department determine the average cost of handling various legal aid cases.[46]

The Regulations also obliges lawyers and law firms engaged in legal aid cases to practice ethics and professional discipline. Article 22 of the Regulations prohibits the lawyers and law firms engaged in legal aid cases from collecting or demanding any property. In cases where a law firm refuses to handle legal aid cases, the judicial administrative department may either warn them or may suspend the firm's business for more than one month to less than three months. For lawyers, the punishment involves suspension from practice for more than one month and less than three months.

2.2.2.2. *Japan*

A) BRIEF

The provisions of free legal aid in Japan find their origin in the Constitution of Japan. Article 34 of the Japanese Constitution mandates that a person's arrest cannot occur without providing him/her the privilege of a legal counsel. Further, Article 37 of Japan's Constitution makes it necessary for an accused to have the assistance of a competent legal practitioner or counsel. In case the accused is incapable of securing any counsel, the state assigns a counsel to the accused. The Government of Japan administers and implements the Comprehensive Legal Support Act (June 2, 2004).

B) ELIGIBILITY OF ENTITLEMENT

A person arrested and detained on criminal charges is eligible for legal aid only if he/she meets the criteria for victims of crime. The act ensures legal aid for suspects facing a prison sentence or death penalty. In terms of civil cases, the state-funded legal aid is for persons belonging to low-income strata of the society, children, and persons with disability. In terms of civil legal aid, the applicant's financial resources must fall below a certain amount. The criteria to decide an applicant's financial status depend on the number of family members and the household savings.[47]An important drawback in Japan's legal aid framework is that it provides no special provisions for women beneficiaries in their LAS. The eligibility provisions focus on household income, not individual income.

C) PROCESS FOR AVAILING OF BENEFITS

Under the Comprehensive Legal Support Act, an entitled beneficiary must prove the status or evidence of low income by submitting supporting documents, such as tax filings in civil cases and personal financial resources in criminal cases. Further, under the Code of Criminal Procedure (Act No. 131 of 1948), the court may also appoint counsel if the accused person is unable to do so.

D) GOVERNANCE OF THE SCHEME – REGULATIONS AND FUNDING

The Japan Legal Support Center ("JLSC"), established by the Comprehensive Legal Support Act, administers legal aid in criminal and civil cases in 2006.[48] It is principally responsible for providing operations for information services, civil legal aid, legal aid for criminal defense, criminal defense measures, and support for victims of crime.[49] Per Article 17 (1) of the act, the Government of Japan funds the JLSC. The minister of justice appoints the president and two inspectors of the JLSC.[50] Further, per Article 29 (1), the JLSC has a judging committee that examines matters related to the characteristics and duties of attorneys-at-law and legal experts concerning the operations of JLSC.

The JLSC has local offices where entitled beneficiaries may apply for legal consultation or assistance. Through these offices, JLSC collects and organizes information to assist its citizenry in the effective use of courts and other legal systems. This information includes the services of attorneys and legal professionals and the cooperation and activities of the Japan Federation of Bar Associations.[51] There exist four types of local offices. The district offices are set up in the 50 locations near the main benches of district courts. District branch offices are set up at different locations in the cities with high populations. Sub-branch offices further extend the services offered by JLSC, and local law offices function in regions where the residents face difficulties accessing legal services due to limited availability of legal aid lawyers or attorneys.

E) TERMS AND CONDITIONS OF ENGAGING LACS

The legal aid providers in Japan vary in terms of engagements in providing legal aid in a civil or criminal case. To be eligible as an attorney, the legal aid providers must have passed the national bar association exam. The JLSC hires attorneys on a contract basis to administer legal aid in Japan. These attorneys or legal aid lawyers are often full-time employees in JLSC. Besides, the bar association and the Ministry of Justice encourage attorneys-at-law through *pro bono* schemes to participate in legal aid cases. Further, apart from attorneys, Japan's legal system has a certified judicial scrivener. A judicial scrivener is a legal professional who assists clients with legal documentation procedures in Japan's judicial framework.

2.2.2.3. South Korea (Republic of Korea)

A) BRIEF

The Republic of Korea constitution provides any person the right to prompt assistance of legal counsel if a defendant is unable to arrange a legal counsel.[52] It further guarantees that all citizens have the right to a trial in conformity with the constitution.[53] Apart from constitutionally guaranteed rights, the Legal Aid Act 1987 provides free legal advice and assistance to any person in the Republic of Korea.[54] The Government of the Republic of Korea operates and maintains legal aid policy.[55]

B) ELIGIBILITY OF ENTITLEMENT

In South Korea, free legal advice and assistance are available to those individuals who face economic difficulties and not "adequately protected enough by the law due to ignorance of the law"[56] Apart from state-sponsored legal aid, victims of sexual crimes,[57] persons requesting adjudication on a constitutional complaint with no financial resources,[58] and persons who fall short of paying the cost of lawsuits under civil proceedings have the right to legal assistance.[59] Persons with no defense counsel in criminal proceedings are eligible for either litigation aid or legal assistance.[60]

C) PROCESS FOR AVAILING OF BENEFITS

The Korean Legal Aid Corporation ("KLAC") determines the procedure and rules for a person to benefit from the legal aid program in South Korea.[61] The applicant needs to submit their written application for legal aid to their respective local legal aid office.[62] The KLAC requests relevant documents from the local government and central administrative agencies to confirm whether an applicant is eligible for free legal aid or not.[63] If the applicant is eligible, the case goes for legal aid, and a suggestion for reconciliation is made. In case no reconciliation is achieved among the parties, the KLAC decides on the litigation aid and appoints a public advocate for the trial based on criminal or civil proceedings.[64]

D) GOVERNANCE OF THE SCHEME – REGULATIONS AND FUNDING

The KLAC is the principal organization responsible for administering the legal aid act in Korea. Founded in 1987, the KLAC is a juristic characteristic and provides legal aid in the form of legal counseling and legal representation by attorneys.[65] The corporation has not more than 14 directors, which includes the president and one auditor.[66] The minister of justice appoints the president of the KLAC. Further, the minister of justice also appoints other directors and auditors per the recommendation of the president.[67] The president exercises overall control over the KLAC. KLAC has an exclusive attorney-at-law that ensures the legal aid services run efficiently under the corporation.

The KLAC also appoints legal aid members for conducting lawsuits concerning any subject related to legal aid.[68] However, the government funds the corporation through contributions and subsidies.[69]The corporation receives funds from cash and other property given by persons, funds borrowed to support a litigation aid, and profits from the corporation's business.[70] The KLAC has three principal branches – the Office of Planning and Coordination, Legal Aid Bureau, and Administrative Bureau – to perform the services enshrined in the Legal Aid Act.[71] The KLAC has its regional legal aid branches all over the Republic of Korea, which is further divided into local KLAC offices.[72] These branch offices and local offices have a legal aid department and a public service department to dispense legal assistance and advise the beneficiaries.[73] The functioning of issues related to legal assistance is delegated to the Legal Aid Bureau of the KLAC. The bureau is responsible for services like the placement of employed lawyers, education on litigation for lawyers and advocates, management of internet legal counseling, victim support, and so on.[74] The Office of Planning and Coordination looks towards establishing and adjusting long-term policies, researching various domestic and foreign LASs, and evaluating the management and business related to companies providing free legal aid contributions.[75] The administrative branch of KLAC holds the role of supervision of human resource affairs, appointments, revealing information, distribution of budget, taxation, and administration of contributions made towards the corporation.[76]

E) TERMS AND CONDITIONS OF ENGAGING LACS

The KLAC takes the representation of lawyers under the corporation for civil and criminal cases under free legal aid. After assessing the cost of litigation aid, KLAC assigns either lawyer under the corporation or public service advocates. These public service advocates are inducted into the LAS to provide benefits of legal assistance or advice to people who scarcely enjoy these services under the Legal Aid Act.[77] These advocates are deemed to be public officials in a fixed-term position.[78] The Ministry of Justice determines their strength every year.[79] The enlisted public service advocates go through extensive training before carrying out their duties (e.g., performing their legal aid or state affairs litigation duties).[80]

Public service advocates have a compulsory service period of three years.[81] In case a public service advocate violates any of his/her duties, the heads of agencies are liable to report such violations.

Further, the Ministry of Justice may deprive a public service advocate if he/she is disqualified or suspended as an attorney-at-law or fails to comply with the training.[82] The Ministry of Justice holds a hearing before deciding on the deprivation or disqualification of a public service advocate.[83] The corporation decides the remuneration of lawyers and public service advocates following the presidential decree and Supreme Court regulations.[84]

2.2.3. *Europe*

2.2.3.1. *Germany*

A) BRIEF

The Constitution of Germany states that every person stands equal before the law.[85] The Constitution further guarantees that lack of means should not hinder access to justice for poor citizens. Maintaining that law applies equally to all individuals, and every citizen can exercise and assert their rights. The legal aid in matters related to civil cases in Germany rests upon two laws – the Code of Civil Procedure and the Act on Advisory Assistance and Representation for Citizens with Low Income, also known as the Advisory Assistance Act.[86] In terms of criminal proceedings, the Code of Criminal Procedure regulates court-ordered representation.

B) ELIGIBILITY OF ENTITLEMENT

Section 1 of the Act on Advisory Assistance grants legal assistance to the applicants who do not have the necessary resources and for whom there are no other possibilities for assistance.

C) PROCESS FOR AVAILING OF BENEFITS

Per Section 4 (2) of the Advisory Assistance Act, an entitled beneficiary can file a written and oral application for legal aid assistance. The application needs to be filed at the local court in the district where the beneficiary has its general authority. The applicant must provide a detailed overview of legal problems and means in their legal aid applications. According to Section 117 (1) of Civil Procedure, the local court assesses the merit and means of the application to decide whether an entitled beneficiary requires advisory assistance or not.[87] The local court then issues a certificate for the applicant to consult a lawyer of his/her choice.[88] Suppose an applicant does not meet the prerequisites for the approval of the advisory assistance, then he/she won't be able to obtain the said services. These prerequisites deal with an applicant's personal and economic circumstances.

In the case of criminal proceedings, it rests upon the judge to qualify or check whether there is a case of necessary representation or not. This necessary representation refers to qualifying the conditions stipulated in Book 2, Section 140 of the German Code of Criminal Procedure.[89]

D) GOVERNANCE OF THE SCHEME – REGULATIONS AND FUNDING

The Code of Civil Procedure elaborates upon the governing aspects of legal aid for court proceedings. Book 1, Chapter 2, Sections 114 to 127a of the code delves into the various aspects of governing legal aid in Germany. As there is no such formal authority of legal aid in Germany, the governance aspects rest before the courts of general authority, the district courts, the high courts, the courts of appeals, and the supreme courts. In terms of funding of the legal aid provisions, there exists no national budget. The Department of Justice in every federal state of Germany funds its respective court systems. The courts are independent in every aspect of the government. Therefore, in Germany, the state court system administers the legal aid provisions, not any central board or foundation.

E) TERMS AND CONDITIONS OF ENGAGING LACS

In Germany, every lawyer is eligible to handle legal aid cases. There exists no system of contracting or franchising a specific group of lawyers. According to the Legal Profession Act, Section 49 (1) for Legal Aid in Criminal Court Procedure, Section 48 (1) for Legal Aid for Non-Criminal Procedure, and Section 49a of Advisory Assistance Act mandate lawyers to accept any assignment to a party supported by legal aid.

In fact, in Germany, the legal aid services are under the pure judicare model, where even low-income individuals must get legal assistance.

In non-criminal legal aid proceedings, the local state funds the remuneration of lawyers. The Code of Civil Procedure exempts the lawyers, handles legal aid cases, pays any court fees for proceedings, and obligates lawyers not to demand any clients' payment. In case the legal aid applicant loses a case, the applicant must bear the cost of the opponent's court fees and lawyer's fees.[90] On the other hand, if the court assigns legal aid in criminal proceedings, the lawyers deal directly with the courts for their remuneration. When the defendant loses the case, the court demands from him/her money in the form of repayment.

2.2.3.2. United Kingdom

A) BRIEF

The Human Rights Act, 1998, of the UK covers the very essence of the right to legal aid in the UK. The act, under Schedule 1, Article 6, guarantees everyone individual to have a fair and public hearing and provides the right to defend themselves through legal assistance of his/her choosing. If the individual cannot pay for legal assistance, the same should be given for free when in the interest of justice.[91] In the UK, the administration governs the legal aid schemes based on various legal instruments based on region – namely, the Legal Aid, Sentencing, and Punishment of Offenders Act 2012 ("LASPO Act 2012"), England and Wales 1999 Access to Justice Act, the Legal Aid Advice and Assistance (Northern Ireland) Order 1981, Access to Justice (Northern Ireland) Order No. 435 of 2003, and Scotland Legal Aid Act 1986.

B) ELIGIBILITY OF ENTITLEMENT

The eligibility criteria are almost the same in every region, depending on their respective legal aid provisions in the UK. In general, it depends on the type of case and the financial circumstances of an applicant. In terms of civil cases, an applicant needs to prove that he/she cannot afford the financial burden of getting either legal assistance or a lawyer. In Northern Ireland, to be eligible for legal advice or assistance in civil cases, an applicant's disposal income should not exceed more than £234 a week. The applicant is a direct or indirect beneficiary of income support, or the applicant's disposable capital does not exceed £1,000.[92] Similarly, in Scotland, a person is eligible for legal advice or assistance for civil legal aid if his/her disposable income does not exceed £26,239 or the disposable capital does not exceed £13,017.[93]

In terms of criminal cases, the eligibility to get legal advice or assistance also rests on the region an applicant belongs to. In England and Wales, legal advice and assistance are available for individuals involved in investigations that may lead to criminal proceedings and individuals who are before a court or tribunal. However, the determination of legal assistance rests on the decisions of the director of the Legal Aid Agency (LAA). In Northern Ireland, the person charged before a court does not have any legal representative. The court may appoint legal aid to the person.[94] Likewise, in Scotland, eligibility is somewhat like legal aid in civil cases.

C) PROCESS FOR AVAILING OF BENEFITS

In England and Wales, the applicant submits the application either over the internet or manually to the LAA. The director of legal aid casework then determines whether the applicant's application is qualified for legal advice or assistance.[95] The determination depends on the types of services and the matters in relation to which these services are available to an applicant. In terms of legal aid in criminal proceedings, it is either the court or the director that decides whether the applicant's representation qualifies for legal aid. The determination depends on Section 21 of the LASPO Act 2012.

In Northern Ireland, the Legal Services Agency determines whether an application is eligible for legal aid based on financial eligibility test. The financial test is based on an applicant's income tax, loans, rent, and maintenance of dependents while determining representation on behalf of an applicant in legal aid in civil proceedings.[96]

For legal aid in criminal cases, if an individual appears before a magistrate court or the judge of any court, and the individual is not able to represent him/herself due to a lack of financial resources, then his/her application can be granted the certificate of legal aid.[97]

Similarly, in Scotland, in the application for civil legal aid, the applicant must have a solicitor to apply for legal aid cases. The application then goes for financial and merit tests to decide whether an applicant qualifies for legal assistance through legal representation. The legal aid board decides whether the applicant needs a solicitor for representation or not.

D) GOVERNANCE OF THE SCHEME – REGULATIONS AND FUNDING

The governance of the legal aid scheme in the UK also rests upon different agencies based on the regions. In England and Wales, the LAA develops and administers both the civil and criminal legal aid schemes. A chief executive appointed by the private secretary of the department heads the LAA. It is the chief executive who is responsible for the leadership of the LAA and its management.[98] The director of legal aid casework, formulated under Part 1, Section 4 of LASPO Act 2012, works with the chief executive for operations and management to deliver legal aid in English and Wales.

Further, the director is responsible for determining whether an applicant qualifies for legal aid or not. Moreover, under Section 7 of the LASPO Act 2012, the director is also responsible for maintaining and producing a director of legal aid casework annual report related to the operation of legal aid in English and Wales. The Parliament provides the funds for legal aid schemes in England and Wales.[99]

Similarly, in Northern Ireland, the Legal Services Agency Northern Ireland ("LSANI") is responsible for administering legal aid schemes under the Legal Aid and Coroners' Courts Act (NI) 2014. The agency also has a chief executive, who is responsible for the governance and operations of the LSANI. The roles and arrangements of the chief executive of LSANI are like the roles stated for LAA in England and Wales. In Northern Ireland, the legal aid framework has a director of legal aid casework under Section 2 (1) of the Legal Aid and Coroners' Courts Act (NI) 2014. In Northern Ireland, the chief executive heads the LSANI board, which focuses on strategy, performance monitoring, service delivery, planning, and budgeting for the agency. The Assembly approves the allocation of funds for the agency.

Further, in Scotland, the Scotland Legal Aid Board is the principal organization for handling legal aid schemes. It came into existence under Part 1, Section 1 of the Legal Aid (Scotland) Act 1986. The board's principal functions are managing the legal aid operations in terms of advice, assistance following the act, and administering the fund allotted to the board.[100] The secretary of state appoints the board members – no less than 11 members and not more than 15 members. Section 4 of the act mandates establishing and maintaining a fund known as the Scottish Legal Aid Fund. This fund takes care of the dues to any solicitors or counsels who provided their services under legal aid.

E) TERMS AND CONDITIONS OF ENGAGING LACS

In Northern Ireland, in terms of civil proceedings, any practicing barrister is eligible to provide advice or assistance or act for persons receiving legal aid unless the General Council of the Bar of Northern Ireland does not prohibit the barrister from practicing.[101] The legal aid fund of the LSANI funds the dues, fees, and expenses that were made while engaging a solicitor and counsel acting for a person receiving legal aid.[102] However, the sums allowed to counsels are restricted up to a certain level. In proceedings in the House of Lords, the Court of Appeal, or the High Court, around 95% or such a larger percentage of the amount allowed on the taxation of the costs.[103] In terms of criminal proceedings, as Articles 36A and 36B of the Legal Aid, Advice, and Assistance (Northern Ireland) Order 1981 states, any person who has a criminal aid certificate may select any solicitor or counsel from the registered solicitor and counsels with the department. A barred solicitor or counsel from practice by the General Council of the Bar of Northern Ireland cannot provide his/her services to a person who has a criminal aid certificate.

In Scotland, as Part 5, Section 26 of the Legal Aid (Scotland) Act 1986 describes, the board employs the solicitors and counsels to give advice and assistance to the individual eligible for legal aid. The organization entrusts these solicitors to assist and guide the legal aid applicants. Further, under Section 28A of the act, the solicitors may be employed to provide criminal legal assistance. In terms of criminal legal assistance in Scotland, the board maintains a Criminal Legal Assistance Register of solicitors and firms who are eligible to provide criminal legal assistance.[104] As registered solicitors, they need to comply with the code of conduct formulated by the board. The board may also remove a solicitor's name from the register if a solicitor fails to comply with the code.

2.2.4. Americas

2.2.4.1. United States of America

A) BRIEF

The Constitution of the USA guarantees the right to a speedy and public trial and to have the assistance of a legal counsel to every individual in case of criminal prosecutions.[105] The precedent set in 1963 with *Gideon v. Wainwright* by the US Supreme Court paved the way and recognized the right to criminal legal aid in the USA.[106] In terms of civil legal assistance or aid, the USA has a varied number of service providers funded by various sources. The Legal Service Cooperation ("LSC") funds most of the civil legal aid programs in the USA. Apart from LSC, non-profit legal aid organizations, law schools, and legal information websites also assist in providing civil legal assistance and aid to US citizens.

B) ELIGIBILITY OF ENTITLEMENT

In the USA, low- and middle-income people face several civil legal issues and, hence, are eligible for free legal assistance.[107] This assistance may revolve around issues concerning non-criminal matters. Further, people living in households whose annual income is at or below 125% of the federal poverty guidelines are also eligible to receive free legal aid under programs funded by LSC.

As stated earlier, the Sixth Amendment guarantees legal aid to every individual in terms of criminal prosecution. The eligibility, in general, is determined by the client's liquid assets and income level, fixed debts, medical expenses, and cost of living in the locality.

C) PROCESS FOR AVAILING OF BENEFITS

Criminal legal aid and civil legal aid are available to every individual upon request from an individual, prosecutor, bar association, or legal aid organization. The court primarily weighs the eligibility for legal aid during the first appearance of the parties.

D) GOVERNANCE OF THE SCHEME – REGULATIONS AND FUNDING

The principal organization in the USA managing and funding the operation of civil legal aid assistance is the LSC. It came into existence in 1974 to promote equal access to justice through funding high-quality civil legal assistance.[108] LSC is a grant-making organization that established maximum income levels for qualified legal assistance under the Legal Services Corporation (LSC) Act.[109]

Per Section 1004 (a) of the LSC Act, the LSC has 11 members on the Board of Directors, each having a three-year term of office. The LSC provides financial assistance to qualified legal aid programs in states and local governments.[110] It also monitors and evaluates civil legal assistance programs offered by private or independent originations.

E) TERMS AND CONDITIONS OF ENGAGING LACS

The terms of engaging legal aid or assistance in terms of representation by a counsel in the criminal prosecutions are followed according to instruments in Title 18, Section 3006 A, Adequate Representation of Defendant, and Rule 44 of the Federal Rules of Criminal Procedure.[111] These instruments ensure that the right to have counsel to represent the defendant is adhered to by the court. With the approval of the circuit's judicial council, the district courts plan the operations of furnishing representation for any person financially unable to obtain a lawyer.

The courts employ attorneys or counsels from a panel of lawyers designated by the court, the bar association, or a legal aid agency.[112] The counselors representing clients under criminal legal aid are paid at an hourly rate with an upper limit for representation. Any appointed attorney is entitled to be compensated at a rate not exceeding $60 per hour for time expended in court and $40 per hour for time expended out of the court.[113] Further, the maximum amount an attorney or legal aid agency, or community defender organization can claim should not exceed $7,000 for each attorney in cases with one or more felonies and $2,000 in a case with misdemeanors.[114]

2.2.4.2. *Canada*

A) BRIEF

In Canada, the Constitution Act, 1982, guarantees the right to legal assistance or aid on arrest or detention to every individual.[115] The constitution obligates federal and state governments in Canada to provide counsel/solicitor from the initial criminal prosecution stage. The legal aid program is a cost-shared venture in Canada, where federal governments provide funding to the provinces and territories. The legal aid boards and commissions at the territorial and provincial levels provide services related to legal advice, assistance, and representation.

B) ELIGIBLY OF ENTITLEMENT

In Canada, economically disadvantaged persons accused of criminal offenses are eligible for free legal aid. Further, under Section 25 (4) of the Youth Criminal Justice Act, every young person at a trial or hearing has the right to obtain counsel if he/she is unable or incapable of obtaining one.[116] In civil matters, the eligibility to be qualified for civil legal aid or assistance depends on various state authorities. However, in general, a major eligibility criterion is a financial threshold determined by various provinces. The commissions in every province provide legal aid or assistance, keeping in mind the gravity, complexity, and merit of the case type.

C) PROCESS FOR AVAILING OF BENEFITS

The process of availing of the benefits is almost similar in every province in Canada. The applicant needs to apply for legal assistance at the local or regional legal aid center. The director of the commission or the center assesses applications based on the merit of an applicant's case and financial eligibility. Once the direction approves the application, a certificate for legal aid is issued by the authorities granting the applicant the beneficiary of legal aid.

D) GOVERNANCE OF THE SCHEME – REGULATIONS AND FUNDING

Since Canada does not have a centrally administered and operational legal aid governing body, the provincial and territorial division has their legal aid instruments. These provinces have their individual legal aid commissions. Canada's federal government runs a legal aid program to fund the legal aid service delivery assisted by the province or territory-led legal aid schemes. This funding gets instrumental through various contribution agreements and Access to Justice Services Agreements ("AJA"). The AJA is the means through which the federal government financially supports the legal aid programs in Canada.[117] Further, a part of the funds is transferred to the provinces and territories through the Canada Social Transfer.[118] A glimpse of legal aid schemes from the provinces in Canada will further clarify the depth of access to justice in Canada.

Alberta In Alberta, the administration of legal aid services takes place in accordance with the Legal Aid Alberta ("LAA"). It is a publicly funded organization that covers the operational aspects of legal aid services in

Alberta. The scope of services includes legal representation in the form of early resolution, limited scope services, full representation, and services by duty counsels.[119] Although a few services are chargeable, LAA does not charge for duty counsel or Brydges counsel services.[120] The LAA provides legal aid to clients who are eligible and have obtained certificates for eligibility. A client or applicant needs to meet the financial eligibility to qualify for legal aid assistance in Alberta. The service eligibility areas in which legal assistance or aid is operational in Alberta include criminal matters, family matters, and civil matters.[121] A client or legal aid applicant should also qualify for financial eligibility, including income and assets levels.[122] The LAA only waives off the fee-only when the LAA determines that paying the fee will bring hardships to the client or the client's family.[123] The LAA is responsible for managing a roster and appointing either a legal staff or lawyer from the roster to a legal aid applicant after he/she qualifies for free legal assistance.[124]

British Columbia In British Columbia, the Legal Services Society ("LSS") governs the delivery of legal aid services.[125] The LSS Act provides legal assistance and aid to individuals who are incapable of affording a lawyer. The LSS board has nine directors, of which four directors are appointed after consultation with the Canadian Bar Association executive's British Columbia branch.[126]The primary objective of the LSS is to assist an individual in resolving legal problems and facilitating access to justice. LSS is responsible for identifying and assessing the legal needs of low-income individuals in British Columbia.[127] The society provides legal aid by providing services of a lawyer, duty counsel, information packages or self-help kits, and funding alternative dispute resolution.[128] Moreover, LSS has the power to appoint lawyers to provide legal aid even if they are not employed with the LSS.[129] The funds for legal aid cases either come from the consolidated funding by the LSS or from the Law Foundation of British Columbia.[130]

Manitoba In Manitoba, legal aid and assistance are looked after by a body corporate known as the Legal Aid Services Society of Manitoba.[131] Legal Aid Manitoba's management council consists of at least seven but no more than nine members.[132] It provides legal aid to applicants without any fees if they are unable to pay for legal aid. The act also has provisions for considering the legal aid or assistance on a judge's request or an officer.[133] An applicant can submit the application for legal aid to the executive director or the area director for the district in which the applicant resides.[134] The executive director decides whether the applicant is eligible to receive legal aid and whether the applicant will pay a portion of legal aid for all the costs.

Further, the executive director appoints a solicitor among the registered panel members to provide legal aid to eligible applicants.[135] The Legal Aid Manitoba maintains a panel of solicitors to furnish legal aid services under the act. Any solicitor can be part of the panel. The lawyer providing their services in Manitoba is paid based on the Legal Aid Manitoba tariff.[136]

New Brunswick In New Brunswick, the governance of legal aid or assistance is taken care of by the New Brunswick Legal Aid Services Commission, formulated by the New Brunswick Legal Aid Act.[137] The commission operates under the legal framework of the New Brunswick Legal Aid Act and Regulations. The commission is empowered to enforce the rights, powers, and privileges of a natural person. The commission has a board of directors, which oversees the financial management of the commission.[138] The commission also appoints lawyers on a contract basis to provide legal assistance.[139] The commission has a legal aid fund under the consolidated fund approved by the legislature of New Brunswick.[140] The commission further delegates its duties to regional legal aid offices and area legal aid committees, which have the duties pertaining to the issuance of legal aid certificates, preparation list of panel lawyers, and so on.[141] The remuneration of lawyers appointed or contracted is according to Section 39 of the Legal Aid Regulation, New Brunswick 2017–12.[142]

Newfoundland and Labrador In Newfoundland and Labrador, legal aid is a program available to assist people with legal issues who cannot afford private clients. The Newfoundland and Labrador Legal Aid Commission was established by the Legal Aid Act of Newfoundland and Labrador.[143] Like in other provinces, the commission has a legal aid fund and has full authority to pay out of the fund in accordance with the legal aid regulations, which includes the fees and disbursements of a solicitor for legal aid.[144] The commission works by further dividing the provinces under legal aid area directors[145] and legal aid centers[146] for efficient operations and legal aid assistance. Commission also provides solicitors employed with it to the applicants who are found eligible for legal aid.[147] The commission also forms a panel of solicitors who agree to provide their professional services to eligible legal aid applicants.[148] The solicitor, other than the one in the panel, if he/she provides his/her services to legal aid applicants, is paid by the commission according to the regulation's tariff set.

Northwest Territories In the Northwest Territories, the Northwest Territories Legal Aid Act provides the instruments through which legal aid services are made available to an individual. The act aims to make legal aid services available to eligible individuals in a cost-effective manner and through a public agency.[149] The Northwest Territories Legal Aid Commission is the principal institution responsible for administering legal aid services in Northwest Territories.[150] An individual seeking legal aid or assistance should apply to the local executive director for recognition of their application as eligible.[151] However, in criminal cases, the executive director allows legal aid based on merit.[152]

As stated previously, the commission maintains a panel. The lawyers who are not a member of public service and capable of providing legal aid services are eligible to be part legal aid panel.[153] The panel lawyer receives an honorarium after submitting a claim for remuneration or reimbursement.[154]

Nova Scotia In Nova Scotia, under Section 3(1) of the Legal Aid Act 1989, the Nova Scotia Legal Aid Commission manages legal aid and assistance services.[155] The commission consists of 15 directors appointed by the governor in council. The commission is responsible for all matters related to legal aid.[156] Legal aid in Nova Scotia is available at any stage of a proceeding before any court.[157] Any applicant can apply for legal aid by making a proper application to the appropriate local area officer.[158] The executive director then assesses the application to determine whether a certificate of eligibility is to be granted to an applicant or not and whether a barrister is to be compensated.[159] The legal aid lawyers are paid in accordance with the tariff sanction by the regulations.[160]

Nunavut The legal aid services in Nunavut are administered by the Legal Service Board, constituting a quorum of five members.[161] An applicant of legal aid in Nunavut submits information and authorization to investigate his/her financial status in the form of an application to the board's executive director.[162] The board's primary objective is to coordinate and review the provision of legal aid services.[163] The board further appoints regional legal services committees for the delivery of free legal assistance in the regions. The board maintains several panel lawyers to provide services related to legal aid.[164] The panel lawyers' appointment is based on their private practice and their consent to provide legal aid.[165] The panel lawyers were inducted at the board level as well as the regional committee level. The board has powers to remove any panel lawyer on the grounds of indiscipline.[166] A lawyer has the right to appeal the removal to a judge of the Nunavut Court of Justice.[167] A lawyer can also withdraw from the panel by submitting a written notice to the executive director.[168]

Ontario The Legal Aid Ontario ("LAO"), a publicly funded institution, manages and administers legal aid services in Ontario. The services of legal aid are operationalized in accordance with the Legal Aid Service Act.[169] The primary role of LAO is to ensure legal aid services are available to low-income individuals and disadvantaged communities in Ontario.[170] LAO is responsible for facilitating coordination among different legal assistance methods or aid and monitoring and supervising legal aid services.[171] LAO delegates the governance to the Law Society. The Law Society assists in degerming the assets and liabilities on plans and funds for legal aid services.[172] In Ontario, an applicant for legal aid is eligible to receive legal aid services if he/she receives a certificate of approval from the area director.[173] The area director assesses the application based on prescribed financial eligibility.

Further, the classes of applicants for legal aid services may differ. The legal aid services classes may be an applicant for certificates, an applicant for legal aid services by duty counsel, or an applicant for legal aid services by a legal aid clinic.[174] The aspect to weigh in these applicants differs from each other in terms of financial eligibility and merit of the case. LAO employs duty counsel on a full-time or part-time basis.[175] The area director establishes the panel of duty counsel. The fees of duty counsels and lawyers providing legal aid services under certificates are calculated based on Schedules 1, 2, 3, 4, and 5 of the General Legal Aid Regulation.[176]

However, the honorarium paid to lawyers for providing services to a legal aid applicant should not exceed $157,500 in a year for a lawyer with four years of certified experience, $177,190 for lawyers with more than four but less than ten years of experience, and $196,875 for a lawyer with more than ten years of experience.[177]

Québec In Québec, it is the *Commission des services juridiques* that administers the legal aid services. The commission delivers legal aid services through various regional legal aid centers headed by a director-general.[178] Further, these regional legal aid centers deliver their services by establishing a legal aid bureau. The Act Respecting Legal Aid and the Provision of Certain Other Legal Services established the commission.[179] The commission consists of 12 members. The chairperson is responsible for the management and administration of the commission.[180] One of the main functions is to promote legal aid programs for the persons eligible for legal aid.

On the other hand, Regional Legal Center's primary functions are to establish legal aid bureaus, engage advocates full-time, and recommend certificates of the local legal aid centers to the commission.[181] The applicants for legal aid submit their applications to the director-general of the regional legal aid center. The director-general has the sole responsibility for approving or disapproving the eligibility of an applicant to get legal aid or not.[182] In most cases, the commission or the center employs its own set of advocates or assists in legal aid services. The commission or the center covers the fees and expenses of advocates or retainers, not on its employ payroll.[183]

Yukon The Yukon Legal Aid Services Society is the principal organization that oversees and manages Yukon's legal aid services. The Legal Services Society Act of Yukon is established under Section (2) of the act.[184] The society provides legal aid or assistance to individuals who are incapable of affording legal services due to financial reasons. The society covers legal aid or assistance in criminal proceedings, civil proceedings, proceedings in domestic disputes, and legal issues threatening a person's livelihood or physical or mental safety.[185]The Government of Yukon or the Government of Canada primarily funds the entire activities of the Society.[186] The society established a panel of lawyers/solicitors to provide services covered under legal aid or assistance under the act.[187] The director decides to select lawyers for the panel and the eligibility criteria for a lawyer to be part of a panel.[188] If a director refuses to include or remove the name of a lawyer from the list of the panel, the director notifies the lawyer of the reasons in writing.[189] These panel lawyers are paid from the funds of the society, following the limit set by the regulation.[190]

E) TERMS AND CONDITIONS OF ENGAGING LACS

The commission or legal aid center often employs full-time lawyers or counsels in most of the provinces. These panel lawyers have a fixed honorarium set out following the legal aid regulation of every province in Canada. If a lawyer takes a legal aid case, the commission reimburses the lawyers who provide his/her legal aid services.

2.2.4.3. *Brazil*

A) BRIEF

The Federal Constitution of Brazil recognizes full and free legal assistance to individuals as a fundamental right.[191] The Constitution obligates the state to provide support for any such endeavor.[192]

To deliver on the constitutionally mandated right, the *Defensoria Pública da União* (Public Defender's Office of the Union; "DPU"), under the Complementary Law No. 18, assigns a federal public defender to administer legal aid services in Brazil.[193]

B) ELIGIBILITY OF ENTITLEMENT

To avail of any kind of legal, judicial, and court assistance from a federal public defender, an individual needs to provide that she/he has no money to afford any kind of legal services.[194] Further, entitlement rests upon the monthly family income and the number of members in the family.[195] The DPU limits the value of economic necessity for free legal assistance at R$ 2,000.[196]

C) PROCESS FOR AVAILING OF BENEFITS

Since the DPU is essential for the state's judicial function, free legal assistance and advice are available to any individual from the state according to the civil and criminal proceedings.[197] The court, by the constitutional mandate, provides free legal assistance to every individual.

On the contrary, legal assistance related to judicial or legal advice has a very different process. A potential legal aid beneficiary files a formal application at their respective local public defender's office. The applicants submit every personal documentation and declaration of the necessity for free legal assistance.[198] After submission, the local public defender office verifies the socioeconomic condition and analyzes whether an applicant passes the hypo sufficiency[199] test or not. If the local DPU denies assistance because the applicant fails the test, the applicant will have 30 days to resubmit the application with documents demonstrating the need for legal assistance.[200] After passing the verification of the test, the DPU promotes the subpoena of the applicant.[201] The applicants have a period of ten days to file an appeal for reconsideration if their appeal is refused for a second time.[202] After applying, the local DPU assigns a titular defender that advises the applicant on the applicant's various legal assistance.[203]

D) GOVERNANCE OF THE SCHEME – REGULATIONS AND FUNDING

The DPU is the principal institution responsible for the governance and administration of FLAS in Brazil.[204] The Constitution guarantees the state DPU's completely functional and administrative autonomy.[205] The federal public defender general heads the DPU.[206] The president of the Federal Republic of Brazil appoints the federal public defender general.[207] The public defender general is responsible for directing the DPU, representing the DPU judicially and extrajudicially, and performing administrative, financial, and personnel management acts.[208] The DPU also consists of an internal affairs department, which performs inspections for the office's efficient working.[209] The DPU has jurisdiction over states, the federal district, and the territories in Brazil. The DPU in each state, in the federal district, and in each territory appoints a chief public defender to perform institutional functions on behalf of the DPU.[210] The chief public defender's principal task is to coordinate the federal public defenders' activities in their respective areas of competence.[211]

The DPU in the states, the federal district, and the territories further delegates its work to nuclei (local) centers.[212] These centers work under the chief public defender only.[213]

E) TERMS AND CONDITIONS OF ENGAGING LACS

The LAS in Brazil has public defenders as LACs who assist and provide legal services on behalf of the DPU, the states, the federal district, and the territories. In the initial stage, the public defenders were inducted into the federal DPU via a national competitive exam.[214] The Federal DPU releases the call for application for the competition, indicating the number of vacant seats in the initial career category.[215] The federal DPU conducts the entrance contest when the number of vacancies exceeds one-fifth of the career's initial positions.[216] The candidates with registration at the Brazilian Bar Association and having at least two years of practice experience are eligible to sit for the entrance contest.[217]

The public defender's career is categorized under three effective positions at the union, state, federal district, and territory levels. A public defender first enters the initial category, then the intermediate category, and finally the special category.[218] In the initial category, the federal public defenders work in the regional federal courts, the regional federal labor courts, and the regional federal electoral courts.[219] The federal public defenders of the intermediate category act together with federal courts, labor courts, electoral boards, maritime courts, military judges, audits, and administrative bodies.[220] The federal public defenders of the special category work in the Superior Court of Justice, the Superior Labor Court, the Superior Electoral Court, and so on.[221]

2.2.5. *Africa*

2.2.5.1. *Nigeria*

A) BRIEF

In Nigeria, the Federal Republic of Nigeria's Constitution mandates the right to legal aid or assistance. Under Article 36 (6) of the Constitution, every person charged with a criminal offense gets adequate time to prepare their defense and has the right to defend themselves in person or by a legal practitioner.[222] Further, the Constitution obligates the National Assembly to render financial or legal assistance to the citizens of Nigeria who are unable to defend their rights.[223] The instrument to provide legal aid or assistance to every individual in Nigeria is governed through the Legal Aid Act, 2011, which focuses on providing legal aid in civil and criminal matters.

B) ELIGIBILITY OF ENTITLEMENT

The eligibility for legal aid in Nigeria is dependent upon the income threshold of an applicant. Per the Legal Aid Act, the individual eligible for free legal aid must have income less than the national minimum wage.[224] However, in exceptional circumstances, the legal aid board can grant legal aid services to a person whose earnings exceed the national minimum wage.[225] Further, the act also ensures that the legal aid council's governing board may approve certain legal aid services on a contributory basis to individuals whose income exceeds ten times the national minimum wage.[226]

C) PROCESS FOR AVAILING OF BENEFITS

An applicant submits the application for legal aid or assistance at the local legal aid center. The local legal aid center assesses the eligibility of the application with the state coordinator to determine whether the applicant qualifies for free legal aid or not based on the area of services an application belongs to.

D) GOVERNANCE OF THE SCHEME – REGULATIONS AND FUNDING

The Legal Aid Council of Nigeria is the principal organization that has the sole responsibility to carry out all the provisions enlisted in the Legal Aid Act.[227] The council comprises the governing board, director general, and legal support staff for the council's efficient working.[228] The council has major departments, such as finance and administration, litigation, international relations, corporate operations and planning, and research, to provide efficient services under the legal aid act.[229] The legal aid framework further divides Nigeria into six geopolitical zonal offices responsible for coordinating state offices and their activities related to legal aid services.[230] The zonal offices head the state coordinators to deliver legal aid services to the citizenry in their respective zones.[231] These state coordinators operate three units – Criminal Defence Unit, Civil Litigation Unit, and Community Legal Services Unit – to cater to legal aid services.[232] Criminal Defence assists indigent persons involved in criminal proceedings, covering access to assistance, advice, and representation before the court.[233] Civil Litigation deals in access to advice, representation, and assistance in court to secure rights, duties, privileges, and other services entitled in the Nigerian legal system.[234] Community Legal Services focuses on promoting individual services for general information about the law and legal system.[235] The council funds its day-to-day administration from the Legal Aid General Fund. The government approves each state's sums.

E) TERMS AND CONDITIONS OF ENGAGING LACS

The panel lawyers providing legal services to the persons receiving legal aid are prepared and maintained by the council.[236] If a legal aid panel lawyer is not satisfied with the removal from the panel and he/she is not satisfied with the decision, the lawyer has the right to refer the matter to the director-general and the governing board.[237]

The legal practitioners are paid by the Legal Aid Fund of the council.[238] Further, the council may also partner with non-governmental or law clinics' services to fulfill the mandate of legal aid.[239]

2.2.5.2. *South Africa*

A) BRIEF

The Republic of South Africa's Constitution provides provisions for legal aid or assistance to selected individuals. For instance, under the constitutional mandate, every child has the right to have a legal practitioner at state expense if facing civil proceedings.[240] Further, the Constitution extends the right to have or assign legal practitioners, at state expense, to detained individuals and sentenced prisoners.[241] It also provides the right to free legal representation for the accused if the accused cannot afford one.[242] Therefore, in South Africa, legal aid is explicitly covered in the form of rights to an individual. In South Africa, the Legal Aid South Africa Act, 2013, provides the ways and methods for delivering legal aid services to every individual in South Africa. Legal Aid South Africa is the principal entity to administer these services in the entire nation.

B) ELIGIBILITY OF ENTITLEMENT

Legal Aid South Africa provides legal assistance to individuals who are incapable of affording legal services due to a lack of financial resources. The individual needs to be a physical resident or a citizen or a permanent resident of the Republic of South Africa.[243]

C) PROCESS FOR AVAILING OF BENEFITS

In South Africa, the legal aid applicant applies at local offices of Legal Aid South Africa or through a Legal Aid employee.[244] The applications go through a means test to qualify for legal aid in civil cases or criminal cases.[245] Under this test, an applicant in a criminal case must have R5,500 a month to qualify for legal aid.[246] In a civil case, an applicant without a spouse must have a monthly income of less than R5,500, and an applicant with a spouse must have a monthly income of less than R5,600 to avail of the benefits under the Legal Aid Act.[247] The applicants are mandated to provide documentary proofs and written disclosure of assets for the means test.[248] Legal Aid South Africa can terminate the legal aid services if a beneficiary of legal aid does not qualify under the means test, fails to appear in court, and makes it impossible for an instructed legal practitioner to carry on its duties.[249]

D) GOVERNANCE OF THE SCHEME – REGULATIONS AND FUNDING

Legal Aid South Africa manages the governance of legal aid services in South Africa, which is primarily through instruments like the Legal Aid South Africa Act 39 of 2014, the Regulation to the Act, the Legal Aid Manual, the provisions of the Standard Operating Procedure of Legal Aid South Africa, the decisions made by the Board of Legal Aid, and directives of the CEO of the Legal Aid South Africa.[250] Legal Aid South Africa aims to provide legal aid and legal representation to persons at state expense.[251] The board governs the operational and management aspects of Legal Aid South Africa.[252] The board consists of 14 voting members.[253] The chief executive officer is responsible for the general administration, supervision of staff, and promotion of Legal Aid South Africa's activities.[254] Legal Aid South Africa is funded by the money granted by South Africa's Parliament or money received from any other sources.[255] The local offices and satellite offices are a further extension of Legal Aid South Africa to provide legal aid and assistance services.

E) TERMS AND CONDITIONS OF ENGAGING LACS

The LAS in South Africa follows a mixed method to deliver FLAS. On the one hand, the board employs full-time legal practitioners and candidate attorneys.[256] On the other, the board also procures PLPs by entering into agreements with them.[257] In terms of PLPs, Legal Aid South Africa often requests their legal aid clients' information and documents for quality and performance assessment.[258] Further, the legal practitioner assigned by Legal Aid South Africa in criminal proceedings is subject to review by the high court at the affected person's instance.[259]

2.2.5.3. *Kenya*

A) BRIEF

The Constitution of Kenya fairly covers the idea of free legal assistance to every individual. The Constitution mandates the state to ensure access to justice for all individuals.[260] Further, under the principle of fair hearing/trial, the Constitution provides the right to choose an advocate and have an advocate assigned or represented on behalf of an accused person at the state's expense.[261] Apart from the constitutional provisions, Kenya also has the Legal Aid Act 2016, which provides free legal advice, representation, and assistance to the poor and needy.

B) ELIGIBLY OF ENTITLEMENT

Under the Legal Aid Act 2016, indigent individuals, children, refugees, victims of human trafficking, internally displaced persons ("IDP"), and stateless persons are eligible for free or state-supported legal aid services.[262] The National Legal Aid Service ("NLAS") determines the person's financial resources for him/her to be eligible for free legal services under the Legal Aid Act 2016.[263] The service only proceeds to grant legal aid if it finds reasonable and justifiable grounds for it.[264]

C) PROCESS FOR AVAILING OF BENEFITS

The applicants need to apply to the NLAS in writing to get FLAS. The applicant needs to apply before the final determination of the matter in court or forum.[265] Further, it is the duty of the court to inform the NLAS to provide legal aid to the accused person.[266] The NLAS assesses the financial means of the person before approving the legal aid service.[267] The NLAS, in whole or in part, grants legal aid assistance to the applicant.[268] The NLAS specifies the conditions under which an applicant is getting FLAS with the legal aid provider's name.[269] The legal aid application is decided within the time limit of 48 hours from the date of receipt by the NLAS.[270] The LAS in Kenya also has a provision of withdrawal of FLAS if the beneficiary's economic condition improves during legal aid.[271] The NLAS keeps an updated record of the financial health of the aided person for the said purpose.[272]

D) GOVERNANCE OF THE SCHEME – REGULATIONS AND FUNDING

The NLAS is the principal body that administers the legal aid scheme that is affordable and sustainable in Kenya.[273] The NLAS aims to promote research in the field of legal aid and access to justice, develop guidelines and standards for legal aid schemes, and establish legal aid services in universities and other institutions.[274] The NLAS is governed by a board that consists of a chairperson appointed by the president of Kenya; a judge of the high court nominated by the chief justice of Kenya; the principal secretary of the ministry; the director of public prosecutions; a person each nominated by the Law Society of Kenya, by the Kenya National Commission on Human Rights, by the Council of Legal Education, and by the National Council of Person with Disabilities; and the director.[275] The NLAS has an established legal aid fund that consists of money allocated by the Parliament, money from grants, and money gained from any other lawful sources.[276]

E) TERMS AND CONDITIONS OF ENGAGING LACS

The NLAS has a pool of accredited legal aid providers and advocates to provide legal aid services enshrined in the Legal Aid Act 2016.[277] These legal aid providers apply directly to the NLAS for accreditation.[278]The NLAS maintains a register of the legal aid providers, including personal details, contact addresses, and the number of cases handled.[279] The accredited legal aid providers are obligated under the Legal Aid Act 2016 to protect the rights and interests of aided person/beneficiary, maintain confidentiality, and have ethical conduct while serving the NLAS.[280] The NLAS has the right to suspend the accreditation if a legal aid service provider breaches the code of conduct, is convicted of an offense, or fails to maintain official records of activities taken on behalf of an aided person.[281] The NLAS determines legal aid providers' fees, which are often less than the legal fee that applies to a person not covered under the Legal Aid Act 2016.[282] Further, if a legal aid provider is dissatisfied with the fees paid by the NLAS, he/she has the right to review the decision.[283]

Notes

1 Dr. Sharma, S. S., Public interest litigations and paralegal services, *Central Law Agency*, p. 42 (2003)
2 Pelletier, George A., Legal aid in France, *Notre Dame Law Review*, 42, p. 627, available at http://scholarship.law.nd.edu/ndlr/vol42/iss5/2 last seen on 08/02/2019

3 Houseman, Alan W., Civil legal assistance for low-income persons: looking back and looking forward, *Fordham Urban Law Journal*, 29(3), pp. 1213–44. HeinOnline, available at https://heinonline.org/HOL/P?h=hein.journals/frdurb29&i=1229 last seen on 08/02/2019
4 NALSA, *Introduction and History of NALSA*, available at https://nalsa.gov.in/about-us last seen on 08/02/2019
5 Article 6(3)(c), The European Convention of Human Rights, 1950
6 Third UN Congress on the *Prevention of Crime and Treatment of Offenders*, 1965, available at *www.unodc.org/congress/en/previous/previous-03.html*, last seen on 11/02/2019
7 Sujan Singh, *Legal aid human right to equality*, Deep & Deep Publications, p. 15 (1996)
8 Art 14(d), International Convention of Civil and Political Right, 1966 (Office of the United Nations High Commissioner for Human Rights)
9 Article 8, Article 21,The American Convention on Human Rights 1969 (Organisation of American States)
10 Convention on International Access to Justice, 1980 (Hague Conference on Private International Law)
11 African Charter On The Rights And Welfare Of The Child 1990 (The African Commission on Human and People's Rights)
12 International Convention On The Protection Of The Rights Of All Migrant Workers And Members Of Their Families 1999 (Office of the United Nations High Commissioner for Human Rights [OHCHR])
13 The Protection of Persons with Mental Illness and the Improvement of Mental Health Care, 1991 (United Nations General Assembly)
14 S. 6 Legal Aid Act, 2054, 1997 (Nepal)
15 Ibid. S. 12 (1)
16 Rule 6 (1) Legal Aid Rules, 2055, 1998 (Nepal)
17 Ibid. Rule 6 (2)
18 Supra 14 at S. 7
19 Supra 16 at Rule 10 (f)
20 S. 3, Legal Aid Services Act, 2000, (Bangladesh)
21 Ibid. S. 16 (1)
22 Ibid. S. 8B (2)
23 Ibid. S. 9 (1)
24 The Constitution of Socialist Republic of Sri Lanka, Article 12 (1)
25 The Legal Aid Law No. 27 of 1978
26 *Legal Aid Beneficiaries*, Legal Aid Commission of Sri Lanka, available at www.legalaid.gov.lk/index.php/legal-aid-beneficiaries, last seen on 15/07/2020
27 *Eligibility*, *Obtain Legal Aid Common Procedure*, Government Information Centre, www.gic.gov.lk/gic/index.php/en/component/info/?id=430&task=info, last seen on 15/07/2020
28 Supra 26, Special Status for Woman in Maintenance Cases
29 Supra 27, Submission Procedure
30 Ibid.
31 Ibid.
32 Supra 25
33 Ibid., S. 4
34 Ibid., S. 5, Constitution of the Commission
35 Ibid., S. 9, Chairman of Commission
36 Ibid., S. 17, Legal Aid Fund
37 Ibid., S. 19, Annual Grant by the Government to the Commission
38 *About Us*, Legal Aid Commission of Sri Lanka, available at www.legalaid.gov.lk/index.php/2016-01-13-09-16-07/about-us, last seen on 15/07/2020

39 The Constitution of People's Republic of China, Article 33 (2)
40 Article 35 and 36, Chapter 4, Criminal Procedure Law 2018 Revision, (People's Republic of China)
41 Article 42, Chapter 4, Lawyers Law 2017 Revision (People's Republic of China)
42 Legal Aid Regulations 2003, (People's Republic of China)
43 Ibid. Article 4
44 Surpa 42. Article 5
45 Surpa 42. Article 21
46 Surpa 42. Article 24
47 *Civil Legal Aid*, Japan Legal Support Centre, available at www.houterasu.or.jp/en/about_jlsc/operations/operation2.html, last seen on 14/05/2020
48 *Implementation of Comprehensive Legal Support*, Japan Legal Support Centre, Ministry of Japan www.moj.go.jp/ENGLISH/issues/issues08.html, last seen on 14/05/2020
49 Article 30 (1) Comprehensive Legal Support Act, (Japan)
50 Ibid. Article 20 (1)
51 Ibid. Article 30 (1) (b)
52 The Constitution of the Republic of Korea Article 12 (4)
53 Ibid. Article 27 (1)
54 Article 1, Purpose, Legal Aid Act (Republic of Korea)
55 Ibid. Article 2(2)(i) Responsibility of State and Local Governments
56 Supra 52, Article 27 (1)
57 Article 27, Act on Special Cases Concerning the Punishment, etc. of Sexual Crimes (Republic of Korea)
58 Article 70, Constitutional Court Act (Republic of Korea)
59 Article 128–133, Section 3, Chapter 3, Civil Procedure Act (Republic of Korea)
60 Article 33, Criminal Procedure Act (Republic of Korea)
61 Article 22, Legal Aid Act (Republic of Korea)
62 *Procedure, Legal Aid System*, Korean Legal Aid Corporation, available at www.klac.or.kr/lang/legalstruct/summary.do, last seen on 20/07/2020
63 Article 22–2 (Request for Providing Material), Legal Aid Act (Republic of Korea)
64 *Procedure, Legal Aid System*, Korean Legal Aid Corporation, available at www.klac.or.kr/lang/legalstruct/summary.do,last seen on 20/07/2020
65 *Fast Facts, About Us*, Korea Legal Aid Corporation, www.klac.or.kr/lang/introduce/companyProfile.do,last seen on 20/07/2020
66 Article 13(1), Executive Officers and Their Terms of Office, Legal Aid Act (Republic of Korea)
67 Ibid. Article 13(2)
68 Article 20 (1), Legal Aid Members, Legal Aid Act (Republic of Korea)
69 Article 24 (1), Financial Resources of Corporation, Legal Aid Act (Republic of Korea)
70 Ibid. Article (2), (3) & (4)
71 *Organization*, Korea Legal Aid Corporation, available at www.klac.or.kr/lang/introduce/organizationChart.do, last seen on 20/07/2020
72 Ibid.
73 Ibid.
74 Ibid. Division of Duties, Legal Aid Bureau
75 Ibid. Division of Duties, Office of Planning and Coordination
76 Ibid. Division of Duties, Administrative Bureau
77 Article 1, Purpose, Chapter 1, General Provisions, Public-Service Advocates Act (Republic of Korea)
78 Article 3 Status, Chapter 2, Training and Assignment of Public Service, Public-Service Advocates Act (Republic of Korea)

79 Article 4 (1), Notifications, etc. of List of Names, Public-Service Advocates Act (Republic of Korea)
80 Article 5 (1), Order for Service, etc., Public-Service Advocates Act (Republic of Korea)
81 Article 8 (1) Period of Compulsory Service, Public-Service Advocates Act (Republic of Korea)
82 Article 16, Deprivation of Status, Public-Service Advocates Act, Republic of Korea
83 Article 18, Hearing, Public-Service Advocates Act, Republic of Korea
84 Article 14, Remuneration, Public-Service Advocates Act, Republic of Korea
85 Article 3 (1), Basic Law (Federal Republic of Germany)
86 Act on Advisory Assistance and Representation for Citizens with a Low Income (Federal Republic of Germany)
87 Section 117 (1), Application, Code of Civil Procedure (Federal Republic of Germany)
88 Section 6 (1) Advisory Assistance Act (Federal Republic of Germany)
89 Book 2, Section 140 of German Code of Criminal Procedure (Federal Republic of Germany)
90 Ibid.Section 123, Code of Civil Procedure, Germany
91 Schedule 1, Article 6 (3) (c), Human Rights Act, 1998, UK Public General Acts (United Kingdom)
92 Part 1, Section 3, Legal Aid, Advice and Assistance Order 1981 (Northern Ireland)
93 Part 3, Section 15, Legal Aid Act 1986 (Scotland)
94 Supra 95, Part 3, Section 28, Legal Aid, Advice and Assistance Order 1981 (Northern Ireland)
95 Part 1, Section 11, Civil Legal Aid, Legal Aid, Sentencing and Punishment of Offenders Act 2012 (United Kingdom)
96 Part 2, Section 14, Assessment of resources etc. Legal Aid, Advice and Assistance Order 1981 (Northern Ireland)
97 Part 3, Section 28, 29, Free Legal Aid in Criminal Proceedings, Legal Aid, Advice and Assistance Order, 1981 (Northern Ireland)
98 *The Chief Executive, Roles, responsibilities and governance*, Legal Aid Agency Framework Document, available at https://assets.publishing.service.gov.uk/government/uploads/system/uploads/attachment_data/file/372206/laa-framework-document.pdf,last seen on 15/06/2020
99 Part 4, Section 150, Financial Provision, Legal Aid, Sentencing and Punishment of Offenders Act 2012, (United Kingdom)
100 Part 1, Section 1(2) The Board, Legal Aid Act 1986 (Scotland)
101 Part 2, Article 15 (1), Solicitors and Counsel, Legal Aid, Advice and Assistance Order 1981 (Northern Ireland)
102 Part 2, Article 13 (1) Remuneration of persons giving legal aid, Legal Aid, Advice and Assistance Order 1981 (Northern Ireland)
103 Schedule 2, Paragraph 1, Legal Aid, Advice and Assistance Order 1981 (Northern Ireland)
104 Part 4 A, Section 25 A (1), Legal Aid Act Act 1986 (Scotland)
105 Sixth Amendment, Rights of Accused in Criminal Prosecutions (United States of America)
106 *Gideon v. Wainwright* 372 US 335 (1963)
107 *Civil Legal Aid 101*, Department of Justice, available at www.govinfo.gov/content/pkg/GPO-CONAN-1992/pdf/GPO-CONAN-1992-10-7.pdf, last seen on 18/06/2020
108 *How We Work*, Legal Services Corporation, available at www.lsc.gov/what-legal-aid/how-we-work, last on seen 18/06/2020

109 Section 1007 (a) Grants and Contracts, Legal Services Corporation Act (United States of America)
110 Section 1006 (a) Powers, Duties, and Limitations, Legal Services Corporation Act (United States of America)
111 Rule 44. Right to Appointment of Counsel, Federal Rules of Criminal Procedure (United States of America)
112 Section 3006 A, (b) Appointment of Counsel, Chapter 201-General Provisions, Title 18 (United States of America)
113 Ibid. (d) (1) Payment for Representation
114 Ibid. (d) (2) Maximum Amounts
115 Section 10 (b), Canadian Charter of Rights and Freedom, Constitution Act, 1982 (Canada)
116 Section 25 (4), Right to Counsel, Youth Criminal Justice Act (Canada)
117 *Access to Justice Services Agreements* (AJA), available at www.justice.gc.ca/eng/fund-fina/gov-gouv/access.html, last seen on 22/06/2020
118 *Legal Aid Program*, available at www.justice.gc.ca/eng/fund-fina/gov-gouv/aid-aide.html, last seen 22/06/2020
119 Section 1.2, Part 1, Legal Aid Rules Alberta 2019 (Alberta)
120 Ibid. Section 1.8.
121 Ibid. Section 3.15
122 Ibid. Section 4.8, Part 4, Financial Eligibility Guidelines
123 Ibid. Section 5.1 & Section 5.5 Part 5
124 Ibid. Section 7.1 & Section 7.6.
125 Section 2 (1) Legal Services Society Act 2002 (Alberta)
126 Ibid. Section 4
127 Ibid. Section 9 (2), Role of the Legal Service Society
128 Ibid. Section 11 (1)
129 Ibid. Section 11 (2)
130 Section 61 (1) (c) Application of funds, Legal Profession Act 1998 (British Columbia)
131 Section 2 (1) The Legal Aid Manitoba Act (Manitoba)
132 Ibid. Section 5 (1) Management Council
133 Ibid. Section 3 (2) Additional Powers
134 Ibid. Section 11 (1) Applying for Legal Aid
135 Ibid. Section 14 (1) No Right to choose lawyer
136 Ibid. Section 16 Solicitor's Bill of Costs
137 Section 3 (1) Commission and Board, New Brunswick Legal Aid Act (New Brunswick)
138 Ibid. Section 6 (1), Board Powers and Duties
139 Ibid. Section 14 (1) Appointments and Contracts
140 Ibid. Section 19 (1) Legal Aid Fund
141 Ibid, Section 24 Legal Aid Offices
142 Section 39, New Brunswick Regulation 2017–12 (New Brunswick)
143 Section 3 (1) The Newfoundland and Labrador Legal Aid Commission, Legal Aid Act, (Newfoundland and Labrador)
144 Ibid. Section 18 (1) & (2), Legal Aid Fund
145 Ibid. Section 28 Area Directors
146 Ibid. Section 29 Legal Aid Centres
147 Ibid. Section 31 Solicitor may be appointed
148 Ibid. Section 35 Cost to be taxed
149 Section 2, Purpose of Act, Northwest Territories Legal Aid Act, (Northwest Territories)
150 Ibid. Section 4 Northwest Territories Legal Aid Commission
151 Ibid. Section 9 (1) Eligible Person

152 Ibid. Section 10 (2) Legal Advice of Lawyer Required in Criminal Appeals
153 Ibid. Section 14 (2) Legal Aid Lawyers
154 Ibid. Section 20 Claim by Panel Lawyers
155 Section 3 (1) Nova Scotia Legal Aid Commission, Legal Aid Act 1989 (Nova Scotia)
156 Ibid. Section 6 (1) Power and Duties of Commission
157 Ibid. Section 16 (1) When Legal Aid Granted
158 Ibid. Section 17 Application for legal aid
159 Ibid. Section 18 Certificate of Eligibility
160 Section 15 Tariff of fees, Legal Aid General Regulations and Tariff of Fees, (Nova Scotia)
161 Section 2 (1) Legal Services Regulation (Nunavut)
162 Ibid. Section 14 (1) Application
163 Section 8 Duties of Board Legal Services Act (Nunavut)
164 Ibid. Section 34 (1) Panels
165 Ibid. Section 34 (2)
166 Ibid. Section 35 (1) Removal from Panel by Board
167 Ibid. Section 35 (2) Appeal
168 Ibid. Section 35 (3)
169 Section 1 (a) Legal Aid Services Act, 1998, (Ontario)
170 Ibid. Section 1(c), (d)
171 Ibid. Section 4 Objects
172 Ibid. Section 11
173 Section 6 (1), Applications, O. Reg. 106/99: Administration Of System For Providing Legal Aid Services (Ontario)
174 Section 1, Ontario Regulation 107/99 (Ontario)
175 Ibid. Section 20 (1)
176 Ibid. Section 3
177 Ibid. Section 5
178 *Profile of the Legal Aid Network*, available at www.csj.qc.ca/IntranetUploads/CSJ/English/Fichiers/Reseau%20ang%202018%2008%2020%20(web).pdf, last seen on 29/06/2020
179 Section 11, Division III, Commission des services juridiques, The Act Respecting Legal Aid and the Provision of Certain Other Legal Services (Quebec)
180 Ibid. Section 17
181 Ibid. Section 32
182 Ibid. Section 66
183 Ibid. Section 6
184 Section 2 (1), Establishment of the Society, Legal Services Society Act (Yukon)
185 Ibid. Section 16 (1) Powers of the Society
186 Ibid. Section (21) & (22), Financial Matters
187 Section 3 (1) Panels of Solicitors, Legal Aid Regulations, Yukon (Yukon)
188 Ibid. Section 4, Application to be on a panel
189 Ibid. Section 5 (4) Panels
190 Ibid. Section 10, Payment for work after removal from panel
191 Article 5, LXXIV, Chapter 1, Individual and Collective Rights and Duties, Title 2, About Fundamental Rights and Guarantees (Brazil)
192 Ibid.
193 *Federal Public Defender*, State Structure, Government of Brazil, available at www.brazil.gov.br/government/how-the-government-works/federal-public-defender, *last seen on 4/07/2020*
194 Ibid.
195 Ibid.

196 *Resolution No. 134* December 07, 2016, available at www.dpu.def.br/conselho-superior/resolucoes/37083-resolucao-n-134-de-07-de-dezembro-de-2016-fixa-o-valor-de-presuncao-de-necessidade-economica-para-fim-de-assistencia-juridica-integral-e-gratuita, *last seen on 4/07/2020*
197 Article 1, General Provisions, Complementary Law No.80/1994 (Brazil)
198 *Article* 9, Resolution No.133, of December 7, 2016, available at www.dpu.def.br/conselho-superior/resolucoes/37078-resolucao-n-133-de-07-de-dezembro-de-2017-dispoe-sobre-a-concessao-de-assistencia-juridica-gratuita-e-da-outras-providencias, *last seen on 4/07/2020*
199 *Hypossuficiency Test*: It is a test of whether natural person belonging to a family nucleus whose gross monthly income does not exceed a certain amount set by the Federal Public Defender's Office, available at www.dpu.def.br/legislacao/instrucoes-normativas/55532-instrucao-normativa-n-70-de-11-de-fevereiro-de-2020-institui-os-procedimentos-do-processo-de-trabalho-atendimento-do-assistido-no-ambito-da-dpu, *last seen on 4/07/2020*
200 Supra 205, Article 14
201 Ibid.
202 Supra 205, Article 16
203 *Initial Service*, Normative Instruction No.70, of February 11, 2020, available at www.dpu.def.br/legislacao/instrucoes-normativas/55532-instrucao-normativa-n-70-de-11-de-fevereiro-de-2020-institui-os-procedimentos-do-processo-de-trabalho-atendimento-do-assistido-no-ambito-da-dpu, *last seen on 4/07/2020*
204 Article 134, The Public Defender Office, Constitution of the Federal Republic of Brazil, 1998 (Brazil)
205 Ibid. Section 2
206 Article 6, Section 1, From Federal Public General Defender, Complementary Law No. 80, of January 12, 1994, (Brazil)
207 Ibid.
208 Ibid, Article 8
209 Ibid, Article 11, Section III, Of the General Ombudsman of the Public Defender of the Union
210 Ibid. Article 15, Section IV
211 Ibid. Article 15 (I), Section IV
212 Ibid. Article 16, Section V, the Nuclei of the Public Defender of the Union in the States, the Federal District, and the Territories
213 Ibid. Article 17
214 Ibid. Article 24
215 Ibid. Article 24 (2)
216 Ibid. Article 25
217 Ibid. Article 26
218 Ibid. Article 19
219 Ibid. Article 21
220 Ibid. Article 20
221 Ibid. Article 22
222 Constitution of the Federal Republic of Nigeria Chapter 4 Fundamental Rights Article 36 (6)
223 Ibid. Article 46 (4) (b)
224 Article 10 (1), Persons entitled for Legal Aid, Legal Aid Act, 2011 (Nigeria)
225 Ibid. Article 10 (2)
226 Ibid. Article 10 (3)
227 Ibid. Article 1(2)
228 Ibid. Article 1 (4)
229 Ibid. Article 6 (1)

230 Ibid. Article 6 (2)
231 Ibid. Article 6 (4)
232 Ibid. Article 6 (5)
233 Ibid. Article 8 (2)
234 Ibid. Article 8 (3)
235 Ibid. Article 8 (7)
236 Ibid. Article 14 (1), Part IV, Legal Practitioners
237 Ibid. Article 14 (3)
238 Ibid. Article 15 (1)
239 Ibid. Article 17 (2)
240 Constitution of the Republic of South Africa s. 28 (h)
241 Ibid. Section 35(2) (c), Arrested, detained, and accused persons
242 Ibid. Section 35 (3) (g)
243 Section 2 (3), General Policy, Legal Aid Regulations South Africa (South Africa)
244 *Section 3.1.1. Legal Aid Applications, Chapter 3*, Applying for legal aid, Legal Aid Manual, pg. 26 https://legal-aid.co.za/wp-content/uploads/2020/04/Legal-Aid-Manual-2020-as-at-01-April-2020.pdf *last seen on 4/07/2020*
245 Section 27 (1), Qualifying for Legal Aid and means test, Legal Aid Regulation (South Afirca)
246 Ibid. Section 27 (2)
247 Ibid. Section 27 (3)
248 Ibid. Section 27 (5)
249 Ibid. Section 33 (1)
250 Governance of the Legal Aid South Africa, p. 22
251 *Section 3, Objectives of Legal Aid South Africa*, the Legal Aid South Africa Act, 2014, www.gov.za/sites/default/files/gcis_document/201412/383159-12act39of2014legalaidsaact2014a.pdf *last seen on 4/07/2020*
252 Ibid. Section 2 (1) Establishment of Legal Aid South Africa and its relationship with Board.
253 Ibid. Section 6 (1) Composition and appointment the Board
254 Ibid. Section 16 (1) Functions of Chief Executive Officer
255 Ibid. Section 21 Finances of Legal Aid South Africa
256 Ibid. Section 4 (a) (i)
257 Ibid. Section 4 (a). (iii)
258 Ibid. Section 19 (1) Protection of client privilege in certain circumstances
259 Ibid. Section 22 (4)
260 Constitution of Kenya Article 48
261 Ibid. Article 50 (2) (g) & (h), Fair Hearing
262 Section 36 (2), Person Eligible for Legal Aid, the Legal Aid Act 2016, (Kenya)
263 Ibid. Section 36 (3)
264 Ibid. Section 36 (4) (l)
265 Ibid. Section 40(1) & (2), Application for the Legal Aid, the Legal Aid Act 2016
266 Ibid. Section 43 (1) & (2), Duties of the Court
267 Ibid. Section 47
268 Ibid. Section 44 (1), Decision on Application for Legal Aid
269 Ibid. Section 44 (2)
270 Ibid. Section 44 (3)
271 Ibid. Section 46 (1)
272 Ibid. Section 47, Financial Information
273 Ibid. Section 7 (1)
274 Ibid. Section 7 (1) Functions of the Services
275 Ibid. Section 9 (1), Establishment of Board of Service
276 Ibid. Section 29 (1) Establishment of Legal Aid Fund

277 Ibid. Section 56, Provision of Legal Aid
278 Ibid. Section 58 (1), Application for Accreditation
279 Ibid. Section 60 (1), Register of Accredited Legal Aid Providers
280 Ibid. Section 61(3), Obligation Relating to the Professional Conduct
281 Ibid. Section 66 (1)
282 Ibid. Section 75 (1)&(4)
283 Ibid. Section 50

3 The State of Access to Justice for Legal Aid Beneficiaries

3.1. Introduction

The idea of FLAS rests on the concept of providing free of cost legal services to every individual from the socially, economically, and culturally strata in a society. This idea aims to guarantee access to justice under the realm of fundamental rights and directive principles of state policy engraved in India's Constitution. To attain this constitutional mandate, the GoI has enacted statutory instruments like the LSA Act, 1987; the Code of Civil Procedure, 1908; and the Code of Criminal Procedure, 1973. Nevertheless, various jurists, scholars, and civil society members have observed that legal aid beneficiaries are taken for granted by their respective LACs. Further, the State Legal Services Authority ("SLSA") and District Legal Services Authority ("DLSA") often focus more on the number of legal services provided to beneficiaries without keeping any tab on those services' quality.

This chapter focuses on evaluating the quality of LACs and legal aid services, in general, from legal aid beneficiaries' perspectives. Overall, field investigators under the principal researcher's supervision, research associate, and assistants collected the data from 18 states. Samples of beneficiaries from two district courts were taken from each state.

To maintain the diversity in data, one rural and one urban district were included in the sample to carry out the empirical research. A team of ten field investigators headed by a research associate and a research assistant was employed to collect the district court premises' primary data in every district. The aim was to collect primary data from beneficiaries of FLAS. The field investigators were allotted different courts in the district court premises, including the DLSA office. The research team visited district courts, sessions courts, special family courts, magistrate courts, fast track courts ("FTCs"), courts dealing with crimes against women ("CAW"), and special SC/ST (scheduled caste/tribe) courts present on the premises of district court center. These courts were selected after a vivid consultation with the secretaries of DLSAs.

3.1.1. *Data Collection*

The data was collected per the structured and unstructured questionnaires. The field investigators commissioned around 3,029 questionnaires in 36

DOI: 10.4324/9781003158325-3

district courts from 18 states in India. One of the most significant aspects of collecting this type of data, which is majorly focusing on the beneficiaries' perspective, is that the data reflects upon many aspects of India's legal aid services and their functioning at the grassroots level. As DLSAs do not maintain any records of daily hearings of cases pending in civil or criminal courts, the data provides a sneak peek into the duration in which a common legal aid beneficiary can claim access to justice.

For the study, the proposed strength of beneficiaries from which questionnaires were to be collected was 50 from each district and subsequently 100 from each state. After completing the study, in total, 3,029 responses under the category of legal aid beneficiaries were collected. The following map gives a broader detail of the state-wise collected data. Table 3.1 and the following map show the difference between the proposed number of beneficiaries and the actual number of beneficiaries who responded.

Table 3.1 Proposed and Actual Responses Received From the Beneficiaries

Zone	*State*	*District*	*Proposed Beneficiaries*	*Actual Beneficiaries*
North	Punjab	Patiala	50	60
		Sangrur	50	33
	Himachal Pradesh	Shimla	50	83
		Solan	50	47
	Haryana	Gurugram	50	76
		Rohtak	50	72
	Uttar Pradesh	Allahabad	50	73
		Gautama Buddha Nagar	50	100
East	West Bengal	Kolkata	50	113
		24 North Pargana	50	97
	Jharkhand	Ranchi	50	86
		Ramgarh	50	53
	Odisha	Bhubaneshwar	50	110
		Cuttack	50	61
West	Rajasthan	Jodhpur	50	47
		Pali	50	40
	Gujarat	Ahmedabad	50	88
		Gandhinagar	50	59
	Maharashtra	Aurangabad	50	139
		Jalna	50	64
South	Karnataka	Bangalore Urban	50	67
		Bangalore Rural	50	58
	Tamil Nadu	Tiruchirappalli	50	70
		Thanjavur	50	54
	Andhra Pradesh	Vizag	50	167
		Vizianagaram	50	79

(*Continued*)

Table 3.1 (Continued)

Zone	*State*	*District*	*Proposed Beneficiaries*	*Actual Beneficiaries*
	Kerala	Pathanamthitta	50	127
		Alappuzha	50	244
Central	Chhattisgarh	Raipur	50	134
		Durg	50	107
	Madhya Pradesh	Indore	50	101
		Dhar	50	39
North East	Meghalaya	Shillong	50	98
		Nongpoh	50	47
		Jowai	50	26
	Assam	Guwahati	50	72
		Amingaon	50	38
	TOTAL		1,850	3,029

3.2. Data Analysis

The research collected data from the country's various zones – namely, North, East, West, South, Central, and North East – to ensure that the data collected and analyzed was an accurate indicator of the situation prevalent in the whole of India. The initial plan was to collect data from at least 3,600 respondents in total, but due to district courts' administrative constraints across all the zones, hesitation. Due to the lack of interest shown by some beneficiaries, the total number of collected samples remained somewhat less at 3,029 (see Table 3.2) – that is, approximately 84% of the stipulated number of respondents for the category of "beneficiaries." The questionnaire for this category was prepared in such a manner as to ascertain the opinions of the legal aid beneficiaries concerning the difficulties faced by them during their legal aid case. The questionnaire's principal aim was to assess the competence and commitment of the LACs in the research universe of 18 states from 6 regional zones in India. As shown in Table 3.2, the highest number of respondents/beneficiaries (866) provided data in the South Zone, while the Nort East Zone recorded the least number of responses (281).

The collection of samples was based on the categories under which a person is eligible for legal aid under the LSA Act, 1987. As shown in Table 3.2, the participation of women beneficiaries/respondents was highest in the South Zone (10.3%) and the North Zone (7%). Further, the participation of beneficiaries with low income was highest in the South Zone (8.8%), followed by the East and West Zones with 6.6% and 6%, respectively (see Table 3.2).

Participation of respondents belonging to the ST category was less than 1% in the North, West, and South Zones. This data shows a clear picture of the level of participation of STs in these zones. It is essential to mention that data collection from SCs and STs took place near SC/ST courts in the

Table 3.2 Details of Respondents (Beneficiaries)

Region		*Women*	*Child*	*SC*	*ST*	*Victim of Trafficking*	*Low Income*	*Disabled Person*	*Victim of a mass disaster, ethnic violence*	*Industrial Woman*	*Person in custody per clause of section 12 of LSA Act, 1987*	*Total*
North	Count	213	8	51	11	1	145	13	4	12	87	545
	%Total	7.00%	0.30%	1.70%	0.40%	0.00%	4.80%	0.40%	0.10%	0.40%	2.90%	18.00%
East	Count	164	4	41	53	10	200	7	12	12	17	520
	%Total	5.40%	0.10%	1.40%	1.70%	0.30%	6.60%	0.20%	0.40%	0.40%	0.60%	17.20%
West	Count	140	3	50	19	0	183	12	8	11	11	437
	%Total	4.60%	0.10%	1.70%	0.60%	0.00%	6.00%	0.40%	0.30%	0.40%	0.40%	14.40%
South	Count	313	5	74	28	3	267	21	7	14	134	866
	%Total	10.30%	0.20%	2.40%	0.90%	0.10%	8.80%	0.70%	0.20%	0.50%	4.40%	28.60%
Central	Count	169	10	33	36	1	93	7	1	16	14	380
	%Total	5.60%	0.30%	1.10%	1.20%	0.00%	3.10%	0.20%	0.00%	0.50%	0.50%	12.50%
North East	Count	35	7	14	114	0	43	3	0	1	64	281
	%Total	1.20%	0.20%	0.50%	3.80%	0.00%	1.40%	0.10%	0.00%	0.00%	2.10%	9.30%
Total	Count	1,034	37	263	261	15	931	63	32	66	327	3,029
	%Total	34.10%	1.20%	8.70%	8.60%	0.50%	30.70%	2.10%	1.10%	2.20%	10.80%	100%

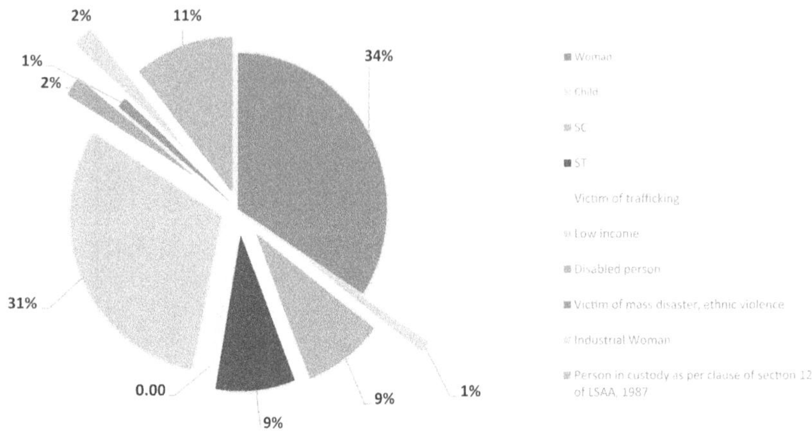

Figure 3.1 All India's Share of Beneficiaries/Respondents Under FLAS (Category-Wise)

respective districts. Therefore, the low percentage of SC/ST involvement in FLAS might be due to their reluctance to opt for the same. Another reason for the low level of participation can be the level of competence and commitment of LACs.

When viewed in its entirety, the data from the various categories of beneficiaries maintained parity within the data set (see Figure 3.1). As is evident from Figure 3.1 and the samples collected from different civil and criminal courts in the 18 states, 34% of samples represent women beneficiaries (see Figure 3.1), while 31% of the samples represent beneficiaries from the low-income category. Further, the samples also represent 9% of beneficiaries under the SC and ST categories. Thus, the research primarily focuses on the beneficiaries irrespective of their gender, caste, class, income, and other parameters. Since this research's primary objective was to evaluate the competence and commitment of the LACs by other stakeholders, heterogeneity in the sample enables it to gather perspectives from all the categories of beneficiaries.

3.2.1. Medium Through Which Beneficiaries Get to Know About Services Offered Under FLAS

In the year 2017–18, SLSAs from across the states in India disbursed around ₹22,38,19,198 on various awareness and literary programs to make aware a potential legal aid beneficiary of FLAS.[1] However, per the empirical study, the trends were not satisfactory. As shown in Figure 3.2, the majority of legal aid beneficiaries in our research universe learned about their right to legal aid either through the DLSA (23%) or through police authorities. It is

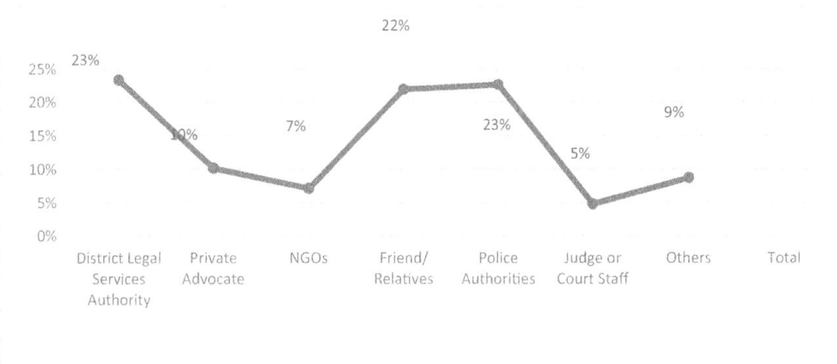

Figure 3.2 Medium Through Which Beneficiaries Get to Know About Services Offered Under FLAS

interesting to note that around 22% of legal aid beneficiaries learned about the legal aid right through their friends, while 5% of legal aid beneficiaries learned about their right to get FLAS from judges or courts.

3.2.1.1. Zonal Analysis of Medium Through Which Beneficiaries Get to Know About FLAS

3.2.1.1.1. DISTRICT LEGAL SERVICES AUTHORITY

The DLSA is the principal authority tasked with running an awareness campaign on FLAS at the district level. As shown in Figure 3.3, in the North Zone, 28.3% of legal aid beneficiaries believed they get to know about FLAS through their DLSAs. In the South Zone and West Zone, 26.8% and 24% of legal aid beneficiaries, respectively, opined that they get to know about FLAS through the DLSA. Further, 20% of legal aid beneficiaries in the North East Zone also noted that the DLSA told them about free legal services. Only 17.5% of legal aid beneficiaries from the East Zone and 18.2% of legal aid beneficiaries from the Central Zone said that they came to know about FLAS from their respective DLSA.

3.2.1.1.2. POLICE AUTHORITIES/POLICE

Police authorities were also the principal medium through which the majority of legal aid beneficiaries get to know about FLAS. The study shows, in Figure 3.3, that the police authority informed around 33.9% of legal aid beneficiaries in the Central Zone and 29.5% of legal aid beneficiaries in the North Zone about free legal services. In the East Zone and West Zone, around 21.9% of legal aid beneficiaries and 20.4% of legal aid beneficiaries

Figure 3.3 Zonal Analysis of Medium Through Which Beneficiaries Get to Know About Services Offered Under FLAS

opined that the police authorities informed them about free legal aid. Legal aid beneficiaries from the South Zone (17.8%) and North East Zone (14%) recorded the lowest percentage of beneficiaries who get to know about FLAS through police authorities.

3.2.1.1.3. FRIENDS AND RELATIVES

We noted in our national assessment that around 20% of legal aid beneficiaries get to know about FLAS from their friends and relatives. In the six zones, 25.4% of legal aid beneficiaries from the West Zone, 23.1% of legal aid beneficiaries from the East Zone, 22.4% of legal aid beneficiaries from the South Zone, and 22% of legal aid beneficiaries from the North East Zone reported that they get to know about FLAS by their friends/relatives. In comparison to other zones, only 16.1% of legal aid beneficiaries from the Central Zone get to know about FLAS from friends or relatives.

3.2.1.1.4. PRIVATE ADVOCATES, NGOS, AND JUDGES/COURTS

Legal aid beneficiaries came to know about FLAS from private advocates, NGOs, judges, or courts. Around 12% of legal aid beneficiaries in the South Zone, 11.5% of legal aid beneficiaries in the East Zone, and around 9% of legal aid beneficiaries in the Central, West, and North East Zones said that a private advocate suggested FLAS.

Non-governmental organizations ("NGOs") also had their share in informing a potential legal aid beneficiary about FLAS. Legal aid beneficiaries from the North East (11%) and East Zone (10.6%) said that they learned about FLAS from NGOs. In the remaining four zones, less than 10% of legal aid beneficiaries said that they came to know about FLAS through NGOs.

The field investigators found that legal aid beneficiaries were informed about FLAS by judges and courts also. Around 8% of legal aid beneficiaries in the North East Zone, 7.9% of legal aid beneficiaries in the Central Zone, 5.5% of legal aid beneficiaries in the West Zone, and 5.2% of legal aid beneficiaries in the South Zone said that judges or courts informed them about FLAS.

3.2.1.1.5. LEGAL SERVICES AUTHORITIES, POLICE AUTHORITIES, AND FRIENDS ARE THE PRINCIPAL MEDIUM

The national trends are following the trends in all the six zones. It is evident from the study that most legal aid beneficiaries came to know about the legal aid services from police authorities, DLSA, and their friends or relatives. Provisions like Article 22 (1) and 39A in the Constitution of India; Section 304 of the Code of Criminal Procedure, 1973; and Section 12 (g) of the Legal Services Authorities Act, 1987 make police authorities the first medium for a potential legal aid beneficiary to know about his/her right to FLAS.

DLSAs are other major institutions through which the majority of legal aid beneficiaries get to know about FLAS. Regulations like the National Legal Services Authority (Free and Competent Legal Services) Regulations, 2010;[2] the National Legal Services Authority (*Lok Adalat*) Regulations, 2009;[3] and the National Legal Services Authority (Legal Services Clinics) Regulations, 2011.[4] The regulation mandates DLSAs to have a front office during court hours that enable many potential beneficiaries to take the benefits of FLAS. Further, the legal aid awareness campaigns run by DLSAs in various *talukas* with the help of PLVs also help in spreading the idea of FLAS. Friends and relatives were another major medium observed by the study through which legal aid beneficiaries got to know about FLAS.

3.2.2. *Rationale Opted by Legal Aid Beneficiaries to Avail of the Services of LACs*

The LSA Act, 1987, mandates the right to legal aid to every individual falling under the purview of the act. Nevertheless, many potential beneficiaries often opt out of the services of LACs, and many avail of the services of LACs. What motivates the latter set of legal aid beneficiaries to take the services of LACs becomes a question of immense consideration because it captures the reasons for which a potential legal aid beneficiary opts for the services of an LAC rather than a PLP.

Legal aid beneficiaries responded in terms of four objective options, such as lack of resources to engage a PLP, the quality of legal services by the LAC,

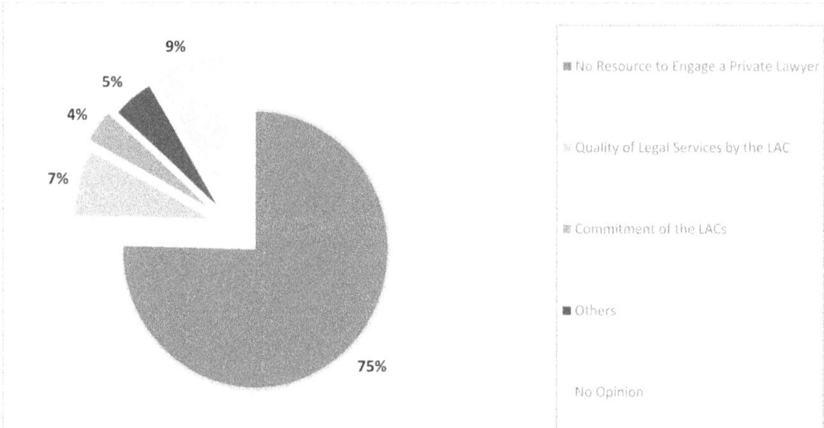

Figure 3.4 Rationale for Opting the Services of an LAC Under FLAS – All Zones

and the LAC's commitment as the rationale for opting for free legal aid. The national trend indicates that most beneficiaries opt for the services of LACs because they do not have the resources to engage a PLP. As Figure 3.4 indicates, around 75% of beneficiaries in our research universe opted for the services of LACs because they had no resources to engage a PLP.

Surprisingly, only 7% of beneficiaries opted for LACs for their quality of legal services, while 4% of beneficiaries opted for LACs because they were satisfied with the commitment of LACs. The national narrative reflects that beneficiaries opt for legal aid services because they have no resources to engage a private legal aid practitioner. A zonal analysis will further clarify the dominant rationale behind beneficiaries opting for the services of LACs in our research universe.

3.2.2.1. Zonal Analysis of Rationale for Opting the Services of an LAC Under FLAS

3.2.2.1.1. NO RESOURCES TO ENGAGE A PLP

The lack of resources to engage PLPs was the sole reason beneficiaries opted for the services of LACs in the first place. It evident from the responses received from six zones. In the North Zone, 77.2% of beneficiaries (see Figure 3.5) claimed that they had no resources to engage PLPs for their litigation. Similarly, most beneficiaries in the East Zone (80.4%), in the West Zone (78.5%), in the South Zone (71.8%), in the Central Zone (70%), and in the North East Zone (84%) also responded that they opted for the services of LACs because they had no resources to engage a private legal aid

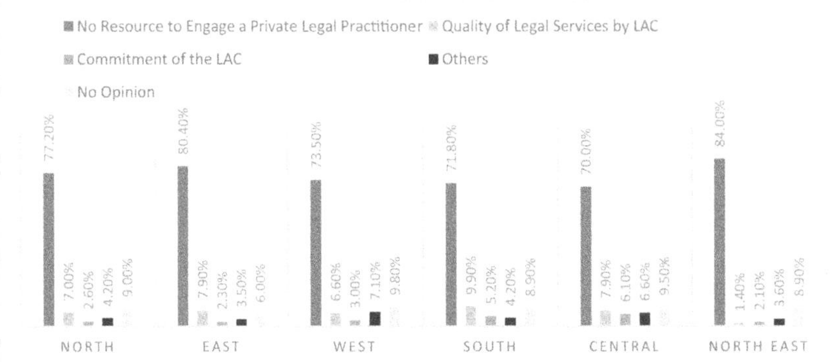

Figure 3.5 Zonal Analysis of Rationale for Opting the Services of an LAC Under FLAS

practitioner. Therefore, in almost every zone, lack of proper resources was the sole reason for a beneficiary to avail of the services of LACs under FLAS.

3.2.2.1.2. QUALITY OF LEGAL SERVICES BY THE LAC AND COMMITMENT OF THE LAC

The rationale to opt for the services of LACs because of the quality of their legal services and their commitment received the lowest response in every zone. LACs' quality of legal services as sole reason received less than 8% of response from the beneficiaries, the only exception being the South Zone, with 9.9% of beneficiaries (see Figure 3.5). On the other hand, around 6.1% of beneficiaries in the Central Zone, 5.2% of beneficiaries in the South Zone, 3% of beneficiaries in the West Zone, 2.6% of beneficiaries in the North Zone, and 2.1% of beneficiaries in the North East Zone opined that they choose the services of LACs because of the level of commitment they showed.

Thus, majority of beneficiaries in every zone opted for LACs based on lack of resources. In contrast, a very minute share of beneficiaries opted for FLAS either for sheer commitment of LACs or quality of legal services offered by the LACs under the LAS.

The data collected and presented here is self-explanatory because people's perception majorly points towards the low quality of services provided by the free LACs. Therefore, the quality and commitment of LACs have largely created apathy in the minds of the intended beneficiaries. It is merely their inability to afford a PLP that is driving the beneficiaries to avail of the services of LACs while they still fail to impose complete faith in the abilities of LACs.

3.2.3. The Level of Awareness Among the Beneficiaries About the Process for Applying to the LSA

The empirical study also explored whether a beneficiary is aware of the process for availing of the services of LACs under FLAS. This becomes an essential aspect of access to justice because it relates to whether the front office well informs a beneficiary of DLSAs or not. The national narrative showed in Table 3.3 indicates that around 61.5% of beneficiaries were aware of the process for applying to the LSA to obtain the services of LACs. Among the beneficiaries who knew the process, only 68.3% of beneficiaries (Table 4.16) from the six zones found the process easy. Beneficiaries were seen hesitant to disclose whether the process of applying was easy enough or not. In most cases, an LAC is seated in the front office and holds the responsibility for explaining a potential beneficiary about getting FLAS.

3.2.3.1. Zonal Analysis of Awareness Among the Beneficiaries

In the six zones, almost 69% of beneficiaries in the East Zone (see Table 3.3) were aware of the process of applying for an LAC at the respective DLSA, followed by the South Zone, where around 65% of beneficiaries (see Table 3.3) knew the process of applying for an LAC under FLAS. Similarly, 61% of beneficiaries both in the North and Central Zones (see Table 3.3) knew about the process of getting an LAC appointed for their case. Further, less than 40% (36%) of beneficiaries in the North East Zone (9.3%) were aware of the very process of applying for the LAC at the DLSA office.

Since being acquainted with a process and the experience of that process are two diverse aspects of service delivery, it was essential to know about

Table 3.3 Are You Aware of the Process for Applying to the LSA to Obtain a LAC?

Region		*Yes*	*No*	*No Response*	*Total*
North	Count	333	178	34	545
	% of Total	61%	33%	6%	18.00%
East	Count	357	134	29	520
	% of Total	69%	26%	5%	17.20%
West	Count	282	134	21	437
	% of Total	64%	31%	5%	14.40%
South	Count	559	261	46	866
	% of Total	65%	30%	5%	28.60%
Central	Count	231	129	20	380
	% of Total	61%	34%	5%	12.50%
North East	Count	102	96	83	281
	% of Total	36%	30%	34%	9.30%
Total	Count	1,864	932	233	3,029
	% of Total	61.50%	30.80%	7.70%	100%

Table 3.4 If Yes, Then Was the Process Easy?

Region		*Yes*	*No*	*No Response*	*Total*
North	Count	216	105	12	333
	% of Total	65%	32%	4%	100%
East	Count	266	58	33	357
	% of Total	75%	16%	9%	100%
West	Count	181	67	34	282
	% of Total	64%	24%	12%	100%
South	Count	411	97	51	559
	% of Total	74%	17%	9%	100%
Central	Count	124	89	18	231
	% of Total	54%	39%	8%	100%
North East	Count	76	20	6	102
	% of Total	75%	20%	6%	100%
Total	Count	1274	436	154	1864
	% of Total	68.30%	23.40%	8.30%	100%

the experiences of the already aware beneficiaries in the six zones in regard to the ease of availing of the services of LACs. In the six zones, 75% of beneficiaries in the East Zone (see Table 3.4) experienced the process for availing of services of an LAC too easy, while 74% of beneficiaries in the South Zone (see Table 3.4) experienced no difficulty in availing of services of an LAC. It is worth mentioning that in the six zones, 32% of beneficiaries in the North Zone (see Table 3.4) experienced the process with a bit of difficulty, although around 65% of beneficiaries (see Table 3.4) found availing of services of an LAC easy. Furthermore, 64% of beneficiaries (see Table 3.4) in the West Zone, 54% of beneficiaries in the Central Zone, and 75% of beneficiaries in the North East Zone experienced ease in the process of availing of the services of an LAC.

The study shows that majority of beneficiaries in the East, West, South, and North East Zones were aware of applying for FLAS. These beneficiaries also find the process easy. The DLSA offices in these zones have the infrastructure facilities, like a front office and a display screen for legal aid campaign, or have the availability of PLVs in enough numbers.

3.2.4. Time Taken by the DLSA to Provide Legal Aid

This section explores the aspect of delay in getting legal aid. This specific question focuses on the number of days it takes for a potential beneficiary to get legal aid from the DLSA. The trends received suggest that beneficiaries faced a significant delay in getting any kind of legal aid from the DLSA. As seen in Figure 3.6, around 29% of beneficiaries, in all the six zones received legal aid from the DLSA office within 1–5 days. On the contrary, almost 27% (27.3%) of beneficiaries received legal aid from the DLSA after more than 15 days.

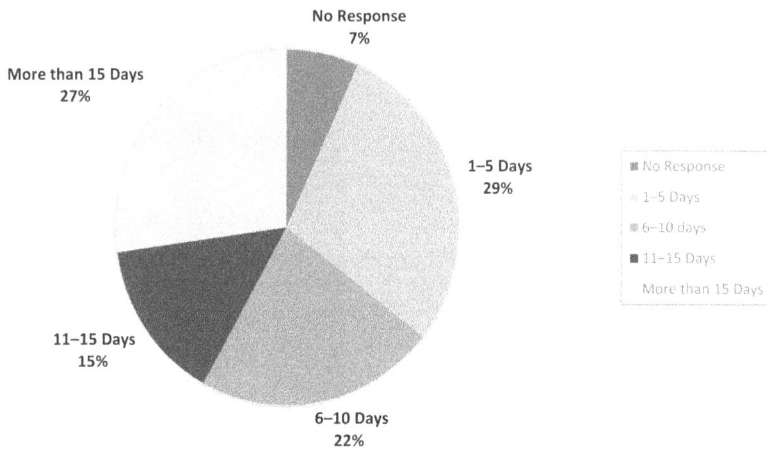

Figure 3.6 Time Taken by the DLSA to Provide Legal Aid

On the other hand, around 23% (22.6%) of beneficiaries received legal aid as late as 6–10 days. Further, 14.7% of beneficiaries received legal aid as late as 11–15 days. Thus, more than 65% (22.6% + 14.7% +27.3%) of beneficiaries responded that the time taken by the DLSA to provide the legal aid was more than 5 days. The situation becomes even grave when the highest number of cases filed under legal aid were criminal cases within the universe.[5]

3.2.4.1. Zonal Analysis of Time Taken by the DLSA to Provide Legal Aid

In the six zones, the time taken by the DLSAs to provide legal aid is highest in the North Zone, according to respondents. In the North Zone, 41% of beneficiaries (see Figure 3.7) reported that it took them more than 15 days to receive any legal aid from the respective DLSA, followed by 34% of beneficiaries in the North East Zone (see Figure 3.7), and 30% of beneficiaries in the Central Zone (see Figure 3.7). Similarly, around 31% of the East Zone beneficiaries (see Figure 3.7) received legal aid from the DLSA as late as 6–10 days. They were followed by 27% of the Central Zone and 23% of beneficiaries in the South zone (see Figure 3.7). The highest percentage of beneficiaries who received legal aid within 1–5 days were in the West Zone (9.4%) (see Figure 3.7), followed by South Zone (6.7%) (see Figure 3.7). Therefore, in the six zones, DLSAs of the East Zone (76%), North East Zone (72%), and Central Zone take the longest time to provide legal aid to their beneficiaries. DLSAs of the North East Zone are the quickest. The inferences also reflect on the commitment of DLSAs since the delay in getting legal aid might cause major hindrances in access to justice and hamper the very mandate of FLAS.

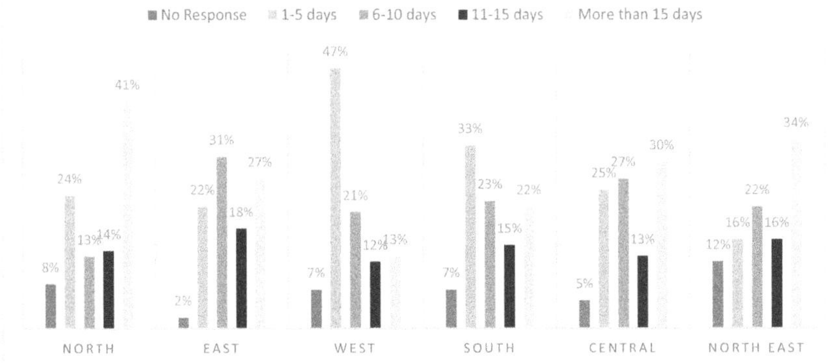

Figure 3.7 Zonal Analysis of Time Taken by the DLSA to Provide Legal Aid

Table 3.5 Did You Approach a PLP Before Approaching the LSA for Free Legal Aid?

Region		*Yes*	*No*	*No Opinion*	*Total*
North	Count	294	228	23	545
	% of Total	54%	8%	4%	100%
East	Count	305	202	13	520
	% of Total	59%	39%	3%	100%
West	Count	219	200	18	437
	% of Total	50%	46%	4%	100%
South	Count	453	359	54	866
	% of Total	52%	41%	6%	100%
Central	Count	163	196	21	380
	% of Total	43%	52%	6%	100%
North East	Count	93	131	57	281
	% of Total	33%	47%	20%	100%
Total	Count	1,527	1316	186	3,029
	% of Total	50%	43%	6%	100%

3.2.5. *Reason(s) for Discontinuing the Services of a PLP*

3.2.5.1. *Beneficiaries Approached a PLP Before Approaching the DLSA for FLAS*

In the previous analysis, the study showed that most beneficiaries took the services of LACs because they have insufficient resources. This section deals with the reasons that compelled a beneficiary to discontinue their PLP's services. The study first segregates those beneficiaries, which approached a PLP before approaching the DLSA, as shown in Table 3.5. In our research universe, around 50% of beneficiaries from the six zones approached PLPs. In comparison, only 43% of beneficiaries did not approach any PLP.

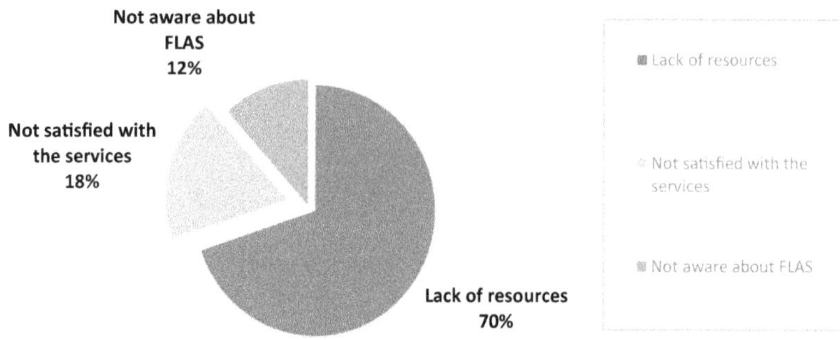

Figure 3.8 Rationale Given by Beneficiaries for Discontinuing the Services of a PLP

In terms of zones, beneficiaries from the East Zone (59%) recorded the highest share of beneficiaries who approached a PLP before approaching the DLSA for FLAS. Similarly, in the North Zone, around 54% of beneficiaries opted for PLPs before approaching FLAS. More around 50% of the South Zone and West Zone beneficiaries also approached a PLP before approaching the DLSA for FLAS. Thus, the study shows that around 50% of beneficiaries in five out of six zones did approach PLPs.

3.2.6. Rationale Given by Beneficiaries for Discontinuing the Services of a PLP

The study further delves into understanding the factors that may have motivated these beneficiaries to opt for free legal aid; the beneficiaries were asked about the reasons for discontinuing a PLP's services, in case they were utilizing such services before. As shown in Figure 3.8, most beneficiaries, around 70%, left the PLP's services because of lack of resources. Another 18% of beneficiaries were not satisfied with PLPs' services, while around 12% of beneficiaries were not aware of FLAS. Lack of resources compelled most beneficiaries to leave PLPs and opt for FLAS.

3.2.6.1. Zonal Analysis of Rationale Given by Beneficiaries for Discontinuing the Services of a PLP

3.2.6.3.1. LACK OF RESOURCES

In almost every zone, around 70% of beneficiaries discontinued PLPs' services and opted for FLAS. As Figure 3.9 shows, around 71% of beneficiaries in the East Zone, West Zone, and South Zone discontinued PLPs'

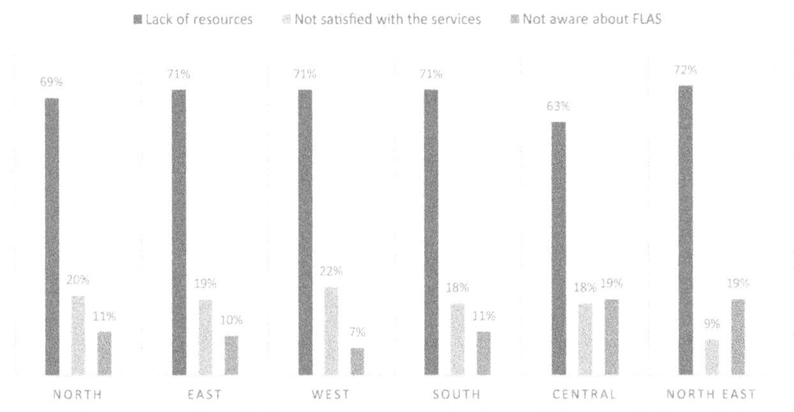

Figure 3.9 Zonal Analysis of Rationale Given by Beneficiaries for Discontinuing the Services of a PLP

services and opted for FLAS. Similarly, 72% of beneficiaries in the North East Zone, 69% of beneficiaries in the North Zone, and 63% of beneficiaries in the Central Zone also discontinued PLPs' services because of a lack of resources.

One of the reasons most people discontinued their PLP's services and opted for FLAS is the higher fees of PLPs and lengthy trial periods. After exhausting all their resources on a PLP, people opt for the services of FLAS.

3.2.6.3.2. NOT SATISFIED WITH THE SERVICES

Around 20% of beneficiaries in the North Zone, 19% of beneficiaries in the East Zone, 22% of beneficiaries in the West Zone, 18% of beneficiaries in the South Zone and Central Zone, and a minuscule 9% of beneficiaries in the North East Zone discontinued the services of a PLP and opted for FLAS because they were not satisfied with the PLP's services. PLPs extend the duration of cases for monetary gains.

3.2.6.3.3. NOT AWARE OF FLAS

Being made aware of FLAS later was also one reason beneficiaries discontinued the services of PLPs. Among the beneficiaries who opted for PLPs before taking the services under FLAS, around 19% of beneficiaries in the Central and North East Zones reported the highest in terms of not being aware of the free legal aid scheme. Similarly, 11% of the North and South Zone beneficiaries also reported the unawarenss reason for discontinuing their PLPs' services and opting for FLAS.

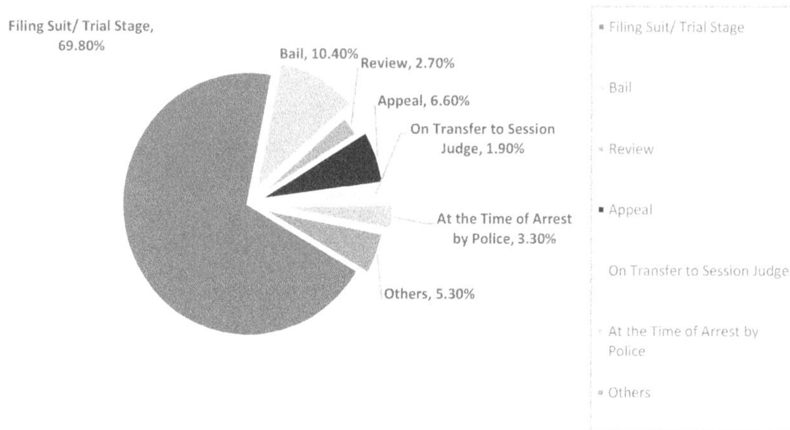

Figure 3.10 Stages at Which a Beneficiary Gets Legal Aid Services From an LAC

3.2.7. *The Stage at Which a Beneficiary Gets Legal Aid Services From LAC*

A potential beneficiary is eligible to avail of legal aid at any stage of a case. Since a potential beneficiary can avail of the services under FLAS at any stage of the case, it becomes crucial to understand at which stage the majority of potential beneficiaries avail of the services offered under FLAS. Per the trends within our research universe, around 69.8% of beneficiaries (see Figure 3.10) availed of the services under FLAS during filling of suit or trial stage. Further, 10% of beneficiaries availed of the services for bail only. Another 6.6% of beneficiaries availed themselves of the legal aid services from LACs during appeals. Furthermore, a minute 3.3% of beneficiaries availed of services under FLAS at the time of arrest, 2.7% of beneficiaries availed of legal aid services from LACs during a review, and 1.9% of beneficiaries availed of the services under legal aid services from LAC when their cases were transferred to a session judge.

3.2.7.1. *Zonal Analysis of Stages at Which Beneficiaries Avail of Legal Aid Services From an LAC*

3.2.7.1.1. FILLING SUIT OR TRIAL STAGE

In almost every zone, most beneficiaries get legal aid at the stage of filing suit or trial stage. As Figure 3.11 shows, around 77% of beneficiaries in the North Zone, 74% of beneficiaries in the West Zone, 72% of beneficiaries in

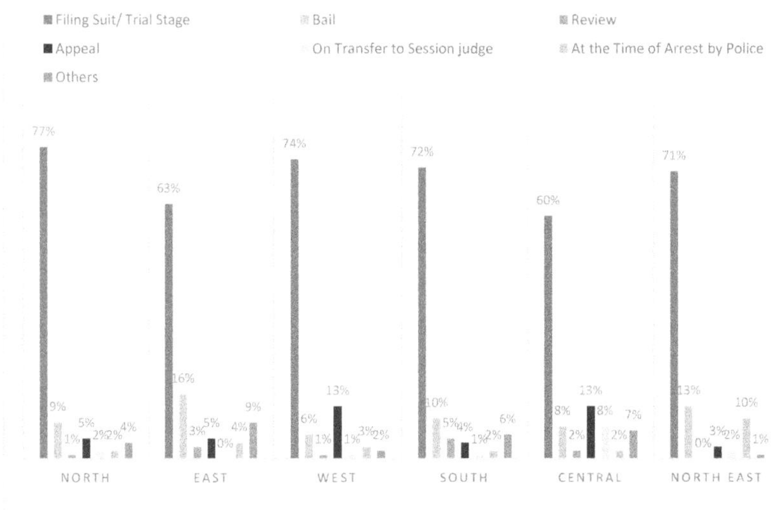

Figure 3.11 Zonal Analysis of Stages at Which a Beneficiary Gets Legal Aid Services From an LAC

the South Zone, 71% of beneficiaries in the North East Zone, 63% of beneficiaries in the East Zone, and 60% of beneficiaries in the Central Zone took the services under FLAS at either filling of suit or trial stage. The majority of beneficiaries get to know about FLAS either from police authorities or through DLSAs. Therefore, the filling stage or trial stage becomes a significant stage for beneficiaries getting legal aid.

3.2.7.1.2. BAIL

Another stage where beneficiaries opted for FLAS services was during bail. As the study shows, 9% of beneficiaries in the North Zone, 16% of beneficiaries in the East Zone, 6% of beneficiaries in the West Zone, 10% of beneficiaries in the South Zone, 8% of beneficiaries in the Central Zone, and 13% of beneficiaries in the North East Zone believed they took FLAS for bail. Often beneficiaries opt for FLAS to get bail and then hire a PLP for their case.

3.2.7.1.3. APPEAL

The appeal was another stage at which a handful of beneficiaries took FLAS. As shown in Figure 3.11, 13% of beneficiaries in the Central Zone and West Zone used FLAS at the appeal stage. On the other hand, 5% of beneficiaries or less in the North Zone, East Zone, South Zone, and North East Zone were also of the opinion that they took services under FLAS at the appeal stage.

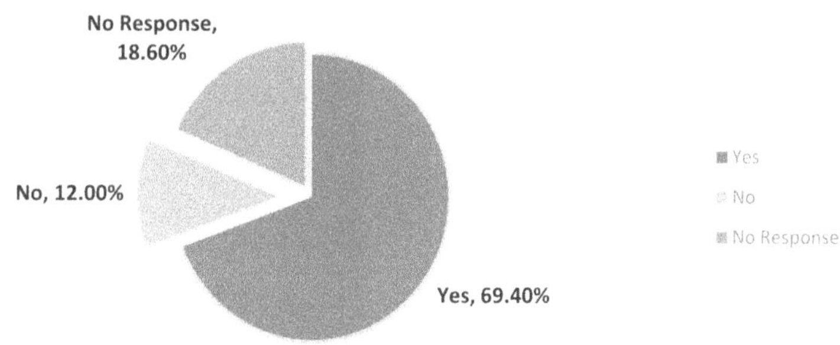

Figure 3.12 Advice and Other Assistance Provided by an LAC

3.2.7.1.4. AT THE TIME OF ARREST BY POLICE OR REVIEW AND ON TRANSFER TO A SESSION JUDGE

Beneficiaries taking the services under FLAS also said they took the services either at the time of arrest by police or review or when their case was transferred to a session judge. The responses falling under these categories were minute, as shown in Figure 3.11.

3.2.8. *The Usefulness of Advice Provided by LACs*

The DLSA allots LACs to legal aid beneficiaries based on the nature of the case. However, is the advice given by their LACs beneficial enough for them? To analyze this aspect, the study first focused on whether a beneficiary received any form of advice or assistance from their respective LACs or not. As Figure 3.12 demonstrates, a majority of beneficiaries in our research universe received advice and other assistance from their LACs. Among the beneficiaries, 60.4% opined that they received advice and other assistance from their LACs, while 12% said the LACs did not provide any form of assistance or advice. Further, 18.6% of beneficiaries did not respond to this specific question, as they were hesitant to say anything about their LACs. This hesitancy arises from an insecurity that LACs might leave their cases if they say anything about them.

3.2.8.1. *Usefulness of an LAC's Advice*

The study further explored how valuable the support was for the beneficiaries who received any form of advice or assistance from their LACs. Among the beneficiaries who were satisfied with the advice and assistance of their LACs, around 24% of beneficiaries believed the assistance that they received was beneficial. Further, around 60% of beneficiaries found the assistance

Table 3.6 Usefulness of Advice in Terms of Preparing for the Dispute

Region		*Very Useful*	*Useful*	*Not at all Useful*	*No Opinion*	*Total*
North	Count	89	148	52	16	305
	% of Total	29%	49%	17%	5%	100%
East	Count	88	222	48	18	376
	% of Total	23%	59%	13%	5%	100%
West	Count	61	194	25	18	298
	% of Total	20%	65%	8%	6%	100%
South	Count	189	446	34	49	718
	% of Total	26%	62%	5%	7%	100%
Central	Count	66	169	29	16	280
	% of Total	24%	60%	10%	6%	100%
North East	Count	17	76	18	13	124
	% of Total	14%	61%	15%	10%	100%
Total	Count	510	1,255	206	130	2,101
	% of Total	24%	60%	10%	6%	100%

usually helpful (see Table 3.6). About 10% of beneficiaries (see Table 3.6) opined that the advice was not helpful to them in preparing for the dispute. Only 6.2% of beneficiaries had no opinion about the level at which the advice and assistance were helpful.

3.2.9. *Issue of LACs Demanding Money From Beneficiaries*

Legal aid services are provided without any cost or charges across the nation. Beneficiaries are not supposed to remunerate LACs for any services rendered by them under the LAS. However, an impression in the field of study was that beneficiaries were compelled to compensate their LACs before the commencement of trial or suits, submission of application, or other litigation stages. The issue of LACs demanding money from their respective beneficiaries was present in every zone. Figure 3.13 shows the national trend in which around 16% of beneficiaries have affirmed that they paid money to their LACs during proceedings, while 71% of beneficiaries either did not pay money or were reluctant to disclose it to the team. The reluctance might be due to the apprehension that their LACs would withdraw from their case if such information were ever disclosed. Such beneficiaries apprehended that in the case of withdrawal of such LACs, they would be stranded in their path to justice.

3.2.9.1. *Zonal Analysis of LACs Demanding Money From Beneficiaries*

The LACs sometimes demand money from their respective beneficiaries during hearings of a case/dispute. However, beneficiaries rarely took the step of lodging an official complaint about them. Furthermore, we also see

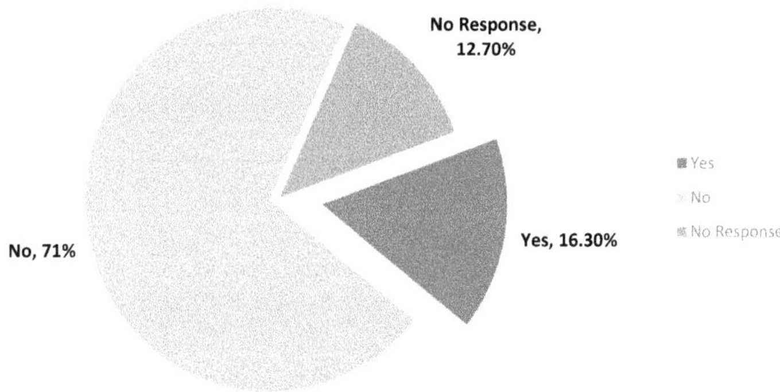

Figure 3.13 Money Demanded From Beneficiaries by LACs to Attend Court Proceedings

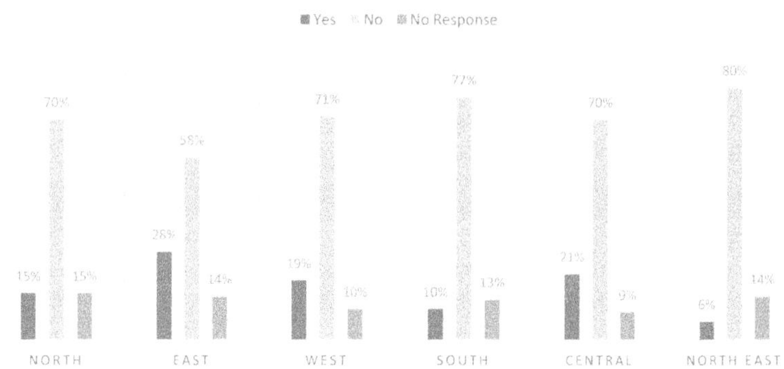

Figure 3.14 Zonal Analysis of Money Demanded From Beneficiaries by LACs to Attend Court Proceedings

that in all the six zones, the percentages of beneficiaries who either did not pay money or were reluctant to disclose are very high.

One of the essential objectives of the LSA Act, 1987, is to provide legal aid free of any cost. Figure 3.14 portrays a picture of the very nature of free legal aid. Responses recorded in the East Zone show that 28% of beneficiaries affirmed that their respective LACs demanded money from them to attend the court. In a similar trend, 21% of beneficiaries in the Central Zone, 19% of beneficiaries in the West Zone, and 15% of beneficiaries in the North Zone responded affirmatively to the point that their LACs

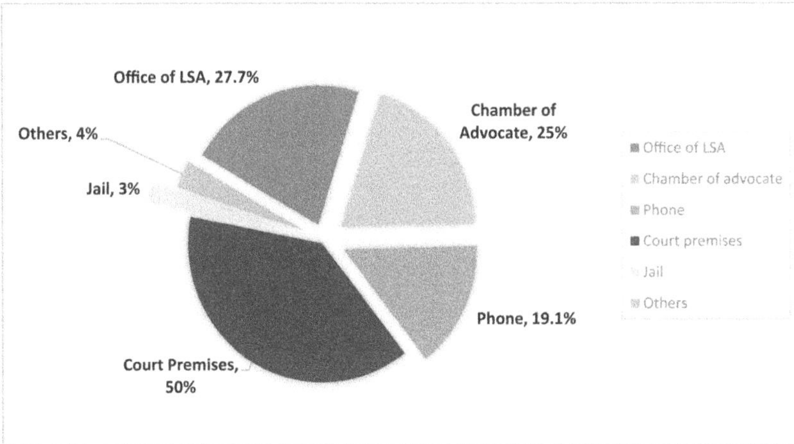

Figure 3.15 Places of LAC Interaction With Beneficiaries*

*Multiple-response question. Percentages are based on respondents.

demanded money for conducting their case or for attending the court proceedings on their behalf. The study thus reports the menace of corruption in the form of LACs illegitimately demanding money from their beneficiaries from all the six zones.

3.2.10. *Places of LAC-Beneficiary Interaction*

The empirical study also focused on the places where a beneficiary and an LAC interact with each other. On the one hand, a place interaction correlates with commitment and availability of LACs for the beneficiaries. On the other, it is also related to the dearth of infrastructure in office DLSAs. The national trend, as shown in Figure 3.15, is that around 50% of beneficiaries interact with their respective LACs either in or near court premises. Another 27.7% of beneficiaries informed that they interact with their LACs in the office of the DLSA. Another 25% of beneficiaries said that their LACs interact with them in their chamber. Surprisingly, for 19.1% of beneficiaries, the LACs also interacted with them via phone calls. Less than 3% of beneficiaries interacted with their LACs on jail premises. These results show that actually, the court premises are where most of the beneficiaries interact with their LACs. Therefore, the court premises' infrastructure capability that facilitates such meetings should be the consideration for future research. It is essential to mention here that many respondents (beneficiaries) opined that they meet and interact with their LACs in more than one place. Thus, we can very well observe an increase in the total percentage.

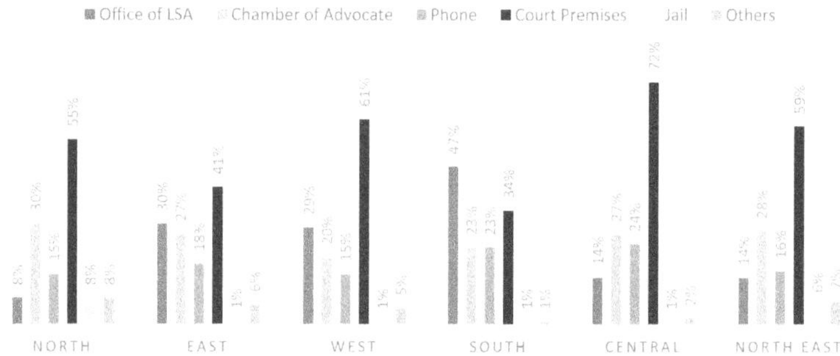

Figure 3.16 Zonal Analysis of Places of LAC Interaction With Beneficiaries*

*Multiple-response question. Percentages are based on respondents.

3.2.10.1. Zonal Analysis of Places of LAC-Beneficiary Interaction

3.2.10.1.1. COURT PREMISES

The majority of beneficiaries interact with their LACs on court premises. According to the study, as shown in Figure 3.16, beneficiaries from the Central Zone (72%) interacted with their LACs the most on court premises. Around 61% of beneficiaries in the West Zone also interacted with their LACs on court premises. Similarly, 59% of the North East Zone beneficiaries and 55% of beneficiaries of the North Zone interacted with their LACs on court premises. Beneficiaries from the East Zone (41%) and South Zone (34%) recorded the lowest percentage of beneficiaries who interacted with their LACs on court premises. The study shows that beneficiaries from the Central Zone, West Zone, North East Zone, and North Zone mostly interact with their LACs on court premises, unlike beneficiaries from the South Zone. Court premises became a central area/place for interaction because of two reasons. First, the LACs, who are also advocates involved in private legal practice, are preoccupied with their private clients. Therefore, the only place they can call or meet a beneficiary is near the court premises when a beneficiary has a hearing or case date. Another reason might be the lack of infrastructure or proper space in DLSA offices. During the field visits, a majority of DLSA offices were congested and lacked proper physical infrastructure.

3.2.10.1.2. OFFICE OF THE DLSA

The office of the DLSA is the place where a majority of potential legal aid beneficiaries, mediators, LACs, and PLVs are present, in general. From a beneficiary's point of view, it is the most accessible place to meet their respective LACs. The study shows that around 47% of the South Zone beneficiaries (see Figure 3.16) reported that the majority of interactions between beneficiaries and LACs take place in the office of the LSA only. Further, 30% of beneficiaries in the East Zone, 29% of beneficiaries in the West Zone, 14% of beneficiaries in the Central and North East Zone, and 8% of the North Zone beneficiaries believed they interacted with their LACs at the office of the LSA (i.e., DLSA).

3.2.10.1.3. CHAMBER OF ADVOCATES

LACs often resist calling or meeting their legal aid beneficiaries at their chambers. In fact, most LACs do not even have their chambers because they are either junior or have no such long experience in advocacy. However, a few LACs meet and interact with their assigned beneficiaries in their chamber. In the six zones, 30% of the North Zone beneficiaries responded that they interact with their LACs in their chamber. Similarly, 27% of beneficiaries in the East Zone and Central Zone, 28% of beneficiaries in the North East Zone, 23% of beneficiaries in the South Zone, and 20% of beneficiaries in the West Zone said that they interact with their LACs in their chamber.

3.2.10.1.4. PHONE

Beneficiaries in our research universe responded that they interacted with their LACs over the phone also. Many times, LACs are unable to meet their beneficiaries due to their engagements with their private client. This compels beneficiaries to discuss the proceedings or case-related progress over the phone. Further, most beneficiaries come from socially or economically vulnerable sections of society, making it difficult to come to the district court to meet their LAC. As shown in Figure 3.16, 24% of beneficiaries in the Central Zone, 23% of beneficiaries in the South Zone, 18% of beneficiaries in the East Zone, 16% of beneficiaries in the North East Zone, and 15% of beneficiaries in the North Zone and West Zone also interacted with their LACs over the phone.

3.2.11. The Difficulties Faced by Beneficiaries While Interacting With LACs

Given the free-of-cost nature of legal services, many LACs take the services for granted. This leads to beneficiaries facing difficulties ranging from LACs showing no keen interest to LACs demanding money. It becomes crucial to mention here that these beneficiaries are vulnerable people from our societies. During the field visits to DLSAs in six zones, beneficiaries were too hesitant to respond to any question concerning their LACs. Many of them believed that their LACs might leave their cases if they spoke anything against them. Therefore, any question concerning the difficulties or issues faced by beneficiaries has a higher response of either "no difficulties" or "no

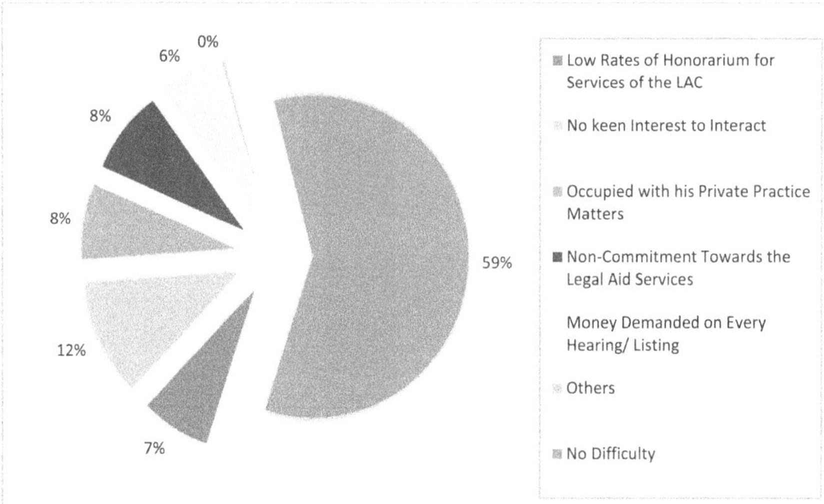

Figure 3.17 Difficulties Faced by Beneficiaries While Interacting With LACs

response" and must be read from this perspective. As shown in Figure 3.17, 59% of beneficiaries responded that they faced no difficulties while interacting with LACs.

Although most beneficiaries showed their reluctance by responding "no difficulties," responses received from a few beneficiaries conveyed the difficulties they faced. As Figure 3.17 shows, 12% of beneficiaries responded that LACs show no keen interest in interacting with them on their cases, while 8% of beneficiaries reported that their LACs are either not committed to legal aid services or occupied with their private practice matters. Further, 7% of beneficiaries said that the low rates of honorarium for services of the LACs are one of the reasons they face difficulty while interacting with LACs. Besides, this low honorarium rate correlates to another difficulty reported by only 6% of beneficiaries: LACs demand money on every hearing or listing within our research universe.

3.2.11.1. Zonal Analysis of Difficulties Faced by Beneficiaries While Interacting With LACs

3.2.11.1.1. NO DIFFICULTIES

The highest percentage of beneficiaries stating that they face no difficulties while interacting with LACs was from the South Zone (88%, See Figure 3.18). In a similar manner, 76% of beneficiaries in the West Zone, 71% of beneficiaries in the North Zone, 69% of beneficiaries in the East Zone,

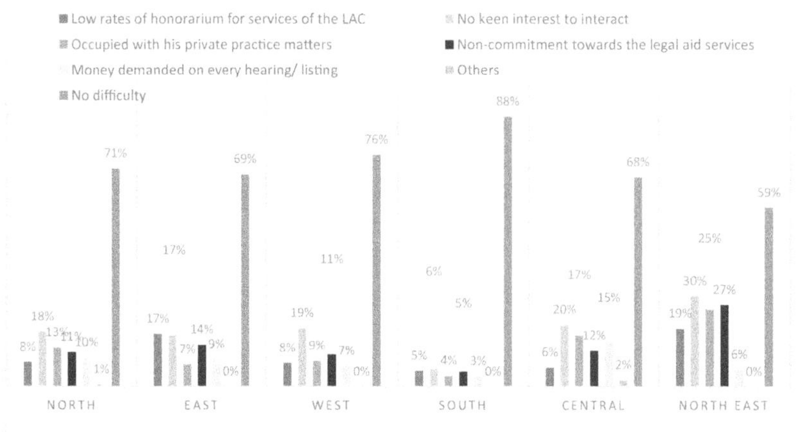

Figure 3.18 Zonal Analysis of Difficulties Faced by Beneficiaries While Interacting With LACs

68% of beneficiaries in the Central Zone, and 59% of beneficiaries in the North East Zone also stated that they face no difficulties while interacting with their LACs.

3.2.11.1.2. NO KEEN INTEREST TO INTERACT

The empaneled LACs also perform their private practices. They are inclined towards clients with higher remuneration rather than low honorarium, which they receive after completing a legal aid case. Therefore, LACs show no keen interest in interacting with beneficiaries. Beneficiaries in every zone flagged this issue. As Figure 3.18 shows, around 30% of the North East beneficiaries flagged the issue of LACs showing no interaction to interact with them. Similarly, 20% of beneficiaries in the Central Zone, 19% of beneficiaries in the West Zone, 18% of beneficiaries in the North Zone, 17% of beneficiaries in the East Zone, and 6% of beneficiaries in the South Zone also responded that their LACs show no keen interest to interact with them.

3.2.11.1.3. NON-COMMITMENT TOWARDS THE LEGAL AID SERVICES AND BEING OCCUPIED WITH PRIVATE PRACTICE

Non-commitment towards the legal aid services and being occupied with the private practice come from the fact that LACs devote more time to their private clients than legal aid beneficiaries. The remunerations attached to legal aid cases are meager compared to private clients' cases, which creates a conflict of interest. Therefore, we see that in the North East, 27% of beneficiaries reported non-commitment of LACs towards legal aid services, and 25% of beneficiaries said that LACs are busy with their private practice matters. A similar pattern is replicated in every zone, as shown in Figure 3.18. In the East Zone, around 14% of beneficiaries said LACs are not committed to legal aid services, while 7% of beneficiaries responded that LACs are busy with their private practice matters. Likewise, in the Central Zone, around 12% of beneficiaries responded that their LACs are not committed to the cause of legal aid services, while 17% of beneficiaries said that LACs are busy with their private practice matters.

North Zone beneficiaries also flagged the issue of non-commitment of LACs and their occupation with private practice matters. Around 11% of the North Zone beneficiaries said that LACs are not committed to legal aid services, and 13% of the North Zone beneficiaries said that LACs are busy with private practice matters. In the West Zone, 11% of beneficiaries said that LACs are not committed to legal aid services, and 17% said LACs are busy with private practice matters. In the South Zone, the percentage of beneficiaries telling about the difficulties in terms of non-commitment of LACs towards legal aid services is 5%, while those beneficiaries who criticized that the LACs are busy with their private practice matters make up 4%, as shown in Figure 3.18.

3.2.11.1.4. LOW RATES OF HONORARIUM AND MONEY DEMANDED

The LSA Act, 1987, and NALSA (Free and Competent Legal Services) Regulations, 2010,[6] define the honorarium of empaneled advocates that they receive for their legal services. The honorarium assigned for LACs is meager when compared to the profit gained by taking a private case. LACs cover expenditure and sometimes bear extra costs while taking a legal aid case. Due to these reasons, beneficiaries often complained about LACs either demanding money or acknowledging that they face issues due to the low honorarium of LACs. As shown in Figure 3.18, 19% of beneficiaries in the North East Zone, 17% of beneficiaries in the East Zone, 8% of beneficiaries in the North and West Zones, 6% of beneficiaries in the Central Zone, and 5% of beneficiaries in the South Zone acknowledged that LACs receive low honoraria for their legal aid services. Similarly, 15% of beneficiaries in the Central Zone, 10% of beneficiaries in the North Zone, 9% of beneficiaries in the East Zone, 7% of beneficiaries in the West Zone, and 6% of beneficiaries in the North East Zone flagged the issue of LACs demanding money on every hearing or listing.

3.2.12 Beneficiaries' Perspective on Commitment and Devotion of LACs

The study also evaluates the commitment and devotion of LACs from the perspective of beneficiaries. The questionnaire had a specific question

Table 3.7 Evaluation of Commitment and Devotion of LACs by Beneficiaries

Region		*Yes*	*No*	*No Response*	*Total*
North	Count	222	193	130	545
	% of Total	41%	35%	24%	100%
East	Count	263	138	119	520
	% of Total	51%	27%	23%	100%
West	Count	243	106	88	437
	% of Total	70%	16%	14%	100%
South	Count	607	141	118	866
	% of Total	70%	16%	14%	100%
Central	Count	195	123	62	380
	% of Total	51%	32%	16%	100%
North East	Count	101	95	85	281
	% of Total	36%	34%	30%	100%
Total	Count	1,631	796	602	3,029
	% of Total	53.8%	26.3%	19.9%	100.%

related to the commitment of LACs. In Table 3.7, we see that around 54% (53.8%) of the beneficiaries from the six zones opined that LACs are committed and devoted to legal aid services. On the contrary, 26.3% of beneficiaries responded that LACs were neither committed nor devoted to the cause of legal aid services. Additionally, around 20% (19.9%) of beneficiaries refrained from answering or commenting on the commitment and devotion of LACs to FLAS.

It is pertinent to point out that 20% of beneficiaries may have been cautious enough to refrain from responding. They refrained because they dreaded that somehow their LACs would come to know about their responses and the beneficiaries would end up losing their LACs' services. Moreover, no response should be counted under the same category as the beneficiaries who are not satisfied with the commitment and devotion of LACs. Thus, cumulatively, around 45% of beneficiaries in our research universe were not satisfied with the commitment and devotion of the LACs.

3.2.12.1. Beneficiaries' Perspective on Commitment and Devotion of LACs

The pattern of beneficiaries being hesitant and not responding is evident in every zone. For instance, in the North Zone (see Figure 3.18), we see that a lesser number of beneficiaries (around 41% of beneficiaries who responded) were satisfied with the services of LACs when compared to the percentage of beneficiaries who either did not respond or were not at all satisfied with the services offered by the LACs.

Similarly, in the North East Zone, the share of beneficiaries being either not satisfied or non-responsive to the question is higher than the share of

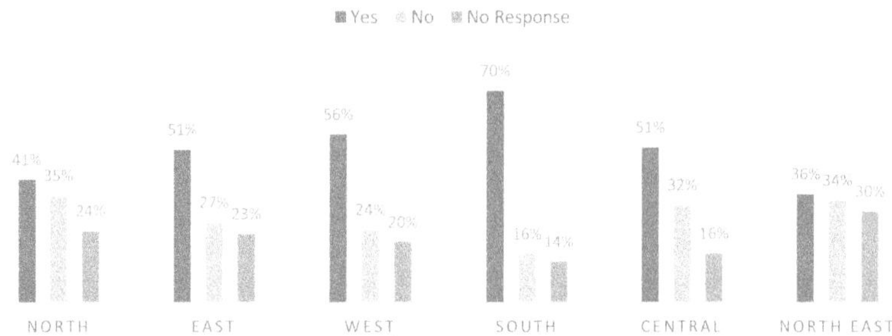

Figure 3.19 Evaluation of Commitment and Devotion of LACs by Beneficiaries

beneficiaries responding that they are satisfied (around 36% of the respondents) with the commitment and devotion of the LACs. In the Central, East, and West Zones, it is seen that the share of beneficiaries satisfied with their LACs is almost like the share of beneficiaries who either are not satisfied with their LACs or had no answer to the specific question. It is only in the South Zone where the share of beneficiaries who are satisfied with the services of LACs is much more than the combined share of beneficiaries who either were not satisfied with the commitment and devotion of LACs or had no answer/opinion.

3.2.13. *Support for Creation of a Permanent Institution of Legal Practitioners for the LAS*

Before asking beneficiaries about their support for a permanent institution of legal practitioners for the LAS, field investigators told them about the procedure of appointing LACs for tenure. Beneficiaries responded to this question to express their inclination towards making the post of LAC a permanent one. As shown in Figure 3.20, around 20% of beneficiaries across the six zones were hesitant to express their opinion on creating a permanent system of legal aid services.

On the other hand, 53% of beneficiaries across the six zones (34.1% "only recommended" and 19.1% "highly recommended") were optimistic about such a change in the existing system. They were hopeful that such a system with the full-time engagement of LACs would help improve the quality of legal aid services. However, around 9.4% of beneficiaries said that such an arrangement is unlikely to improve LACs' commitment and quality. These beneficiaries were not very hopeful about creating such a system in which LACs are engaged on a full-time basis.

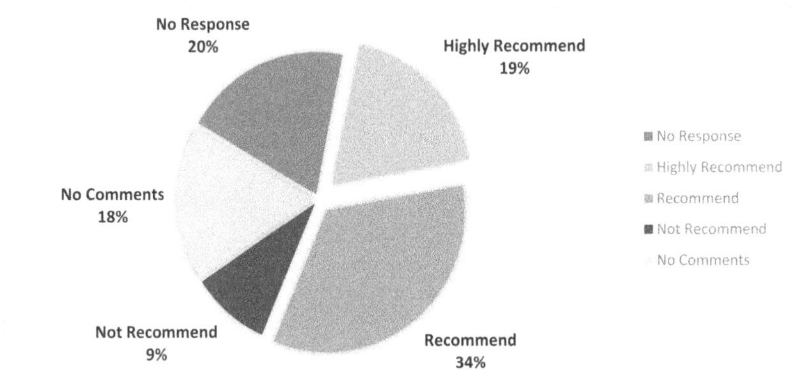

Figure 3.20 Support for Creation of a Permanent Institution of Legal Practitioners for the LAS

3.2.13.1. *Zonal Analysis of Support for Creation of a Permanent Institution of Legal Practitioners for the LAS*

3.2.13.1.1. HIGHLY RECOMMEND

Beneficiaries from the Central Zone were the highest to highly recommend the creation of a permanent institution of legal practitioners for the legal system. Further, as Figure 3.21 shows, 23% of beneficiaries in the East Zone, 21% of beneficiaries in the South Zone, 16% of beneficiaries in the North Zone, 15% of beneficiaries in the West Zone, and 11% of beneficiaries in the North East Zone highly recommended creating a permanent institution of legal practitioners for the LAS.

3.2.13.1.2. RECOMMEND

In terms of recommendation, around 48% of the South Zone beneficiaries reported the highest in recommending the creation of a permanent institution of legal practitioners for the LAS. Similarly, 38% of beneficiaries in the Central Zone, 34% of beneficiaries in the East Zone, 25% of beneficiaries in the North East Zone, 24% of beneficiaries in the North Zone, and 22% of beneficiaries in the West Zone also recommended for creation of a permanent institution of legal practitioners for the LAS.

3.2.13.1.3. NOT RECOMMEND

The study came across the beneficiaries who did not recommend a permanent institution of legal practitioners for the LAS. As shown in Figure 3.21,

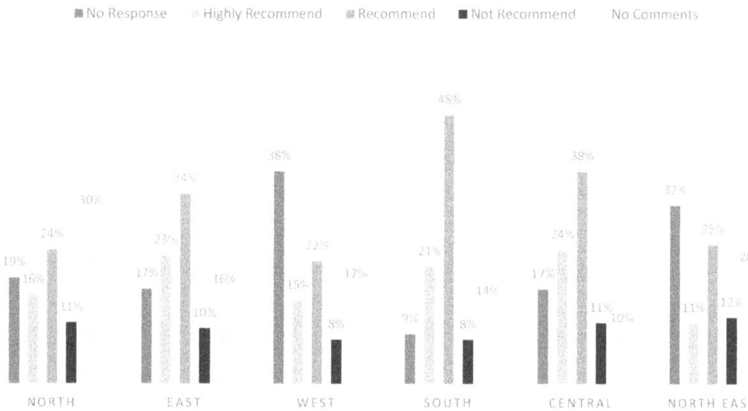

Figure 3.21 Zonal Analysis of Support for Creation of a Permanent Institution of Legal Practitioners for the LAS

12% of beneficiaries in the North East, 11% of beneficiaries in the North and Central Zones, 10% of beneficiaries in the East Zone, and 8% of beneficiaries in the West and South Zones did not recommend the creation of a permanent institution of legal practitioners for the LAS.

3.2.13.1.4. NO RESPONSE AND NO COMMENTS

A significant percentage of beneficiaries also responded with either no comments or no response. As shown in Figure 3.21, 30% of the North Zone beneficiaries responded with "no comments," while 19% of beneficiaries did not respond to this specific question in the North Zone. In the same pattern, in the East Zone, 17% of beneficiaries did not respond to this specific question, while 16% preferred to mark "no comments." In the West Zone, most beneficiaries, around 38%, did not respond to this specific question, while 17% of beneficiaries marked "no comments" as their response. Only 9% of the South Zone beneficiaries did not prefer not to respond, while 14% of the South Zone beneficiaries marked "no comments" for this specific question. Around 34% of beneficiaries chose not to respond in the North East Zone, while 20% marked "no comments" for this question.

3.2.14. *Other Issues Faced by Beneficiaries – Open-Ended Questions and Their Answers*

In the research universe, the questionnaire given to the beneficiaries also consisted of open-ended questions to include insights from the perspective of the beneficiaries; this allowed them to throw some light on any aspect

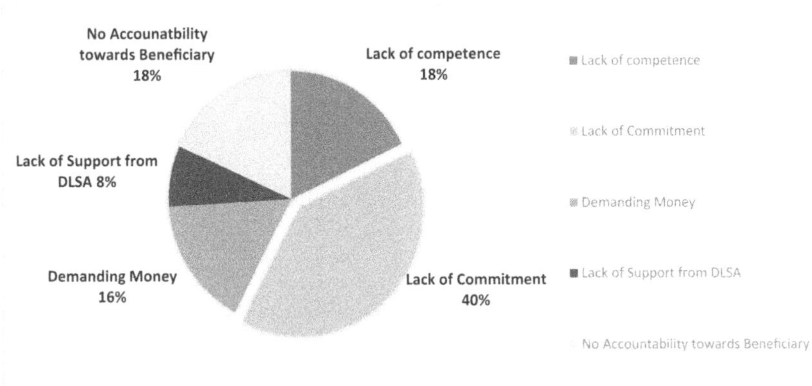

Figure 3.22 Issues Faced by Beneficiaries While Availing of the Services of LACs – Open-Ended Question

that the questionnaire failed to cover. The focus was more on knowing the beneficiaries' issues while availing of the services of LACs. The data represented as a pie chart in Figure 3.22 represents samples who have answered this open-ended question. The blank samples were not considered because the idea behind the open-ended question was to decipher any other issue faced by beneficiaries that they could not express through the structured questionnaire.

It is evident in Figure 3.22 that around 40% of beneficiaries in the six zones claimed that the lack of commitment of their LACs is the most critical issue they face. Further, 18% of beneficiaries questioned the competence aspect of LACs. This is also a reflection on the quality of LACs selected in the legal aid services and raises specific questions concerning the quality of legal services available. Also, 16% of beneficiaries complained that their LACs demanded money. Furthermore, another 18% of beneficiaries complained about how LACs were not accountable to them. The research also reveals that beneficiaries sometimes face difficulties due to the lack of proper support from DLSA offices. Here, we may conclude that more than 90% of beneficiaries, which responded to this open-ended question, faced issues related to the lack of competence and lack of commitment of LACs.

3.2.14.1. Zonal Analysis of Issues Faced by Beneficiaries – Open-Ended Questions and Their Answers

3.2.14.1.1. LACK OF COMPETENCE

When asked an open-ended question, among the beneficiaries who responded to the question, the beneficiaries in the West Zone (27%; see Figure 3.23)

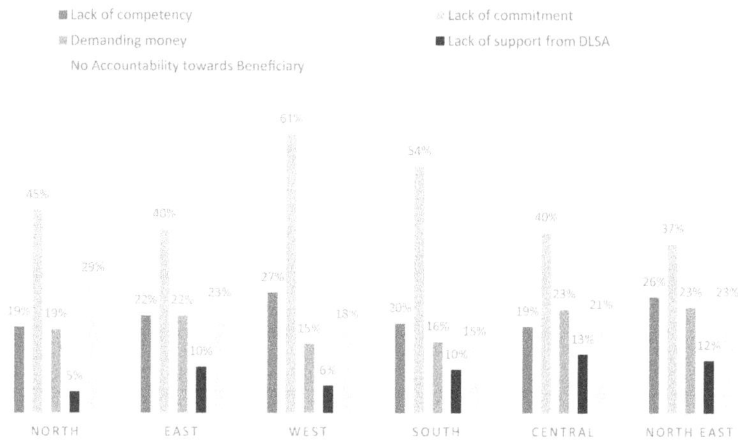

Figure 3.23 Zonal Analysis of Issues Faced by Beneficiaries While Availing of the Services of LACs – Open-Ended Question

were the highest to report a lack of competence of LACs, which is a significant issue. Similarly, 26% of beneficiaries in the North East Zone, 22% of beneficiaries in the East Zone, 20% of beneficiaries in the South Zone, and 19% of beneficiaries in the North and Central Zones also complained about LACs' lack of competence as one of the major issues they faced.

3.2.14.1.2. LACK OF COMMITMENT

In terms of issues related to lack of commitment, around 61% of the West Zone beneficiaries responded that LACs are not committed to their services. Beneficiaries from other zones also flagged the same issue when asked in the form of an open-ended question. As shown in Figure 3.23, 54% of beneficiaries in the South Zone, 45% of beneficiaries in the North Zone, 40% of beneficiaries in the East and Central Zones, and 37% of beneficiaries in the North East Zone also flagged the issue of lack of commitment as the central issue faced by them while availing of the services of LACs. Figure 3.23 demonstrates that in each of the six zones, most beneficiaries said that lack of commitment was the significant issue they faced.

3.2.14.1.3. DEMANDING MONEY

Beneficiaries answering the open-ended question also wrote about LACs demanding money. Among the beneficiaries who answered this specific question, 23% of beneficiaries in the North East and Central Zones responded that LACs demanded money for their legal aid services. Similarly, around 22% of beneficiaries in the East Zone, 19% of beneficiaries in the North Zone, 16% of beneficiaries in the South Zone, and 15% of beneficiaries in the West Zone also complained about LACs demanding money from beneficiaries. It is crucial to note that to a direct close-ended question on money demanded by LACs, the percentage of beneficiaries who responded "Yes" was too low. However, in terms of open-ended, most beneficiaries were open to comment on the aspect of demanding money.

3.2.14.1.4. LACK OF SUPPORT FROM THE DLSA

The beneficiaries also raised the issue related to the lack of support from the DLSA. As Figure 3.23 represents, 13% of beneficiaries in the Central Zone, 12% of beneficiaries in the North East Zone, 10% of beneficiaries in the South and East Zones, 6% of beneficiaries in the West Zone, and 5% of beneficiaries in the North Zone also responded that lack of support from the DLSA is one of the significant issues. Beneficiaries often complain about this aspect, as many times they are unable to locate either the assigned LAC or the DLSA office is taking too much time in addressing their grievances.

3.2.14.1.5. NO ACCOUNTABILITY TOWARDS THE BENEFICIARY

In answering the open-ended question about other issues, a few beneficiaries complained about the accountability aspect of LACs. Around 29% of beneficiaries believed LACs are not accountable to North Zone beneficiaries, while 23% of beneficiaries in the North East and East Zones also raised non-accountability among LACs towards beneficiaries. Further, as shown in Figure 3.23, 21% of beneficiaries in the Central Zone, 18% of the beneficiaries in the West Zone, and 15% of the beneficiaries in the South Zone also commented that LACs show no accountability towards beneficiaries.

3.2.15. Recommendations Made by Beneficiaries to Improve the Quality of Legal Aid Services

The study examined recommendations from the perspective of beneficiaries. In another open-ended question, the beneficiaries were requested to provide their views on the free legal aid vis-à-vis LACs. The rationale behind the inclusion of this open-ended question was that a beneficiary of a legal aid service would be better positioned to offer an insight into the complications faced by a common beneficiary in the legal aid services realm and recommend solutions to resolve those complications. Therefore, this section covers the feedback from beneficiaries about the viable solutions to improve the quality of legal services and counteract the lack of commitment by LACs. The data used in the analysis also covers respondents who refrained from commenting or writing any recommendations in the questionnaire. These

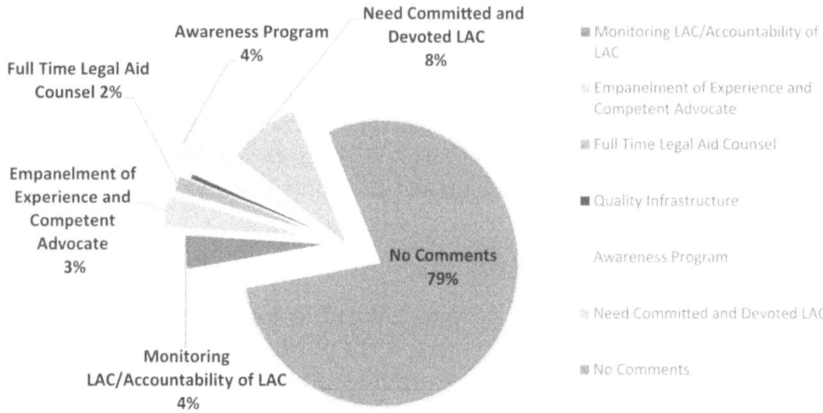

Figure 3.24 Recommendations Made by Beneficiaries to Improve the Quality of Legal Aid Services

respondents were grouped under the category of "no comments." The percentage of beneficiaries having no comments is high, probably due to their inability to understand the legal system's practical details and lack of legal literacy.

As we see in Figure 3.24, 79% of beneficiaries in all the six zones did not suggest anything to enhance the quality of legal aid services. The high share of such beneficiaries points towards two major trends: First, the research universe's beneficiaries lacked understanding and knowledge of the LAS. Second, the front offices of the DLSAs do not brief the beneficiaries, both actual and intended, in a proper manner. Further, around 8% of beneficiaries responded that since the current LACs lack commitment and devotion, there is an urgent need to bring more committed and devoted LACs into the LAS. Moreover, almost a similar percentage of beneficiaries in the research universe suggested that a monitoring mechanism should be introduced to make LACs more accountable to beneficiaries.

Notes

1 NALSA, *Activity-wise Annual Expenditure by the SLSAs (including DLSAs, HCLSCs, TLSCs) During 2017–18*, available at https://nalsa.gov.in/grants-and-accounts/expenditure-of-slsa/activity-wise-annual-expeenditure-by-the-slsas-including-dlsa-hclscs-tlscs-during-2017-18, last seen on February 24, 2020

2 THE NATIONAL LEGAL SERVICES AUTHORITY (FREE AND COMPETENT LEGAL SERVICES) REGULATIONS, 2010, available at https://nalsa.gov.in/acts-rules/regulations/national-legal-services-authority-free-and-competent-legal-services-regulations-2010, last seen on February 23, 2020

3 THE NATIONAL LEGAL SERVICES AUTHORITY (LOK ADALAT) REGULATIONS, 2009, available at https://nalsa.gov.in/acts-rules/regulations/national-legal-services-authority-lok-adalat-regulations-2009, last seen on February 23, 2020
4 NATIONAL LEGAL SERVICES AUTHORITY (LEGAL SERVICES CLINICS) REGULATIONS, 2011, available at https://nalsa.gov.in/acts-rules/regulations/national-legal-services-authority-legal-services-clinics-regulations-2011, last seen on February 23, 2020
5 Refer to Appendix Table on Nature of Cases for legal aid
6 THE NATIONAL LEGAL SERVICES AUTHORITY (FREE AND COMPETENT LEGAL SERVICES) REGULATIONS, 2010, available at https://nalsa.gov.in/acts-rules/regulations/national-legal-services-authority-free-and-competent-legal-services-regulations-2010, last seen on March 11, 2020

4 Women in Legal Aid and Access to Justice

4.1. Introduction

The most important stakeholders for this research are the legal aid beneficiaries eligible to avail of services under the ambit of free legal aid. For the research, it was crucial to know the perceptions of beneficiaries eligible for free legal aid, yet they did not prefer to take its benefits and the reasons behind that situation. Under the LSA Act, 1987, the eligibility criteria for the beneficiaries cover many grounds, in the sense that many people are eligible to avail of such services. When they are on district court premises, identifying and locating each of them is not plausible given the limitations of resources and time. Therefore, the principal researcher decided that data should be collected from women beneficiaries entitled to free legal aid (as a separate category) and unaware women beneficiaries who were entitled to free legal aid yet opted out of the services. This type of classification serves two purposes. First, it closely studies the reasons that compel legal aid beneficiaries to opt for a PLP's services instead of those by an LAC. Second, the data on unaware women eligible for legal aid and yet opted out reflects the trust a potential beneficiary has over an LAC's services. The principal objective of including this category of respondents in this empirical study was to understand why they (entitled women beneficiaries) are not utilizing the free services offered by LACs but prefer to pay fees to PLPs.

Further, respondents from this category also shared their own opinions and comments vis-à-vis the level of commitment and competence of the empaneled LACs in their respective district courts. This category's questionnaire specifically focused on women's reluctance to seek legal aid schemes' benefits even though the scheme covers them as eligible beneficiaries. The data collection took place from civil courts, CAW (crimes against women) courts, family courts, POCSO (Protection of Children from Sexual Offences Act, 2012) courts, SC/ST courts, fast track courts (FTC), and magistrate courts situated on the premises of district court centers. The research staff collected data from 3,120 women respondents on the premises of 36 district courts in 18 states. The district-wise and

DOI: 10.4324/9781003158325-4

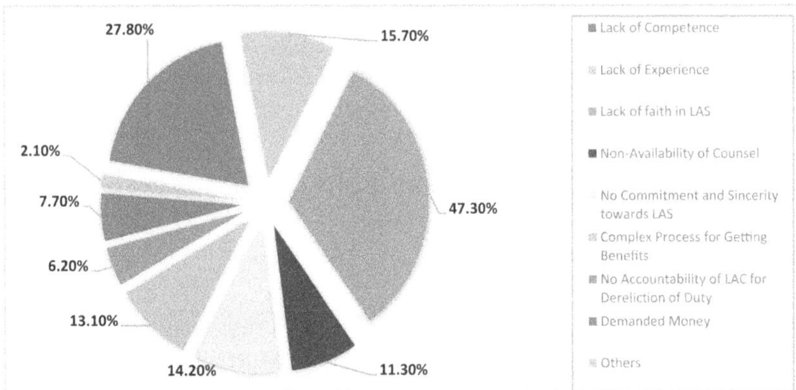

Figure 4.1 Reasons for Either Not Opting For or Discontinuing the Services of LACs Under FLAS in the Six Zones

state-wise distribution of the proposed number of women respondents and the actual number of women respondents from whom data was collected is given in the next section. The responses received bring various issues faced by beneficiaries that demotivate them from taking the services of LACs.

4.1.1. Reasons for Either Not Opting For or Discontinuing the Services of LACs

The questionnaire focused on getting the reasons from these respondents for not taking the services of LACs under FLAS. As seen from Figure 4.1, in the six zones, 47.3% of women respondents did not have faith in the system of free legal aid, and that became the reason for them not opting for FLAS. Further, around 27.8% of women beneficiaries in the six zones questioned the level of competence of LACs. Besides, 15.7% of women respondents did not approve of the sufficiency of experience of LACs. Another 14.2% of women respondents did not choose to avail of LAC services or discontinued their services because LACs were not committed and sincere towards the LAS.

Similarly, around 11.3% of women respondents also discontinued the service of LACs because of their non-availability during the trial. Another 13.3% of women respondents believed the process of availing of the services of LAC is very complex, and therefore, they refrained from opting for the services of LAC. Furthermore, 7.7% of women respondents even complained that the LACs demanded money. Other than these, 6.2% of women respondents pointed out that the non-accountability of LACs was the key reason for them not opting for or discontinuing the services of

LACs. Hence, it is evident that most women respondents were not interested in getting the benefits of FLAS. Otherwise, most of the respondents were in a sound financial position to engage PLPs. The only condition they would have opted for legal aid services would have fewer or no resources to engage a PLP.

4.1.1.1. Zonal Analysis of Reasons for Either Not Opting For or Discontinuing the Services of LACs

4.1.1.1.1. LACK OF FAITH IN THE LAS

One of the most critical aspects of this study was that respondents did not have enough faith in the LAS. Almost in every zone, respondents were vocal about the lack of faith in the LAS. This lack of faith stems from their perception that LACs either do not have ample experience or lack competence in dealing with a legal case. Therefore, they are not willing to risk their legal case on the LAS. As seen in Figure 4.2, 63% of women respondents did not opt for the services of LACs because they lacked faith in the LAS. A similar pattern is seen in the West and South Zones, where around 51% of women respondents cited lack of faith as the reason for either not opting for or discontinuing the services of LACs. Around 46% of women respondents in the Central Zone, 44% of women respondents in the North East Zone, and 43% of women respondents in the East Zone also said that they did not opt for LAC services because they do not have any faith in the LAS.

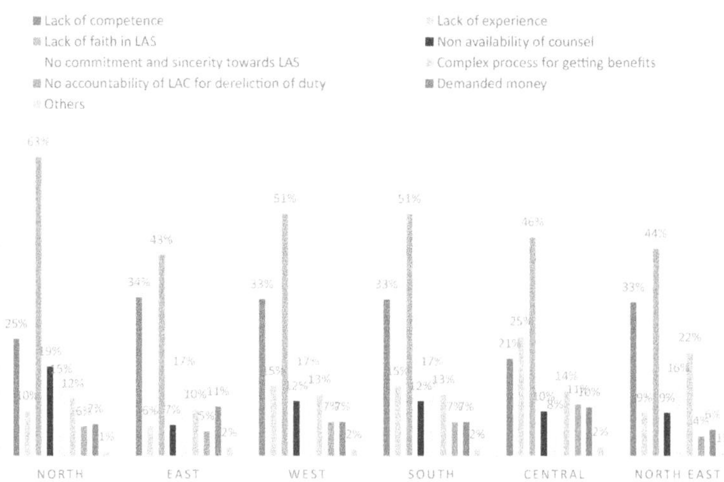

Figure 4.2 Zonal Analysis of Reasons for Either Not Opting For or Discontinuing the Services of LACs

4.1.1.1.2. LACK OF COMPETENCE

Women respondents who did not opt for FLAS were vocal in pointing out the lack of competence among the LACs. These perceptions were about low competence among empaneled advocates observed and pointed out by the beneficiaries off the record during the field visits. In Figure 4.2, we see that 34% of women respondents did not opt for the services of LACs due to a lack of competence in the East Zone. In a similar pattern, around 33% of women respondents in the West, South, and North East zones did not opt for the services of LACs because of a lack of competence in LACs. In the North Zone, around 25% of women respondents, and in the Central Zone, around 21% of women respondents believed that they did not opt for FLAS because LACs were not competent enough.

4.1.1.1.3. LACK OF EXPERIENCE

Women respondents were also concerned about the experience of the LACs. Often LACs join by either a young advocate or an advocate who does not have any experience. Women respondents considered lack of proper experience as one of the reasons for either discontinuing or not opting for the services of LACs. Around 25% of women respondents in the Central Zone were the highest to report a lack of experience of LACs as one of the reasons to either discontinue or not opt for the services offered by LACs under FLAS. Similarly, as shown in Figure 4.2, 15% of women respondents in the West and South Zones pointed out that lack of experience among the LACs is one of the reasons they opted out of the services of LACs. Further, 10% of women respondents in the North Zone, 9% of women respondents in the North East Zone, and 6% of women respondents in the East Zone were also of the opinion that LACs do not have enough experience; hence, these women did not opt for the services of LACs.

4.1.1.1.4. NON-AVAILABILITY OF COUNSEL

These results from the study note that lack of faith was one reason for these women respondents not opting for the services offered by LACs even though these respondents were eligible for FLAS. The reason for the lack of faith stems from LACs being not available for many beneficiaries. The questionnaire provided to women respondents also had options related to the non-availability of counsels. As shown in Figure 4.2, women respondents from all the six zones flagged the non-availability of LACs. Around 19% of women respondents in the North Zone and 12% of women respondents in the West and South Zones cited that non-availability of LACs for the beneficiaries was one of the reasons they did not opt for LACs. On the other side, only 10% of women respondents in the Central Zone, 9% of women respondents in the North East Zone, and 7% of women respondents in the East Zone did not opt for or discontinued their services LACs because of their non-availability.

4.1.1.1.5. COMPLEX PROCESS FOR GETTING BENEFITS

The beneficiaries under the Legal Aid Act 1987 come from the most underprivileged strata of society. They often seem not to understand the complex processes related to courts and other legal activities. Women respondents also cited the complex process for getting the benefits under FLAS as one of the reasons for not opting for the services of LACs. In the six zones, as shown in Figure 4.2, 22% of women respondents in the North East Zone, 14% of women respondents in the Central Zone, and 13% of women respondents in the South and West Zones reported that they did not opt for the services of LACs because the process for getting benefits was complex for them. Further, 12% of women respondents in the North Zone and 10% of women respondents in the East Zone also responded that they did not opt for the services of LACs because the process of getting benefits is complex.

4.1.1.1.6. NO COMMITMENT TOWARDS LEGAL AID SERVICES

The lack of commitment and sincerity towards legal aid services was also among the reasons that most of the women respondents did not opt for the services of LACs. This reason for not opting for the services of LACs should be in congruence with the reasons cited previously, as it contributes to a lack of faith in a potential beneficiary. As seen in Figure 4.2, around 17% of women respondents in the West, South, and East Zones marked the lack of commitment and sincerity towards legal aid services as the reason for not taking the services of LACs. Likewise, 16% of women respondents in the North East Zone and 12% of women respondents in the North Zone also stated that LACs are neither committed nor sincere towards LAS. Only in the Central Zone, less than 10% of women respondents believed due to a lack of commitment and sincerity of LACs towards legal aid services, they did not opt for the services of LACs.

4.1.1.1.7. DEMANDING MONEY AND LACK OF ACCOUNTABILITY OF LAC FOR DERELICTION OF DUTY

Women respondents also gave other reasons, such as LACs demanding money and LACs not being accountable for the dereliction of duty, for either discontinuing the services of LACs or not opting for their services. These reasons are less than 10% in most of the six zones.

4.1.2. Persons Who Advised Women Not to Opt for Legal Aid Services

The study further delves into deciphering the people advising these women respondents not to take the services of LACs under FLAS. Thus, the

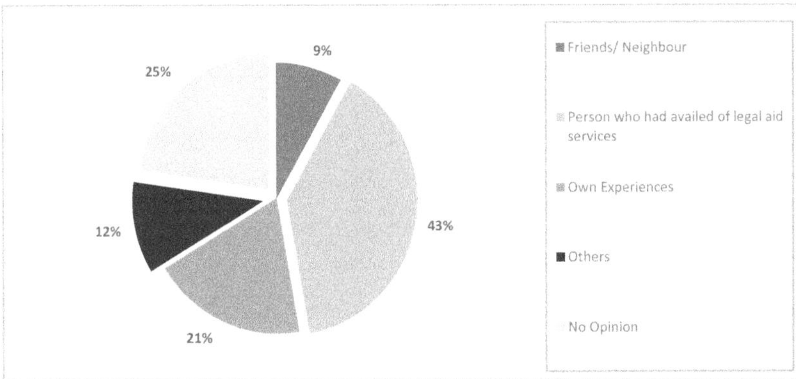

Figure 4.3 Persons Who Advised Women Not to Opt for Legal Aid Services in the Six Zones

responses confirm that most of the people who had opted for legal aid services suggested that these women not opt for legal aid services. As seen from Figure 4.3, around 43% of women respondents believed a person who had availed of LAS advised them not to opt for an LAC's services but instead opt for a PLP's. It reflects the state of poor services offered under LAS as the beneficiaries are discouraging others from opting for the services of LACs under FLAS. Further, 21% of women respondents did not opt for LAS because of their own experience.

In contrast, friends or neighbors advised around 9% of women respondents not to opt for LAS. A significant percentage of women respondents, around 25% of women respondents, had no opinion on who advised them not to opt for FLAS. Thus, many women respondents were discouraged from opting for FLAS by the beneficiaries who had opted for these services.

4.1.2.1. *Zonal Analysis of Persons Who Advised Women Not to Opt for Legal Aid Services*

4.1.2.1.1. PERSON WHO AVAILED OF LEGAL AID SERVICES

It is evident in Figure 4.4 that the people who had availed of LAS advised women respondents earlier not to opt for FLAS. Women respondents in the West Zone, around 49% of women respondents, were the highest in responding that people who had availed of LAS at any point in time advised them not to opt for FLAS. Similarly, 46% of women in the East Zone, 43% of women respondents in the North and Central Zones, and 40% of women responded that the same group of people advised them not to opt for FLAS. In the North East Zone, around 34% of women responded that they did

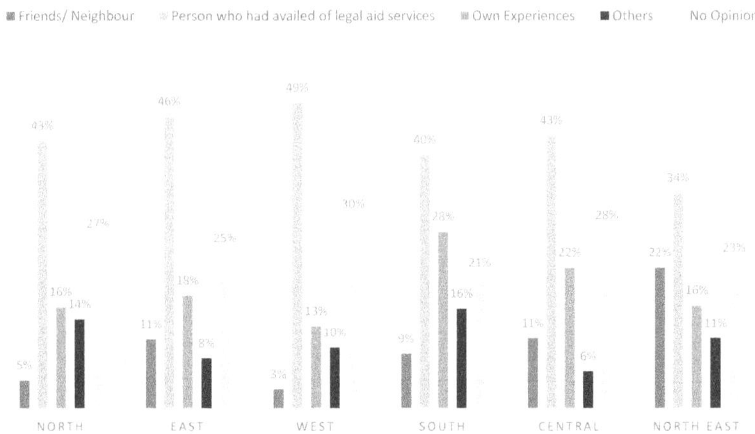

Figure 4.4 Zonal Analysis of Persons Who Advised Women Not to Opt for Legal Aid Services in the Six Zones

not opt for FLAS because they knew a person who had obtained LAS who advised them not to take these services.

4.1.2.1.2. OWN EXPERIENCES

Women respondents' own experience was also a significant reason for not opting for the services of LACs under FLAS. Around 28% of women respondents in the South Zone, 22% of women respondents in the Central Zone, 18% of women respondents in the East Zone, and 16% of women respondents in the North and North East Zones did not opt for the LAS because of their own experiences. Further, 13% of women respondents in the West Zone also relied on their own experiences to opt out of FLAS.

4.1.2.1.3. FRIENDS AND NEIGHBORS

Friends and neighbors were also a few people who advised women respondents not to opt for services of LACs under FLAS. In the study, as shown in Figure 4.3, around 22% of women respondents in the North East Zone responded that their friends and neighbors advised them not to opt for FLAS. Likewise, their neighbors advised 11% of women respondents in the East Zone and Central Zone not to opt for FLAS. Simultaneously, less than 10% of women respondents in the South Zone, North Zone, and East Zone reported that their friends and neighbors advised them not to opt for FLAS.

4.1.2.1.4. OTHERS AND NO OPINIONS

Women respondents in every zone responded with many other reasons beyond the study's scope or the given options. These responses were marked as "others" in their respective questionnaires. Further, "no opinion" as a response has a significant presence – more than 20% of women respondents in every zone. Many women respondents were hesitant to respond or reveal the person advised them not to opt for FLAS and hence preferred to mark "no opinion."

4.1.3. Reasons for Engaging PLPs

The subsequent set of responses focuses on the reasons that compelled women respondents to engage PLPs instead of LACs even when they were eligible for FLAS. The women respondents marked multiple responses for the reasons to engage PLPs. As shown in Figure 4.5, in the six zones, 93% of women (2,817 out of 3,003) cited accountability for dereliction of duties as the single most important criteria for them to engage a PLP. Similarly, 59.5% of women respondents marked the ability to control the litigation process and outcomes through a PLP (1,786 out of 3,003) as one of the reasons. Further, commitment or competence also accounted for a significant reason to opt for a PLP, as 31% of women respondents marked that as one reason. Thus, as the empirical evidence reflects, accountability, control, commitment, and competence remain the principal reasons behind these women respondents engaging a PLP instead of an LAC.

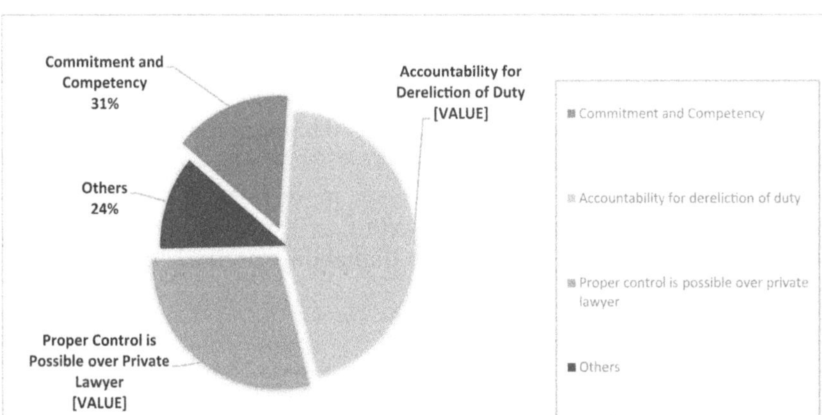

Figure 4.5 Reasons for Engaging PLPs in the Six Zones*

*Multiple-response question. Percentages are based on respondents.

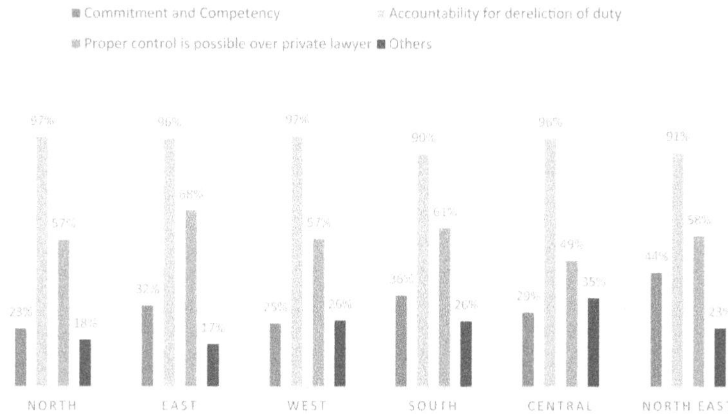

Figure 4.6 Zonal Analysis of Reasons for Engaging PLPs in the Six Zones*
*Multiple-response question. Percentages are based on respondents.

4.1.3.1. Zonal Analysis of Reasons for Engaging PLPs in the Six Zones

4.1.3.1.1. ACCOUNTABILITY FOR DERELICTION OF DUTY

One of the most evident rationales given by these women respondents is accountability for dereliction of duty. As seen in Figure 4.6, in almost every zone, more than 90% of women respondents cited PLPs' accountability aspect over LACs. The respondents must have developed a perception that LACs are often not accountable for any negligence in dealing with legal aid cases. Women respondents were confident that since they pay a PLP, he/she can be accountable for any negligence. The responses received reflect the confidence of women respondents, as 97% of women respondents in the North and West Zones, 96% of women in the Central and East Zones, 91% of women respondents in the North East Zone, and 90% of women respondents in the South Zone cited accountability for dereliction of duty as the reason for engaging PLPs.

4.1.3.1.2. PROPER CONTROL POSSIBLE OVER A PRIVATE LAWYER

The aspect related to command and control over their lawyers also made these women respondents engage PLPs instead of LACs under FLAS. As shown in Figure 4.6, 68% of women respondents in the East Zone, 61% of women respondents in the South Zone, 58% of women respondents in the North East Zone, 57% of women respondents in the North and West

Zones, and 49% of women respondents in the Central Zone said that they engaged a PLP so that they can have proper control over them.

4.1.3.1.3. COMMITMENT AND COMPETENCE

Commitment and competence of PLPs are also among the major reasons that compelled women respondents to engage PLPs instead of LACs. Around 44% of women respondents in the North East Zone, 36% of women respondents in the South Zone, 32% of women respondents in the East Zone, 29% of women respondents in the Central Zone, 25% of women respondents in the West Zone, and 23% of women respondents in the North Zone flagged that they preferred to engage a PLP over an LAC. Per the conversation, women respondents were vocal about the lack of commitment and competence shown by LACs towards legal aid beneficiaries.

4.1.4. Major Issues Faced by Women Beneficiaries

The questionnaire also consisted of two open-ended questions focusing on women beneficiaries' significant issues and any suggestions to better the services. It is evident from Figure 4.7 that most of the women respondents were reluctant to share any such open-ended issues. Around 71% of women respondents did not answer the open-ended question. The hesitation in responding or conversing freely on this issue might have resulted from societal notions. "No comments" was provided to the open-ended questions probably because of the fear of getting into a controversy. However, the open-ended questions must be seen from the viewpoint of women beneficiaries' various issues rather than the number of responses. Among the

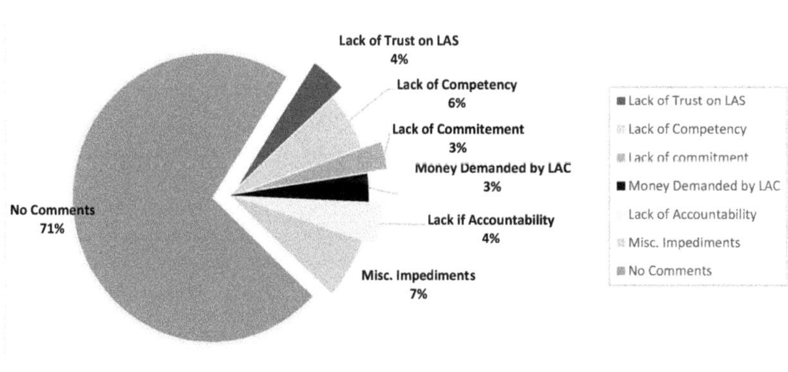

Figure 4.7 Major Issues Faced by Women Beneficiaries

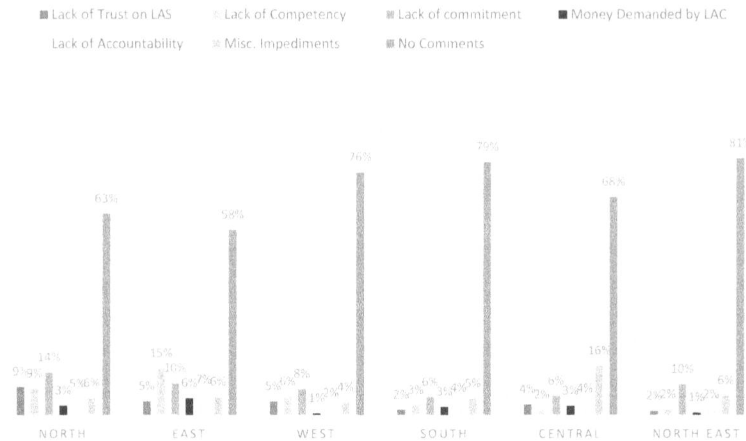

Figure 4.8 Zonal Analysis of Major Issues Faced by Women Beneficiaries

major issues women respondents faced, 4% of women respondents flagged the issue of lack of trust, 6% of women respondents wrote that LACs are not competent, and 3% of women respondents were concerned about the lack of commitment shown by the LACs. Similarly, 3% of women respondents raised the issue of LACs demanding money, and another 4% of women respondents also raised the issue of lack of accountability among the LACs.

4.1.4.1. *Zonal Analysis of Major Issues Faced by Women Beneficiaries*

4.1.4.1.1. LACK OF TRUST IN THE LAS

As seen in Figure 4.8, around 9% of women respondents in the North Zone, 5% of women respondents in the East and West Zones, 4% of women respondents in the Central Zone, and 2% of women respondents in the South and North East Zones raised the issue of lack of trust in the LAS as one of the major issues faced by women beneficiaries.

4.1.4.1.2. LACK OF COMPETENCE

Women respondents also raised the issue of lack of competence among the LACs in every zone. All in all, 15% of women respondents in the East Zone, 9% of women respondents in the North Zone, 6% of women respondents in the West Zone, and 3% of women respondents in the South Zone were vocal about the lack of competence in the LAS. Likewise, 2% of women respondents in the Central and North East Zones also complained about the low level of competence in the LAS.

4.1.4.1.3. LACK OF COMMITMENT

The low level of competence of LACs is evident in the responses received from the women respondents. In Figure 4.8, 14% of women respondents in the North Zone, 10% of women respondents in the East and North East Zones, 8% of women respondents in the West Zone, and 6% of women respondents in the South and Central Zones wrote about the lack of competence among the empaneled advocates in their responses to this open-ended question.

4.1.4.1.4. MONEY DEMANDED BY LACS

In the open-ended format, a few women respondents raised the issue of money demanded by LACs to perform their duties under FLAS. In the East Zone, 6% of women respondents raised the issue of LACs demanding money from women beneficiaries. Further, 3% of women respondents in the North Zone, South Zone, and Central Zone were vocal about the issue of money demanded by LACs. Only 1% of women respondents in the North East Zone and West Zone raised the issue of money demanded by LACs.

4.1.4.1.5. LACK OF ACCOUNTABILITY

Another issue that came forward in the open-ended question is the lack of accountability among LACs. In the East Zone, around 7% of women responded that LACs show no accountability towards the legal aid beneficiaries. Similarly, 5% of women respondents in the North Zone, 3% of women respondents in the South Zone and Central Zone, and 2% of women respondents in the West Zone and North East Zone also commented that lack of accountability is an issue faced by women beneficiaries under FLAS.

4.1.5. Suggestions for Improving the Services Provided by LACs

Most of the women respondents did not respond to this open-ended question, citing a lack of time to fill in or respond. As seen in Figure 4.9, where women respondents managed to respond, they suggested a need for devoted and committed LACs in the LAS. The respondents also put forth the proposition that the potential legal aid beneficiaries should receive sensitization about the LAS. Further, a few were vocal about the need to empanel competent and experienced LACs.

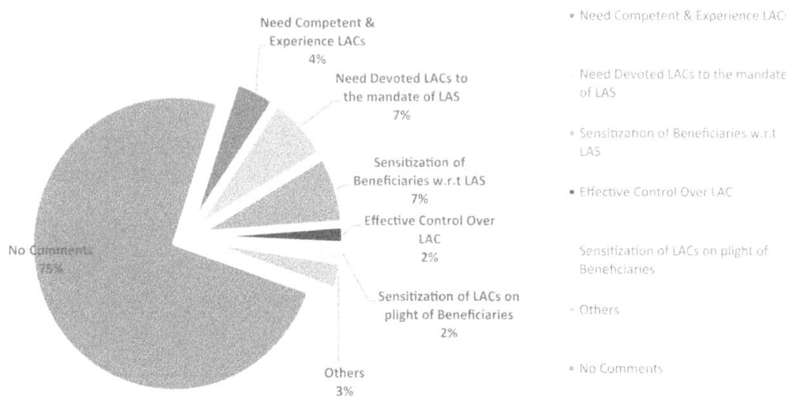

Figure 4.9 Suggestions for Improving the Services Provided by LACs

4.1.5.1. *Zonal Analysis of Suggestions for Improving the Services Provided by LACs*

4.1.5.1.1. NEED FOR COMPETENT AND EXPERIENCED LACS

Women respondents suggested that the LAS needs to empanel competent and experienced advocates to improve FLAS services. In Figure 4.10, we see that 12% of women respondents in the East Zone suggested that the need for competent and experienced LACs in the LAS is increasing. Similarly, 4% of women respondents in the North Zone and Central Zone, 3% of women respondents in the South Zone, and 1% of women respondents in the West Zone and North East Zone suggested that LAS needs competent and experienced LACs to improve the services of LACs.

4.1.5.1.2. NEED FOR LACS DEVOTED TO THE MANDATE OF THE LAS

The women respondents also suggested that the LAS needs devoted LACs. This very suggestion stems from their experience of seeing LACs showing dereliction in their duties while dealing with other legal aid beneficiaries. Figure 4.10 shows that in almost every zones, women respondents voiced this suggestion. Around 13% of women respondents in the North Zone, 12% of women respondents the East Zone, 8% of women respondents in the Central Zone, and 4% of women respondents in the West Zone, South Zone, and North East Zone suggested that there is a need to empanel LACs devoted to the mandate of the LAS.

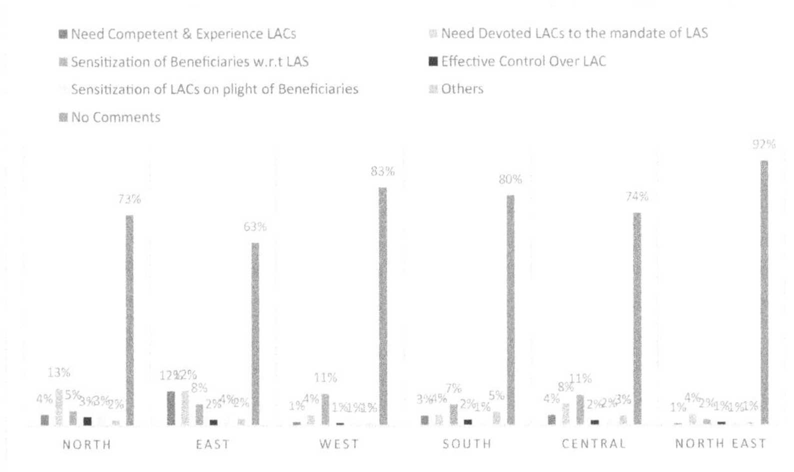

Figure 4.10 Zonal Analysis of Suggestions for Improving the Services Provided by LACs

4.1.5.1.3. SENSITIZATION OF BENEFICIARIES CONCERNING THE LAS

The open-ended question brought up the suggestion of sensitization of beneficiaries concerning the LAS. All in all, 11% of women respondents in the West Zone and Central Zone suggested the LAS's sensitization. Similarly, 8% of women respondents in the East Zone, 7% of women respondents in the South Zone, 5% of women respondents in the North Zone, and 2% of women respondents in the North East Zone also suggested the sensitization of beneficiaries concerning the LAS.

4.1.5.1.3. EFFECTIVE CONTROL OVER LAC

In the preceding sections, the study shows women respondents preferred PLPs to have proper control over them. They suggested the same for LACs. Around 3% of women respondents in the North Zone and 2% of women respondents in the East Zone, South Zone, and Central Zone have suggested having effective control over LACs. In North East and Central Zone, around 1% of women respondents suggested the same.

4.1.5.1.4. SENSITIZATION OF LACS ON THE PLIGHT OF BENEFICIARIES

Women respondents suggested that LACs should be aware of the plight of beneficiaries. They suggested for sensitization of LACs on the plight of beneficiaries. Around 4% of women respondents in the East Zone, 3% of women respondents in the North Zone, 2% of women respondents in the Central

Zone, and 1% of women respondents in the West Zone, South Zone, and North East Zone suggested sensitizing LACs on the plight of beneficiaries.

4.2. Unaware Women's Perception About Legal Aid Services

Every year, the NALSA, with other legal aid services institutions, undertakes several activities and programs to make people aware of their right to legal aid and understand legal aid services' functioning. However, these programs and activities do not seem to have any impact on the ground. Further, the preceding section analyzed the perceptions of aware women about legal aid services and why they were unwilling to opt for legal aid services. In this section, the study assesses the perception of unaware women respondents vis-à-vis FLAS. To weigh in these ground realities of the awareness program and test the hypothesis that beneficiaries opt for legal aid services due to lack of resources, the research delved into the study of the unaware women beneficiaries of the LAS in selective district courts. During the study, researchers collected data from 8,539 unaware women respondents from 36 districts in 18 states.

4.2.1. Willing and Unwilling Unaware Women (Unaware About FLAS)

The field investigators collected the data near the courtrooms, particularly family courts and courts dealing with CAW, in which the majority of cases or disputes are related to females or women in general. The field investigators informed and explained to these unaware women respondents about FLAS and subsequently asked whether they were willing or unwilling to opt for FLAS? The field investigator further asked why their willingness and unwillingness to opt for the free services offered to them under the LSA Act, 1987. As Figure 4.11 demonstrates, around 67% of unaware women respondents were willing to opt for services because they lacked the resources to engage a PLP.

In comparison, only 33% of unaware women respondents showed their unwillingness to opt for FLAS as they do not trust LAS. Thus, most unaware women respondents, when told about the benefits of FLAS, were willing to opt for FLAS due to a lack of resources. On the other hand, those unaware women respondents who were unwilling to take services offered under FLAS cited that they do not trust LAS.

4.2.1.1. Zonal Analysis of Willing and Unwilling Unaware Women (Unaware About FLAS)

4.2.1.1.1. UNAWARE WOMEN WILLING, DUE TO LACK OF RESOURCES

More than 60% of unaware women respondents were willing to take the services offered under FLAS in most regions. As seen in Figure 4.12, around

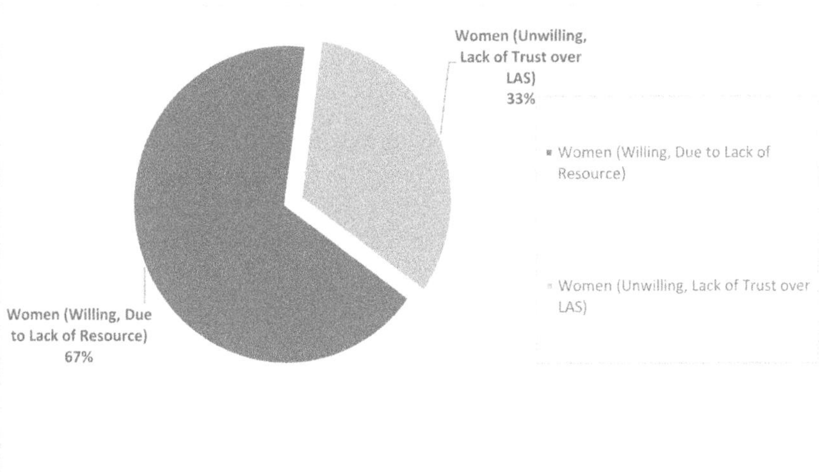

Figure 4.11 Willing and Unwilling Unaware Women (Unaware About FLAS)

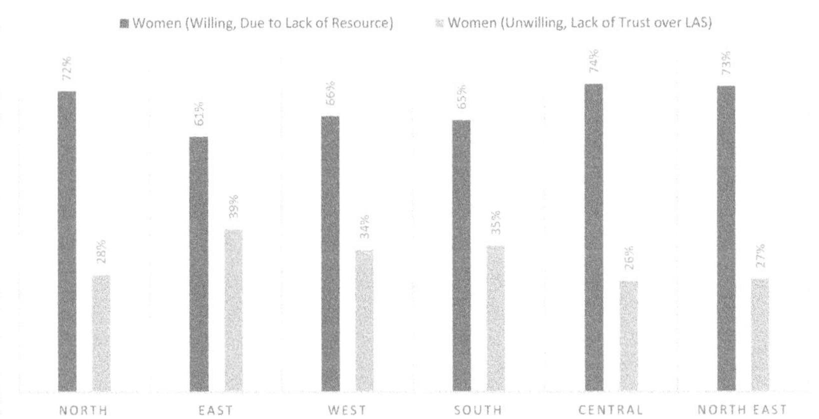

Figure 4.12 Zonal Analysis of Willing and Unwilling Unaware Women (Unaware About FLAS)

72% of unaware women respondents in the North Zone, 74% of unaware women respondents in the Central Zone, and 73% of unaware women respondents in the North East Zone were willing to take the services of LACs offered under FLAS. Similarly, 66% of unaware women respondents in the West Zone, 65% of unaware women in the South Zone, and 61% of unaware women respondents in the East Zone were also willing to opt for FLAS. It is evident that the unaware women respondents were only willing to take the services of LACs because they do not have enough resources to engage a PLP for their cases.

4.2.1.1.2. UNAWARE WOMEN UNWILLING, DUE TO LACK OF TRUST

A few unaware women respondents were unwilling to opt for FLAS. Around 39% of unaware women respondents in the East Zone, 35% of unaware women respondents in the South Zone, and 34% of unaware women respondents in the West Zone were unwilling to opt for FLAS because they do not trust LAS. The trend was visible in other zones also, as 28% of unaware women respondents in the North Zone, 27% of unaware women respondents in the North East Zone, and 26% of unaware women respondents in the Central Zone were unwilling to benefit from FLAS due to lack of trust in the LAS. The study, therefore, demonstrates that beneficiaries are willing to opt for FLAS only because they lack the resources to engage a PLP. Further, beneficiaries often opt out because they do not have any trust in the LAS.

5 Regulators of the Legal Aid Services

5.1. Introduction

The LSA Act, 1987, in Section 9 of Chapter 3, mandates that the district court should constitute a DLSA to implement the mandate of FLAS in the district. The district judge is the chairperson of the DLSA. However, in practice, it is the secretary or the regulator who manages the daily affairs of the DLSA/SLSA, and he/she is appointed after consulting with the chairman of the DLSA. The regulator belongs to the State Judicial Services, and he/she should not be lower than the rank of a subordinate judge or civil judge. A regulator is responsible for the empanelment, allocation of legal aid cases, and regulating the overall conduct of LACs.

This empirical study included regulators to understand the issues and challenges they faced in dealing with legal aid's daily affairs related to LACs and beneficiaries in their respective DLSAs. Regulators in the research universe of the study received a copy of the questionnaire designed explicitly for them. It is worthwhile to bring an observation related to regulators. The regulators were ardent to know about the questionnaire and questions asked to the empaneled advocates and legal aid beneficiaries.

During the empirical study, regulators from every district were cordial and amiable towards the research staff. The scope of interaction with these regulators dealt with assessing the competence and commitment of the LACs. The questionnaire focused on taking inputs from the regulators about LACs' drafting skills, articulation skills, and communication skills. Further, they were requested to answer the questionnaire in light of the quality of services offered by LACs in their respective districts. The questionnaire also covered the operational aspect of the DLSA office.

DOI: 10.4324/9781003158325-5

In total, 33 regulators willingly submitted their questionnaires with great appreciation for the research done on legal aid services. The district-wide list of regulators is shown in the following table:

Table 5.1 Proposed and Actual Responses Received From the Regulators

Zone	*State*	*District*	*Proposed Regulator*	*Actual Regulator*
North	**Punjab**	Patiala	1	1
		Sangrur	1	1
	Himachal Pradesh	Shimla	1	1
		Solan	1	1
	Haryana	Gurugram	1	1
		Rohtak	1	1
	Uttar Pradesh	Allahabad	1	1
		Gautam Buddha Nagar	1	1
East	**West Bengal**	Kolkata	1	1
		24 North Pargana	1	1
	Jharkhand	Ranchi	1	1
		Ramgarh	1	1
	Odisha	Bhubaneshwar	1	0
		Cuttack	1	1
West	**Rajasthan**	Jodhpur	1	1
		Pali	1	1
	Gujarat	Ahmedabad	1	0
		Gandhinagar	1	1
	Maharashtra	Aurangabad	1	1
		Jalna	1	1
South	**Karnataka**	Bangalore Urban	1	1
		Bangalore Rural	1	1
	Tamil Nadu	Tiruchirappalli	1	1
		Thanjavur	1	1
	Andhra Pradesh	Vizag	1	1
		Vizianagaram	1	1
	Kerala	Pathanamthitta	1	1
		Alappuzha	1	1
Central	**Chhattisgarh**	Raipur	1	1
		Durg	1	1
	Madhya Pradesh	Indore	1	1
		Dhar	1	1
North East	**Meghalaya**	Shillong	1	1
		Nongpoh	1	1
		Jowai	1	0
	Assam	Guwahati	1	1
		Amingaon	1	0
	Total		37	33

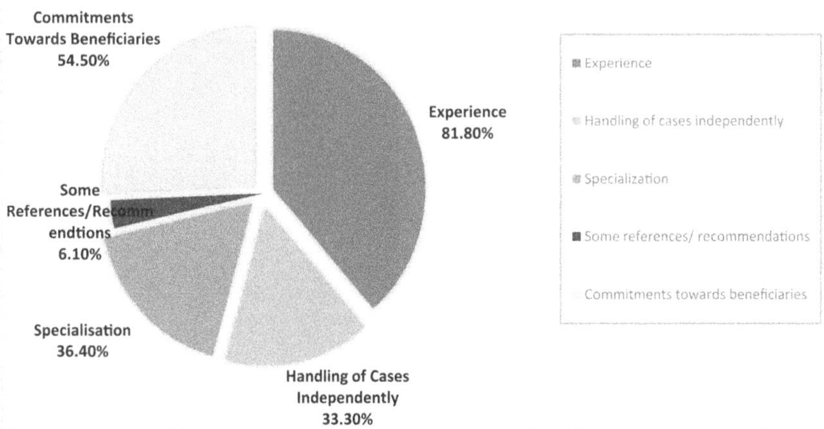

Figure 5.1 Preferential Qualification for the Empanelment of LACs in the Six Zones*

*Multiple-response question. Percentages are based on respondents.

5.2. Data Analysis

5.2.1. Preferential Qualification for the Empanelment of LACs

The empirical study first focused on deciphering regulators' criteria in selecting the empaneled advocates to deliver FLAS in their respective districts. In multiple-response questions, the questionnaire asked various criteria they prefer, in general, to select an LAC. As seen in Figure 5.1, around 81% of regulators preferred the experience of LACs as one of the significant criteria. Then 54.5% of regulators marked the level of commitment shown by an advocate towards beneficiaries as one of the selection criteria or a preferred qualification for empaneling an advocate as an LAC. Further, 36.4% of regulators considered a specialization of an advocate, while 33.3% of regulators considered a number of cases handled by an advocate as one of the criteria to qualify an advocate for empanelment as an LAC. Indeed, experience is a significant element in selecting an advocate for empanelment, followed by an advocate's competence and commitment.

5.2.1.1. Zonal Analysis of Preferential Qualification for the Empanelment of LACs

5.2.1.1.1. EXPERIENCE

The regulators' first and foremost criterion for selecting a panel lawyer or LAC is the advocate's experience in terms of practice in the bar. As seen

Figure 5.2 Zonal Analysis of Preferential Qualification for the Empanelment of LACs*

*Multiple-response question. Percentages are based on respondents.

in Figure 5.2, 100% of regulators in the North Zone and Central Zone gave preference to the advocate's experience for empaneling him/her as an LAC. Similarly, 80% of regulators in the East Zone, 63% of regulators in the South Zone, and 60% of regulators in the West Zone and North East Zone preferred the experience of an advocate for the empanelment of LACs. The preference for experience comes from the NALSA (Free and Competent Legal Services) Regulations, 2010, Section 8, para. 3, which mandates that LACs should have no less than three years of experience at the bar.

5.2.1.1.2. COMMITMENT TOWARDS BENEFICIARIES

The NALSA (Free and Competent Legal Services) Regulations, 2010, in Section 8, para. 5, states that when empaneling the lawyers for legal aid, regulators should consider the integrity, competence, and suitability of lawyers. Regulators in almost every zone preferred to take commitment shown by lawyers as one of the qualifications to empanel LACs. In Figure 5.2, we see that around 88% of regulators in the South Zone and 50% of regulators in the Central Zone preferred commitment shown by lawyers as one of the criteria for the empanelment of LACs. Further, around 40% of regulators in the North East Zone, West Zone, and East Zone also considered this very aspect while selecting lawyers for empanelment as LACs. Only 38% of regulators in the North Zone believed they preferred commitment towards beneficiaries as a qualification for the empanelment of LACs.

5.2.1.1.3. HANDLING OF CASES INDEPENDENTLY

Regulators even considered several cases handled by a lawyer independently as one of the qualifications for the empanelment of LACs. Regulators believed that as an LAC, lawyers would handle legal aid cases independently. Therefore, he/she must have handled enough cases independently. Around 50% of regulators in the North Zone, 40% of regulators in the East Zone, 38% of regulators in the South Zone, 25% of regulators in the Central Zone, and 20% of regulators in the West Zone preferred a number of cases handled by a lawyer independently as one of the criteria for the empanelment of LACs.

5.2.1.1.4. SPECIALIZATION

A regulator often deals with varied issues related to legal aid beneficiaries. Per the NALSA (Free and Competent Legal Services) Regulations, 2010, panel lawyers should have specialized lawyers also. Regulators consider specialization as one of the qualifications for the empanelment of LACs in almost every zone. In Central Zone, around 75% of regulators preferred specialization as one of the criteria for the empanelment of LACs. Similarly, 50% of regulators in the North Zone, 40% of regulators in the East Zone, 25% of regulators in the South Zone, and 20% of regulators in the West Zone also preferred specialization lawyers as one of the qualifications for the empanelment of LACs.

5.2.1.1.5. SOME REFERENCES/RECOMMENDATIONS

Regulators in almost all the zones did not consider references or recommendations as one of the qualifications for the empanelment of LACs. However, as shown in Figure 5.2, only 25% of regulators in the North Zone considered a reference or recommendation by any senior advocate or judge as a qualification for the empanelment of LACs.

5.2.2. Justification by LACs for Joining the LAS

The commitment of LACs to the LAS is directly related to the objectives of joining FLAS. The next set of questions demonstrates a regulator's rationale for LAC to join legal aid services. Regulators often act as a conduit between beneficiaries and their respective LACs to address both stakeholders' grievances. Since regulators are also stakeholders in the legal aid services, it becomes essential to know their perception about the sole motivation of LACs joining the legal aid services. As seen in Figure 5.3, 73% of regulators responded that LACs join the LAS to provide services to the poor, whereas 36% of the regulators responded that LACs see the LAS as an employment

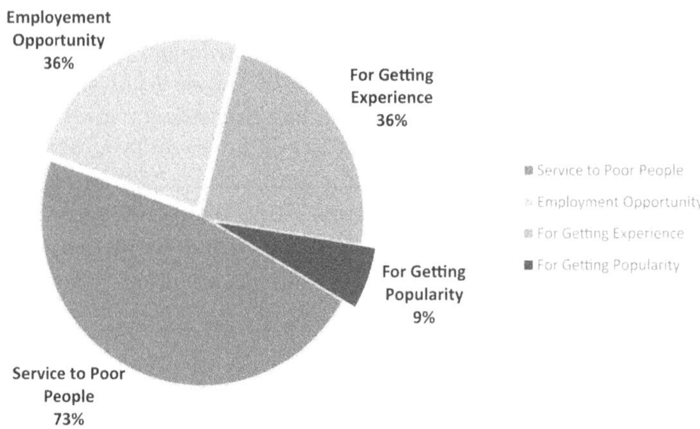

Figure 5.3 Justification by LACs for Joining the LAS*

*Multiple-response question. Percentages are based on respondents.

opportunity. Similarly, 36% of regulators believed LACs join the LAS to get acquainted with the profession. Only 9% of regulators responded that LACs join the LAS to gain some popularity.

5.2.2.1. *Zonal Analysis of Justification by LACs for Joining the LAS*

5.2.2.1.1. SERVICE TO POOR PEOPLE

As stated, regulators are one of the stakeholders in FLAS. They are involved in selecting panel lawyers. Their perception regarding the justification given by LACs while telling us what motivates lawyers to be in the panel. Since the legal aid is for the poor and lower stratum of the society, most of the LACs, per regulators, justified their joining the service to serve the poor. As seen in Figure 5.4, 100% of regulators in the East Zone, 80% of regulators in the West Zone, 75% of regulators in the South Zone, 66% of regulators in the North East Zone, and 63% of regulators in the North Zone told that LACs joined the services to serve poor people as one of the justifications for joining LAS.

5.2.2.1.2. EMPLOYMENT OPPORTUNITY

Regulators were also of the opinion that LACs also justify their joining to gain employment opportunities. Around 88% of regulators in the North Zone, 75% of regulators in the Central Zone, and 33% of regulators in the

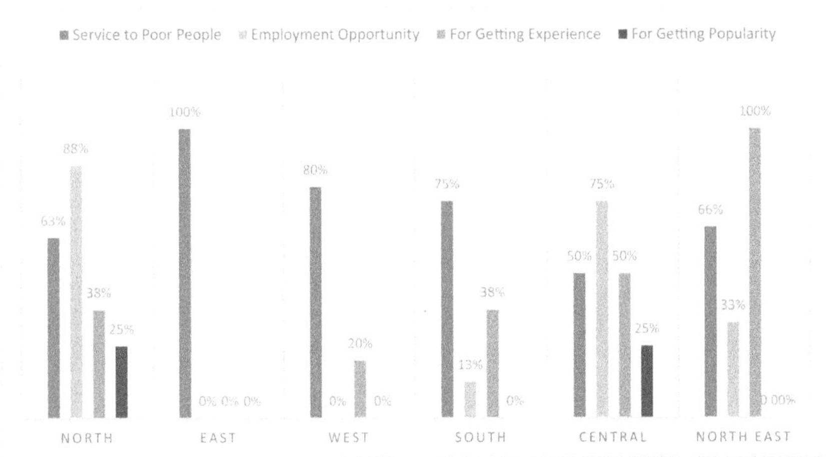

Figure 5.4 Zonal Analysis of Justification by LACs for Joining the LAS

North East Zone responded that LACs join the LAS because of employment opportunities. In contrast, only 13% of the South Zone regulators opined that LACs join the LAS as an employment opportunity.

5.2.2.1.3. GETTING EXPERIENCE

Panel lawyers in the LAS often have less experience when compared to other senior practicing lawyers. These LACs often lack experience and join the LAS to gain experience by handling poor people's legal cases.

As seen in Figure 5.4, 100% of regulators in the North East Zone, 50% of regulators in the Central Zone, and 38% of regulators in the South Zone and North Zone said that LACs join the LAS to gain some experience. Only 20% of regulators in the West Zone said that getting experience is one of the justifications LACs cite for joining LAS.

5.2.2.1.4. GAINING POPULARITY

Regulators in two zones also responded that often LACs join the LAS to gain popularity in the district court. Around 25% of regulators in the North and Central Zones said LACs justify their joining the LAS because they want to gain popularity.

5.2.3. Availability of the LACs for Discussion with Clients

Throughout the empirical study, the LACs were not available for discussion with their respective clients. Regulators' interface for discussing and

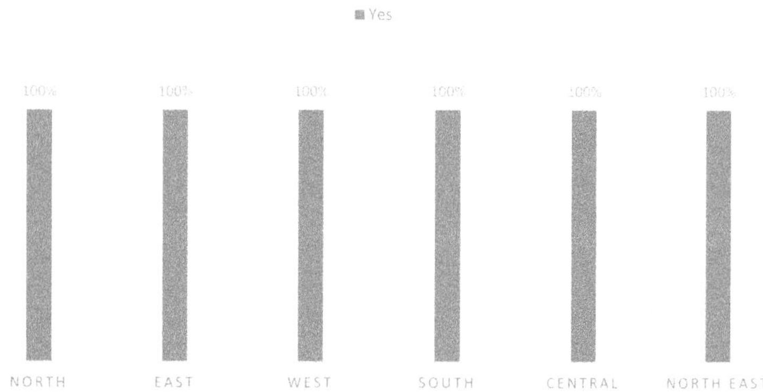

Figure 5.5 Availability of the LACs for Discussion With Clients

defending the interests of LACs and beneficiaries is essential for bridging the trust deficit gap. It further supports promoting the mandate of the LAS. As we can see from Figure 5.5, every regulator of each zone (100%) agreed that LACs must be available for discussion with clients.

5.2.4. Places of LAC Interaction With Beneficiaries in the Six Zones (From Regulators' Perspective)

The regulators were also asked about the places where most of the interaction between LACs and beneficiaries occurs. As shown in Figure 5.6, 63.3% of regulators believed LACs and beneficiaries meet in court or on court premises. This meeting may happen before or after the scheduled hearing on the given date. On the other hand, 66.7% of regulators said that LACs interact with their respective beneficiaries at the office of the DLSA. Similarly, 40% of Regulators felt that most LACs interact with their respective clients over the phone. Further, 33.3% of Regulators were also of the view that LACs often interact with legal aid beneficiaries at the chambers of LACs. Henceforth, we can conclude that from a regulator's perspective, the office of the DLSA and court premises are two major places of interaction between LACs and beneficiaries.

5.2.4.1. Zonal Analysis of Places of LAC Interaction With Beneficiaries

5.2.4.1.1. OFFICE OF THE LSA

Beneficiaries of legal aid are people from the most vulnerable strata of society. Regulators often meet them directly after assigning their case to

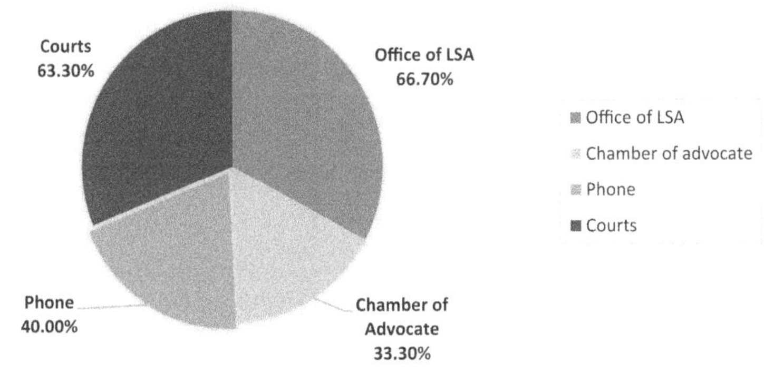

Figure 5.6 Places of LAC Interaction With Beneficiaries*

*Multiple-response question. Percentages are based on respondents.

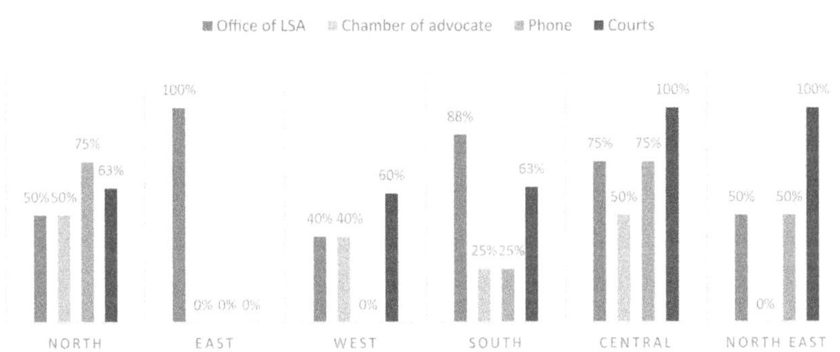

Figure 5.7 Zonal Analysis of Places of LAC Interaction With Beneficiaries*

*Multiple-response question. Percentages are based on respondents.

an LAC. Since most of the LACs have less experience, they do not have any chamber. Therefore, LACs meet/interact with their respective legal aid beneficiaries in the office of the DLSA only. As shown in Figure 5.7, 100% of regulators in the East Zone, 88% of regulators in the South Zone, 75% of regulators in the Central Zone, and 50% of regulators in the North and North East Zones said that interaction between LACs and their respective beneficiaries takes place in the office of the DLSA. Only 40% of regulators in the West Zone opined that interaction between beneficiaries and their respective LACs takes place in the office of the DLSA.

5.2.4.1.2. COURTS

Regulators believed that beneficiaries also interact with their LACs near the court premises after or before a scheduled appearance in a hearing. In Figure 5.7, we see that 100% of regulators in the Central Zone and North East Zone said that court premises are places where LACs interact with their beneficiaries. Similarly, 63% of regulators in the South Zone and North Zone and 60% of regulators in the West Zone also marked the court as one of the many places where LACs interact with their beneficiaries.

5.2.4.1.3. PHONE

Since LACs are often engaged in their private practices, they often tend to interact with their beneficiaries over a phone call regarding any briefing related to beneficiaries' cases. Regulators from every zone validated this with their responses. As seen in Figure 5.7, around 75% of regulators in the North Zone and Central Zone opined that LACs interact with their respective beneficiaries over the phone. Similarly, 50% of regulators in the North East Zone and 25% of regulators in the South Zone also responded that LACs interacted with their beneficiaries over the phone.

5.2.4.1.4. CHAMBER OF ADVOCATES

A few regulators believed the chamber of advocates are also places where interaction between LACs and beneficiaries occurs. Around 50% of regulators in the North Zone and Central Zone said that the chamber of advocates is one place where interaction between LACs and beneficiaries occurs. Further, 40% of regulators in the West Zone and 25% of regulators in the South Zone cite the respondent's chamber of advocates as one of the places where LACs interact with beneficiaries.

5.2.5. *Duration of Interaction/Discussion/Briefing Between LACs and Beneficiaries*

During this research study, most LACs were involved in legal aid cases on an ad hoc or case-by-case basis, and no regular appointment or engagement was made. Further, the legal aid cases become a secondary priority of the LACs. Moreover, LACs give low priority to legal aid cases. Therefore, it becomes crucial to know, from a regulator's perspective, the duration of interaction between LACs and beneficiaries because regulators act as the linchpin between LACs and beneficiaries.

As shown in Table 5.2, per the data collected from the district courts of six zones, around 84.8% of regulators assessed that the average time taken for interaction/discussion between the LACs and beneficiaries is not more than one to three hours per case. Further, around 12.1% of regulators

Table 5.2 Duration of Interaction/Discussion/Briefing Between LACs and Beneficiaries

Region		*1–3 hours*	*4–6 hours*	*7–9 hours*	*Total*
North	Count	7	0	1	8
	% of Total	88%	0%	13%	100%
East	Count	4	1	0	5
	% of Total	80%	20%	0%	100%
West	Count	5	0	0	5
	% of Total	100%	0%	0%	100%
South	Count	6	2	0	8
	% of Total	75%	25%	0%	100%
Central	Count	3	1	0	4
	% of Total	75%	25%	0%	100%
North East	Count	3	0	0	3
	% of Total	100%	0%	0%	100%
Total	Count	28	4	1	33
	% of Total	84.80%	12.10%	3.00%	100%

believed LACs and beneficiaries interacted for an average of about four to six hours per case. On the contrary, a minute, 3% of regulators believed that LACs interact for about seven to nine hours per case with their legal aid beneficiaries. Accordingly, the time spent by LACs per case is indeed way less when compared to private ones.

Researchers involved in the study believe that the duration of interaction may also be dependent upon the nature of disputes involved, availability of infrastructure, and willingness or commitment of LACs to support the cause of the beneficiaries. Separate and detailed research to further inquire the specific issue of interaction between the stakeholders can be covered under future research agendas.

5.2.6. Average Duration of Trial of Cases Involving LACs: Criminal and Civil Cases

Prompt and economic justice is an integral part of the Constitution of India. In the justice system, the time taken for a trial is vital for access to justice. Therefore, the next set of sections is based on the spirit of justice delayed is justice denied. The questionnaire circulated to the regulators also focused on the duration of trial cases involving LACs. It is worth mentioning that all the stakeholders answered this set of questions, as it dealt with the commitment and competency of the LACs. In criminal cases, as shown in Table 5.3, 90.9% of regulators said the average disposal time of trial cases involving LACs is from one to three years. It also shows that per regulators in almost all the zones, most legal aid cases of criminal nature take an average of one to three years.

Table 5.3 Average Duration of Trial of Criminal Cases Involving LACs

Region		*1–3 Years*	*4–6 Years*	*Total*
North	Count	7	1	8
	% of Total	88%	13%	100%
East	Count	5	0	5
	% of Total	100%	0%	100%
West	Count	5	0	5
	% of Total	100%	0%	100%
South	Count	7	1	8
	% of Total	88%	13%	100%
Central	Count	4	0	4
	% of Total	100%	0%	100%
North East	Count	2	1	3
	% of Total	100%	50%	100%
Total	Count	30	3	33
	% of Total	90.90%	9.10%	100%

Table 5.4 Average Duration of Trial of Civil Cases Involving LACs

Region		*1–3 Years*	*4–6 Years*	*7–10 Years*	*Total*
North	Count	6	2	0	8
	% of Total	75%	25%	0%	100%
East	Count	4	1	0	5
	% of Total	80%	20%	0%	100%
West	Count	2	3	0	5
	% of Total	40%	60%	0%	100%
South	Count	4	3	1	8
	% of Total	50%	38%	13%	100%
Central	Count	2	1	1	4
	% of Total	50%	25%	25%	100%
North East	Count	2	1	0	3
	% of Total	66%	33%	0%	100%
Total	Count	20	11	2	33
	% of Total	60.60%	33.30%	6.10%	100%

On the other hand, in civil cases, as shown in Table 5.4, around 60.6% of regulators responded that the average time of trial cases involving LACs is from one to three years. Similarly, 9.1% of regulators feel that the average time taken to dispose of a criminal case where LACs are involved is from four to six years.

Further, in civil cases, 33.3% of regulators believed that it takes around four to six years to dispose of a case where LACs are involved. Around 6.1% of regulators were also of the view that sometimes it takes from seven to ten years to dispose of a civil case where LACs are involved.

One can comprehend that the average time taken in most civil cases is more than in criminal cases. One explanation or reason for this disparity between criminal and civil cases is that LACs largely want to conclude criminal cases as early as possible to claim the specified honorarium. The outcome of cases is not relevant to the payment of honorarium. Moreover, protection and promotion of the interests of the beneficiaries are the least priority of LACs.

5.2.7. Regulators' Perspective on the Difficulties Faced by LACs

To assess the quality of interaction between the LACs and the beneficiaries, the regulators' questionnaire also asked about various difficulties faced by the LACs while dealing with beneficiaries. It is crucial to assess the difficulties faced by LACs while pursuing their duties under FLAS with the legal aid beneficiaries from a regulator's perspective because a regulator also acts as a medium between LACs and beneficiaries.

As shown in Figure 5.8, 51.7% of regulators from the six zones said that LACs are occupied with their private practice matters and cannot interact with the legal aid beneficiaries. Similarly, 51.7% of regulators believed the low quality or lack of infrastructure is one of the difficulties faced by LACs while interacting with beneficiaries. Further, almost 38% (37.9%) of regulators blamed the beneficiaries for the problems experienced by LACs. It is peculiar to notice that the system, which exists because of the legal aid beneficiaries, is blaming the beneficiaries for the problems faced by the LACs.

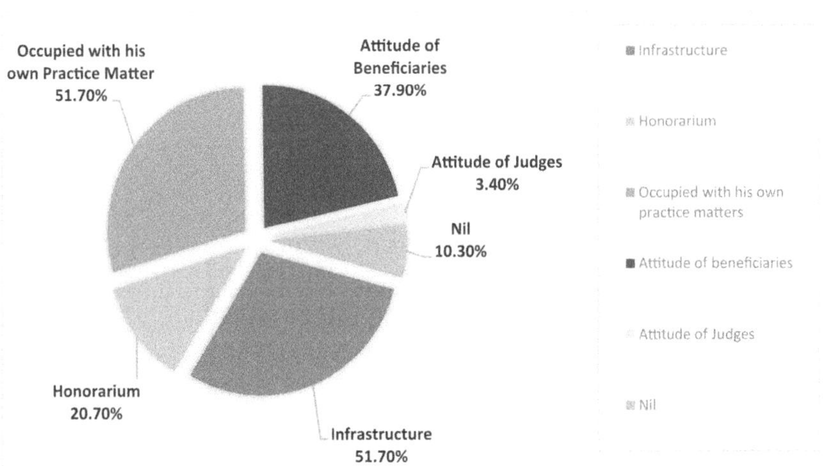

Figure 5.8 Regulators' Perspective on the Difficulties Faced by LACs*

*Multiple-response question. Percentages are based on respondents.

Additionally, 20.7% of regulators also pointed out that the low rate of honorarium created difficulties for LACs to devote time to beneficiaries. A minute 3.4% of regulators said that sometimes judicial officers create difficulties for LACs to interact with their beneficiaries. Interestingly, only 10.3% of regulators from the six zones responded that LACs face no difficulties interacting with the legal aid beneficiaries. Accordingly, per regulators, difficulties faced by LACs revolve around LACs being occupied with their private practice, lack of infrastructure, beneficiaries' attitudes, untimely or low honorarium, and judges' attitudes.

5.2.7.1. Zonal Analysis of Regulators' Perspective on the Difficulties Faced by LACs

5.2.7.1.1. BEING OCCUPIED WITH THEIR PRIVATE PRACTICE MATTERS

Serving legal aid beneficiaries is not the only focus area for LACs. The LSA Act, 1987, and NALSA (Free and Competent Legal Services) Regulations, 2010, did not bind them to practice their private practice matters. Regulators refer to this as one of the difficulties faced by LACs. Since their private practice matters take a significant amount of time, LACs are often unable to concentrate on legal aid beneficiaries' matters.

As shown in Figure 5.9, around 100% of regulators in the Central Zone, 75% of regulators in the East Zone, 50% of regulators in the North Zone and West Zone, and 29% of regulators in the South Zone opined that one of the difficulties faced by LACs is that they are occupied with their private practice matters.

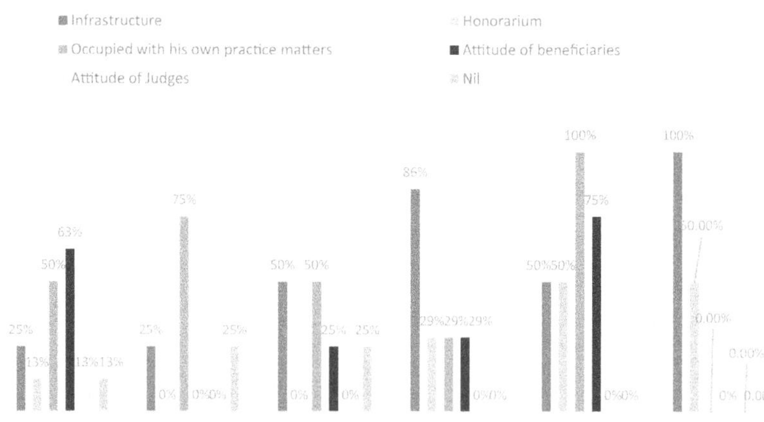

Figure 5.9 Zonal Analysis of Regulators' Perspective on the Difficulties Faced by LACs

5.2.7.1.2. INFRASTRUCTURE

Another difficulty faced by LACs, according to regulators, is the lack of infrastructure. Since most LACs are legal practitioners with less experience, they do not have their chambers. This makes their interaction with their beneficiaries difficult. Around 100% of regulators in the North East Zone, 86% of regulators in the South Zone, and 50% of regulators in the Central Zone and West Zone cited lack of infrastructure as one of the difficulties faced by LACs. Only in the North Zone, around 25% of regulators responded that lack of infrastructure is one of the difficulties faced by LACs.

5.2.7.1.3. ATTITUDE OF BENEFICIARIES

Regulators also pointed out the attitude of beneficiaries as one of the difficulties faced by LACs. Regulators believed beneficiaries expect too much from the assigned LACs and assume LACs to work on their whim. As shown in Figure 5.9, around 75% of regulators in the Central Zone, 63% of regulators in the North Zone, 29% of regulators in the South Zone, and 25% of regulators in the West Zone said that the attitude of beneficiaries is one of the difficulties faced by LACs.

5.2.7.1.4. HONORARIUM

Regulators also acknowledged that the low rate of honorarium and delay in receiving honorarium are a few difficulties faced by LACs. As shown in Figure 5.9, around 50% of regulators in the North East Zone and Central Zone responded that LACs face difficulties in honorarium. Likewise, 29% of regulators in the South Zone and 13% of regulators in the North Zone also said LACs faced difficulties in honorarium.

5.2.8. Nature of Complaints/Observations From Judges About the Services of LACs

5.2.8.1. Status of Complaints Received by Regulators From Judges About the Services of LACs

In any system of governance, grievance redressal is one of the major ways to improve the system. The office of the DLSA has a system of filing grievances against the LACs and Regulators for the problems faced by judicial officers while hearing the legal aid cases. However, according to the regulators, most of the complaints against LACs are verbal/oral. As shown in Figure 5.10, 33% of regulators from the six zones affirmed that they had received complaints from judicial officers against LACs on various grounds. On the contrary, 46% of regulators denied that they had received complaints against LACs from any judicial officer. Furthermore, 21% of regulators from the six zones did not respond to this specific question. It is important to note that

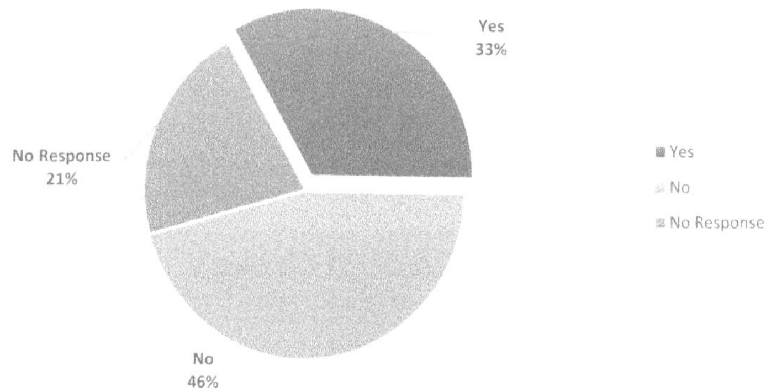

Figure 5.10 Whether Regulators Received Any Complaint Against LACs From Judicial Officers

the observations and data collected from judicial officers contradict such an observation.

5.2.8.1.1. ZONAL ANALYSIS OF STATUS OF COMPLAINTS RECEIVED BY REGULATORS FROM JUDICIAL OFFICERS ABOUT THE SERVICES OF LACS

5.2.8.1.1.1. Yes Regulators were asked whether they had received any complaints from judicial officers or judges about the services offered by LACs. As seen in Figure 5.11, around 62.5% of regulators in the North Zone, 50% of regulators in the Central Zone, 37.5% of regulators in the South Zone, and 20% of regulators in the West Zone said that they received complaints from judicial officers or judges about the services offered by LACs.

5.2.8.1.1.2. No The study finds that regulators in a few zones denied receiving any such complaints from judicial officers or judges against the services of LACs. As seen in Figure 5.11, 80% of regulators in the East Zone, 60% of regulators in the West Zone, and 50% of regulators in the South Zone and Central Zone opined that they did not receive any such complaints against LACs from either judicial officers or judges. Similarly, 33.33% of regulators in the North East Zone and 12.5% of regulators in the North Zone also denied that any complaints were filed against LACs by judicial officers or judges.

5.2.8.1.1.3. No Response A few regulators did not wish to respond to this question. As seen in Figure 5.11, 66.7% of regulators in the North East Zone, 25% of regulators in the North Zone, and 20% of regulators in the

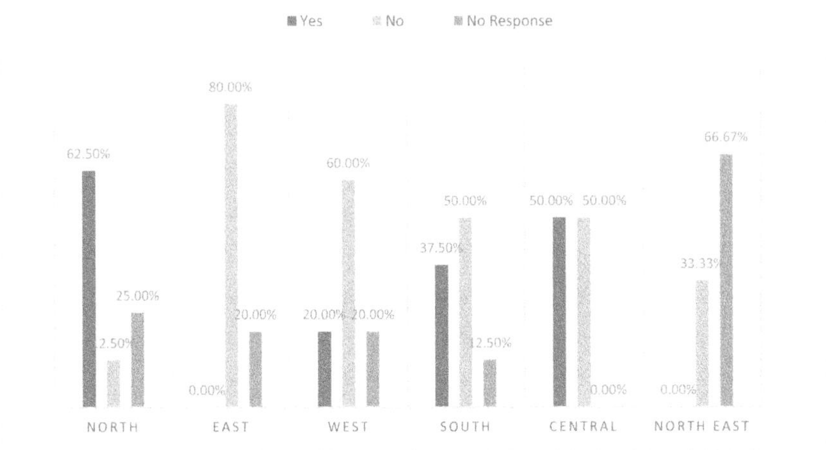

Figure 5.11 Zonal Analysis Whether Regulators Received Any Complaint Against LACs From Judicial Officers

East Zone and West Zone did not respond to this question. In the South Zone also, 12.5% of regulators did not wish to respond to the question of whether they received any complaints from judicial officers or judges against the services of LACs.

5.2.8.2. Nature of Complaints/Observations From Judges About the Services of LACs

Regulators who responded yes in the previous section elaborated on the nature of complaints they received from judicial officers or judges. Figure 5.12 and Figure 5.13 show responses received from the regulators in the North Zone, West Zone, South Zone, and Central Zone. As shown in Figure 5.12, regulators from the four zones have acknowledged that they have mostly received complaints about the quality of arguments made by LACs (28%) being unsatisfactory from the judicial officers. Further, judicial officers have also complained about LACs for their lack of preparation for arguments (18%), late attendance (18%), deliberately seeking of frequent adjournments (18%), not protecting the interests of beneficiaries (9.1%), and even not interacting with beneficiaries (9%).

The nature of complaints, such as lack in quality of arguments, not being prepared for the arguments, being late for appearance in court on the specified date, and seeking unnecessary adjournments, reflects a lack of commitment of LACs. These complaints are widespread in every zone and have affected the governance of legal aid services across.

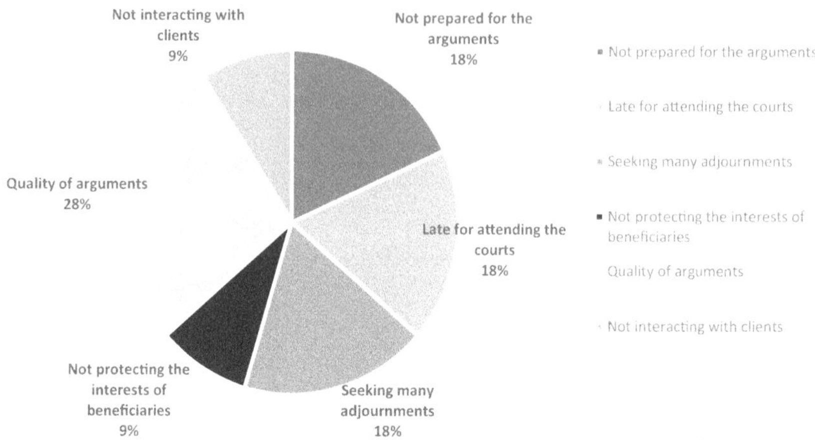

Figure 5.12 Nature of Complaints/Observations From Judges About the Services of LACs

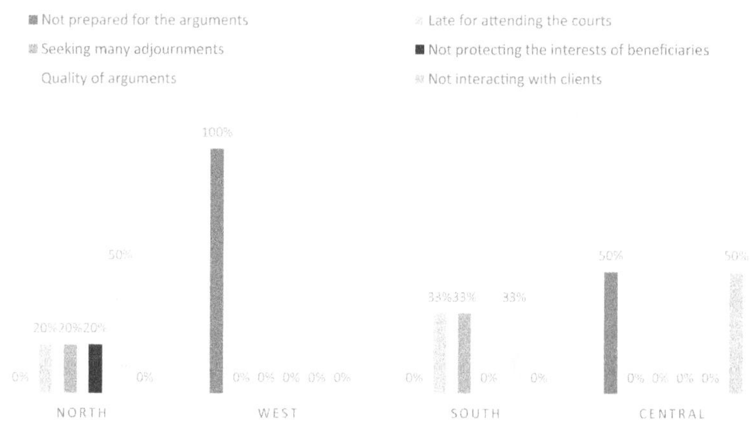

Figure 5.13 Zonal Analysis of Nature of Complaints/Observations From Judges About the Services of LACs

5.2.8.2.1. ZONAL ANALYSIS OF NATURE OF COMPLAINTS/OBSERVATIONS FROM JUDGES ABOUT THE SERVICES OF LACS

5.2.8.2.1.1. Quality of Arguments As stated earlier by regulators that one of the justifications given by LACs to join the LAS is to gain experience. Regulators received complaints from judicial officers or judges about LACs not making quality arguments. This might be because most LACs are inexperienced in terms of practice and lack the competence required to make quality arguments. As seen in Figure 5.13, around 50% of regulators in the North Zone and 33% of regulators in the South Zone received a complaint against the services of LACs from the judicial officers on this very aspect.

5.2.8.2.1.2. Being Unprepared for Arguments Judicial officers also complained about LACs not being prepared for arguments while representing legal aid beneficiaries. LACs are often not prepared for arguments because they focus more on private clients or they lack LAS commitment. In Figure 5.13, we see that 100% of regulators in the West Zone and 50% of regulators in the Central Zone received complaints from judicial officers pertaining to LACs being prepared for arguments.

5.2.8.2.1.3. Being Late for Attending the Courts Since LACs focus more on their private practice matters. They often tend to attend and prepare for private cases more. Hence, they often show up late in court cases dealing with legal aid beneficiaries. In Figure 5.13, we see that regulators in the South Zone (33%) and regulators in the North Zone (20%) received complaints of this nature from the judicial officers or judges.

5.2.8.2.1.4. Seeking Many Adjournments Due to lack of preparedness or unavailability of legal aid beneficiaries at times, LACs request adjournments. As shown in Figure 5.13, around 33% of regulators in the South Zone and 20% of regulators in the North Zone received complaints from judicial officers or judges that LACs seek many adjournments in the legal aid cases.

5.2.8.2.1.5. Not Interacting With Clients Since LACs focus more on their private clients and do not have their chambers or places to interact with beneficiaries, they do not interact with legal aid beneficiaries. In Figure 5.13, we see that 50% of regulators in the Central Zone received complaints from judicial officers that LACs are not interacting with their legal aid clients.

5.2.8.2.1.6. Not Protecting the Interests of Beneficiaries Around 20% of regulators in the North Zone received complaints from judicial officers or judges that LACs are not protecting beneficiaries' interests. LACs not protecting the interest of beneficiaries highlights a lack of commitment by LACs towards legal aid. This might be due to low honorarium factors involved with legal aid cases or favoring the opposing advocate for monetary benefits.

5.2.9. Information/Complaints Against LACs for Demanding Money From Judicial Officers

Legal aid services aim to aid and assist the socially and economically weaker section of the society. It is free of any cost for the people entitled to such services. It is public money that funds these services. NALSA and SLSA

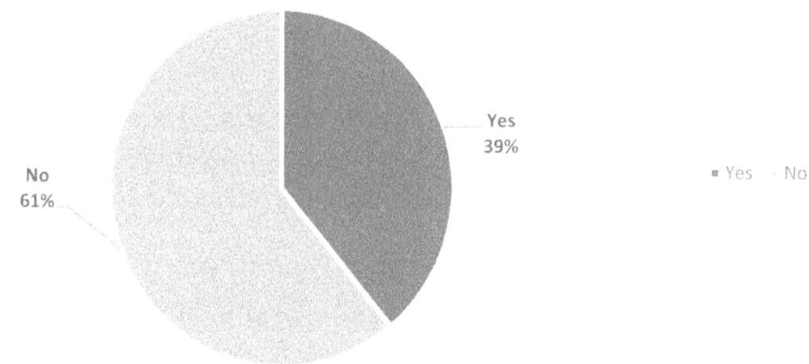

Figure 5.14 Whether There Are Complaints Received From Judicial Officers Against LACs for Demanding Money

regulate the services offered under the LSA Act, 1987, in every state. LACs are paid honoraria in three stages for dealing with legal aid cases. However, in actual practice, the situation is not the same. As shown in Figure 5.12, around 39% of regulators confirmed that they had received judicial officers' or judges' complaints against LACs demanding money before and after court hearings. In comparison, 61% of regulators denied any such complaints by judicial officers or judges against LACs.

5.2.9.1. *Zonal Analysis of Whether There Are Complaints Received From Judicial Officers Against LACs for Demanding Money*

5.2.9.1.1. YES

As shown in Figure 5.15, around 100% of regulators in the Central Zone, 50% of regulators in the South Zone and North Zone, and 20% of regulators in the East Zone opined that they did receive complaints from judicial officers that LACs are demanding money. It is worth mentioning that not all regulators were vocal enough to affirm that LACs demand money. Nevertheless, a few regulators confirmed that LACs demand money. These regulators cited the low honorarium for legal services as one reason LACs are compelled to demand money from legal aid beneficiaries.

5.2.9.1.2. NO

In the study, not all regulators were vocal enough to affirm that LACs demand money from their legal aid beneficiaries. As seen in Figure 5.15,

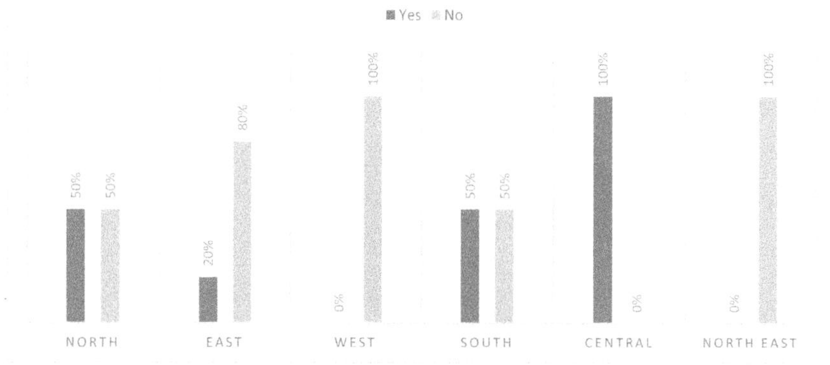

Figure 5.15 Zonal Analysis of Complaints Received From Judicial Officers Against LACs for Demanding Money

100% of regulators in the North East Zone and West Zone and 80% of regulators in the East Zone denied any such complaints from judicial officers or judges. Further, 50% of regulators in the South Zone and North Zone also denied any such complaints from the judicial officers or judges that LACs demand money for the services rendered by them.

5.2.10. Action Taken by Legal Services Authority (LSA) for Demanding Money

The data presented earlier validates that regulators often receive judicial officers' complaints against LACs for demanding money from beneficiaries. Consequently, it becomes pertinent to know the nature of action regulators take to curb this menace. Regulators of India's legal aid services have minimal powers under the LSA regulations and rules framed for regulating India's legal aid services. A regulator cannot give disciplinary actions but can give warnings and replace or remove the name of the said counsel from the panel of LACs. As shown in Figure 5.16, around 15% of regulators acknowledged that the LSA replaced those LACs who demanded money from their beneficiaries. Further, almost 12% of regulators responded that the LSA only warned the LACs about their misconduct.

Additionally, 6% of regulators across the six zones acknowledged that the LSA removed LACs from the group of panel LACs for demanding money from their legal aid beneficiaries. Another 6% of regulators responded that they suspended from the panel those LACs who demanded money from their beneficiaries (see Figure 5.16). It is pertinent to mention that this research study did not find a single instance where the SLSA or DLSA ever

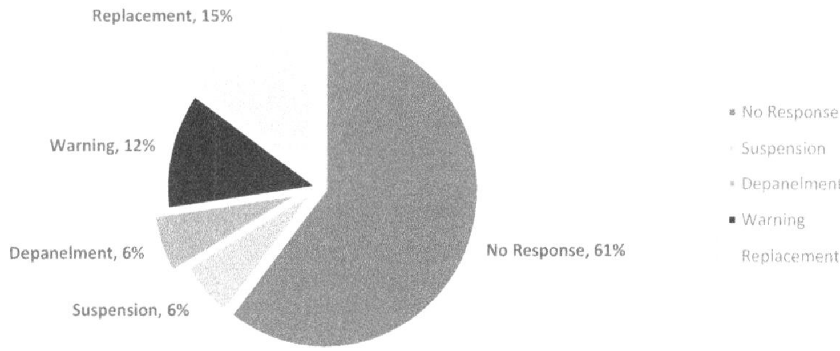

Figure 5.16 Action Taken by the LSA for Demanding Money in the Six Zones (on Complaints From Judicial Officers)

approached the Bar Council of India for suspension or termination of LACs (in case of severe misconduct) from the bar.

The study highlights regulators' inability to ensure accountability on behalf of LACs, the nature of complaints received from judicial officers, and the action taken against those LACs. The extent of complaints from judicial officers to regulators covertly reflects upon the lack of commitment of LACs towards the mandate of FLAS. No such mechanism exists by which regulators can keep a check on LACs and hold them accountable too. This lack of empowerment to ensure the accountability of LACs leads to low quality of services and low commitment of LACs. This leads to the absence of trust in legal aid services by the beneficiaries also.

5.2.10.1. Zonal Analysis Action Taken by the LSA for Demanding Money in the Six Zones (on Complaints From Judicial Officers)

5.2.10.1.1. REPLACEMENT

After receiving complaints from judicial officers or judges, regulators replaced LACs on the cases with a new LAC. As shown in Figure 5.17, 75% of regulators in the Central Zone and 20% of Regulators in the West Zone said they replaced LACs after receiving a complaint from judicial officers or judges about LACs demanding money.

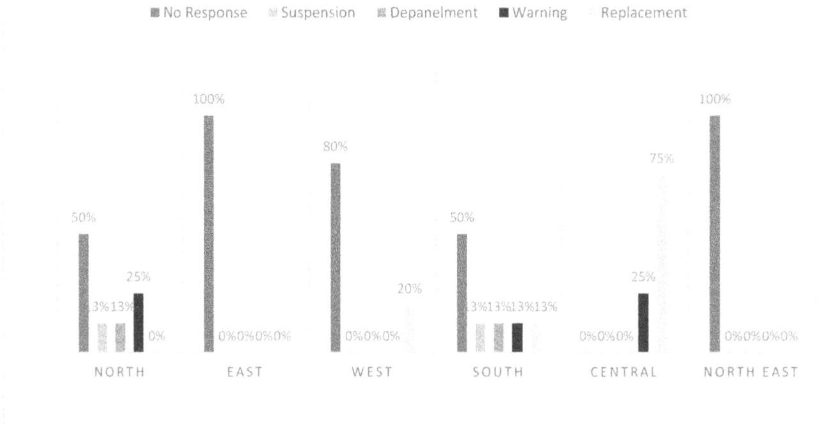

Figure 5.17 Zonal Analysis Action Taken by the LSA for Demanding Money in the Six Zones (on Complaints From Judicial Officers)

5.2.10.1.2. WARNING

Regulators often warned LACs when they received any complaints from judicial officers or judges that LACs were demanding money. As shown in Figure 5.17, 25% of regulators in the North Zone and Central Zone warned the LACs after receiving any complaints related to demanding money from their legal aid clients. Similarly, 13% of regulators in the South Zone also warned LACs when they received complaints from judicial officers or judges.

5.2.10.1.3. DE-EMPANELMENT AND SUSPENSION

A few regulators also resorted to the de-empanelment of LACs from the panel after receiving complaints that LACs are demanding money. Around 13% of regulators in the South Zone and North Zone preferred to de-empanel those LACs who demanded money. As seen in Figure 5.17, 13% of regulators in the North Zone and South Zone said they even suspended the LACs after receiving complaints from judicial officers or judges.

5.2.11. Nature of Complaints Filed Against LACs by Beneficiaries Before the LSA

5.2.11.1. Whether Any Complaints Were Filed Against LACs by Beneficiaries Before the LSA

This question was based on the nature of complaints filed by the beneficiaries against LACs while receiving FLAS from the DLSA. Regulators interact

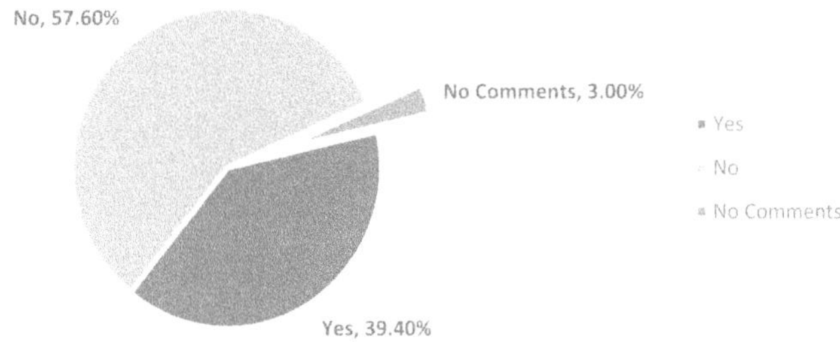

Figure 5.18 Whether Any Complaints Were Filed Against LACs by Beneficiaries Before the LSA

with beneficiaries if they face any issues about the services offered under legal aid. The regulators' questionnaire had a question focusing on any complaints received from beneficiaries against LACs. Although the filing of a written complaint is not in practice at any DLSA, regulators consider oral complaints from beneficiaries on a case-by-case basis.

As shown in Figure 5.18, 39.4% of regulators in the six zones acknowledged that beneficiaries had filed complaints against the LACs before the LSA, whereas 57.6% of regulators denied any complaints filed by the beneficiaries before the LSA. According to the NALSA manual for India's legal aid services, every DLSA front office should have a complaint box. However, during this study, researchers did not find any complaint box at the front of the office in most of the DLSAs. Further, most of the beneficiaries were hesitant to file a complaint against LACs, fearing a backlash from them.

5.2.11.1.1. ZONAL ANALYSIS OF WHETHER ANY COMPLAINTS WERE FILED AGAINST LACS BY BENEFICIARIES

5.2.11.1.1.1. Yes Regulators were hesitant to affirm that beneficiaries filed any complaints against LACs. As seen in Figure 5.19, around 75% of regulators in the North Zone, 50% of regulators in the Central Zone, and 37.5% of regulators in the South Zone affirmed that beneficiaries filed complaints against their respective LACs. Further, 20% of regulators in the East Zone and West Zone also affirmed that beneficiaries filed complaints against LACs at the DLSA.

5.2.11.1.1.2. No Most of the regulators denied any such complaints filed by beneficiaries against their LACs. In North East Zone, as shown in Figure 5.19, around 100% of regulators denied the existence of any such complaints filed

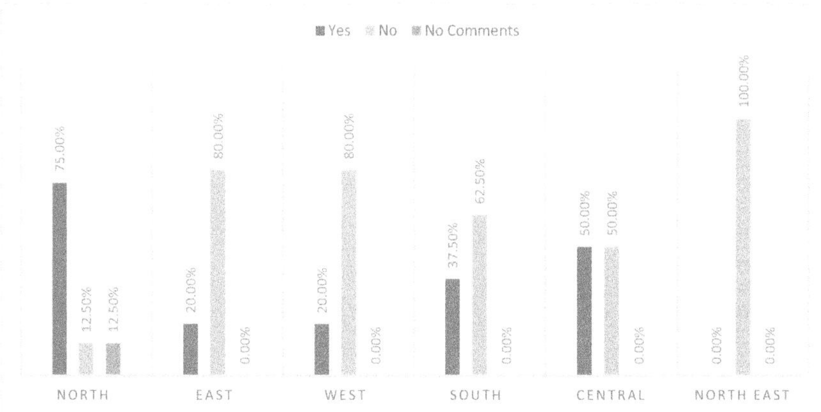

Figure 5.19 Zonal Analysis of Whether Any Complaints Were Filed Against LACs by Beneficiaries

by beneficiaries against their respective LACs. Similarly, around 80% of regulators in the East Zone and West Zone, 62.5% of regulators in the South Zone, 50% of regulators in the Central Zone, and 12.5% of regulators in the North Zone also denied any complaints made by beneficiaries.

5.2.11.2. Nature of Complaints Filed Against LACs by Beneficiaries Before the LSA

In the previous section, regulators affirmed that they had received complaints by beneficiaries against their respective LACs. This section covers the nature of complaints with which beneficiaries are coming up to regulators. The questionnaire asked about the nature of complaints from regulators who marked "yes" as an option.

As shown in Figure 5.20, the majority of complaints (30.8%) regulators received from the beneficiaries were related to a lack of communication between beneficiaries and LACs. It is important to note that many of the beneficiaries believed LACs did not interact with beneficiaries during this research. Another set of complaints from beneficiaries about the services of LACs, which regulators received, was about LACs being late for court hearings (26.9%). Judicial officers or judges also raised similar complaints against LACs to regulators. Similarly, beneficiaries complained about the LACs seeking many adjournments (11.5%), not protecting their interests (11.5%), and being unable to present a quality argument to defend a beneficiaries' case (11.5%). Moreover, few regulators received complaints from beneficiaries that LACs were not even prepared for the arguments at the time of the court hearing. The nature of complaints that beneficiaries filed

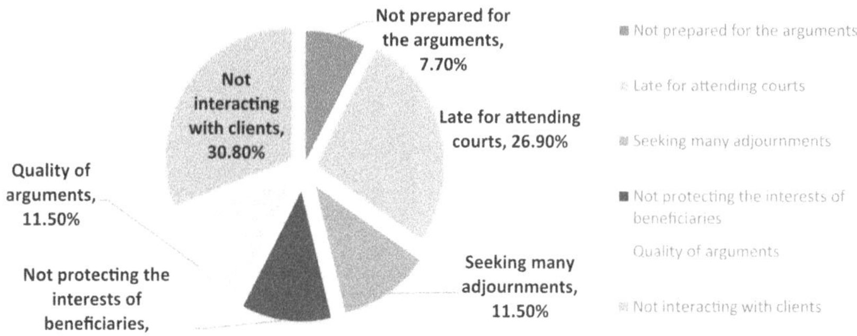

Figure 5.20 Nature of Complaints Filed Against LACs by Beneficiaries Before the LSA*

*Multiple-response question. Percentages are based on respondents.

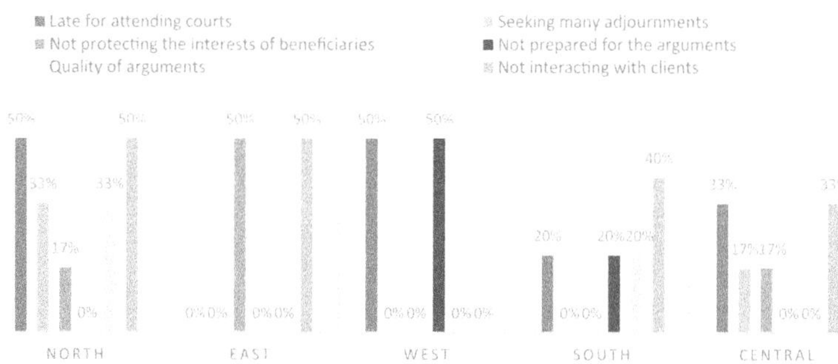

Figure 5.21 Zonal Analysis of Nature of Complaints Filed Against LACs by Beneficiaries*

*Multiple-response question. Percentages are based on respondents.

to the regulators rests upon a low level of or lack of commitment of LACs, which seemed to be omnipresent across the zones.

5.2.11.2.1. ZONAL ANALYSIS OF NATURE OF COMPLAINTS FILED AGAINST LACS BY BENEFICIARIES

5.2.11.2.1.1. Not Interacting with Clients Regulators in most of the zones were vocal about LACs not interacting with their legal aid beneficiaries. As seen in Figure 5.21, around 50% of regulators in the North Zone and East

Zone, 40% of regulators in the South Zone, and 33% of regulators in the Central Zone responded that beneficiaries have complained about LACs not interacting with them as one of the many complaints.

5.2.11.2.1.2. Being Late for Attending the Court LACs being late for attending the courts is one of the complaints filed by actual beneficiaries also. This highlights that even beneficiaries suffer from such a lack of commitment by LACs. As seen in Figure 5.21, around 50% of regulators in the North Zone and West Zone, 33% of regulators in the Central Zone, and 20% of regulators in the South Zone said that beneficiaries often complained about LACs being late to attend the court.

5.2.11.2.1.3. Seeking Many Adjournments LACs' seeking of many adjournments in legal aid cases is also a complaint that regulators received from beneficiaries. As shown in Figure 5.21, 33% of regulators in the North Zone and 17% of regulators in the Central Zone responded that beneficiaries complained about their LACs seeking many adjournments. LACs take adjournments because either they are not prepared for arguments or they are busy with their private practice matters.

5.2.11.2.1.4. Not Protecting the Interests of Beneficiaries Beneficiaries also complained to regulators about LACs not protecting the interest of beneficiaries. Since the honorarium for legal aid is low, LACs tend to not focus on winning the case; instead, LACs focus on making monetary gains from the opposite party in a dispute at the behest of his/her beneficiaries.

In Figure 5.21, around 50% of regulators in the East Zone and 17% of regulators in the North Zone and Central Zone said that one of the complaints they received from beneficiaries was LACs not protecting their interests.

5.2.11.2.1.5. Being Unprepared for Arguments Another complaint regulators received from beneficiaries was that LACs are not prepared for arguments. This may be because LACs are inclined to prepare for their private practice matters. As shown in Figure 5.21, 50% of regulators in the West Zone and 20% of regulators in the South Zone received a similar complaint from beneficiaries about their LACs not being prepared for arguments.

5.2.11.2.1.6. Quality of Arguments Regulators in the six zones received complaints pertaining to the low quality of arguments raised by LACs by beneficiaries. As seen in Figure 5.21, 33% of regulators in the North Zone and 20% of regulators in the South Zone said that beneficiaries complained about LACs making low-quality arguments in their cases.

5.2.12. Nature of Disciplinary Action Taken Against LACs by the LSA on Complaints From Beneficiaries

5.2.12.1. Whether Disciplinary Action Was Taken Against LACs by the LSA on Complaints From Beneficiaries

During this research, most of the DLSA's front office did not have a proper complaint/suggestion box in which beneficiaries could drop-in feedback forms for any complaints about LACs. Further, the complaints or issues raised by beneficiaries were mainly oral. Therefore, it becomes evident to look at the actions taken by the DLSA on any complaints raised by legal aid beneficiaries.

As shown in Figure 5.22, 49% of regulators did not take any disciplinary actions against LACs for not following the legal aid service mandate. Additionally, 12% of regulators from the six zones refrained from responding to this question. Among the regulators from six zones, only 39% of regulators acknowledged that they had taken appropriate warning, replacement, or removal measures from the panel based on the beneficiaries' complaints. Thus, most regulators are not keen to protect beneficiaries' interests, as more than 50% of regulators were cynical about taking any action against the LACs.

5.2.12.1.1. ZONAL ANALYSIS OF WHETHER DISCIPLINARY ACTION WAS TAKEN AGAINST LACS BY THE LSA ON COMPLAINTS FROM BENEFICIARIES

5.2.12.1.1.1. Yes As seen in Figure 5.23, around 75% of regulators in the Central Zone, 63% of regulators in the North Zone, 60% of regulators in the West Zone, and 25% of regulators in the South Zone affirmed that they had taken disciplinary actions against LACs on complaints made by beneficiaries.

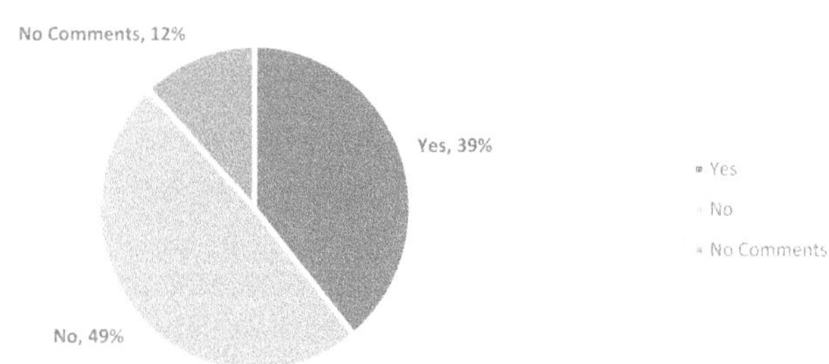

Figure 5.22 Whether Disciplinary Action Was Taken Against LACs by the LSA on Complaints From Beneficiaries

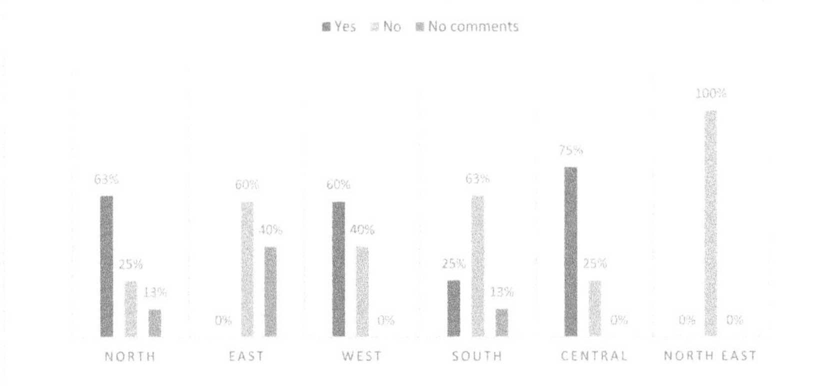

Figure 5.23 Zonal Analysis of Whether Disciplinary Action Was Taken Against LACs by the LSA on Complaints From Beneficiaries

5.2.12.1.1.2. No A few regulators from almost every zone did not take any disciplinary action against LACs. In Figure 5.23, we see that 100% of regulators in the North East Zone, 63% of regulators in the South Zone, 40% of regulators in the West Zone, and 25% of regulators in the North Zone did not take any disciplinary actions against LACs despite receiving complaints from beneficiaries.

5.2.12.2. Nature of Disciplinary Action Taken Against LACs by the LSA on Complaints From Beneficiaries

The analysis of the nature of disciplinary action taken against LACs by the LSA on complaints received from beneficiaries is based on the 39% of regulators who responded "yes." As seen in Figure 5.24, upon receiving complaints, 46.2% of regulators preferred to replace the LAC.

On the other hand, around 31% of regulators responded that they issued warnings to LACs against any beneficiaries' complaints. Further, 7.7% of regulators agreed to remove LACs from the group of empaneled LACs. Another 15.4% of regulators used "nil" as their response, meaning that they did not specify their disciplinary action.

5.2.12.2.1. NATURE OF DISCIPLINARY ACTION TAKEN AGAINST LACS BY THE LSA ON COMPLAINTS FROM BENEFICIARIES

5.2.12.2.1.1. Replacement In Figure 5.25, around 66% of regulators in the Central Zone, 60% of regulators in the North Zone, and 33% of regulators in the West Zone responded that they replaced the LACs against whom

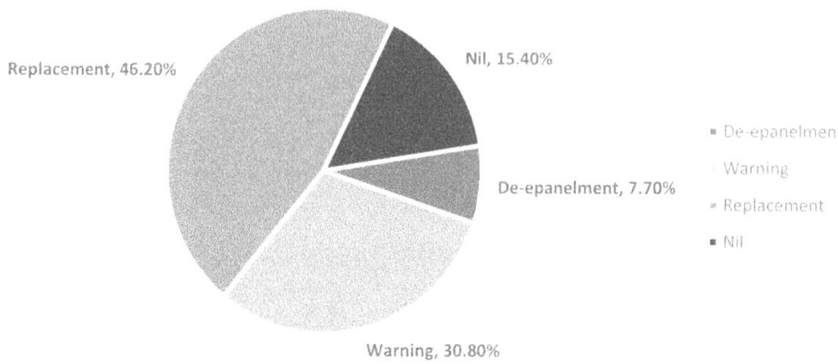

Figure 5.24 Nature of Disciplinary Action Taken Against LACs by the LSA on Complaints From Beneficiaries

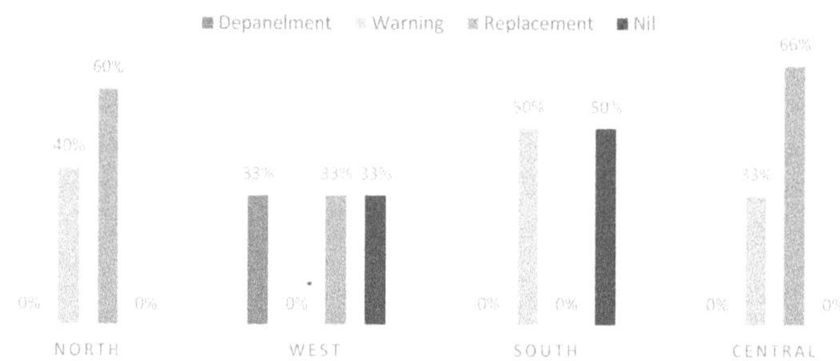

Figure 5.25 Nature of Disciplinary Action Taken Against LACs by the LSA on Complaints From Beneficiaries in Four Zones*

*Regulators from the East and North East Zones are omitted because they did not take any action against LACs on complaints by beneficiaries.

they received any complaints from beneficiaries. Regulators do not have any other power. At most, they can replace an LAC.

5.2.12.2.1.2. De-empanelment De-empanelment is punitive action against LACs. Regulators can only exercise de-empanelment of LACs in consultation with the chairperson of the DLSA (i.e., the district judge). As seen in Figure 5.25, only 33% of regulators in the West Zone took de-empanelment as disciplinary action against LACs on complaints from beneficiaries.

5.2.12.2.1.3. Warning Regulators often tend to warn LACs verbally or orally in case they receive any complaints from beneficiaries. As shown

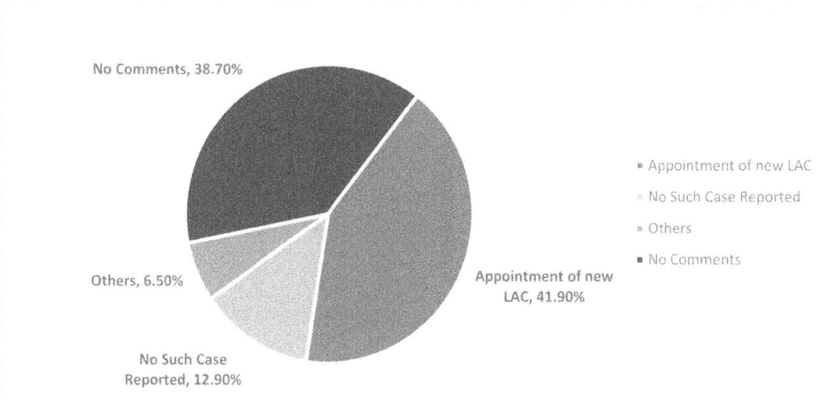

Figure 5.26 The LSA Taking Action in Case an LAC Leaves/Resigns Voluntarily

in Figure 5.25, 50% of regulators in the South Zone, 40% of regulators in the North Zone, and 33% of regulators in the Central Zone preferred to warn the LACs against whom they received any complaints from beneficiaries.

5.2.13. The LSA Taking Action in Case an LAC Leaves/Resigns Voluntarily

An empaneled lawyer may resign or discontinue the service of the LSA anytime. No provision can hold an LAC accountable for premature withdrawal before completing a stipulated tenure of engagement. Per Section 8, para. 15 of NALSA (Free and Competent Legal Services) Regulations, 2010, LACs may withdraw from any legal aid case after stating the reason to the member secretary or regulator. However, even if this process relieves any concerned LACs from their duties, any premature withdrawal adversely affects the continuity of the litigation process and the claims/rights of the beneficiaries.

As shown in Figure 5.26, around 38.7% of regulators were reluctant to express any opinion on actions taken if any LAC leaves or resigns voluntarily from the services of the LSA. Further, around 13% of regulators responded that none of the LACs either left or resigned voluntarily from any legal aid case during their tenure. On the other hand, around 42% (41.9%) of regulators said they appointed a new LAC whenever they come across a case where an LAC withdraws from the services of the LSA. Indeed, as LACs are not bound to any of the services, a regulator's only option is to assign a new LAC to the affected beneficiary.

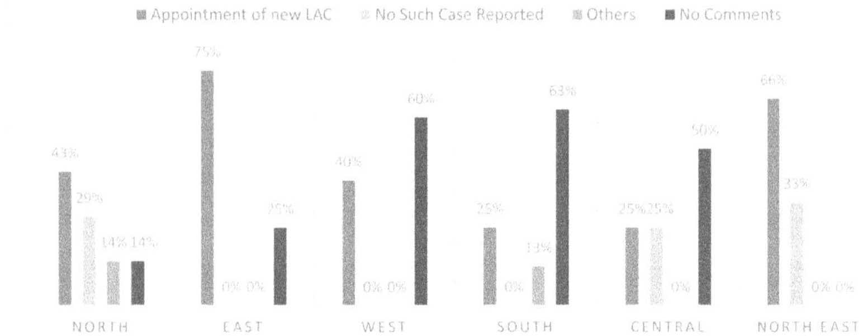

Figure 5.27 Zonal Analysis of Action Taken by the LSA in Case an LAC Leaves/Resigns Voluntarily

5.2.13.1. Zonal Analysis of Action Taken by the LSA in Case an LAC Leaves/Resigns Voluntarily

5.2.13.1.1. APPOINTMENT OF NEW LACS

Figure 5.27 shows that regulators in every zone appoint a new LAC if in case an LAC leaves or voluntarily resigns from a legal aid case. In East Zone, around 75% of regulators appointed a new LAC to those beneficiaries whose LACs either left their cases or voluntarily resigned from a legal aid case. Similarly, 66% of regulators in the North East Zone, 43% of regulators in the North Zone, 40% of regulators in the West Zone, and 25% of regulators in the South Zone and Central Zone responded that they appointed a new LAC.

5.2.13.1.2. NO SUCH CASE REPORTED

Regulators in a few zones also reported that they did not come across any such cases where LACs have left or resigned from legal aid cases. Around 33% of regulators in the North East Zone, 29% of regulators in the North Zone, and 25% of regulators in the Central Zone said they did not come across any such legal aid cases where LACs left or voluntarily resigned.

5.2.13.1.3. OTHER AND NO COMMENTS

A few regulators even reported issues that were beyond the purview of the study. The "others" option covered these responses from regulators. Further, a few regulators did not wish to comment on the action taken by them if an LAC left or voluntarily resigned. Around 63% of regulators in the South Zone, 60% of regulators in the West Zone, 50% of regulators in the Central Zone, 25% of regulators in the East Zone, and 14% of regulators in the North Zone refrained from commenting on the issue.

5.2.14. Action Taken in Case an LAC Fails to Live Up to the Expectations of Beneficiaries

The previous section scrutinizes regulators' decision-making capabilities under FLAS if he/she receives any complaint against LACs. This section aims to examine the monitoring capability of the regulatory system. It is pertinent that a regulator initiates an action based on a complaint from either a beneficiary or judicial officer. To ensure an effective control mechanism over the LACs, a pro-active regulatory system becomes a prerequisite for promoting the LAS.

Therefore, the regulators' questionnaire also focused on their actions in case of failure of LACs to live up to the expectations of the beneficiaries. The responses were overwhelming. As shown in Figure 5.28, around 42% of regulators responded that they changed or replaced the LACs if they felt they lacked in performance. Further, 7% of regulators in the six zones even denied any such case when beneficiaries complained about LACs not living or working up to their expectations. Interestingly, 36% of regulators refrained from commenting on the specific question. Indeed, regulators at most change or replace LACs but cannot take any strict disciplinary actions against LACs for not performing the mandated task under the LSA Act, 1987.

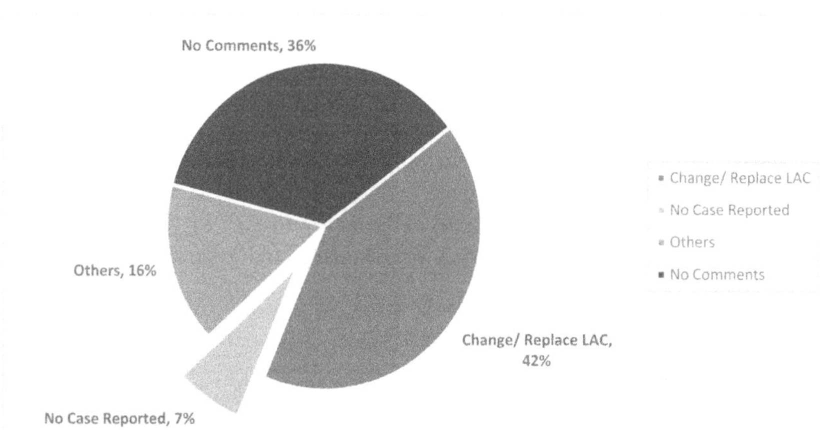

Figure 5.28 Action Taken in Case an LAC Fails to Live Up to the Expectations of Beneficiaries

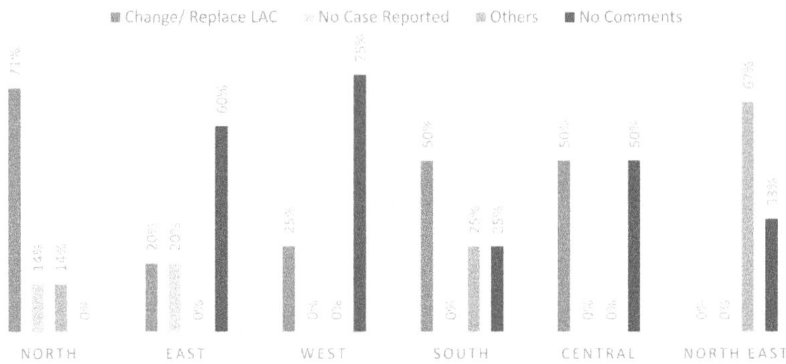

Figure 5.29 Zonal Analysis of Action Taken in Case an LAC Fails to Live Up to the Expectations of Beneficiaries

5.2.14.1. Zonal Analysis of Action Taken in Case an LAC Fails to Live Up to the Expectations of Beneficiaries

5.2.14.1.1. CHANGED OR REPLACED LACS

Regulators do not have any such statutory power to take any drastic action against LACs if he/she fails to live up to beneficiaries' expectations. At most, a regulator can only change or replace the LACs of beneficiaries. As shown in Figure 5.29, around 71% of regulators in the North Zone, 50% of regulators in the South and Central Zones, 25% of regulators in the West Zone, and 20% of regulators in the West Zone replaced the LACs of beneficiaries if they failed to live up to a beneficiary's expectation.

5.2.14.1.2. NO CASE REPORTED

A few regulators even reported that no such case has occurred in their tenure where LACs failed to live up to beneficiaries' expectations. Around 20% of regulators in the East Zone and 14% of regulators in the North Zone opined that they had not received any such issues from beneficiaries.

5.2.14.1.3. NO COMMENTS AND OTHERS

Most of the regulators in our research universe did not opt to answer this question related to action they might have taken if LACs failed to live up to beneficiaries' expectations. As shown in Figure 5.29, around 75% of regulators in the West Zone, 60% of regulators in the East Zone, 50% of regulators in the Central Zone, 33% of regulators in the North East Zone, and 25% of regulators in the South Zone refrained from commenting on whether they have taken any action against LACs who failed to live up to the expectations of beneficiaries. Regulators in the North East Zone, South Zone, and North Zone marked "others" as their actions. In an oral discussion, they opined that not much is in their hands and that lawyers' influence in their district is stronger.

5.2.15. Grievance Settlement Mechanism for Beneficiaries by the LSA in the Six Zones

There is no dearth of resources and legal protection for legal aid services. LACs, per the LSA Act, 1987, and NALSA Regulations, 2010, are engaged by the DLSA. It is essential to mention that the LACs are empaneled under the regulator's authority (member secretary) to provide quality legal aid services, and it is the responsibility of the regulators to exert control over the conduct of LACs. However, in practice, such a control mechanism struggles to seek accountability of LACs in case of misconduct. This section deals with this same grievance mechanism system and the methods opted by regulators. As shown in Figure 5.30, 61% of regulators acknowledged that the LSA has a grievance settlement mechanism to decide beneficiaries' grievances. In contrast, almost 40% of regulators were either not aware or denied the existence of any such mechanism.

5.2.15.1. Zonal Analysis of Grievance Settlement Mechanism for Beneficiaries by the LSA

5.2.15.1.1. YES

Regulators in every zone affirmed that they have a grievance settlement mechanism for beneficiaries in the DLSA. As shown in Figure 5.31, 100% of regulators

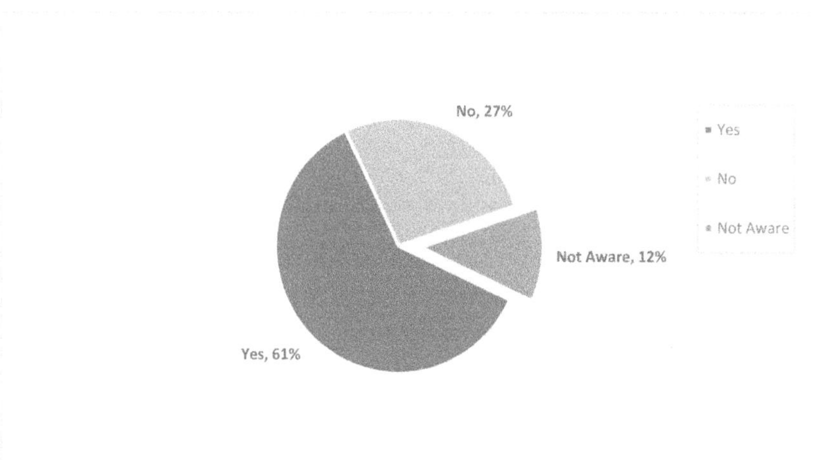

Figure 5.30 Grievance Settlement Mechanism for Beneficiaries by the LSA

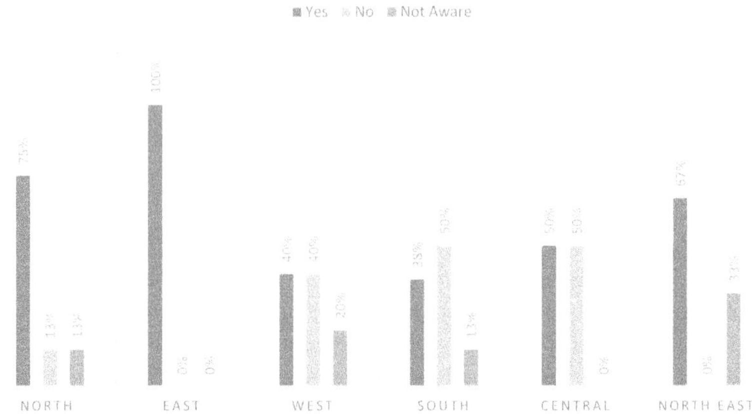

Figure 5.31 Zonal Analysis of Grievance Settlement Mechanism for Beneficiaries by the LSA

in the East Zone, 76% of regulators in the North Zone, 67% of regulators in the North East Zone, 50% of regulators in the Central Zone, 40% of regulators in the West Zone, and 38% of regulators in the South Zone affirmed to have a grievance settlement mechanism for beneficiaries at the DLSA.

5.2.15.1.2. NO

A few regulators opined that they do not have any such grievance mechanism at the DLSA. In Figure 5.31, around 50% of regulators in the Central Zone and South Zone, 40% of regulators in the West Zone, and 13% of regulators in the North Zone denied the presence of any grievance settlement mechanism for beneficiaries at the DLSA.

5.2.15.1.3. NOT AWARE

Interestingly, in a few zones, regulators were unaware of any such grievance settlement mechanism for beneficiaries. In the North East Zone, around 33% of regulators responded that they are not aware of any such mechanism at the DLSA. Similarly, 20% of regulators in the West Zone and 13% of regulators in the North Zone and South Zone responded that they are not aware of any grievance settlement mechanism for beneficiaries at the DLSA.

5.2.16 The Mechanism for Monitoring LACs

The NALSA (Free and Competent Legal Service) Regulations, 2010, Section 20, mandates for creation of a monitoring committee at the district

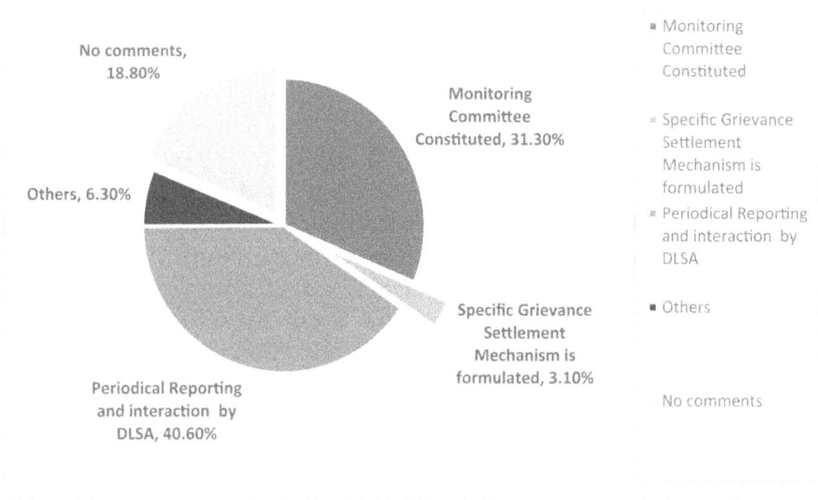

Figure 5.32 The Mechanism for Monitoring LACs

level for close monitoring of legal aid cases. In this light, the regulators' questionnaire consists of questions focusing on regulators' various mechanisms to monitor LACs under the DLSA. As shown in Figure 5.32, 40.6% of regulators responded that they periodically interact with the LACs regarding cases allotted to them under the LSA Act, 1987. On the other hand, only 31.3% of regulators were aware of any monitoring committee constituted per the guidelines of NALSA. Further, 18.8% of regulators refrained from even commenting on the question. A minute 3.1% of regulators acknowledged the formulation of a specific grievance settlement mechanism to deal with a particular situation. In most DLSA offices, regulators fail to furnish any such record of meetings and monitoring despite requesting documented evidence. Thus, as seen from the following analysis, regulators in most zones are unaware of any monitoring mechanism for LACs. Regulators only rely on verbal or oral interaction from LACs.

5.2.16.1. Zonal Analysis of the Mechanism for Monitoring LACs

5.2.16.1.1. PERIODICAL REPORTING AND INTERACTION BY DLSA

Regulators in most of the zones rely on verbal questioning and interaction with LACs. Regulators keep no record of these interactions, and these interactions are random. As observed by the field agents, regulators' interaction with LACs happens only either when LACs get a legal aid case or are scheduled to receive an honorarium. As shown in Figure 5.31, around 75% of regulators in the East Zone, 50% of regulators in the North Zone and South Zone, 33% of regulators in the North East Zone, and 25% of regulators in the Central Zone said that they periodically interact with LACs to monitor their working on legal aid cases.

5.2.16.1.2. MONITORING COMMITTEE CONSTITUTED

In almost every zone, a few regulators were aware of the monitoring committee mandated in NALSA Regulations, 2010. Around 66% of regulators in the North East Zone, 50% of regulators in the North Zone, 25% of regulators in the East Zone and Central Zone, 20% of regulators in the West Zone, and 13% of regulators in the South Zone have constituted a monitoring committee to monitor LACs in their district courts.

5.2.16.1.3. SPECIFIC GRIEVANCE SETTLEMENT MECHANISM IS FORMULATED

Regulators from the South Zone were the only ones to formulate a specific grievance settlement mechanism in their district courts. As shown in Figure 5.33, around 13% of regulators in the South Zone said they had formulated a specific grievance settlement mechanism at the DLSA.

5.2.16.1.4. OTHERS AND NO COMMENTS

Regulators also responded by either not commenting on the specific question or their responses were beyond the scope of the research. Such responses are under the categories of “no comments” and “others.”

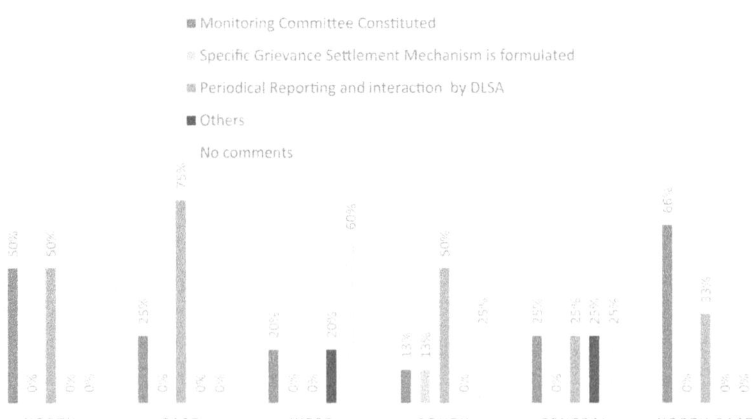

Figure 5.33 Zonal Analysis of the Mechanism for Monitoring LACs

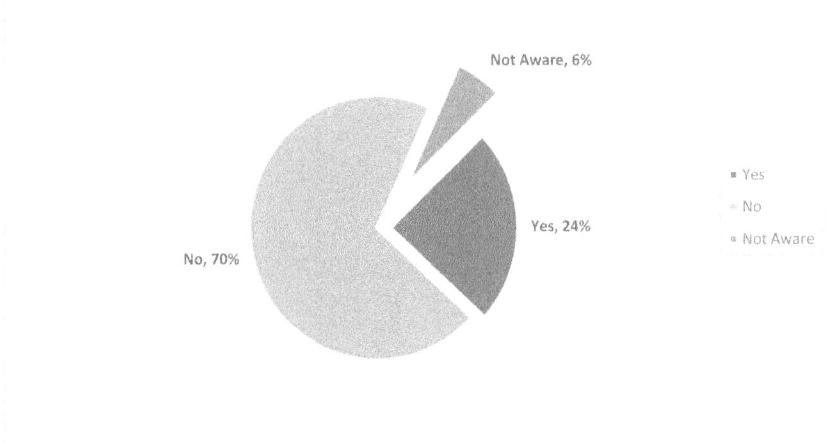

Figure 5.34 Beneficiaries' Feedback System to Evaluate the Services of LACs

5.2.17. Beneficiaries' Feedback System to Evaluate the Services of LACs

The assessment of any public policy rests upon the public's perspective or experiences at the receiving end of that policy. Similarly, a beneficiary of legal aid services is better positioned to assess the quality of commitment and competence of the LACs. Feedback from the beneficiaries is an effective tool to enhance the quality of service of the LACs. Other countries like Austria, Canada, and the UK have used this kind of feedback system to advance quality legal aid services.

In India, according to NALSA guidelines, there is a provision to provide feedback forms to beneficiaries by the DLSA. However, during this research study, no such feedback form was available to the beneficiaries. Accordingly, approximately 24% of regulators across the six zones agreed that there is a beneficiaries' feedback system to evaluate the services of the LACs (see Figure 5.34). On the contrary, approximately 70% of the regulators denied any existence of this feedback system.

5.2.17.1. Zonal Analysis of Beneficiaries' Feedback System to Evaluate the Services of LACs

5.2.17.1.1. YES

In Figure 5.35, around 60% of regulators in the East Zone, 38% of regulators in the North Zone, 25% of regulators in the Central Zone, and 13% of

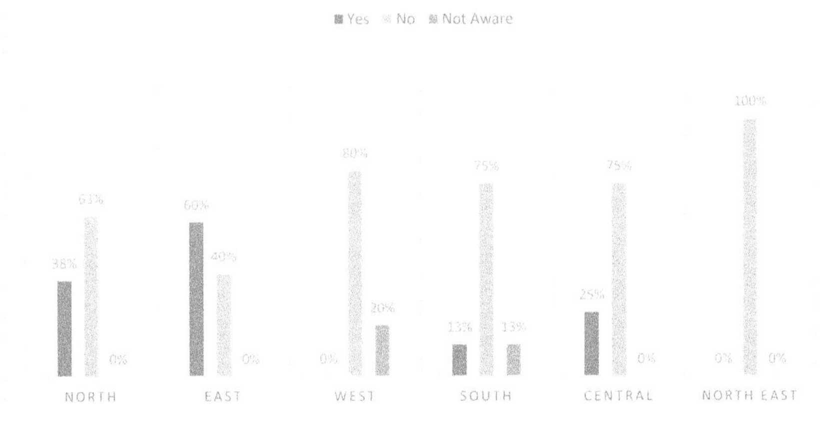

Figure 5.35 Zonal Analysis of Beneficiaries' Feedback System to Evaluate the Services of LACs

regulators in the South Zone affirmed that they have a beneficiary feedback system to evaluate the services of LACs.

5.2.17.1.2. NO

Contrary to the affirmation of a few regulators, as shown in Figure 5.35, 100% of regulators in the North East Zone, 80% of regulators in the West Zone, 75% of regulators in the South Zone and Central Zone, 63% of regulators in the North Zone, and 40% of regulators in the East Zone denied any existence of beneficiaries' feedback system to evaluate services of LACs at their DLSA. Further, around 20% of regulators in the West Zone were unaware of any beneficiary feedback system.

5.2.18 Methods of Ensuring the Accountability of LACs

Accountability towards the LAS is one of the objectives of this study which aims to analyze the competency and commitment of LACs. The questionnaire further focused on the various methods adopted by the regulators in all the six zones to ensure the accountability of LACs. As shown in Figure 5.36, 60.7% of regulators responded that they do not offer a second term of empanelment in the legal panel if any LAC is involved in any misconduct. Similarly, 57.1% of regulators were vocal about removing the name of LACs from the empaneled group of lawyers as one of the methods to ensure accountability. Further, 39.3% of regulators in the

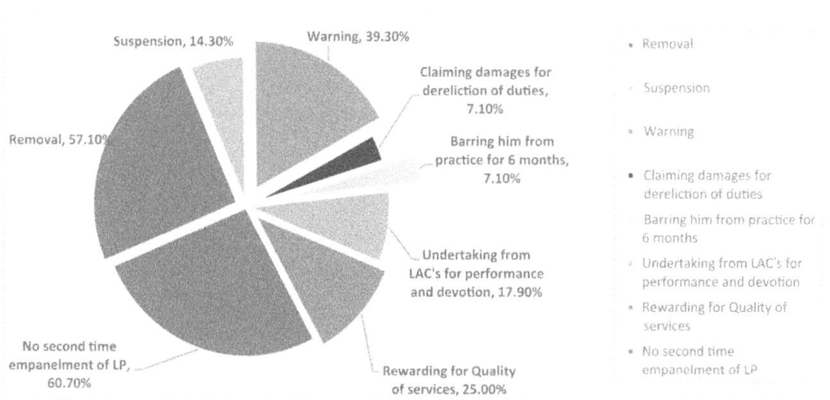

Figure 5.36 Methods of Ensuring the Accountability of LACs*
*Multiple-response question. Percentages are based on respondents.

six zones also preferred warning LACs as one of the methods to ensure accountability.

Around 18% (17.9%) of regulators made LACs sign an undertaking for performance and devotion. Additionally, 14.3% of regulators held a view that they often suspend LACs involved in any serious misconduct to ensure accountability. Furthermore, 7.1% of regulators even made LACs claim the damages caused by LACs during their dereliction of duties. Moreover, barring LACs from practice for six months is also a method to ensure accountability, according to 7.1% of the regulators. Surprisingly, 25% of regulators acknowledged that they offered LACs rewards for quality services to ensure the accountability of LACs.

5.2.18.1. Zonal Analysis of Methods of Ensuring the Accountability of LACs

5.2.18.1.1. NO SECOND-TIME EMPANELMENT OF LEGAL PRACTITIONERS

Regulators ensured that if they know that any LAC is involved in any misconduct, they will not empanel an LAC for a second term. As shown in Figure 5.37, around 100% of regulators in the North East Zone, 80% of regulators in the West Zone, and 75% of regulators in the North Zone opined that they do not empanel legal practitioners for a second time as one of the methods to ensure accountability of LACs. Similarly, 43% of regulators in the South Zone and 33% of regulators in the East Zone and Central Zone each also adopt no second-time empanelment to ensure the accountability among LACs.

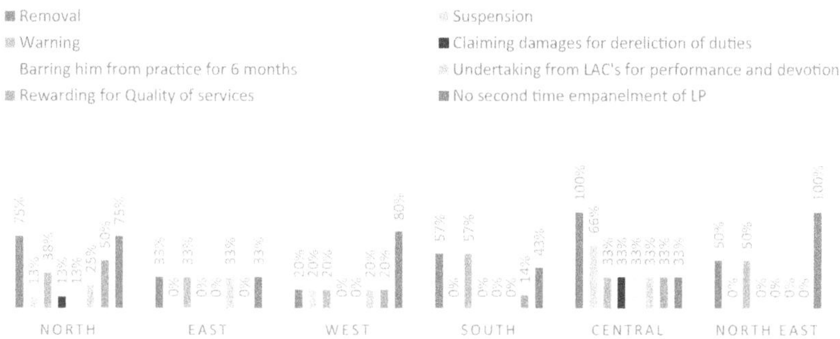

Figure 5.37 Zonal Analysis of Methods of Ensuring the Accountability of LACs*
*Multiple-response question. Percentages are based on respondents.

5.2.18.1.2. REMOVAL

Regulators do not have much say in the conduct of LACs. However, after consulting the chairperson of the DLSA, the regulators can remove any LACs if he/she is not living up to the expectations. As seen in Figure 5.37, 100% of regulators in the Central Zone, 75% of regulators in the North Zone, 57% of regulators in the South Zone, 50% of regulators in the North East Zone, 20% of regulators in the West Zone, and 33% of regulators in the East Zone adopted the removal of LACs from legal aid cases as one of the methods to ensure the accountably among them.

5.2.18.1.3. WARNING

Regulators also considered warning LACs as one of the methods to ensure accountability of LACs. In Figure 5.37, around 57% of regulators in the South Zone, 50% of regulators in the North East Zone, 38% of regulators in the North Zone, 33% of regulators in the Central Zone and East Zone, and 20% of regulators in the West Zone said that they often warned LACs to ensure accountability.

5.2.18.1.4. REWARD FOR QUALITY OF SERVICES

A few regulators are inclined towards rewarding LACs if they perform well in legal aid cases. This reward ranged from getting an honorarium on time to getting cases related to the LAC's specialization. As shown in Figure 5.37, around 50% of regulators in the North Zone, 33% of regulators in the Central Zone, 20% of regulators in the West Zone, and 14% of regulators in the South Zone said that rewarding LACs for quality services is one of the methods that ensured accountability among LACs.

5.2.18.1.5. UNDERTAKING FROM LACS FOR PERFORMANCE AND DEVOTION

Regulators are aware that LACs are not that devoted to legal aid cases in general and lawyers use the platform for gaining experience, getting famous, and getting employment. Regulators started taking an undertaking from LACs for their performance and devotion. As shown in Figure 5.37, 33% of regulators in the Central Zone and East Zone, 25% of regulators in the North Zone, and 20% of regulators in the West Zone responded that they took an undertaking from LACs for performance and devotion to ensure accountability.

5.2.18.1.6. SUSPENSION

Regulators in a few zones suspended LACs to ensure accountability. In Figure 5.37, 66% of regulators in the Central Zone, 20% of regulators in the West Zone, and 13% of regulators in the North Zone adopted suspension as one method to ensure accountability of LACs.

5.2.18.1.7. CLAIMING DAMAGES FOR DERELICTION OF DUTIES

Regulators even responded that they even made LACs pay damages for dereliction of duties. As shown in Figure 5.37, 33% of regulators in the Central Zone and 13% of regulators in the North Zone said they made LACs pay for damages caused to beneficiaries for dereliction of duties.

5.2.18.1.8. BARRING LACS FROM PRACTICE FOR SIX MONTHS

Regulators, in extreme cases, also barred LACs from practicing for six months as a method to ensure accountability. As shown in Figure 5.37, 33% of regulators in the Central Zone and 13% of regulators in the North Zone responded that they bar LACs from practice for six months to ensure accountability.

5.2.19. Maintenance of Records for the Grievances Against LACs

As seen in Figure 5.36, in the six zones, 45.5% of regulators responded that they do not maintain any records of the grievances filed against LACs. Further, the figure highlights that around 9.1% of regulators said they could not maintain the records of grievances filed against LACs. Thus, it also demonstrates a low level of efficiency through which the grievances handling system of legal aid services goes through. On the other hand, around 30% (30.3%) of regulators said they maintain records for grievances filed against LACs.

These regulators abide by the NALSA guidelines for legal aid that focus on beneficiary feedback mechanisms to deal with a beneficiary's grievances. However, a large share of non-maintenance of records for grievances filed against LACs might also be due to the paucity of resources and infrastructure.

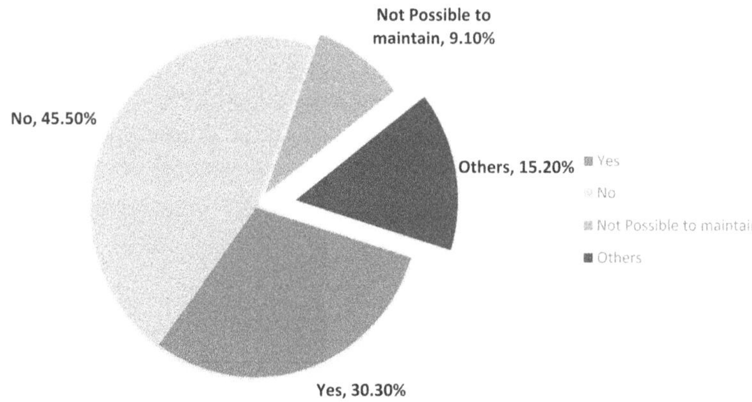

Figure 5.38 Maintenance of Records for the Grievances Against LACs

In an oral discussion with regulators, it came out that staff and infrastructure's insufficient strength is one of the principal reasons that make it challenging to maintain a record for grievances and monitor those grievances.

5.2.19.1. Zonal Analysis of Maintenance of Records for the Grievances Against LACs

5.2.19.1.1. YES

Regulators who were aware of the NALSA regulation pertaining to maintaining a register on LACs and recording grievances against LACs responded that they maintain records for the grievances against LACs. As shown in Figure 5.39, 50% of regulators in the North Zone, 38% of regulators in the South Zone, 25% of regulators in the Central Zone, and 20% of regulators in the East Zone and West Zone said that they maintain records for the grievances against LACs at their DLSA offices.

5.2.19.1.2. NO

Contrary to regulators who maintained records of grievances, a few regulators did not practice any recordkeeping. One of the significant reasons that regulators give for the same is insufficient staff and lack of infrastructure.

In Figure 5.39, around 75% of regulators in the Central Zone, 67% of regulators in the North East Zone, 50% of regulators in the South Zone,

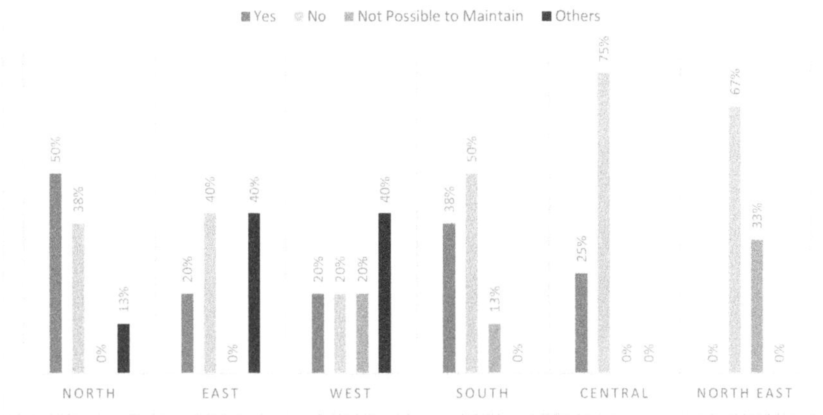

Figure 5.39 Zonal Analysis of Maintenance of Records for the Grievances Against LACs

40% of regulators in the East Zone, 38% of regulators in the North Zone, and 20% of regulators in the West Zone affirmed that they do not maintain any record for the grievances against LACs.

5.2.19.1.3. NOT POSSIBLE TO MAINTAIN AND OTHERS

Regulators who knew about a record maintaining mechanism also preferred not to maintain one in their DLSA offices. They cited that the pool of LACs is too long to keep, and hence, it is not possible to maintain a record on such a large scale. Around 33% of regulators in the North East, 20% of regulators in the West Zone, and 13% of regulators in the South Zone opined that they could not maintain records for the grievances against LACs. Further, around 40% of regulators in the East Zone and South Zone and 13% of regulators in the North Zone marked "others" as their response but did not elaborate on it.

5.2.20. *Taking Account of Complaints Against LACs for Subsequent Empanelment*

In the previous section, some regulators revealed that whether they maintain any records of grievances or not. This section delves into whether Regulators consider any complaint against LACs as one of the criteria in selecting LACs for the subsequent empanelment or not. Surprisingly, as shown in Figure 5.40, 61% of regulators agreed that they consider any complaints filed against LACs for subsequent empanelment. This share of acknowledgment contradicts regulators' last stand, as only 30.3% of regulators (see

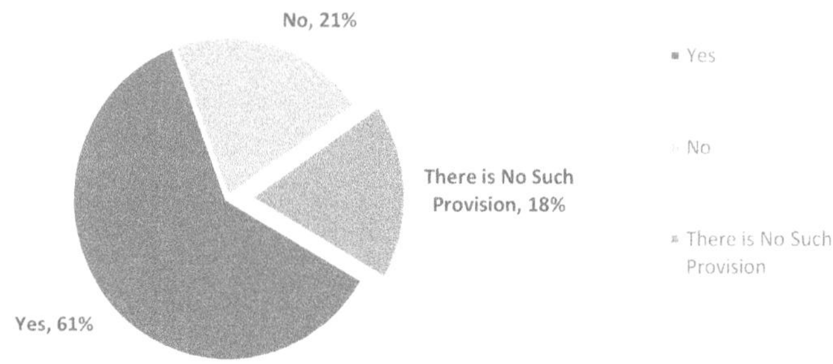

Figure 5.40 Taking Account of Complaints Against LACs for Subsequent Empanelment

Figure 5.36) confirmed maintaining a record for grievances. It seems that regulators maintained a record but did not want to share it with the research team. As it is, only by maintaining a proper record of complaints against LACs, regulators consider taking into account complaints against LACs for subsequent empanelment or not.

Indeed, it is not plausible to consider complaints of every LAC without systematic maintenance of records while deciding to empanel an LAC. This irregularity among two sets of data exposes the level of discrepancy in the operation of DLSA concerning LAS. In addition to this, around 49% (21.2% + 18.2%) of regulators either denied or described no provision to take the complaints into account for subsequent empanelment. This raises questions over the system of empanelment of the LACs. The current system of empanelment of LACs neither reprimands the non-performing LACs nor rewards the performing LACs to promote legal aid services.

5.2.20.1. Zonal Analysis of Taking Account of Complaints Against LACs for Subsequent Empanelment

5.2.20.1.1. YES

As shown in Figure 5.41, around 100% of regulators in the West Zone, 67% of regulators in the North East Zone, and 63% of regulators in the

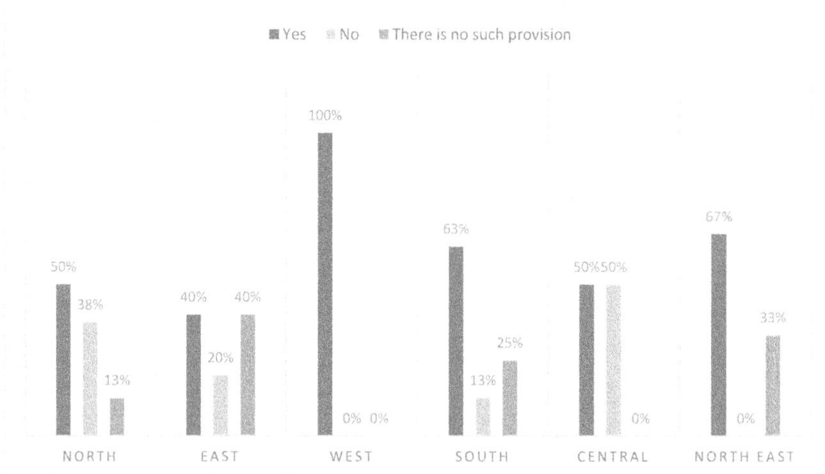

Figure 5.41 Zonal Analysis of Taking Account of Complaints Against LACs for Subsequent Empanelment

South Zone affirmed that they consider complaints against LACs for subsequent empanelment. Similarly, around 50% of regulators in the Central Zone and North Zone and 40% of regulators in the East Zone consider complaints against LACs for subsequent empanelment.

5.2.20.1.2. NO

Some regulators responded that they do not consider any previous complaints against LACs for the subsequent empanelment. As shown in Figure 5.41, 50% of regulators in the Central Zone, 38% of regulators in the North Zone, 20% of regulators in the East Zone, and 13% of regulators in the South Zone did not consider complaints against LACs for subsequent empanelment. Regulators believe that most LACs are early-career legal practitioners, and at times they might make mistakes. These mistakes should not withhold their empanelment.

5.2.20.1.3. THERE IS NO SUCH PROVISION

In some of the zones, regulators denied any such provision present or practiced at their DLSA offices. Around 40% of regulators in the East Zone, 33% of regulators in the North East Zone, 25% of regulators in the South Zone, and 13% of regulators in the North Zone responded that no such provision exists in which the selection committee considers complaints against LACs for subsequent empanelment.

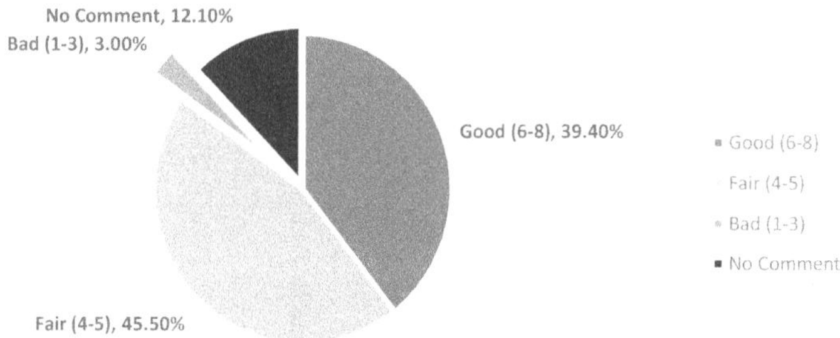

Figure 5.42 Regulators' Perspective on the Quality of Arguments

5.2.21. Rating of Services of LACs

The questionnaire distributed to regulators consists of questions related to measuring the competency aspects of LACs. Professional competency is one of the tenants of quality services in any profession. The system of LAS cannot flourish without a competent and committed LAC. If an LAC happens not to be well versed with the laws and practice in the relevant subject matter, then the entire LAS is jeopardized.

Therefore, LACs are one of the main stakeholders in servicing legal aid to beneficiaries. The next set of sections focuses on the competency of LACs on parameters like quality of presentation, arguments, and drafting skills for the enhancement of services offered by LACs.

5.2.21.1. Regulators' Perspective on the Quality of Arguments

As shown in Figure 5.42, 39.4% of regulators from the six zones rated that the argument skills of LACs are of a good standard, whereas 45.5% of regulators responded that LACs have an acceptable quality of arguments. Further, 12% of regulators refrained from commenting on the quality of argument of LACs. Another 3% of regulators marked the quality of arguments made by LACs as bad. Therefore, in terms of quality of argument majority of regulators rated that LACs have reasonable argument skills in their respective subject matter.

5.2.21.1.1. ZONAL ANALYSIS OF REGULATORS' PERSPECTIVE ON THE QUALITY OF ARGUMENTS

5.2.21.1.1.1. Fair Regulators in most of the zones rated the argument skills of LACs as fair. As shown in Figure 5.43, 75% of regulators in the

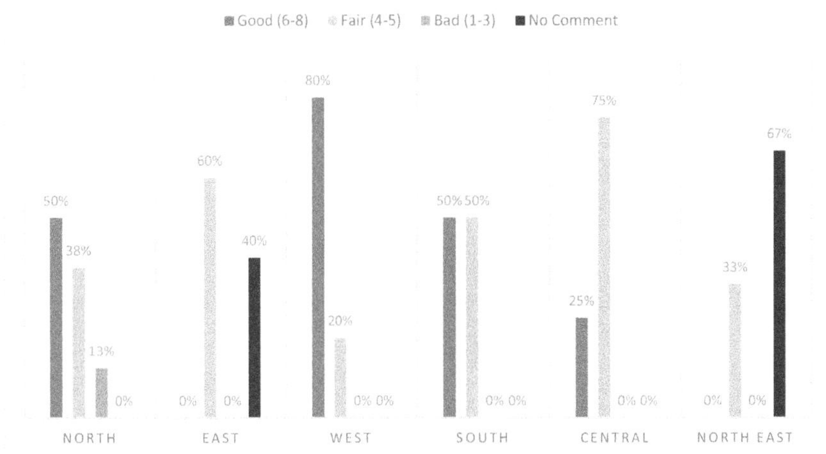

Figure 5.43 Zonal Analysis of Regulators' Perspective on the Quality of Arguments

Central Zone, 60% of regulators in the East Zone, 50% of regulators in the South Zone, 38% of regulators in the North Zone, 33% of regulators in the North East Zone, and 20% of regulators in the West Zone rated the argument skills of LACs as fair.

5.2.21.1.1.2. Good Similarly, around 80% of regulators in the West Zone, 50% of regulators in the North Zone and South Zone, and 25% of regulators in the Central Zone marked the skills of LACs arguments as good in quality.

5.2.21.1.1.3. Bad A few regulators also marked the quality of argument skills by LACs as "bad." In Figure 5.43, only 13% of regulators in the North Zone rated the quality of arguments made LACs as bad.

5.2.21.1.1.4. No Comments Regulators in two zones refrained from answering this section. As shown in Figure 5.43, 67% of regulators in the North East Zone and 40% of regulators in the East Zone did not rate the quality of arguments made by LACs.

5.2.21.2. Regulators' Perspective on the Quality of Presentation

The next skill that regulators rated was the quality of presentation made by LACs. As shown in Figure 5.44, a meager 6.1% of regulators responded that the quality of presentation skills of LACs are very good. Further, 27.3% of regulators rated the quality of presentation and articulation skills of LACs as good quality. In comparison, 45.5% of regulators responded that the

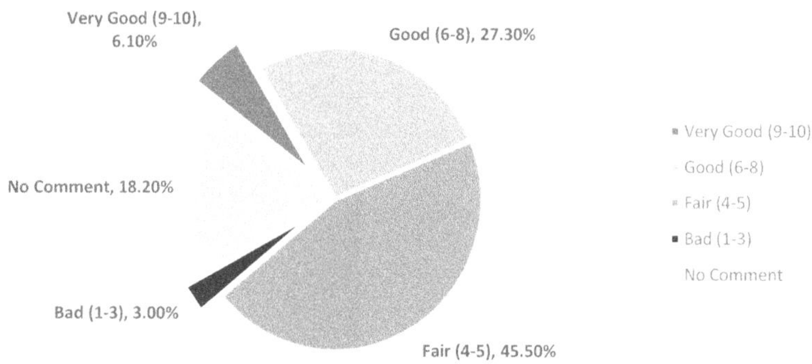

Figure 5.44 Regulators' Perspective on the Quality of Presentation

quality of presentation and articulation of LACs are average in quality. In addition to this, 3% of regulators also pointed out that the quality of presentation and articulation made by LACs is bad in quality. Another 18.2% of regulators refrained from commenting on the quality of presentation and articulation skills of LACs. Hence, most of the regulators opined that LACs have very average presentation and articulation skills.

5.2.21.3. Zonal Analysis of Regulators' Perspective on the Quality of Presentation

5.2.21.3.1. FAIR

The quality of presentation of LACs is another skill that defines their competency. As shown in Figure 5.45, 75% of regulators in the Central Zone, 63% of regulators in the South Zone, 40% of regulators in the West Zone, 38% of regulators in the North Zone, 33% of regulators in the North East Zone, and 20% of regulators in the East Zone rated the quality of presentation skills of LACs as fair.

5.2.21.3.2. GOOD

Some regulators find the LACs under their DLSA have good presentation skills. As shown in Figure 5.45, 40% of regulators in the West Zone, 38% of regulators in the North Zone, 25% of regulators in the South Zone and

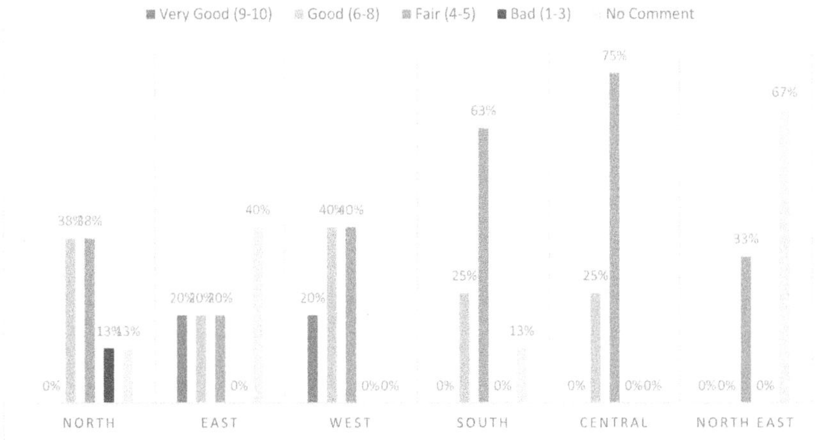

Figure 5.45 Zonal Analysis of Regulators' Perspective on the Quality of Presentation

Central Zone, and 20% of regulators in the East Zone responded that LACs have good presentation skills.

5.2.21.3.3. VERY GOOD

A very few regulators opined that LACs have very good presentation skills. Around 20% of regulators in the East Zone and West Zone rated the quality of presentation skills of LACs as very good.

5.2.21.3.4. BAD

A small percentage of regulators from the North Zone (13%) was the only one to rate the quality of presentation skills of LACs as bad.

5.2.21.3.5. NO COMMENTS

Some regulators preferred to refrain from rating the presentation skills of LACs. As seen in Figure 5.45, 67% of regulators in the North East Zone, 40% of regulators in the East Zone, and 13% of regulators in the North Zone and South Zone each preferred not to rate the quality of presentation skills of LACs.

5.2.21.4. Regulators' Perspective on the Quality of Drafting Skill

This section evaluates the drafting skills of LACs from the perspective of regulators. As shown in Figure 5.46, 3% of regulators rated the drafting

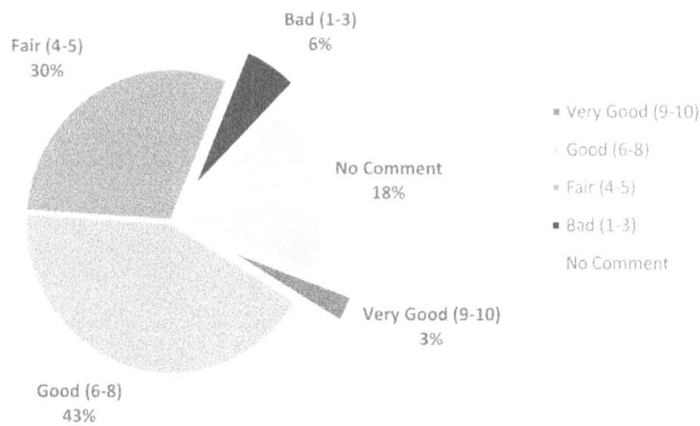

Figure 5.46 Regulators' Perspective on the Quality of Drafting Skill

skills of LACs as very good. At the same time, 43% of regulators from the six zones rated the drafting skills of LACs as good in quality. Further, 30% of regulators were also of the view that the LACs have an average drafting skill, whereas 6.1% of regulators even responded that the drafting skills of LACs are bad. Another 18% of regulators did not comment on this question. Thus, the data reflects most regulators are of the considerate opinion that LACs have a fairly good quality of drafting skills.

5.2.21.4.1. ZONAL ANALYSIS OF REGULATORS' PERSPECTIVE ON THE QUALITY OF DRAFTING SKILL

5.2.21.4.1.1. Good As shown in Figure 5.47, 60% of regulators in the East Zone and West Zone, 50% of regulators in the North Zone and Central Zone, 33% of regulators in the North East Zone, and 13% of regulators in the South Zone find the quality of drafting skills among LACs as good in quality.

5.2.21.4.1.2. Fair A few regulators rated the drafting skills of LACs as fair. In Figure 5.47, around 75% of regulators in the South Zone, 25% of regulators in the North and Central Zones, and 20% of regulators in the West Zone responded that LACs have a fair quality of drafting skills.

5.2.21.4.1.3. Bad Only in two zones did regulators rate the drafting skills of LACs as bad. 25% of regulators in the Central Zone and 13% of regulators in the North Zone said LACs have bad drafting skills.

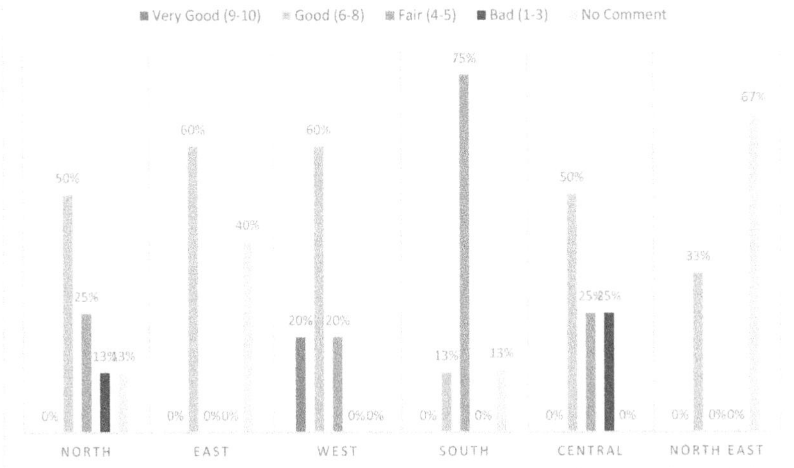

Figure 5.47 Zonal Analysis of Regulators' Perspective on the Quality of Drafting Skill

5.2.21.4.1.4. Very Good Very few regulators rated the quality of drafting skills of LACs as very good in quality. As shown in Figure 5.47, 20% of regulators in the West Zone were the only ones who rated the quality of LACs as very good.

5.2.21.4.1.5. No Comments Regulators in some zones also preferred not to rate the quality of drafting skills of LACs. Around 67% of regulators in the North East Zone, 40% of regulators in the East Zone, and 13% of regulators in the South Zone did not comment or rate the drafting skills quality.

5.2.21.5. Regulators' Perspective on the Overall Degree of Satisfaction

This section narrates the regulator's perspective on the degree of overall satisfaction in terms of overall competency skills of LACs. As shown in Figure 5.58, only 3% of regulators from the six zones believed the overall competency skills of LACs are very good, whereas another 48.5% of regulators believed that the overall competency skills of LACs are good enough. Further, 24.2% of regulators from the six zones were of the considerate opinion that LACs have an average level of overall competency skill set, and 6.1% of regulators even felt that the overall competency skill set of LACs was bad. From a regulator's perspective, the overall competency skills of LACs are fair and good. However, in two out of three skills, most of the regulators marked LACs as average in their skills.

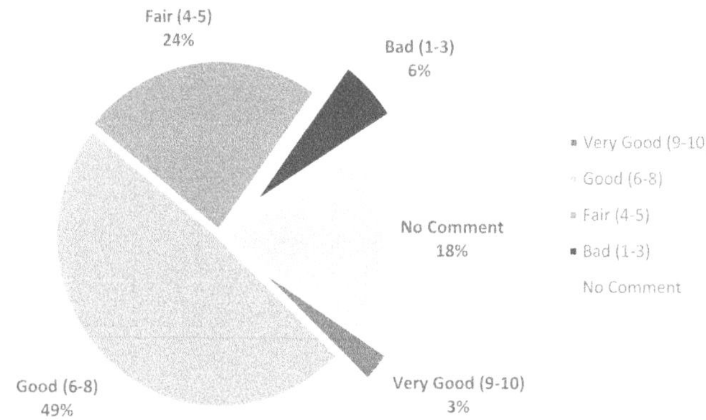

Figure 5.48 Regulators' Perspective on the Overall Degree of Satisfaction

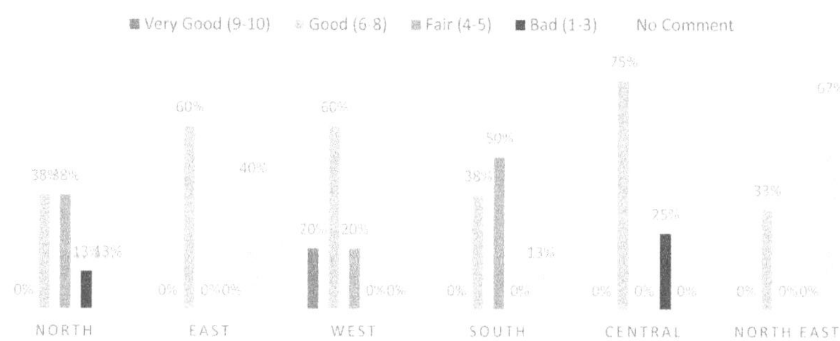

Figure 5.49 Zonal Analysis of Regulators' Perspective on the Overall Degree of Satisfaction

5.2.21.5.1. ZONAL ANALYSIS OF REGULATORS' PERSPECTIVE ON THE OVERALL DEGREE OF SATISFACTION

5.2.21.5.1.1. Good Regulators in all the zones were satisfied with the quality of the overall skills of LACs. As shown in Figure 5.49, 75% of regulators in the Central Zone and 60% of regulators in the East Zone and West

Zone rated the overall satisfaction level as good. Similarly, 38% of regulators in the North Zone and South Zone and 33% of regulators in the North East Zone also rated the overall satisfaction with LACs as good.

5.2.21.5.1.2. Fair Regulators also rated the overall degree of satisfaction as fair in a few zones. As shown in Figure 5.49, 50% of regulators in the South Zone, 38% of regulators in the North Zone, and 20% of regulators in the West Zone rated the degree of overall satisfaction with the skills of LACs as fair.

5.2.21.5.1.3. Bad Some regulators' overall degree of satisfaction with the skills of LACs was not good enough. In Figure 5.49, 25% of regulators in the Central Zone and 13% of regulators in the North Zone rated the degree of overall satisfaction level as bad.

5.2.21.5.1.4. Very Good Around 20% of regulators in the West Zone were the only ones who marked that their degree of overall satisfaction with the skills of LACs is very good. The reason for regulators marking their degree of satisfaction as very good might be because some LACs in the West Zone must be senior or competent LACs.

5.2.21.5.1.5. No Comments Around 67% of regulators in the North East Zone, 40% of regulators in the East Zone, and 13% of regulators in the North Zone and South Zone refrained from commenting on their overall degree of satisfaction with the skills of LACs.

5.2.22. Regulators' Perspective on the Full-Time Empanelment of LACs

The existing system of legal aid engages LACs on an ad hoc basis. The empanelment of LACs happens for a specific term period, and they get a specific honorarium for civil and criminal cases on a stage-by-stage basis. They are not full-time employees at the DLSA. An idea of appointing LACs for full-time empanelment was put forth in front of regulators. They were asked if they would recommend this kind of setup to ensure better accountability and full-time commitment from LACs.

As shown in Figure 5.50, around 27.3% of regulators recommended creating such kind of setup in the legal aid framework, while 18.2% of regulators in six zones highly recommended such employment within the legal framework aid system in India. However, 33.3% of regulators were skeptical about creating permanent employment, and 21.2% of regulators did not respond to this specific question. Indeed, as it is evident from Figure 5.50, the majority, a total 45.5% (18.2% + 27.3%) of regulators, recommended the creation of a permanent and full-time scheme for the empanelment of LACs for the promotion of legal aid services across the nation.

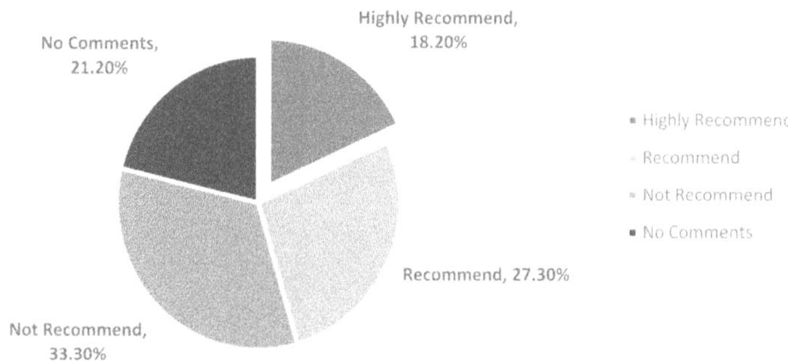

Figure 5.50 Regulators' Perspective on the Full-Time Empanelment of LACs

5.2.22.1. *Zonal Analysis Regulators' Perspective on the Full-Time Empanelment of LACs*

5.2.22.1.1. NOT RECOMMEND

In Figure 5.51, around 60% of regulators in the West Zone, 50% of regulators in the Central Zone, and 38% of regulators in the North Zone did not recommend full-time empanelment LACs. Similarly, 33% of regulators in the North East Zone and 25% of regulators in the South Zone preferred not to recommend full-time empanelment of LACs.

5.2.22.1.2. RECOMMEND

Regulators in almost every zone recommended full-time empanelment of LACs. As shown in Figure 5.51, around 40% of regulators in the West Zone, 33% of regulators in the North East Zone, and 25% of regulators in the North, South, and Central Zones recommended the formulation of full-time empanelment of LACs to ensure accountability and commitment from them.

5.2.22.1.3. HIGHLY RECOMMEND

A few regulators even highly recommended the formulation of full-time empanelment of LACs; 33% of regulators in the North East Zone, 25% of regulators in the South and Central Zones, 20% of regulators in the East Zone, and 13% of regulators in the North Zone highly recommended the formulation of full-time empanelment of LACs.

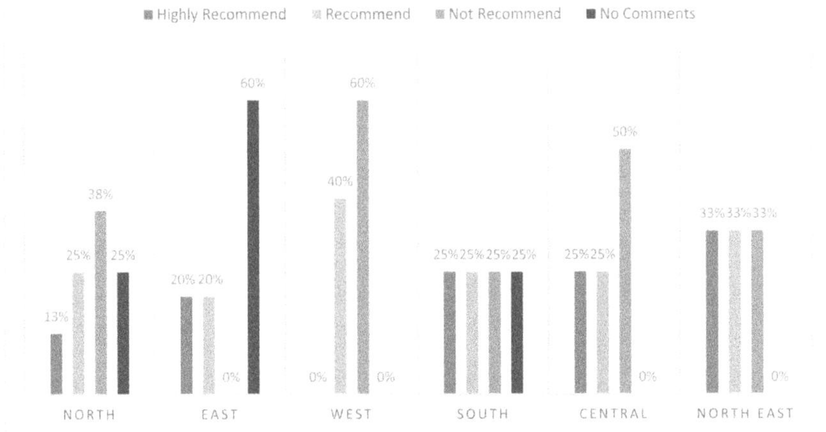

Figure 5.51 Zonal Analysis of Regulators' Perspective on the Full-Time Empanelment of LACs

5.2.22.1.4. NO COMMENTS

As seen in Figure 5.51, 60% of regulators in the East Zone and 25% of regulators in the South, Central, and North Zones preferred not to comment on whether they recommend or not recommend the formulation of a full-time empanelment of LACs.

5.2.23. Major Issues Faced Regulators While Dealing With LACs

Regulators are a part of the LAS, and they act as a linchpin among various stakeholders. They are the only stakeholders who interact with LACs, beneficiaries, and judicial officers. Figure 5.52 shows the major issues faced by the regulators while dealing with LACs across the six zones. Regulators' issues must be seen in terms of making the system more efficient rather than focusing frequency of the data. According to 27.3% of regulators, the commitment of LACs is a major issue faced by them while dealing with LACs. Honoraria and the competence of LACs are the other major issues reported by 12.1% of regulators. However, 27.3% of regulators did not comment on this question.

5.2.23.1. Zonal Analysis Major Issues Faced by Regulators While Dealing With LACs

5.2.23.1.1. COMMITMENT

Regulators, in answering an open-ended question, highlighted the commitment of LACs as a significant issue they face while dealing with LACs. As

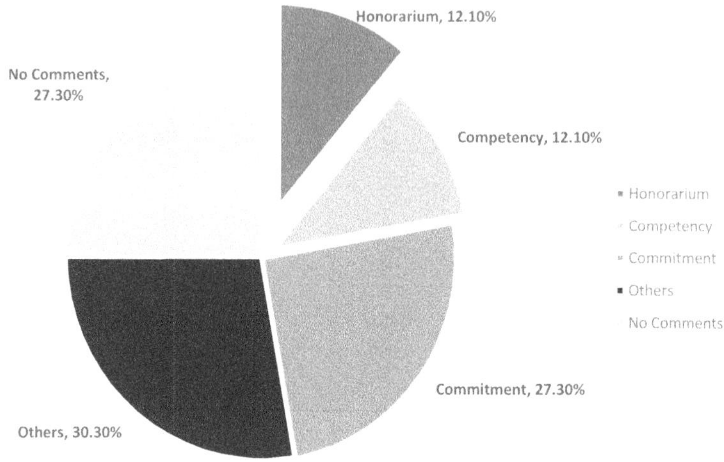

Figure 5.52 Major Issues Faced by Regulators While Dealing With LACs

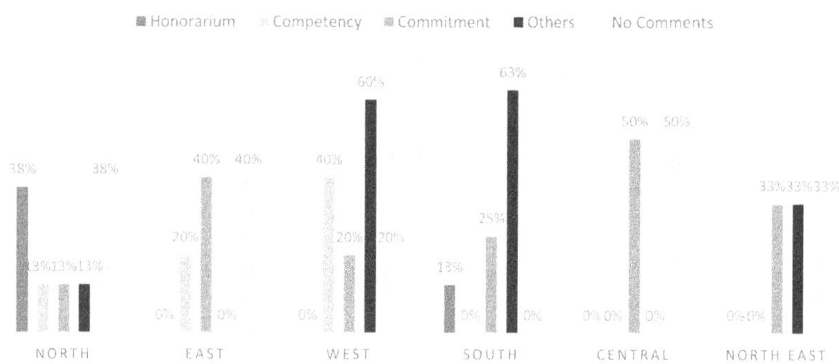

Figure 5.53 Zonal Analysis of Major Issues Faced by Regulators While Dealing With LACs

shown in Figure 5.53, around 50% of regulators in the Central Zone, 20% of regulators in the West Zone, 33% of regulators in the North East Zone, 25% of regulators in the South Zone, and 13% of regulators in the North Zone raised the issues of the commitment of LACs while dealing with them.

5.2.23.1.2. HONORARIUM

Another significant issue regulators face while dealing with LACs is related to the honorarium of LACs. Regulators are aware of the hardships beneficiaries face because LACs either get a low honorarium or do not get an honorarium on time. As shown in Figure 5.53, 38% of regulators in the North Zone and 13% of regulators in the South Zone raised that the honorarium of LACs is a major issue they face dealing with LACs.

5.2.23.1.3. COMPETENCE

Although regulators did rate the skills of LACs in the previous sections, they did mention that the competence of LACs is another issue faced by them while dealing with LACs. As shown in Figure 5.53, around 40% of regulators in the West Zone, 20% of regulators in the East Zone, and 13% of regulators in the North Zone raised the low level of competence among LACs as a significant issue they face while dealing with LACs.

5.2.23.1.4. OTHERS AND NO COMMENTS

In answering the open-ended question on major issues faced by regulators while dealing with LACs, Regulators often tend to write issues beyond the study's scope. Those responses are covered under the category of "others." Further, a few regulators in every zone did not respond to the specific question. Those responses are covered under the "no comments" category.

5.2.24. Suggestions for Improving Services Provided by LACs

One of the most pertinent issues this study deals with is finding the solution to the problems ailing FLAS. This last part is focused on gathering specific solutions from the stakeholders themselves after documenting the problems. As mentioned earlier, the study aims to outline practical solutions that stakeholders suggest. Like the problems, suggested solutions also differ from zone to zone. However, it is apparent from Figure 5.54 that the most popular suggestion is the training of LACs. Around 39.3% of regulators suggested training the LACs after empaneling them to provide legal services. Another 14.3% of regulators suggested the appointment of experienced LACs to provide legal aid. Further, 10.7% of regulators suggested bringing in a mechanism for monitoring LACs.

5.2.24.1. Zonal Analysis of Suggestions for Improving Services Provided by LACs

5.2.24.1.1. TRAINING OF LACS

Regulators suggested proper training of LACs after inducting them into panel lawyers. Regulators often see a lack of competence among the empaneled LACs in terms of knowledge of the law, drafting skills, and argument skills (i.e., why a few regulators suggested training LACs). As shown in

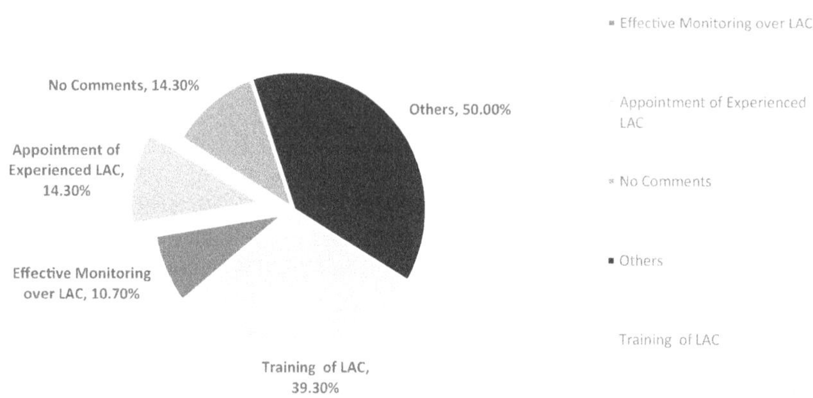

Figure 5.54 Suggestions for Improving Services Provided by LACs

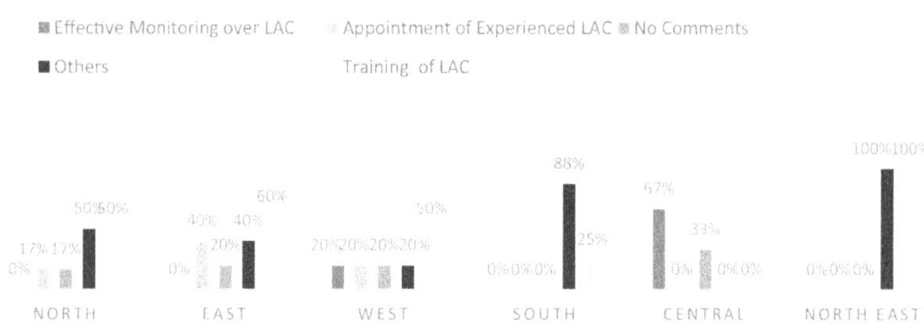

Figure 5.55 Zonal Analysis of Suggestions for Improving Services Provided by LACs

Figure 5.55, 100% of regulators in the North East Zone, 60% of regulators in the East Zone, 50% of regulators in the North and East Zone, and 25% of regulators in the South Zone suggested proper training of LACs to improve the services provided by LACs.

5.2.24.1.2. APPOINTMENT OF EXPERIENCED LACS

Regulators were vocal enough to suggest the appointment of experienced LACs as one of the ways to improve services provided by LACs. As shown in Figure 5.55, around 40% of regulators in the East Zone, 20% of regulators in the West Zone, and 17% of regulators in the North Zone were vocal enough to suggest the appointment of experienced LACs to improve the services provided by LACs.

5.2.24.1.3. EFFECTIVE MONITORING OF LACS

Regulators also suggested effective monitoring of LACs to improve the services offered by LACs. In Figure 5.55, 67% of regulators in the Central Zone and 20% of regulators in the West Zone suggested effective monitoring of LACs to improve services provided by LACs.

6 Judges' and Judicial Officers' Perspective on Legal Aid

6.1. Introduction

Judicial officers or Judges are other significant stakeholders whose perspectives on the level of commitment and competence of LACs will prove valuable input to analyze the Indian LAS's pitfalls. Previous chapters analyzed responses received from the beneficiaries and regulators. This chapter focuses on the views and inputs received from the judicial officers or judges in around 36 district courts in 18 states. To highlight an unbiased approach, the study considered judicial officers or judges from all the courts presently taking cases under legal aid services

The research team relied either on distributing a personally administered questionnaire to individual judicial officers or judges or circulating it with the member secretary's assistance to the court operating on the district court premises. The field investigators and research team collected 609 filed questionnaires from judicial officers or judges. Most of the judicial officers or judges presided over metropolitan magistrate courts, chief metropolitan magistrate courts, additional session judges' courts, family courts, or special courts covering cases related to narcotic drugs and psychotropic substances ("NDPS"), SC/ST ("Scheduled Caste/ Scheduled Tribe"), protection of children from sexual offenses ("POCSO"), and crimes against women ("CAW").

The fundamental objective of collecting primary data from more than 600 judicial officers or judges across 18 states was to ascertain the assessment of senior and junior judges on the involvement of the LACs and amicus curiae in serious offenses, such as rape, murder, narcotics, grievances, and culpable homicide not amounting to murder. Although a majority of the judicial officers were critical of the judicial infrastructure, it seemed that they were unsatisfied with the services offered or work performed by LACs in their respective courts. The questionnaires explicitly questioned the level of commitment and quality of services offered by the LACs However, when asked whether they have forwarded any formal complaints, judicial officers or judges were mainly reluctant to talk about the issue.

For this study, the proposed strength of collected questionnaires from judicial officers or judges was 20 from each district court and subsequently

DOI: 10.4324/9781003158325-6

Table 6.1 Proposed and Actual Responses Received From the Judges and Judicial Officers

Zone	*State*	*District*	*Proposed Number*	*Actual Number*
North	Punjab	Patiala	20	20
		Sangrur	20	13
	Himachal Pradesh	Shimla	20	13
		Solan	20	9
	Haryana	Gurugram	20	12
		Rohtak	20	8
	Uttar Pradesh	Allahabad	20	11
		Gautama Buddha Nagar	20	9
East	West Bengal	Kolkata	20	29
		24 North Pargana	20	14
	Jharkhand	Ranchi	20	24
		Ramgarh	20	10
	Odisha	Bhubaneshwar	20	9
		Cuttack	20	10
West	Rajasthan	Jodhpur	20	14
		Pali	20	8
	Gujarat	Ahmedabad	20	31
		Gandhinagar	20	19
	Maharashtra	Aurangabad	20	34
		Jalna	20	20
South	Karnataka	Bangalore Urban	20	19
		Bangalore Rural	20	11
	Tamil Nadu	Tiruchirappalli	20	21
		Thanjavur	20	24
	Andhra Pradesh	Vizag	20	25
		Vizianagaram	20	17
	Kerala	Pathanamthitta	20	13
		Alappuzha	20	31
Central	Chhattisgarh	Raipur	20	26
		Durg	20	31
	Madhya Pradesh	Indore	20	19
		Dhar	20	10
North East	Meghalaya	Shillong	20	11
		Nongpoh	20	4
	Assam	Jowai	20	0
		Guwahati	20	20
		Amingaon	20	10
	TOTAL		740	609

40 from each state. Table 6.1 shows the difference between the proposed number of judges or judicial officers and the actual number of judicial officers or judges who responded.

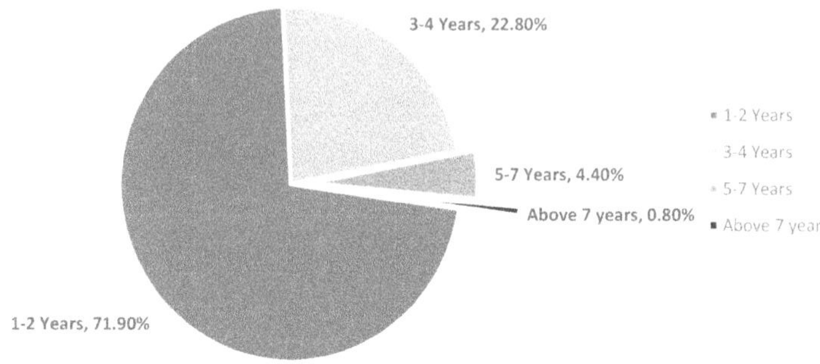

Figure 6.1 Average Time Taken to Conclude a Civil Case Under FLAS

6.2. Data Analysis

6.2.1. *Average Time Taken to Conclude a Civil Case Under FLAS*

It has been a preconceived notion that LACs extend the legal aid cases to gain some monetary benefits from beneficiaries. To know whether the same is true for an average legal aid case of a civil nature, the questionnaire for judicial officers or judges had a question related to the average time taken to conclude a civil case under FLAS. As shown in Figure 6.1 that mostly, a civil case under FLAS did not take more than two years to conclude. Around 71.9% of judicial officers or judges responded that civil cases under FLAS reached their conclusion in one to two years. On the other hand, 22.8% of judicial officers or judges said it takes around three to four years to conclude a civil case under FLAS. Further, 4.4% of judicial officers or judges said that it might take five to seven years, and just 0.8% of judicial officers or judges responded that the civil cases under FLAS take more than seven years.

6.2.1.1. *Zonal Analysis of Average Time Taken to Conclude a Civil Case Under FLAS*

6.2.1.1.1. ONE TO TWO YEARS

In most cases, judicial officers or judges opined that a civil case under FLAS takes an average of one to two years to reach its conclusion. Figure 6.2 demonstrates that 80% of judicial officers or judges in the North East Zone, 78% of judicial officers or judges in the East Zone, 75% of judicial officers or judges in the West Zone, 71% of judicial officers or judges in the South Zone, 66% of judicial officers or judges in the North Zone, and 64% of

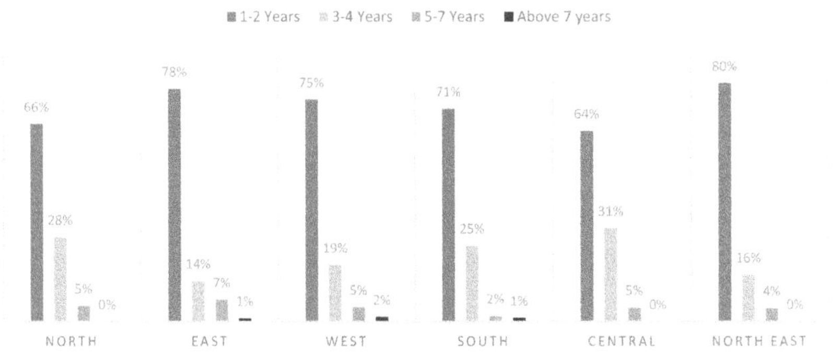

Figure 6.2 Zonal Analysis of Average Time Taken to Conclude a Civil Case Under FLAS

judicial officers or judges in the Central Zone responded that the average time taken to conclude a civil case under FLAS ranged from one to two years.

6.2.1.1.2. THREE TO FOUR YEARS

A few judicial officers or judges also replied that it takes around three to four years to conclude a civil case under FLAS. In Figure 6.2, around 31% of judicial officers or judges in the Central Zone, 28% of judicial officers or judges in the North Zone, 25% of judicial officers or judges in the South Zone, 19% of judicial officers or judges in the West Zone, 16% of judicial officers or judges in the North East Zone, and 14% of judicial officers or judges in the East Zone said that it takes around three to four years to conclude a civil case under FLAS.

6.2.1.1.3. FIVE TO SEVEN YEARS

In some zones, judicial officers or judges said that sometimes it takes around five to seven years to conclude a civil case under FLAS. As shown in Figure 6.2, 7% of judicial officers or judges in the East Zone, 4% of judicial officers or judges in the North East Zone, 2% of judicial officers or judges in the South Zone, and 5% of judicial officers or judges in the North, West, and Central Zones replied that it takes five to seven years to conclude a civil case under FLAS.

6.2.1.1.4. ABOVE SEVEN YEARS

A very minute percentage of judicial officers or judges responded that it takes more than seven years to conclude a civil case under FLAS. As shown in Figure 6.2, 2% of judicial officers or judges in the West Zone and 1% in the East Zone and South Zone responded that it takes more than seven years to conclude a civil case under FLAS.

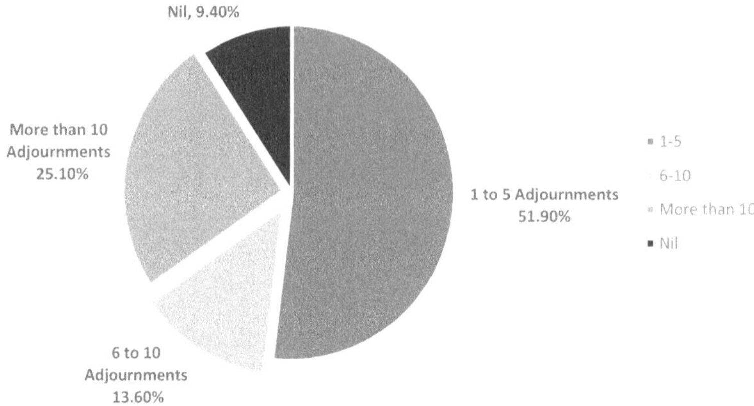

Figure 6.3 Average Number of Adjournments Taken by LACs in Civil Cases Under FLAS

6.2.2. *Average Number of Adjournments Taken by LACs in Civil Cases Under FLAS*

Figure 6.3 provides judicial officers' or judges' responses on the average number of adjournments taken by LACs in civil cases under FLAS. As shown in Figure 6.3, most judicial officers or judges (around 52%) responded that LACs, on average, take around one to five adjournments throughout the course of a civil case under FLAS. On the other hand, around 25.1% of judicial officers or judges said that in civil cases under FLAS, LACs often take more than ten adjournments.

6.2.2.1. *Zonal Analysis of Average Number of Adjournments Taken by LACs in Civil Cases Under FLAS*

6.2.2.1.1. ONE TO FIVE ADJOURNMENTS

Judicial officers or judges in most of the zones opined that the average number of adjournments taken by LACs in a civil case under FLAS is around one to five adjournments. As shown in Figure 6.4, 64% of judicial officers or judges in the North East Zone, 57% of judicial officers or judges in the East Zone, 53% of judicial officers or judges in the South Zone, and 51% of judicial officers or judges in the Central Zone responded that LACs take around one to five adjournments in a civil case under FLAS. Likewise, around 48% of judicial officers or judges in the West Zone and 44% of judicial officers or judges in the North Zone also responded that LACs take around one to five adjournments in civil cases under FLAS.

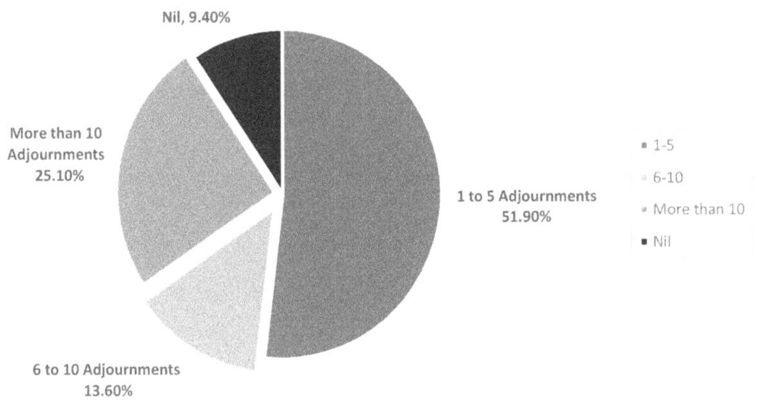

Figure 6.4 Zonal Analysis of Average Number of Adjournments Taken by LACs in Civil Cases Under FLAS

6.2.2.1.2. SIX TO TEN ADJOURNMENTS

Around 19% of judicial officers or judges in the North Zone, 14% of judicial officers or judges in the East and West Zone, 16% of judicial officers or judges in the South Zone opined that LACs take around six to ten adjournments in civil cases under FLAS. Similarly, 7% of judicial officers or judges in the Central Zone and North East Zone opined that LACs take around six to ten adjournments in civil cases under FLAS.

6.2.2.1.3. MORE THAN TEN ADJOURNMENTS

Judicial officers or judges responding to more than ten adjournments taken by LACs for a Civil case under FLAS were in considerable percentage in every zone. As shown in Figure 6.4, 34% of judicial officers or judges in the North Zone, 30% of judicial officers or judges in the Central Zone, 27% of judicial officers or judges in the South Zone, and 23% of judicial officers or judges in the West Zone opined that LACs take more than ten adjournments in civil cases under FLAS. Further, 19% of judicial officers or judges in the East Zone and 9% of judicial officers or judges in the North East Zone had a similar opinion.

6.2.2.1.4. NIL

Some judicial officers or judges responded that LACs did not take any adjournments in civil cases under FLAS. Around 20% of judicial officers or judges in the North East Zone, 14% of judicial officers or judges in the West Zone, 12% of judicial officers or judges in the Central Zone, 10%

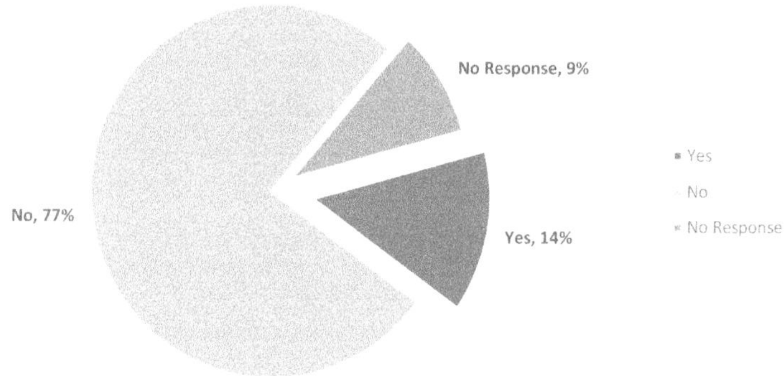

Figure 6.5 LACs Warned/Not Warned by Judges or Judicial Officers Without Filing Complaints

of judicial officers or judges in the East Zone, 4% of judicial officers or judges in the South Zone, and 3% of judicial officers or judges in the North Zone reported that LACs did not take any adjournments in civil cases under FLAS.

6.2.3. *LACs Warned/Not Warned by Judges or Judicial Officers Without Filing Complaints*

Figure 6.5 outlines whether judicial officers or judges warned any LACs without filling complaints to the DLSA for lack of commitment or not. As shown in Figure 6.5, judicial officers or judges did not warn most LACs. In total, around 77% of judicial officers or judges responded that they have never warned LACs in case of any misconduct. However, around 14% of judicial officers or judges affirmed that they did warn LACs but did not file any complaints.

6.2.3.1. *Zonal Analysis of LACs Warned/Not Warned by Judges or Judicial Officers Without Filing Complaints*

6.2.3.1.1. YES

A few judicial officers or judges responded that they did warn LACs. In Figure 6.6, around 25% of judicial officers or judges in the North Zone, 22% of judicial officers or judges in the North East Zone, 21% of judicial officers or judges in the Central Zone, 10% of judicial officers or judges in

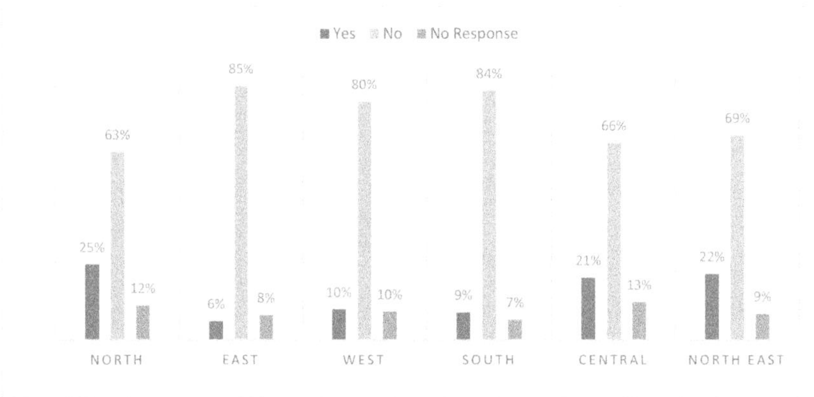

Figure 6.6 Zonal Analysis of LACs Warned/Not Warned by Judges or Judicial Officers Without Filing Complaints

the West Zone, 9% of judicial officers or judges in the South Zone, and 6% of judicial officers or judges in the East Zone did warn LACs without filing a complaint at the DLSA.

6.2.3.1.2. NO

As shown in Figure 6.6, 85% of judicial officers or judges in the East Zone, 84% of judicial officers or judges in the South Zone, 80% of judicial officers or judges in the West Zone, and 69% of judicial officers or judges in the North East Zone responded that they did not warn LACs. Similarly, 66% of judicial officers or judges in the Central Zone, and 63% of judicial officers or judges in the North Zone also responded that they did not warn LACs.

6.2.3.1.3. NO RESPONSE

Some judicial officers or judges did not respond to this question. Around 13% of judicial officers or judges in the Central Zone, 12% of judicial officers or judges in the North Zone, 10% of judicial officers or judges in the West Zone, 9% of judicial officers or judges in the North East Zone, 8% of judicial officers or judges in the East Zone, and 7% of judicial officers or judges in the South Zone did not respond to this question.

6.2.4. *Instances of Judges/Judicial Officers Warning LACs for Lack of Commitment*

Judicial officers or judges often informally warn LACs if they come across any LACs not performing his/her mandated duties under the guidelines of

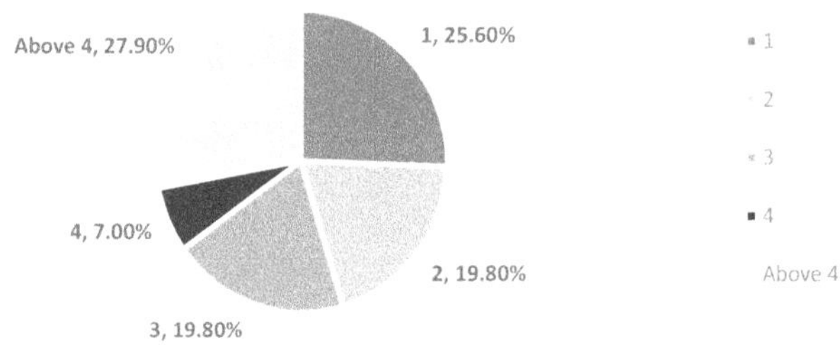

Figure 6.7 Instances of Judges/Judicial Officers Warning LACs for Lack of Commitment

NALSA Regulations, 2010. This section emphasizes that judicial officers or judges had warned LACs about their lack of commitment and dereliction of their duties. Figure 6.7 illustrates the number of times judicial officers or judges had warned LACs informally. In most cases, judicial officers or judges have responded that they have warned LACs in more than four instances. The judicial officers or judges who had warned LACs checked on the quality of work and commitment of LACs. As shown in Figure 6.7, among the judicial officers or judges who warned or scolded LACs, almost 28% (27.9%) of them affirmed that they warned LACs about their lack of commitment more than four times during the trial. Further, around 20% (19.8%) of judicial officers or judges also affirmed that they had warned LACs, during the trial, two to three times for their lack of commitment towards legal aid services. Around 26% (25.9%) of judicial officers or judges responded that they had warned LACs only once throughout a trial.

6.2.4.1. *Zonal Analysis Instances of Judges/Judicial Officers Warning LACs for Lack of Commitment*

6.2.4.1.1. WARNING ONE TIME

As shown in Figure 6.8, around 67% of judicial officers or judges in the East Zone, 31% of judicial officers or judges in the West Zone, 30% of judicial officers or judges in the North East Zone, 22% of judicial officers or judges in the Central Zone, 21% of judicial officers or judges in the North Zone, and 13% of judicial officers or judges in the South Zone opined that they had warned LACs for lack of commitment at one instance.

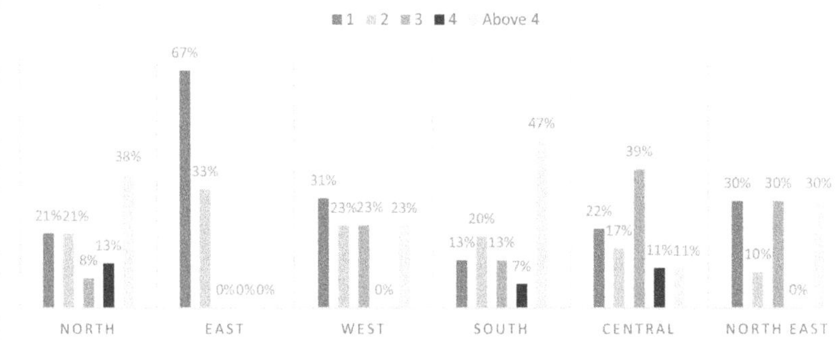

Figure 6.8 Zonal Analysis of Instances of Judges/Judicial Officers Warning LACs for Lack of Commitment

6.2.4.1.2. WARNING TWO TIMES

All in all, 33% of judicial officers or judges in the East Zone, 23% of judicial officers or judges in the West Zone, around 21% of judicial officers or judges in the North Zone, 20% of judicial officers or judges in the South Zone, 17% of judicial officers or judges in the Central Zone, and around 10% of judicial officers or judges in the North East Zone responded that they had warned LACs twice for lack of commitment.

6.2.4.1.3. WARNING THREE TIMES

A few judicial officers or judges even warned LACs thrice for lack of commitment. As shown in Figure 6.8, 39% of judicial officers or judges in the Central Zone, 30% of judicial officers or judges in the North East Zone, 23% of judicial officers or judges in the West Zone, 13% of judicial officers or judges in the South Zone, and 8% of judicial officers or judges in the North Zone warned LACs thrice for lack of commitment.

6.2.4.1.4. WARNING FOUR TIMES

Some of the judicial officers or judges even warned LACs four times for their lack of commitment. As shown in Figure 6.8, 13% of judicial officers or judges in the North Zone, 11% of judicial officers or judges in the Central Zone, and 7% of judicial officers or judges in the South Zone warned LACs four times for lack of commitment during a legal aid case.

6.2.4.1.5. WARNING MORE THAN FOUR TIMES

Judicial officers or judges often warned LACs more than four times during a legal aid case. Figure 6.8 shows that around 47% of judicial officers or

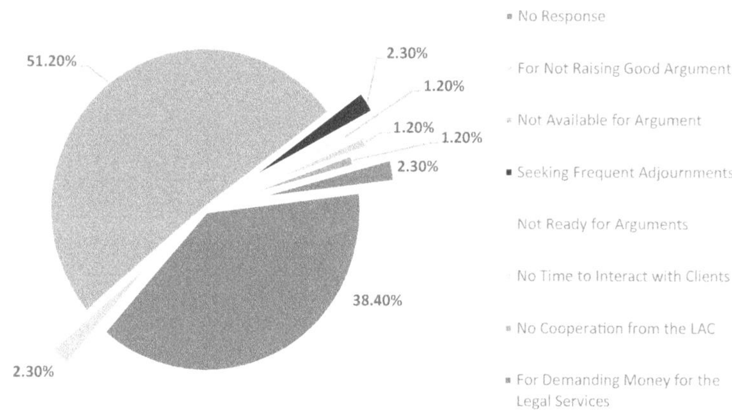

Figure 6.9 Nature of Default by LACs for Which Judicial Officers or Judges Issued Warning

judges in the South Zone, 38% of judicial officers or judges in the North Zone, 30% of judicial officers or judges in the North East Zone, 23% of judicial officers or judges in the West Zone, and 11% of judicial officers or judges in the Central Zone responded that they had warned LACs about four times during the hearing of a legal aid case.

6.2.5. *Nature of Default by LACs for Which Judicial Officers or Judges Issued Warning*

The previous section covered the number of instances judicial officers or judges warned LACs for their lack of commitment. It becomes significant to identify the nature of complaints and observations (informally) raised by the judicial officers about the services of LACs during a trial. It is important to note here that most judicial officers or judges, almost half in some zones, refrained from answering or telling the nature of default made by LACs. As shown in Figure 6.9, most judicial officers or judges opined that the LACs were not available for arguing (around 51.2%) their respective cases under FLAS.

6.2.5.1. *Zonal Analysis Nature of Default by LACs for Which Judicial Officers or Judges Issued Warning*

6.2.5.1.1. NOT AVAILABLE FOR ARGUMENTS

LACs do not only take legal aid cases, but they rely on private practice matters as it earns them more monetary benefits than a legal aid case. They tend to devote most of their time to attending or preparing for their private practice matters rather than on cases related to legal aid. At times, hearing their

Figure 6.10 Zonal Analysis of Nature of Default by LACs for Which Judicial Officers or Judges Issued Warning

private practice matters and legal aid cases clash, or sometimes they are not prepared for the argument. This compels them to skip the court proceedings of legal aid cases. As shown in Figure 6.10, 80% of judicial officers or judges in the South Zone, 60% of judicial officers or judges in the North East Zone, 50% of judicial officers or judges in the North Zone, 44% of judicial officers or judges in the Central Zone, 33% of judicial officers or judges in the East Zone, and 31% of judicial officers or judges in the West Zone warned LACs for not being available for arguments at the time of hearing of a legal aid case.

6.2.5.1.2. NOT RAISING GOOD ARGUMENTS

Judicial officers or judges in the two zones also warned LACs for not raising good arguments. In Figure 6.10, around 8% of judicial officers or judges in the West Zone and 4% of judicial officers or judges in the North Zone warned LACs for not raising good arguments.

6.2.5.1.3. SEEKING FREQUENT ADJOURNMENTS

Seeking frequent adjournments is another nature of the default. Judicial officers or judges warned the LACs while hearing a legal aid case. Around 17% of judicial officers or judges in the East Zone and 6% of judicial officers or judges in the Central Zone responded that they had warned LACs about seeking frequent adjournments.

6.2.5.1.4. NOT READY FOR ARGUMENTS

Only in the West Zone, around 8% of judicial officers or judges warned LACs because they were not ready for arguments in the court.

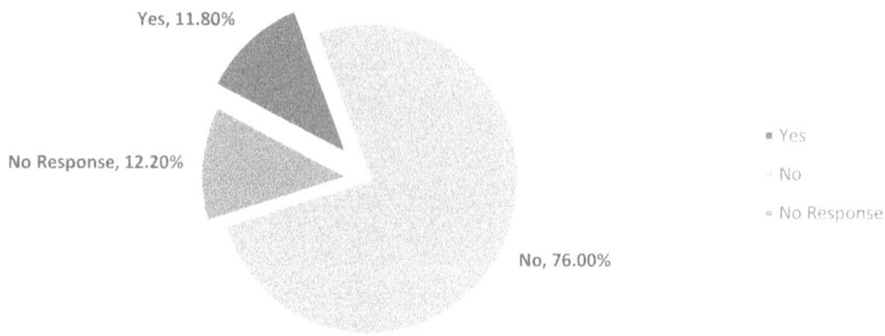

Figure 6.11 Complaints Made by Beneficiaries to Judicial Officers or Judges Against Services of LACs

6.2.5.1.5. NO TIME TO INTERACT WITH CLIENTS, NO COOPERATION FROM LACS, AND DEMANDING MONEY FOR LEGAL SERVICES

Judicial officers or judges also issued warnings to LACs for demanding money, not cooperating with beneficiaries, and not interacting with beneficiaries during court hearings.

6.2.6. *Complaints and Observations by the Beneficiaries to the Judges/Judicial Officers About Services*

Legal aid beneficiaries come from the most vulnerable sections of society. At times legal aid beneficiaries are unable to complain about the services LACs provide to them. However, sometimes beneficiaries are vocal enough to complain about the services of LACs to judicial officers or judges presiding in their cases. Figure 6.11 outlines whether any complaints or observations were made against the LACs by the beneficiaries to the judicial officers or judges. Overwhelmingly, most judicial officers or judges did not receive any observations or complaints about the services of the LACs by the beneficiaries under FLAS.

6.2.6.1. *Zonal Analysis of Complaints and Observations by the Beneficiaries to the Judges/Judicial Officers About Services*

6.2.6.1.1. YES

A few judicial officers or judges affirmed that they did receive complaints and observations against LACs from beneficiaries. As shown in Figure 6.12, around 17% of judicial officers or judges in the North Zone, 15% of judicial officers or judges in the Central Zone, 12% of judicial officers or judges in the

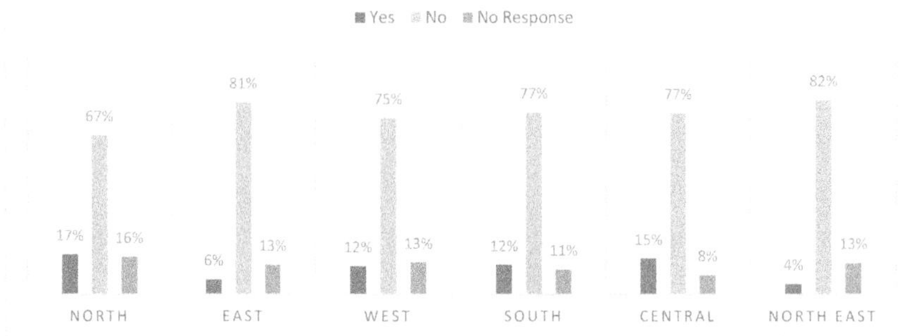

Figure 6.12 Zonal Analysis of Complaints Made by Beneficiaries to Judicial Officers or Judges Against Services of LACs

West and South Zones, 6% of judicial officers or judges in the East Zone, and 4% of judicial officers or judges in the North East Zone acknowledged that they did receive complaints and observations against LACs from beneficiaries.

6.2.6.1.2. NO

As shown in Figure 6.12, around 82% of judicial officers or judges in the North East Zone, 81% of judicial officers or judges in the East Zone, 77% of judicial officers or judges in the Central and South Zones, 75% of judicial officers or judges in the West Zone, and 67% of judicial officers or judges in the North Zone responded that they did not receive any complaints from beneficiaries against LACs.

6.2.6.1.3. NO RESPONSE

Judicial officers or judges in every zone did not respond to this specific question. Around 16% of judicial officers or judges in the North Zone, 11% of judicial officers or judges in the South Zone, 8% of judicial officers or judges in the Central Zone, and 13% of judicial officers or judges in the West, East, and North East Zones did not respond on whether they received any complaint from beneficiaries or not.

6.2.7. *Types of Complaints Made by the Beneficiaries to Judicial Officers or Judges*

In the previous section, judicial officers or judges responded about whether they received any complaints from beneficiaries or not. This section focuses on the responses of that 11.8% of judicial officers or judges (see Figure 6.11) who affirmed that they did receive complaints from beneficiaries against the

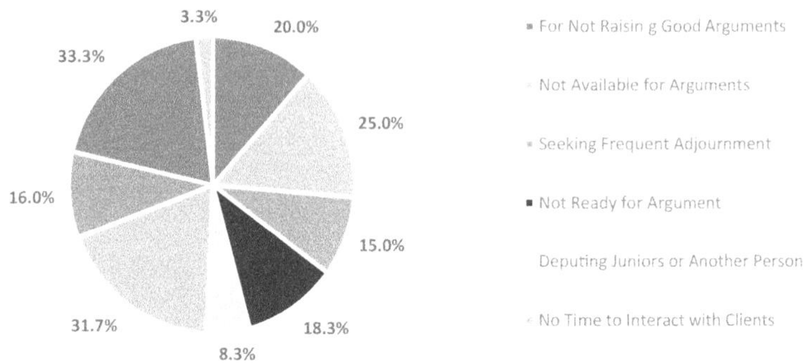

Figure 6.13 Types of Complaints Made by the Beneficiaries to Judicial Officers or Judges

services of LACs. The complaints or observations hold importance because it helps to ascertain issues faced by beneficiaries. As shown in Figure 6.13, there are several complaints of various nature filed by the beneficiaries about the services of LACs to the judicial officers or judges.

Around 33.3% of judicial officers or judges responded that beneficiaries often complained about their LACs demanding money to provide legal services. On the other hand, almost 32% (31.7%) of judicial officers or judges responded that beneficiaries complained that LACs do not interact with them (beneficiaries). Further, 25% of judicial officers or judges said that beneficiaries complained about LACs not being available for court arguments. Besides, 20% of judicial officers or judges also affirmed that beneficiaries often complained about their respective LACs not raising good arguments.

6.2.7.1. *Zonal Analysis of Types of Complaints Made by the Beneficiaries to Judicial Officers or Judges*

6.2.7.1.1. NOT RAISING GOOD ARGUMENTS

Judicial officers or judges received complaints that LACs were not raising good arguments. As shown in Figure 6.14, 38% of judicial officers or judges in the South Zone, 19% of judicial officers or judges in the North Zone, 15% of judicial officers or judges in the Central Zone, and 10% of judicial officers or judges in the West Zone received complaints from beneficiaries that LACs are not raising good arguments.

6.2.7.1.2. BEING NOT AVAILABLE FOR ARGUMENTS

In some zones, judicial officers or judges received complaints against LACs for not being available for arguments. As shown in Figure 6.14, 50% of judicial

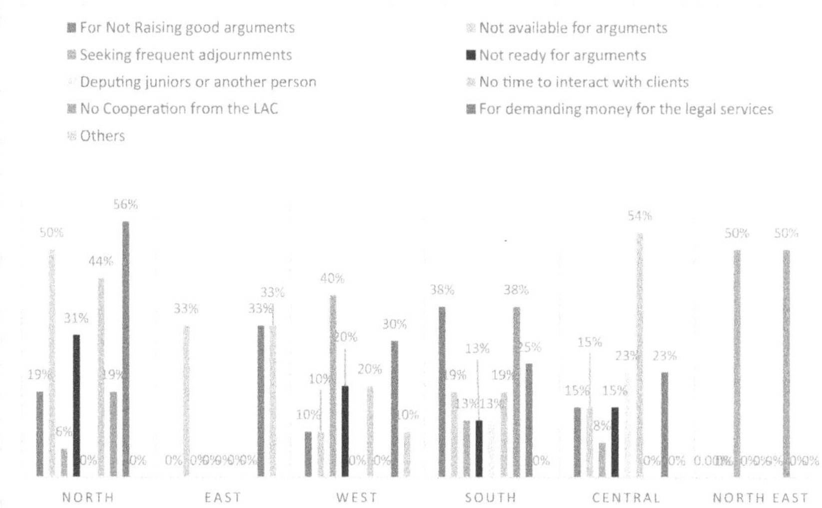

Figure 6.14 Zonal Analysis of Types of Complaints Made by the Beneficiaries to Judicial Officers or Judges

officers or judges in the North Zone, 33% of judicial officers or judges in the East Zone, 19% of judicial officers or judges in the South Zone, 15% of judicial officers or judges in the Central Zone, and 10% of judicial officers or judges in the West Zone received complaints by beneficiaries that LACs are not available for arguments. The non-availability of LACs for arguments is one of the major issues raised by judicial officers or judges while warning LACs.

6.2.7.1.3. SEEKING FREQUENT ADJOURNMENTS

Seeking frequent adjournments is also one of the complaints received by judicial officers or judges from beneficiaries. Around 50% of judicial officers or judges in the North East Zone, 40% of judicial officers or judges in the West Zone, 13% of judicial officers or judges in the South Zone, and 8% of judicial officers or judges in the Central Zone received complaints from beneficiaries about LACs seeking frequent adjournments.

6.2.7.1.4. BEING NOT READY FOR ARGUMENTS

Judicial officers or judges also received complaints regarding LACs not being ready for arguments. As Figure 6.14 demonstrates, around 31% of judicial officers or judges in the North Zone, 20% of judicial officers or judges in the West Zone, 15% of judicial officers or judges in the Central Zone, and 13% of judicial officers or judges in the South Zone received complaints from beneficiaries that their LAC is not ready for arguments.

6.2.7.1.5. DEPUTING JUNIORS OR ANOTHER PERSON

A few senior advocates who happen to be LACs depute a junior with no or zero experience to handle legal aid cases. Judicial officers or judges also received a few complaints from beneficiaries against LACs on this very matter. As shown in Figure 6.14, 23% of judicial officers or judges in the Central Zone and 13% of judicial officers or judges in the South Zone received complaints from beneficiaries that their LACs are deputing junior advocates for their cases.

6.2.7.1.6. NO TIME TO INTERACT WITH CLIENTS

Beneficiaries also complained about LACs giving no time to interact with them. As shown in Figure 6.14, 54% of judicial officers or judges in the Central Zone, 44% of judicial officers or judges in the North Zone, 20% of judicial officers or judges in the West Zone, and 19% of judicial officers or judges in the South Zone received complaints from beneficiaries that their LACs are not giving any time to interact.

6.2.7.1.7. NO COOPERATION FROM LACS

Around 50% of judicial officers or judges in the North East Zone, 38% of judicial officers or judges in the South Zone, and 19% of judicial officers or judges in the North Zone received complaints from beneficiaries that LACs are not cooperating with them appropriately.

6.2.7.1.8. DEMANDING MONEY FOR LEGAL SERVICES

Beneficiaries were vocal even about LACs demanding money from them. Judicial officers or judges received complaints from beneficiaries that LACs are demanding money for the legal services rendered to them under FLAS. As shown in Figure 6.14, 56% of judicial officers or judges in the North Zone, 50% of judicial officers or judges in the North East Zone, 33% of judicial officers or judges in the East Zone, 30% of judicial officers or judges in the West Zone, 25% of judicial officers or judges in the South Zone, and 23% of judicial officers or judges in the Central Zone, received complaints from beneficiaries that their LACs are demanding money from them for legal services.

6.2.8. *Complaints Made During the Trial Against LACs by Judges/Judicial Officers to the LSA*

Figure 6.15 narrates whether any complaints were made during the trial against the LACs by judicial officers or judges to the DLSA or not. As shown, more than 80% (82.11%) of judicial officers or judges, 520 out of 609 judicial officers or judges, did not file any complaints. Unquestionably, most judicial officers or judges are often heavily burdened with their daily workload, and making a formal complaint to the DLSA does not seem feasible for any judicial officer or judge.

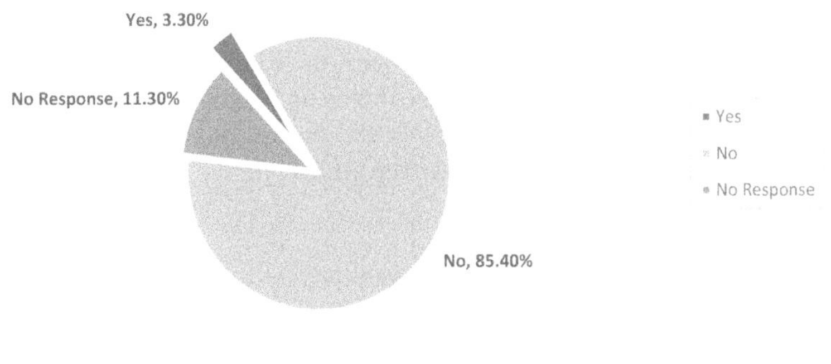

Figure 6.15 Complaints Made During the Trial Against LACs by Judges/Judicial Officers to the LSA

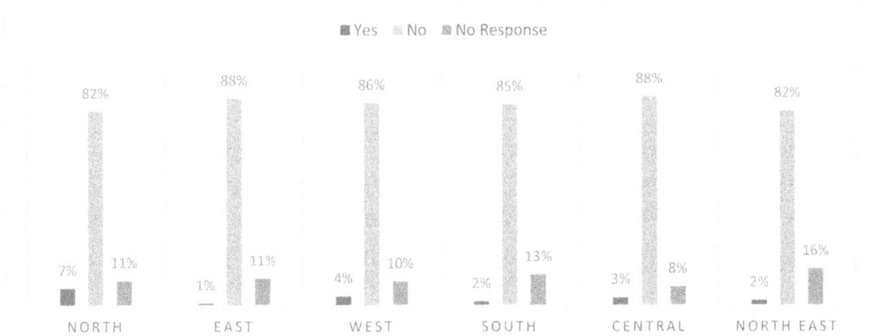

Figure 6.16 Zonal Analysis of Complaints Made During the Trial Against LACs by Judges/Judicial Officers to the LSA

6.2.8.1. *Zonal Analysis Complaints Made During the Trial Against LACs by Judges/Judicial Officers to the LSA*

6.2.8.1.1. YES

A very few judicial officers or judges responded that they had made complaints against LACs during the trial proceedings of legal aid cases. As shown in Figure 6.16, 7% of judicial officers or judges in the North Zone, 4% of judicial officers or judges in the West Zone, 3% of judicial officers or judges in the Central Zone, 2% of judicial officers or judges in the North East Zone, and 1% of judicial officers or judges in the East Zone said that they did complain to the DLSA about LACs during trial proceedings of legal aid cases.

6.2.8.1.2. NO

Judicial officers or judges denied the very existence of them making any formal or informal complaints to the DLSA against LACs during trial proceedings of legal aid cases. As shown in Figure 6.16, 88% of judicial officers or judges in the East and Central Zones, 86% of judicial officers or judges in the West Zone, 85% of judicial officers or judges in the South Zone, and 82% of judicial officers or judges in the North and North East Zones did not complain against any LACs at the DLSA.

6.2.8.1.3. NO RESPONSE

Some judicial officers or judges did not respond on whether they filed any complaints against LACs or not. As shown in Figure 6.16, 16% of judicial officers or judges in the North East Zone, 13% of judicial officers or judges in the South Zone, 11% of judicial officers or judges in the North and East Zones, 10% of judicial officers or judges in the West Zone, and 8% of judicial officers or judges in the Central Zone did not respond on the issue.

6.2.9. *Difficulties Faced by Beneficiaries While Interacting With Their LACs*

Even though judicial officers or judges do not interact with beneficiaries about the issues they face while interacting with their LACs, there are several difficulties that judicial officers or judges might highlight. Judicial officers' or judges' perspective becomes important as beneficiaries do not have anywhere else to turn to. As shown in Figure 6.17,

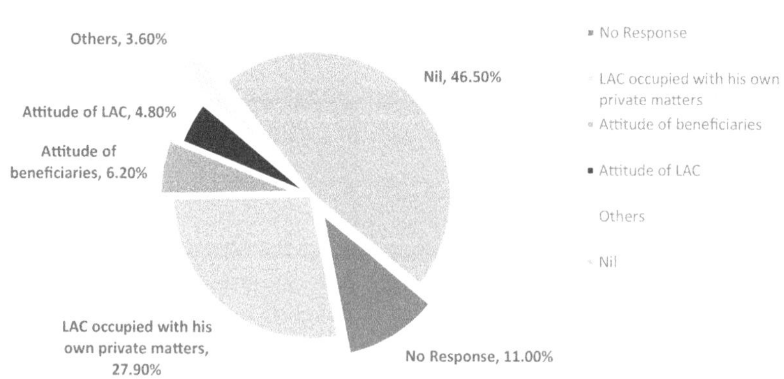

Figure 6.17 Difficulties Faced by Beneficiaries While Interacting With Their LACs

most judicial officers or judges opined that beneficiaries do not face any difficulties while interacting with their LACs. This response can be attributed to the fact that judicial officers or judges are often preoccupied with daily court proceedings and are unable to pay attention to beneficiaries. On the other hand, around 27.9% of judicial officers or judges responded that LACs are preoccupied with their private practice matters, which is one of the issues faced by beneficiaries while interacting with LACs. Further, 6.2% of judicial officers or judges cited that beneficiaries' attitude is also an issue. Another 4.8% of judicial officers or judges opined that beneficiaries sometimes face difficulties due to the attitude of LACs.

6.2.9.1. Zonal Analysis of Difficulties Faced by Beneficiaries While Interacting With Their LACs

6.2.9.1.1. LACS OCCUPIED WITH PRIVATE PRACTICE MATTERS

Judicial officers or judges in most of the zones cited that LACs' preoccupation with their private practice matters creates difficulties for beneficiaries. As shown in Figure 6.18, around 40% of judicial officers or judges in the Central Zone, 33% of judicial officers or judges in the North Zone, 29% of judicial officers or judges in the West and South Zones, 16% of judicial officers or judges in the East Zone, and 13% of judicial officers or judges in the North East Zone responded that since LACs are preoccupied with their private practice matters, they tend to focus less on the beneficiaries.

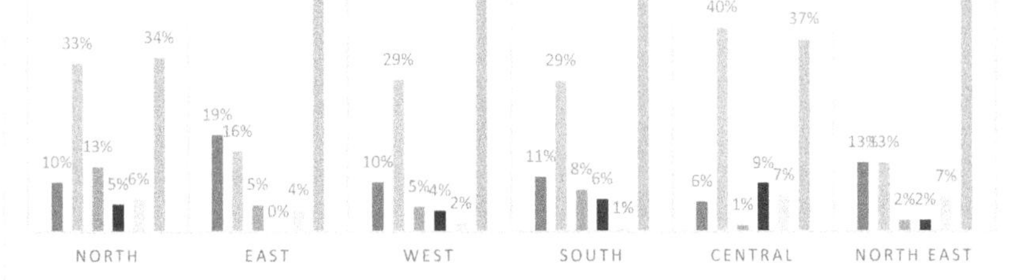

Figure 6.18 Zonal Analysis of Difficulties Faced by Beneficiaries While Interacting With Their LACs

6.2.9.1.2. ATTITUDE OF BENEFICIARIES

Around 13% of judicial officers or judges in the North Zone, 8% of judicial officers or judges in the South Zone, 5% of judicial officers or judges in the East and West Zones, and 2% of judicial officers or judges in the North East Zone responded that beneficiaries face difficulties because of their attitude as they expect too much from LACs in terms of legal services.

6.2.9.1.3. ATTITUDE OF LACS

Judicial officers or judges in a few zones responded that the attitude of LACs is also one of the difficulties faced by beneficiaries. As shown in Figure 6.18, 9% of judicial officers or judges in the Central Zone, 6% of judicial officers or judges in the South Zone, 5% of judicial officers or judges in the North Zone, 4% of judicial officers or judges in the West Zone, and 2% of judicial officers or judges in the North East Zone said that the attitude of LACs is one of the many difficulties faced by beneficiaries.

6.2.10. *Commitment and Devotion of LACs as Rated by Judicial Officers or Judges*

The quality of work and devotion of LACs are directly responsible for the success or failure of the legal aid scheme. If the beneficiaries do not feel that the LACs are willing to render the mandated services properly, then even fewer people will opt for legal aid, although it is their lawful right. The questionnaire for judicial officers or judges consisted of a section devoted to weighing in on the commitment and devotion of LACs towards the services. Figure 6.19 shows that most judicial officers or judges (54.5%) believe that LACs show partial devotion towards the services under legal aid. On the other hand, around 25.8% of judicial officers or judges believed that LACs show strong devotion towards the mandate of legal aid services in India. Further, around 8.5% of judicial officers or judges even said that LACs show no devotion towards the mandate of legal aid.

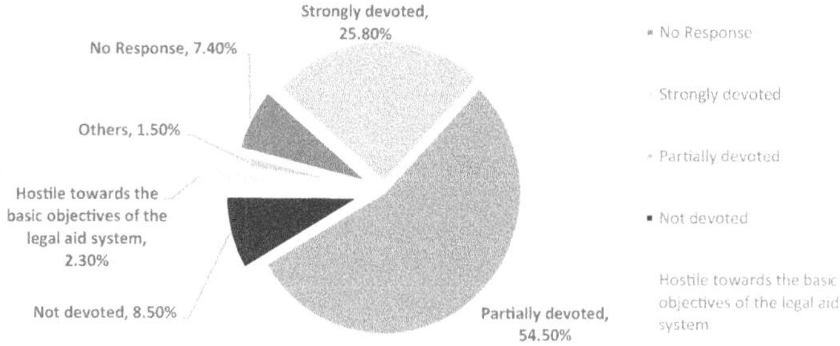

Figure 6.19 Commitment and Devotion of LACs as Rated by Judicial Officers or Judges

6.2.10.1. *Zonal Analysis of Commitment and Devotion of LACs as Rated by Judicial Officers or Judges*

6.2.10.1.1. PARTIALLY DEVOTED

As shown in Figure 6.19, 63% of judicial officers or judges in the West Zone, 58% of judicial officers or judges in the North Zone, 53% of judicial officers or judges in the South Zone, 51% of judicial officers or judges in the Central Zone, 49% of judicial officers or judges in the North East Zone, and 48% of judicial officers or judges in the East Zone said that LACs show partial devotion towards the services under FLAS.

6.2.10.1.2. STRONGLY DEVOTED

Contrary to the partial devotion, a few judicial officers or judges stated that LACs show strong devotion towards the services under FLAS. As shown in Figure 6.20, 40% of judicial officers or judges in the East Zone, 31% of judicial officers or judges in the North East Zone, 28% of judicial officers or judges in the North Zone, 27% of judicial officers or judges in the South Zone, and 16% of judicial officers or judges in the Central and West Zone opined that LACs show strong devotion towards the services under FLAS.

6.2.10.1.3. NOT DEVOTED

Judicial officers or judges in some zones were vocal about LACs showing no devotion towards FLAS. As shown in Figure 6.20, 14% of judicial officers or judges in the Central Zone, 10% of judicial officers or judges in the South and West Zones, 8% of judicial officers or judges in the North Zone, 4% of judicial officers or judges in the North East Zone, and 2% of judicial officers or judges in the East Zone responded that LACs show no devotion towards the services under FLAS.

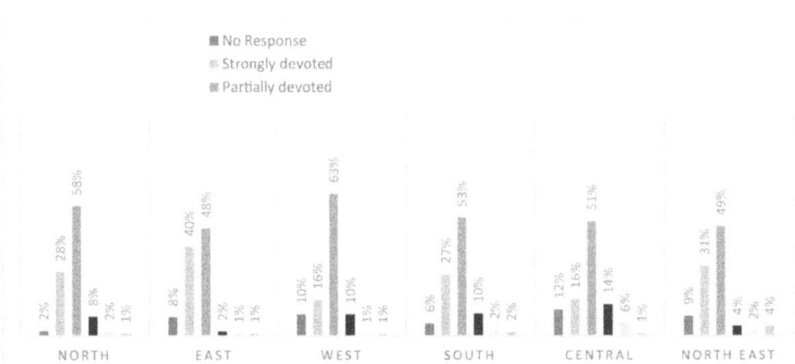

Figure 6.20 Zonal Analysis of Commitment and Devotion of LACs as Rated by Judicial Officers or Judges

Figure 6.21 Overall Performance of LACs as Rated by Judicial Officers or Judges

6.2.10.1.4. HOSTILE TOWARDS BASIC OBJECTIVE OF THE LAS

A very minute group of judicial officers or judges marked LACs as being hostile towards the objective of FLAS. As shown in Figure 6.20, 6% of judicial officers or judges in the Central Zone, 1% of judicial officers or judges in the East and West Zones, and 2% of judicial officers or judges in the North, North East, and South Zones responded that LACs are hostile towards the basic objective of FLAS.

6.2.11. Overall Performance of LACs as Rated by Judicial Officers or Judges

The questionnaire distributed to judicial officers or judges consisted of a question focusing on the overall performance of LACs. As shown in Figure 6.21, around 73.7% of judicial officers or judges rated the overall performance of LACs as satisfactory, whereas 10% of judicial officers or judges rated the overall performance of LACs as unsatisfactory. Further, only 4.3% of judicial officers or judges opined that the overall performance of LACs is highly satisfactory, and a minute 1.6% of judicial officers or judges rated the overall performance of LACs as highly unsatisfactory.

6.2.11.1. Zonal Analysis of Overall Performance of LACs as Rated by Judicial Officers or Judges

6.2.11.1.1. SATISFACTORY

Judicial officers or judges in almost every zone rated the overall performance of LACs as satisfactory. As shown in Figure 6.22, 80% of judicial officers or judges in the East Zone, 77% of judicial officers or judges in the North Zone, 73% of judicial officers or judges in the West and South Zones, 72% of judicial officers or judges in the Central Zone, and 62% of judicial officers or judges in the North East Zone rated the overall performance of LACs as satisfactory.

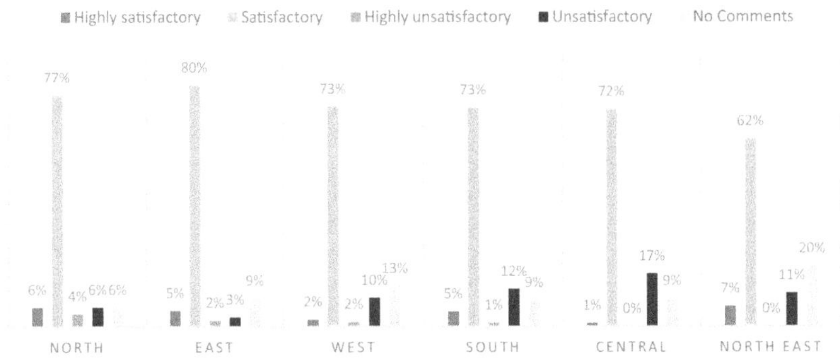

Figure 6.22 Zonal Analysis of Overall Performance of LACs as Rated by Judicial Officers or Judges

6.2.11.1.2. HIGHLY SATISFACTORY

Very few judicial officers or judges rated the overall performance of LACs as highly satisfactory. All in all, 7% of judicial officers or judges in the North East Zone, 6% of judicial officers or judges in the North Zone, 5% of judicial officers or judges in the East and South Zones, 2% of judicial officers or judges in the West Zone, and 1% of judicial officers or judges in the Central Zone rated the overall performance of LACs as highly satisfactory.

6.2.11.1.3. HIGHLY UNSATISFACTORY

As shown in Figure 6.22, around 4% of judicial officers or judges in the North Zone, 2% of judicial officers or judges in the East and West Zones, and 1% of judicial officers or judges in the South Zone rated the overall performance of LACs as highly unsatisfactory.

6.2.11.1.4. UNSATISFACTORY

Around 17% of judicial officers or judges in the Central Zone, 12% of judicial officers or judges in the South Zone, 11% of judicial officers or judges in the North East Zone, 10% of judicial officers or judges in the West Zone, 6% of judicial officers or judges in the North Zone, and 3% of judicial officers or judges in the East Zone rated the overall performance of LACs as unsatisfactory.

6.2.12. Quality of Arguments Made by LACs According to Judicial Officers or Judges

Judicial officers or judges interact with LACs in their legal aid cases and private practice matters. They are aware of the quality of argument skills. As shown in Figure 6.23, 38.1% of judicial officers or judges rated the quality

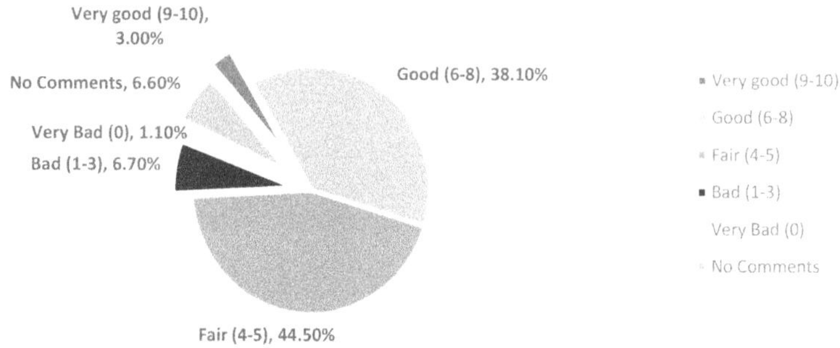

Figure 6.23 Quality of Arguments Made by LACs According to Judicial Officers or Judges

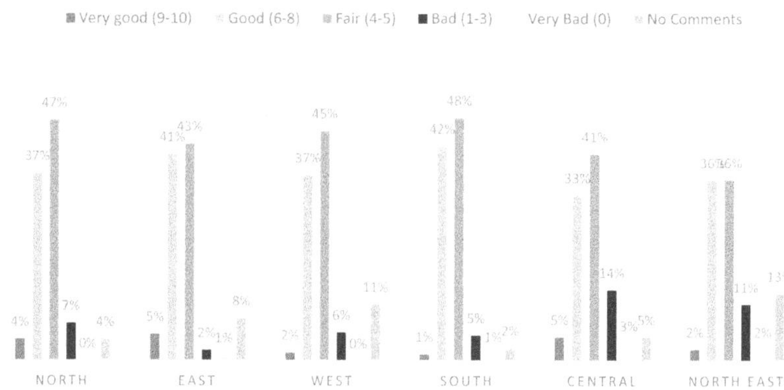

Figure 6.24 Zonal Analysis Quality of Arguments Made by LACs According to Judicial Officers or Judges

of arguments skills of LACs as good. Interestingly, most judicial officers or judges rated the quality of arguments made by LACs as fair quality. Further, 6.7% of judicial officers or judges rated the quality of arguments made by LACs as bad, and 3% of judicial officers or judges rated the quality of arguments made by LACs as very good.

6.2.12.1. *Zonal Analysis of Quality of Arguments Made by LACs According to Judicial Officers or Judges*

6.2.12.1.1. VERY GOOD

In Figure 6.24, 5% of judicial officers or judges in the East Zone and Central Zone, 4% of judicial officers or judges in the North Zone and East

Zone, 2% of judicial officers or judges in the West Zone and North East Zone, and 1% of judicial officers or judges in the South Zone rated the quality of argument made by LACs as very good.

6.2.12.1.2. GOOD

Around 42% of judicial officers or judges in the South Zone, 41% of judicial officers or judges in the East Zone, 37% of judicial officers or judges in the West Zone and North Zone, 36% of judicial officers or judges in the North East Zone, 33% of judicial officers or judges in the Central Zone rated the quality of arguments made by LACs as good.

6.2.12.3. FAIR

Most of the judicial officers or judges rated the quality of arguments made by LACs as fair. This may be because most judicial officers or judges did not want to rate them as bad. As shown in Figure 6.24, 48% of judicial officers or judges in the South Zone, 47% of judicial officers or judges in the North Zone, 45% of judicial officers or judges in the West Zone, 43% of judicial officers or judges in the East Zone, 41% of judicial officers or judges in the Central Zone, and 36% of the judicial officers or judges in the North East Zone rated the quality of arguments made by LACs as fair.

6.2.12.4. BAD AND VERY BAD

Very few judicial officers or judges rated the quality of arguments made by judicial officers or judges as bad or very bad. As shown in Figure 6.24, around 14% of judicial officers or judges in the Central Zone, 11% of judicial officers or judges in the North East Zone, 7% of judicial officers or judges in the North Zone, 6% of judicial officers or judges in the West Zone, 5% of judicial officers or judges in the East Zone and South Zone rated the quality of arguments skills of LACs as bad.

Further, around 3% of judicial officers or judges in the Central Zone, 2% of judicial officers or judges in the North East Zone, and 1% of judicial officers or judges in the East Zone rated the quality of arguments made by LACs as very bad.

6.2.13. Quality of LACs' Presentation and Articulation According to Judges/Judicial Officers

Figure 6.25 demonstrates the quality of presentation and articulation skills rated by judicial officers or judges. As shown, 46.5% of judicial officers or judges rated the quality of presentation and articulation skills of LACs as fair, whereas 38.4% of judicial officers or judges rated the quality of presentation and articulation skills of LACs as good. Further, 5.4% of judicial officers or judges rated the quality of presentation and articulation skills

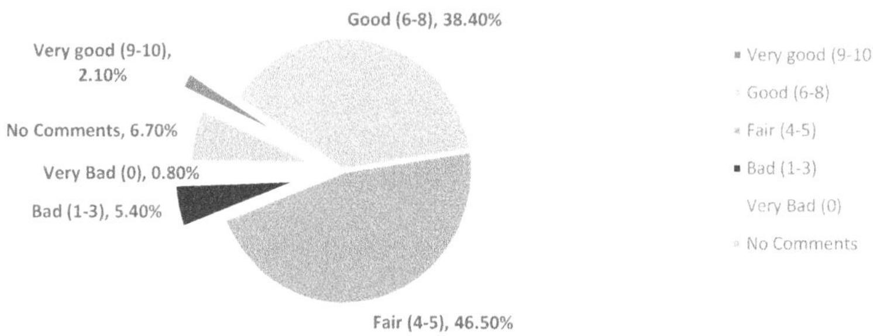

Figure 6.25 Quality of LACs' Presentation and Articulation According to Judges/Judicial Officers

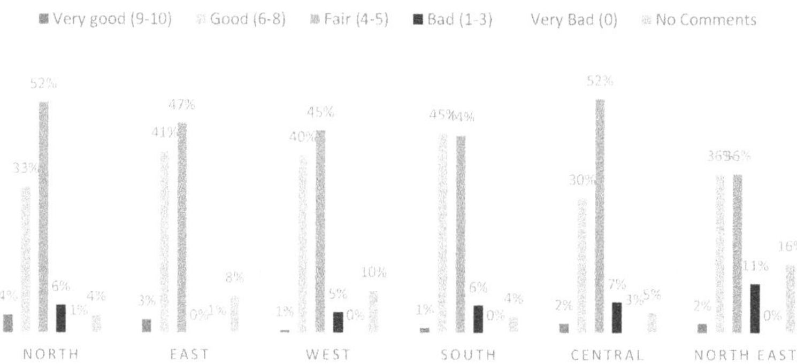

Figure 6.26 Zonal Analysis of Quality of LACs' Presentation and Articulation According to Judges/Judicial Officers

of LACs as bad, and 2.1% of judicial officers or judges responded that the presentation and articulation skills of LACs are very bad.

6.2.13.1. *Zonal Analysis of Quality of LACs' Presentation and Articulation According to Judges/Judicial Officers*

6.2.13.1. VERY GOOD

As shown in Figure 6.26, 4% of judicial officers or judges in the North Zone, 3% of judicial officers or judges in the East Zone, 2% of the judicial officers or judges in the Central Zone and North East Zone, and 1% of judicial officers and judges in the West and South Zones opined that LACs have a very good quality of presentation and articulation skills.

6.2.13.2. GOOD

A significant percentage of judicial officers or judges also rated the presentation and articulation made by LACs as good. As shown in Figure 6.26, around 45% of judicial officers or judges in the South Zone, 41% of judicial officers or judges in the East Zone, 40% of judicial officers or judges in the West Zone, 36% of judicial officers or judges in the North East Zone, 33% of judicial officers or judges in the North Zone, and 30% of judicial officers or judges in the Central Zone responded that the quality of presentation and articulation skills of LACs is good.

6.2.13.3. FAIR

Most judicial officers or judges rated the quality of presentation skills of LACs as fair quality. As shown in Figure 6.26, around 52% of judicial officers or judges in the North Zone and Central Zone, 47% of judicial officers or judges in the East Zone, 45% of judicial officers or judges in the West Zone and South Zone, and 36% of judicial officers or judges in the North East Zone responded that LACs have a fair quality of presentation and articulation skills.

6.2.13.4. BAD AND VERY BAD

As shown in Figure 6.26, 11% of judicial officers or judges in the North East Zone, 7% of judicial officers or judges in the Central Zone, and 6% of judicial officers or judges in the North Zone and South Zone rated the quality of presentation and articulation made by LACs as bad.

Further, around 3% of judicial officers or judges in the Central Zone and 1% of judicial officers or judges in the North Zone and East Zone responded that LACs have very bad presentation and articulation skills.

6.2.14. *Quality of Drafting Skills of LACs According to Judicial Officers or Judges*

As shown in Figure 6.27, around 46.6% of judicial officers or judges rated the quality of drafting skills of LACs as fair, while 33.3% of judicial officers or judges responded that the drafting skills of LACs are good in quality.

Further, 8.4% of judicial officers or judges rated the drafting skills of LACs as bad, and 1.1% rated the drafting skills of LACs as very bad. Only

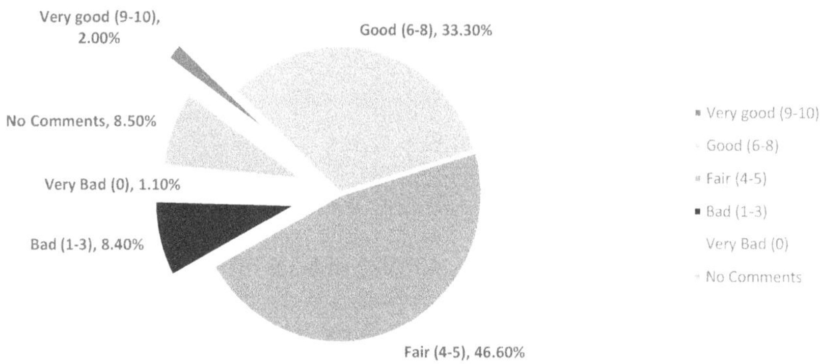

Figure 6.27 Quality of Drafting Skills of LACs According to Judicial Officers or Judges

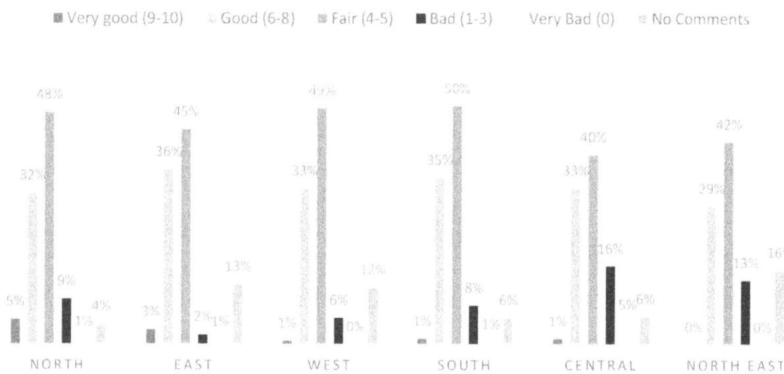

Figure 6.28 Zone Analysis of Quality of Drafting Skills of LACs According to Judicial Officers or Judges

2% of judicial officers or judges rated the drafting skills of LACs as very good.

6.2.14.1. *Zone Analysis of Quality of Drafting Skills of LACs According to Judicial Officers or Judges*

6.2.14.1.1. VERY GOOD

In Figure 6.28, 5% of judicial officers or judges in the North Zone, 3% of judicial officers or judges in the East Zone, and 1% of judicial officers or judges in the West Zone, South Zone, and Central Zone rated the drafting skills of LACs as very good.

6.2.14.1.2. GOOD

Around 36% of judicial officers or judges in the East Zone, 35% of judicial officers or judges in the South Zone, 33% of judicial officers or judges in the West Zone and Central Zone, 32% of judicial officers or judges in the North Zone, and 29% of judicial officers or judges in the North East Zone rated the quality of drafting skills by LACs as good.

6.2.14.1.3. FAIR

Judicial officers or judges also rated the drafting skills of LACs as fair in quality. As shown in Figure 6.28, around 50% of judicial officers or judges in the South Zone, 49% of judicial officers or judges in the West Zone, 48% of judicial officers or judges in the North Zone, 45% of judicial officers or judges in the East Zone, 42% of judicial officers or judges in the North East Zone, and 40% of judicial officers or judges in the Central Zone responded that LACs have a fair quality of drafting skills.

6.2.14.1.4. BAD AND VERY BAD

A few judicial officers or judges rated the drafting skills by LACs as bad and very bad in terms of quality. As shown in Figure 6.28, around 16% of judicial officers or judges in the Central Zone, 13% of judicial officers or judges in the North East Zone, 9% of judicial officers or judges in the North Zone, 8% of judicial officers or judges in the South Zone, 6% of judicial officers or judges in the West Zone, and 3% of judicial officers or judges in the East Zone responded that LACs have a bad quality of drafting skills.

6.2.15. Degree of Overall Satisfaction With the Skills of LACs According to Judicial Officers or Judges

Judicial officers or judges also responded to the overall satisfaction they have from the professional skills of LACs. As shown in Figure 6.29, around 45.6% of judicial officers or judges rated the overall professional skills of LACs as fair. In comparison, around 34% of judicial officers or judges responded that the overall professional skills of LACs are good in quality. Around 3.1% of judicial officers or judges even rated the quality of professional skills of LACs as very good. Further, around 7.2% of judicial officers or judges rated the overall professional skills of LACs as bad, while 1% of judicial officers or judges rated the quality of professional skills of LACs as very bad.

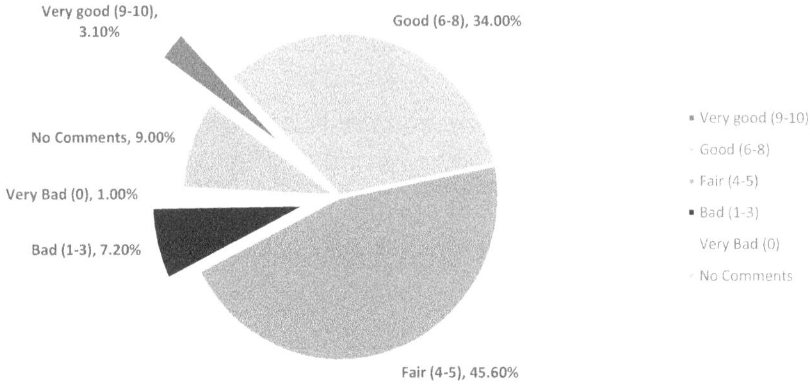

Figure 6.29 Degree of Overall Satisfaction With the Skills of LACs According to Judicial Officers or Judges

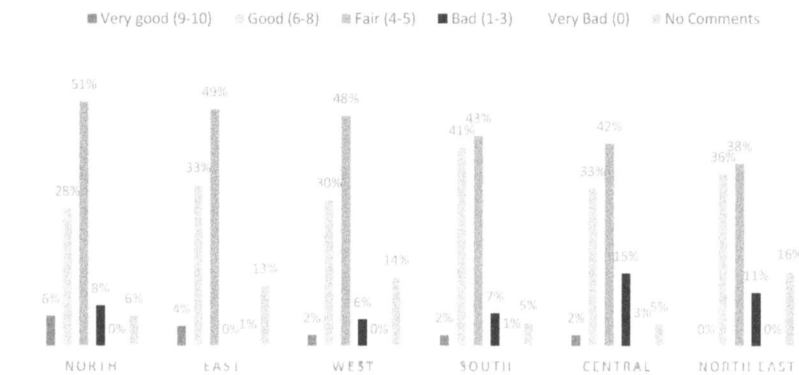

Figure 6.30 Zonal Analysis of Degree of Overall Satisfaction With the Skills of LACs According to Judicial Officers or Judges

6.2.15.1. *Zonal Analysis of Degree of Overall Satisfaction With the Skills of LACs According to Judicial Officers or Judges*

6.2.15.1.1. VERY GOOD

In Figure 6.30, around 6% of judicial officers or judges in the North Zone, 4% of judicial officers or judges in the East Zone, and 2% of judicial officers or judges in the West Zone, South Zone, and Central Zone responded that LACs are very good in terms of overall professional skills.

6.2.15.1.2. GOOD

Judicial officers or judges also rated the overall professional skills of LACs as good. As shown in Figure 6.30, around 41% of judicial officers or judges in the South Zone, 36% of judicial officers or judges in the North East Zone, 33% of judicial officers or judges in the East Zone and Central Zone, 28% of judicial officers or judges in the North Zone responded that the overall professional skills of LACs are good quality.

6.2.15.1.3. FAIR

Most judicial officers or judges rated the quality of overall professional skills of LACs as fair. As shown in Figure 6.30, around 51% of judicial officers or judges in the North Zone, 49% of judicial officers or judges in the East Zone, 48% of judicial officers or judges in the West Zone, 42% of judicial officers or judges in the Central Zone, and 38% of judicial officers or judges in the North East Zone rated the quality of overall professional skills in LACs as fair.

6.2.15.1.4. BAD AND VERY BAD

A few judicial officers or judges also rated the quality of overall professional skills by LACs as bad and very bad. As shown in Figure 6.30, around 15% of judicial officers or judges in the Central Zone, 11% of judicial officers or judges in the North East Zone, 8% of judicial officers or judges in the North Zone, 7% of judicial officers or judges in the South Zone, and 6% of judicial officers or judges in the West Zone rated the quality of overall professional skills of LACs as bad.

Further, around 3% of judicial officers or judges in the Central Zone and 1% of judicial officers or judges each in the East Zone and South Zone responded that the overall professional skills of LACs are very bad.

7 Legal Aid Counsels

7.1. Introduction

LACs play a pivotal role in providing legal aid services. LACs are undoubtedly the most important stakeholder in delivering access to justice to the beneficiaries under the LAS. Moreover, LACs are at the axis of the justice delivery system per the Legal Services Authority Act, 1987. The LAS is bound to fail in case LACs do not perform or live up to the mandate of the LSA Act, 1987. Providing legal aid to the beneficiaries is directly proportional to the level of commitment and competence of the LACs engaged with their respective beneficiaries.

LACs are also important stakeholders in the delivery of FLAS. The questionnaire given to LACs consisted of questions pertaining to their perceptions, the difficulties they faced, and their narrative in the delivery of services under FLAS. The aim was to interpret their level of commitment, their assessment of their own services, and their recommendations to improve the quality of services under legal aid in India.

Initially, a list of panel lawyers at every DLSA was prepared using data available on the NALSA website. Thereafter, the team of researchers approached the respective regulators to tally the list available at their DLSA office and select the LACs based on experience. For the questionnaire-based interview, LACs who had more than ten years of experience or handled more than ten cases under the LAS were selected. The questionnaires were distributed in cohorts of ten LACs at a time at every DLSA to maintain the sanctity of individual LAC's perceptions. In a span of five days, the required number of questionnaires was collected from every district court. Table 7.1 shows the number of proposed samples and collected samples from each state in the research universe of this study.

The questionnaires to the LACs (empaneled in 36 district courts) were provided to them personally. The LACs are the conduit between the LAS and the recipients of said aid in India. They are the face of the program, and their competence reflects that of the system. This makes it imperative to understand the ground realities from their perspectives. Since they are the ones working closely with the recipients and the legal system, their thoughts and ideas have significant importance. The design of this focuses on assessing the level of expertise of the LACs, generating awareness of the challenges they face, and seeking remedies from them.

DOI: 10.4324/9781003158325-7

Table 7.1 Proposed and Actual Responses Received From the LACs

Zone	*State*	*District*	*Proposed Number of LACs*	*Actual Number of LACs*
North	Punjab	Patiala	30	21
		Sangrur	30	30
	Himachal Pradesh	Shimla	30	27
		Solan	30	15
	Haryana	Gurugram	30	17
		Rohtak	30	14
	Uttar Pradesh	Allahabad	30	5
		Gautam Buddha Nagar	30	21
East	West Bengal	Kolkata	30	20
		24 North Pargana	30	31
	Jharkhand	Ranchi	30	32
		Ramgarh	30	15
	Odisha	Bhubaneshwar	30	19
		Cuttack	30	20
West	Rajasthan	Jodhpur	30	18
		Pali	30	21
	Gujarat	Ahmedabad	30	50
		Gandhinagar	30	19
	Maharashtra	Aurangabad	30	46
		Jalna	30	34
South	Karnataka	Bangalore Urban	30	38
		Bangalore Rural	30	23
	Tamil Nadu	Tiruchirappalli	30	48
		Thanjavur	30	36
	Andhra Pradesh	Vizag	30	38
		Vizianagaram	30	32
	Kerala	Pathanamthitta	30	28
		Alappuzha	30	33
Central	Chhattisgarh	Raipur	30	34
		Durg	30	34
	Madhya Pradesh	Indore	30	78
		Dhar	30	38
North East	Meghalaya	Shillong	30	17
		Nongpoh	30	13
		Jowai	30	7
	Assam	Guwahati	30	11
		Amingaon	30	24
	TOTAL		1,110	1,007

7.2. Data Analysis

7.2.1. LACs' Area of Specialization

The NALSA (Free and Competent Legal Services) Regulations, 2010, mandates the selection of empaneled lawyers with reference to their

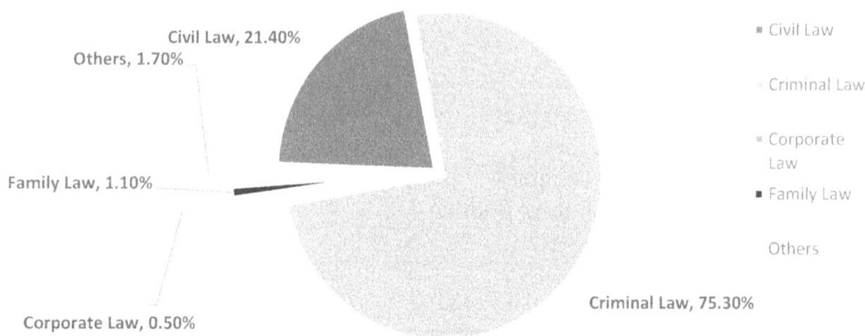

Figure 7.1 LACs' Area of Specialization

area of specialization. The section analyzes whether the heterogeneity in types of area of specialization among the panel lawyers at DLSAs is present or not. As shown in Figure 7.1, around 75.3% of LACs have specialization in criminal law, whereas only 21.4% of LACs have specialization in civil law. Further, only 1.1% of LACs have specialization in family law, and 0.5% of LACs have specialization in corporate law. Certainly, an overwhelming majority of the LACs specialize in criminal law. The specializations in environmental law, constitutional law, labor law, matrimonial disputes, and juvenile justice are missing from empaneled LACs.

7.2.1.1. Zonal Analysis of LACs' Area of Specialization

7.2.1.1.1. CRIMINAL LAW

Since most of the legal practitioners have a common specialization in criminal law in their early stages of careers, the proportion of specialization in this area is in the majority. As shown in Figure 7.2, 92% of LACs in the North East Zone, 87% of LACs in the North Zone, 80% of LACs in the Central Zone, 77% of LACs in the West Zone, 74% of LACs in the East Zone, and 61% of LACs in the South Zone have specialization in the area of criminal law.

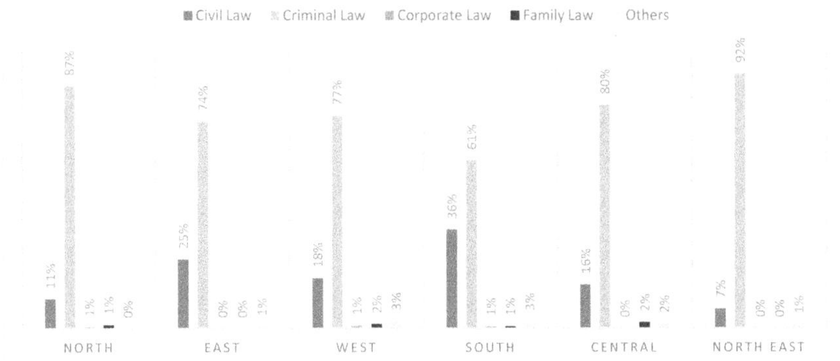

Figure 7.2 Zonal Analysis of LACs' Area of Specialization

7.2.1.1.2. CIVIL LAW

The specialization in civil law among the LACs happens to be lower than in criminal law. In Figure 7.2, around 36% of LACs in the South Zone, 25% of LACs in the East Zone, 18% of LACs in the West Zone, 16% of LACs in the Central Zone, 11% of LACs in the North Zone, and 7% of LACs in the North East Zone have specialization in civil law.

7.2.1.1.3. CORPORATE LAW

Since the cases pertaining to corporate law are very rare to land as a legal aid case, the specialization in this area falls short. As shown in Figure 7.2, a meager 1% of LACs in the North Zone, West Zone, and South Zone responded that they have specialization in corporate law.

7.2.1.1.4. FAMILY LAW

In terms of specialization in family law, the percentage of LACs happens to be lower than required. As shown in Figure 7.2, around 2% of LACs in the Central Zone and West Zone and 1% of LACs in the South Zone responded that they specialize in family law.

7.2.2. Empanelment of LACs in Different Panels

This section covers the empanelment of LACs into different panels present at their DLSA. As shown in Figure 7.3, around 36% of LACs are empaneled in criminal courts, 32.7% of LACs are empaneled in both criminal and civil courts, and around 15.9% of LACs are empaneled in criminal courts.

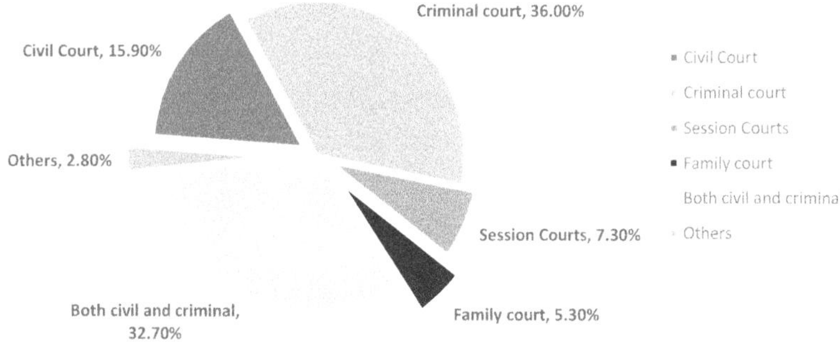

Figure 7.3 Empanelment of LACs in Different Panels

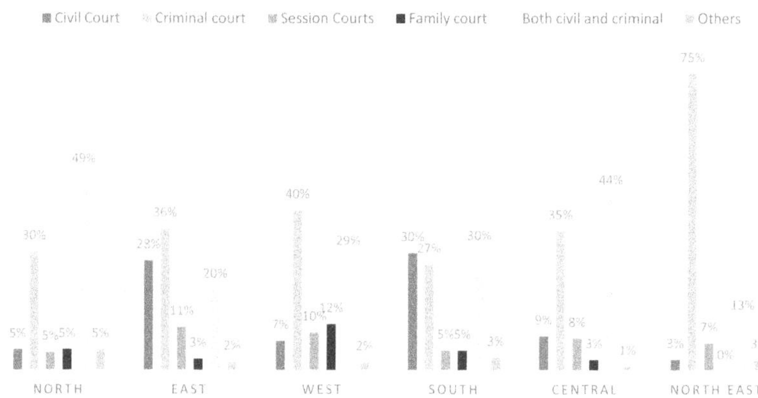

Figure 7.4 Zonal Analysis of Empanelment of LACs in Different Panels

Similarly, 7.3% of LACs are empaneled in sessions courts, and 5.3% of LACs are empaneled in family courts.

7.2.2.1. *Zonal Analysis of Empanelment of LACs in Different Panels*

7.2.2.1.1. CRIMINAL COURTS

In Figure 7.4, we see that 75% of LACs in the North East Zone, 40% of LACs in the West Zone, 36% of LACs in the East Zone, 35% of LACs in the Central Zone, 30% of LACs in the North Zone, and 27% of LACs in the South Zone are empaneled in criminal courts.

7.2.2.1.2. BOTH CRIMINAL AND CIVIL COURTS

A few LACs are empaneled in both civil and criminal courts. As shown in Figure 7.4, around 49% of LACs in the North Zone, 44% of LACs in the Central Zone, 30% of LACs in the South Zone, 29% of LACs in the West Zone, and 20% of LACs in the East Zone are empaneled in both criminal and civil courts.

7.2.2.1.3. CIVIL COURTS

The percentage of LACs empanelment in civil courts remains low when compared to criminal court. As shown in Figure 7.4, 30% of LACs in the South Zone, 28% of LACs in the East Zone, 9% of LACs in the Central Zone, 7% of LACs in the West Zone, 5% of LACs in the North Zone, and 3% of LACs in the North East Zone are empaneled in civil courts.

7.2.2.1.4. SESSIONS COURTS

The share of LACs in sessions courts was also very low. As shown in Figure 7.4, 11% of LACs in the East Zone, 10% of LACs in the West Zone, 8% of LACs in the Central Zone, 7% of LACs in the North East Zone, and 5% of LACs in the North Zone are empaneled in sessions courts.

7.2.2.1.5. FAMILY COURTS

The empanelment of LACs in family courts stands low in all the zones. Around 12% of LACs in the West Zone, 5% of LACs in the North and Zone, and 3% of LACs in the Central and East Zone are empaneled in family courts.

7.2.3. Duration of Association as LACs With FLAS

The empanelment of LACs takes place over the cycle of three years. A few LACs continue to be panel lawyers in the subsequent cycle. The duration of association of a panel lawyer as an LAC in the LAS reflects the experience of the LAC in general in handling legal aid cases. As shown in Figure 7.5, 40.9% of LACs responded that they have been associated with FLAS for around one to three years. Further, 26.4% of LACs said that they have been associated with FLAS as LACs for four to six years. Around 12.2% of LACs have been associated with FLAS for seven to nine years, whereas 20.5% of LACs have been associated with FLAS for more than nine years.

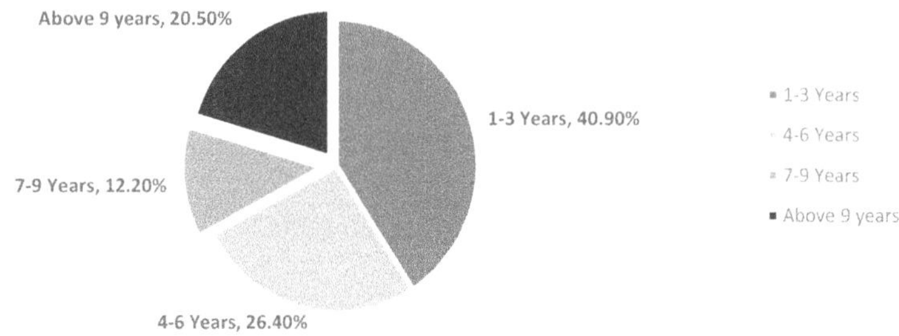

Figure 7.5 Duration of Association as LACs With FLAS

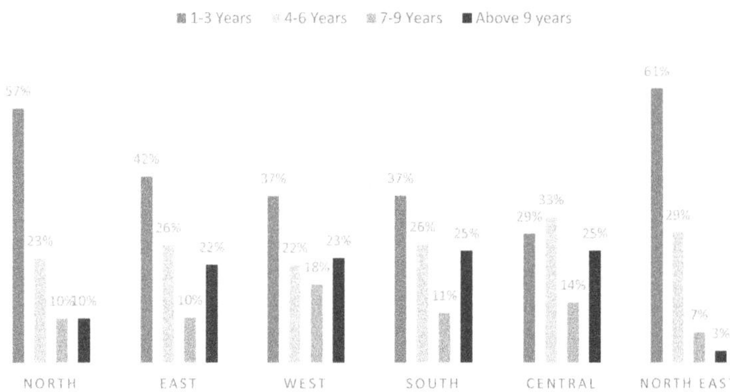

Figure 7.6 Zonal Analysis of Duration of Association as LACs With FLAS

7.2.3.1. *Zonal Analysis of Duration of Association as LACs With FLAS*

7.2.3.1. ONE TO THREE YEARS

LACs in most of the zones have been associated with FLAS for around one to three years. As shown in Figure 7.6, 61% of LACs in the North East Zone, 57% of LACs in the North Zone, 42% of LACs in the East Zone, 37% of LACs in the West and South Zone, and 33% of LACs in the Central Zone responded that they have been associated with FLAS from one to three years.

7.2.3.2. FOUR TO SIX YEARS

Some of the LACs in all the zones have been associated with FLAS for around four to six years. In Figure 7.6, we see that 33% of LACs in the

Central Zoe, 29% of LACs in the North East Zone, 26% of LACs in the East and South Zone, 23% of LACs in the North Zone, and 22% of LACs in the West Zone responded that their association as LACs with FLAS is from four to six years.

7.2.3.3. SEVEN TO NINE YEARS

A few LACs responded that they have been associated with FLAS for the past seven to nine years. In Figure 7.6, around 18% of LACs in the West Zone, 14% of LACs in the Central Zone, and 11% of LACs in the South Zone have been associated with FLAS for the past seven to nine years.

7.2.3.4. MORE THAN NINE YEARS

A considerate percentage of LACs in each zone has been associated with FLAS for more than nine years. As shown in Figure 5.6, around 25% of LACs in the Central and South Zone, 23% of LACs in the West Zone, 22% of LACs in the East Zone, 10% of LACs in the North Zone, and 3% of LACs in the North East Zone have been associated with FLAS for more than nine years.

7.2.4. Nature of Engagement of the LACs With FLAS

Under the Indian LAS, panel lawyers are not bounded by any law to leave their private practice matter while pursuing to serve as LACs at the DLSA. However, the nature of their engagement with FLAS highlights their level of commitment towards the services under FLAS in India. As shown in Figure 7.7, 63% of LACs responded that their engagement with FLAS is part-time, whereas only 25.6% of LACs affirmed that they are engaged with FLAS on a full-time basis. Further, around 5.8% of LACs said their engagement with FLAS is on ad hoc basis. Therefore, most LACs consider FLAS as part-time work, which entails less commitment and devotion.

7.2.4.1. Zonal Analysis of Nature of Engagement of the LACs With FLAS

7.2.4.1.1. PART-TIME ENGAGEMENT

In most of the zones, LACs affirmed that their engagement with FLAS is part-time. One of the reasons that LACs prefer to be engaged with FLAS on a part-time basis is that it gives them some extra money in the form of an honorarium. Another reason for their part-time engagement is low honorarium amount. As shown in Figure 7.8, 71% of LACs in the East Zone, 70% of LACs in the South Zone, 63% of LACs in the North and West Zones,

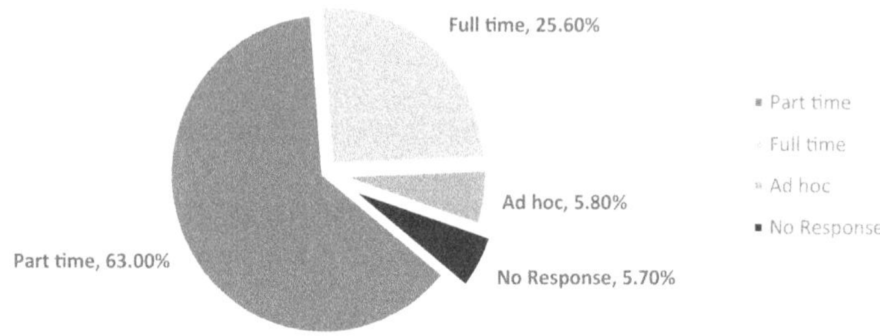

Figure 7.7 Nature of Engagement of the LACs With FLAS

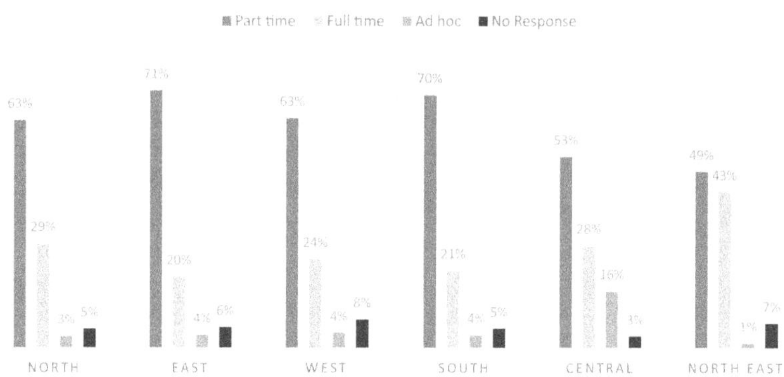

Figure 7.8 Zonal Analysis of Nature of Engagement of the LACs With FLAS

53% of LACs in the Central Zone, and 49% of LACs in the North East Zone responded that their engagement with FLAS is on a part-time basis.

7.2.4.1.2. FULL-TIME ENGAGEMENT

A few LACs across the zones responded that their engagement with FLAS is full-time. As shown in Figure 7.8, around 43% of LACs in the North East Zone, 29% of LACs in the North Zone, 28% of LACs in the Central Zone, 24% of LACs in the West Zone, 21% of LACs in the South Zone, and 20%

of LACs in the East Zone responded that their engagement with FLAS is full-time.

7.2.4.1.3. AD HOC

LACs in some zones also reported that they are engaged with FLAS on an ad hoc basis. As shown in Figure 7.8, around 4% of LACs in the East Zone, West Zone, and South Zone stated their engagement with FLAS is ad hoc. Similarly, 3% of LACs in the North Zone and Central Zone and 1% of LACs in the North East Zone responded that their engagement with FLAS is on an ad hoc basis.

7.2.5. Time Spent by LACs on Legal Aid Services per Week

In the previous chapters on beneficiaries, regulators, and judicial officers comes an impression that LACs do not spend an ample amount of time on legal aid services. This section and the succeeding section deal primarily with the time LACs spend on legal aid services and private practice matters. As shown in Figure 7.9, 36.6% of LACs spend around two to five hours on legal aid services per week. On the other hand, 23.1% of LACs spend an average of ten to fifteen hours per week on legal aid services. Moreover, 19.3% of LACs spend around six to nine hours on services related to legal aid, and another 13.5% of LACs responded that they spend more than fifteen hours on legal aid services per week.

7.2.5.1. Zonal Analysis of Time Spent by LACs on Legal Aid Services per Week

7.2.5.1.1. TWO TO FIVE HOURS

In almost every zone, most of the LACs tend to spend around two to five hours on legal aid services. As shown in Figure 7.10, 49% of LACs in the

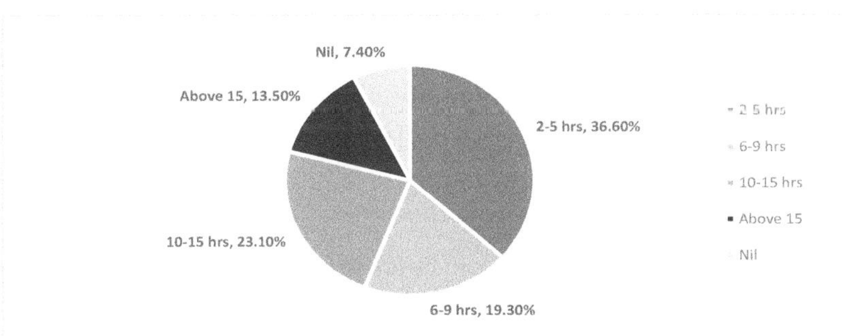

Figure 7.9 Time Spent by LACs on Legal Aid Services per Week

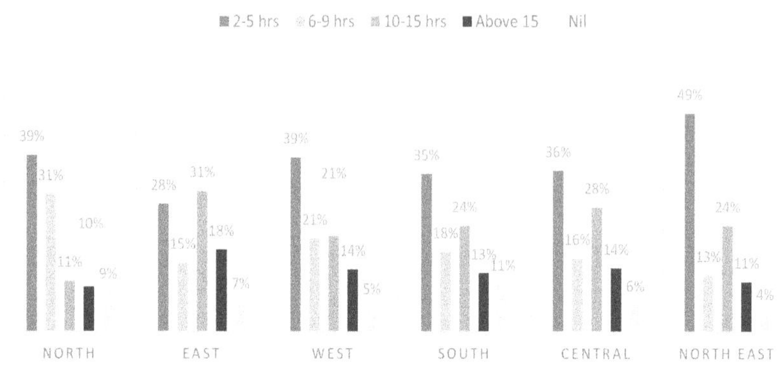

Figure 7.10 Zonal Analysis of Time Spent by LACs on Legal Aid Services per Week

North East Zone, 39% of LACs in the North Zone and West Zone, 36% of LACs in the Central Zone, 35% of LACs in the South Zone, and 28% of LACs in the East Zone responded that they spend around two to five hours on legal aid services per week.

7.2.5.1.2. SIX TO NINE HOURS

In Figure 7.10, we see that around 31% of LACs in the North Zone, 21% of LACs in the West Zone, 18% of LACs in the South Zone, 16% of LACs in the Central Zone, 15% of LACs in the East Zone, and 13% of LACs in the North East Zone responded that they spend around six to nine hours on legal aid services per week.

7.2.5.1.3. TEN TO FIFTEEN HOURS

A few LACs also spend ten to fifteen hours on legal aid services. As shown in Figure 7.10, 31% of LACs in the East Zone, 28% of LACs in the Central Zone, 24% of LACs in the South and North East Zones, and 21% of LACs in the West Zone spend around ten to fifteen hours per week on legal aid services.

7.2.5.1.4. ABOVE FIFTEEN HOURS

Some LACs devote more than fifteen hours per week to legal aid services. As shown in Figure 7.10, 18% of LACs in the East Zone, 14% of LACs each in the West and Central Zones, 13% of LACs in the South Zone, and 10% of LACs in the North Zone responded that they spend more than fifteen hours per week on legal aid services.

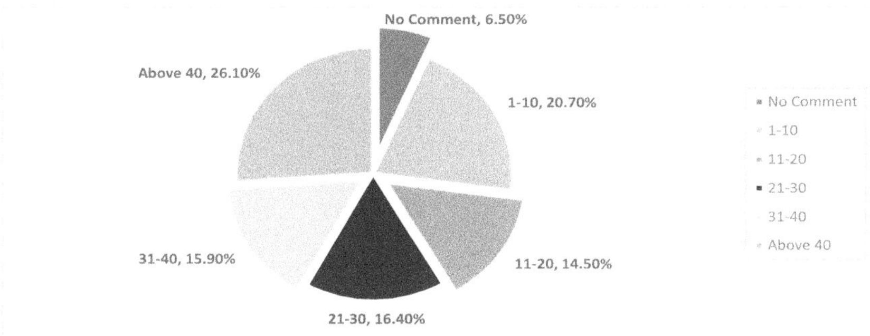

Figure 7.11 Time Spent by LACs on Private Practice per Week

7.2.6. Time Spent by LACs on Private Practice

As stated earlier, LACs are not bound to cease their private practice while they serve as panel lawyers. They are free to pursue private practice. Figure 7.11 shows the average time spent by LACs on their private practice per week. As shown in Figure 7.11, 26.1% of LACs spend above 40 hours per week on private practice, whereas 20.7% of LACs spend around 1 to 10 hours on their private practice per week. Further, around 16.4% of LACs responded that they spend 21 to 30 hours per week on private practice. Moreover, around 15.9% of LACs were vocal enough to affirm that they spend 31 to 40 hours per week on private practice. Comparing this to the average time spent by LACs on legal aid service cases per week, it reflects the quality of legal aid received by the beneficiaries and the attitude of the LACs towards the system.

7.2.6.1. Zonal Analysis of Time Spent by LACs on Private Practice

7.2.6.1.1. 1 TO 10 HOURS

In terms of hours spent in private practice, as shown in Figure 7.12, around 39% of LACs in the North East Zone, 23% of LACs in the North Zone, and 20% of LACs in the Central Zone responded that they spend around 1 to 10 hours on their private practice per week. Similarly, 19% of LACs in the West and South Zones and 15% of LACs in the East Zone said that they spend around 1 to 10 hours per week on private practice.

7.2.6.1.2. 11 TO 20 HOURS

Some of the LACs in the six zones responded that they spend 11 to 20 hours per week in their private practice. As shown in Figure 7.12, 20% of LACs

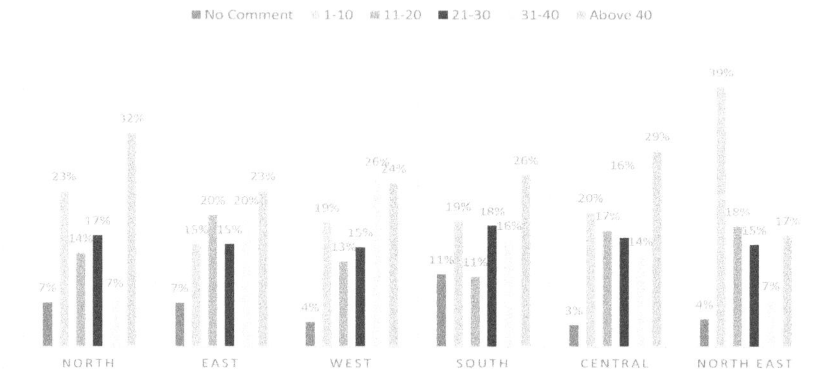

Figure 7.12 Zonal Analysis of Time Spent by LACs on Private Practice per Week

in the East Zone, 18% of LACs in the North East Zone, and 17% of LACs in the Central Zone stated that they spend around 11 to 20 hours per week on their private practice. Further, 14% of LACs in the North Zone, 13% of LACs in the West Zone, and 11% of LACs in the South Zone also replied that they spend around 11 to 20 hours on their private practice.

7.2.6.1.3. 21 TO 30 HOURS

In Figure 7.12, we see that around 18% of LACs in the South Zone, 17% of LACs in the North Zone, 16% of LACs in the Central Zone, and 15% of LACs in the East, West, and North East Zones responded that they spend around 21 to 30 hours on their private practice.

7.2.6.1.4. 31 TO 40 HOURS

A few LACs work in their private practice for around 31 to 40 hours per week. As shown in Figure 7.12, 26% of LACs in the West Zone, 20% of LACs in the East Zone, 16% of LACs in the South Zone, and 14% of LACs in the Central Zone responded that they worked on their private practice matters for 31 to 40 hours per week. Further, 7% of LACs in the North Zone and North East Zone also spend 31 to 40 hours per week on their private practice.

7.2.6.1.5. ABOVE 40 HOURS

Around 32% of LACs in the North Zone, 29% of LACs in the Central Zone, 26% of LACs in the South Zone, and 24% of LACs in the West Zone

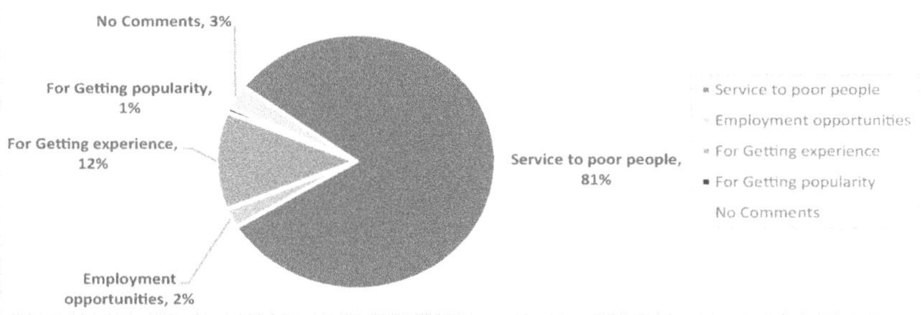

Figure 7.13 LACs' Motives for Joining the Legal Aid Services

responded that they spend more than 40 hours per week on private practice. Similarly, around 23% of LACs in the East Zone and 17% of LACs in the North East Zone spend more than 40 hours per week on their private practice.

7.2.7. LACs' Motives for Joining the Legal Aid Services

This section covers LACs' motives for joining the legal aid services. As shown in Figure 7.13, around 81% of LACs responded that they joined the legal aid services to serve poor people. Another 12% of LACs joined the legal aid services to get experience in practice. Further, 2% of LACs joined the legal aid services for employment opportunities, while only 1% of LACs joined to be popular.

7.2.7.1. LACs' Motives for Joining the Legal Aid Services

7.2.7.1.1. SERVICE TO PEOPLE

In almost every zone, LACs said that they joined the legal aid services to serve the poor people. As shown in Figure 7.14, 87% of LACs in the West Zone, 86% of LACs in the East Zone, 81% of LACs in the North Zone, 79% of LACs in the South and Central Zones, and 74% of LACs in the North East Zone gave service to poor as the motive join the legal aid services.

7.2.7.1.2. EMPLOYMENT OPPORTUNITIES

A few LACs also cited that they joined legal aid services for employment opportunities. In Figure 7.14, we see that around 4% of LACs in the North East and Central Zones, 3% of LACs in the West Zone, 2% of LACs in the

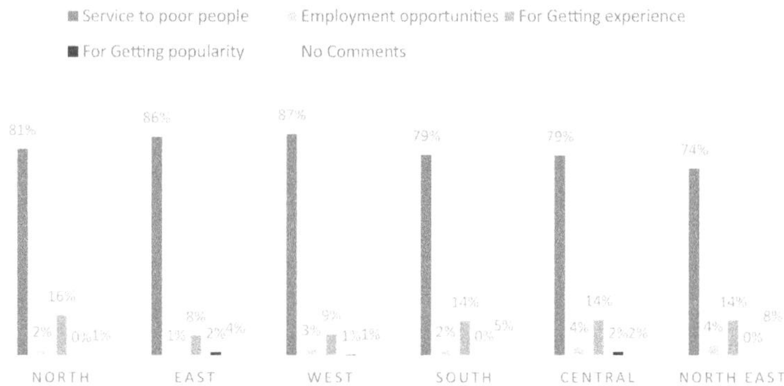

Figure 7.14 Zonal Analysis of LACs' Motives for Joining the Legal Aid Services

North and South Zones, and 1% of LACs in the East Zone said that they joined legal aid services for employment opportunities.

7.2.7.1.3. FOR GETTING EXPERIENCE

Another set of LACs, as shown in Figure 7.14, joined the legal aid services to get some experience. Around 16% of LACs in the North Zone, 9% of LACs in the West Zone, 8% of LACs in the East Zone, and 14% of LACs in the South, Central, and North East Zones responded that their motive for joining the legal aid services was to get experience.

7.2.7.1.4. FOR GETTING POPULAR

LACs also joined the legal aid services to gain popularity in the district courts. As shown in Figure 7.14, 2% of LACs in the East Zone and Central Zone and 1% of LACs in the North Zone joined the legal aid services to be popular in the district court.

7.2.8. Whether LACs Received Training at the Time of Joining Services by the LSA

Figure 7.15 consolidates data collected on whether LACs, after joining the services, received any kind of rejuvenation or induction training or not. Out of the total respondents, 40.32% of LACs received training to deal with FLAS cases, 52.5% of LACs did not receive any training at the time of joining FLAS, and 7.1% of LACs did not answer the question.

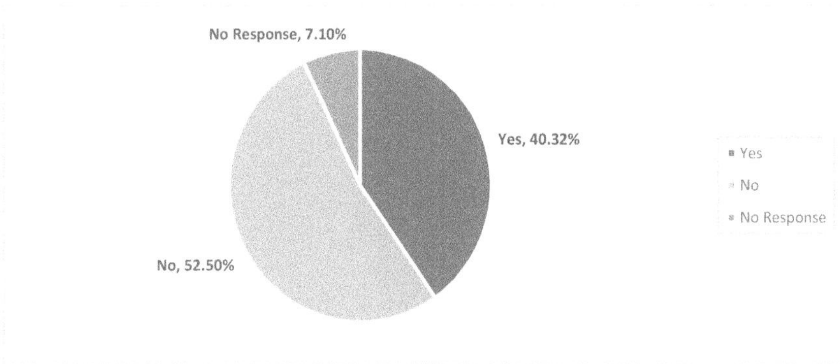

Figure 7.15 Whether LACs Received Training at the Time of Joining Services by the LSA

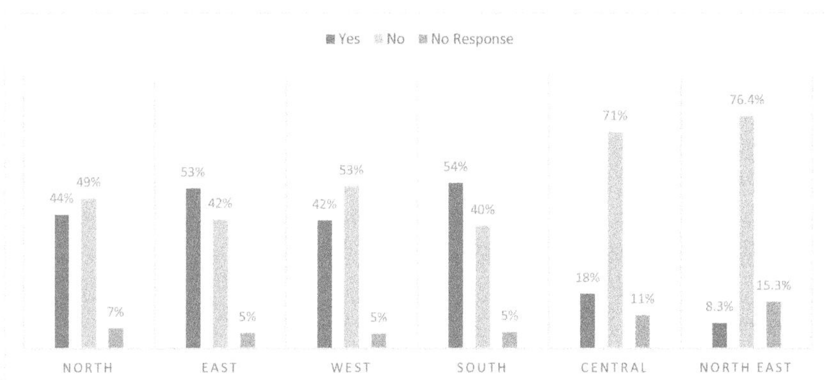

Figure 7.16 Zonal Analysis of Whether LACs Received Training at the Time of Joining Services by the LSA

7.2.8.1. *Zonal Analysis of Whether LACs Received Training at the Time of Joining Services by the LSA*

7.2.8.1.1. YES

As shown in Figure 7.16, 54% of LACs in the South Zone, 53% of LACs in the East Zone, 44% of LACs in the North Zone, and 42% of LACs in the West Zone affirmed that they did receive training at the time of joining the legal aid services by the DLSA. Similarly, 18% of LACs in the Central Zone and 8.3% of LACs in the North East Zone responded that they did receive training at the time of joining the legal aid services.

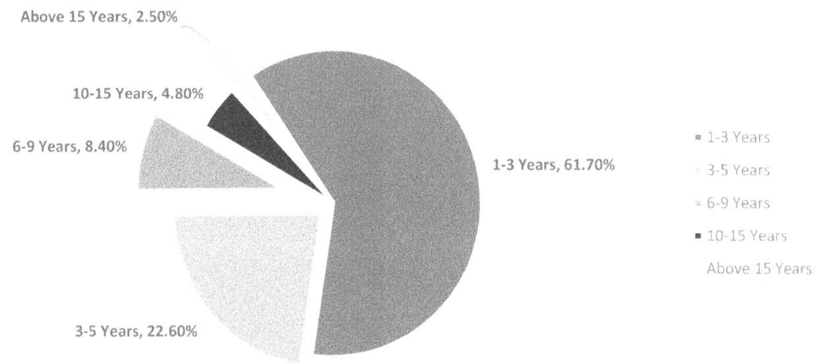

Figure 7.17 Duration of Legal Aid Cases for Trial in Civil Cases

7.2.8.1.2. NO

Some LACs in every zone denied that they received any such training at the time of joining the services by the DLSA. As shown in Figure 7.16, around 76.4% of LACs in the North East Zone, 71% of LACs in the Central Zone, 53% of LACs in the West Zone, 49% of LACs in the North Zone, and 42% of LACs in the East Zone responded that they did not receive any training at the time of joining the legal aid services by the DLSA.

7.2.9. Duration of Legal Aid Cases for Trial in Civil Cases

Figure 7.17 shows the average duration of the civil trials under FLAS. Out of the total respondents in the universe of the research, 61.7% of LACs responded that it takes one to three years to conclude a civil trial under FLAS. Further, 22.6% of LACs said that it takes around three to five years to conclude a trial in civil cases under FLAS. Similarly, 8.4% of LACs said that it takes six to nine years to conclude civil cases under FLAS, 4.8% of LACs said that it takes ten to fifteen years, and 2.5% of LACs said that it takes more than fifteen years.

7.2.9.1. Zonal Analysis of Duration of Cases for Trial in Civil Cases

7.2.9.1.1. ONE TO THREE YEARS

As shown in Figure 7.18, around 72% of LACs in the North East Zone, 65% of LACs in the North Zone, 62% of LACs in the South Zone, 60%

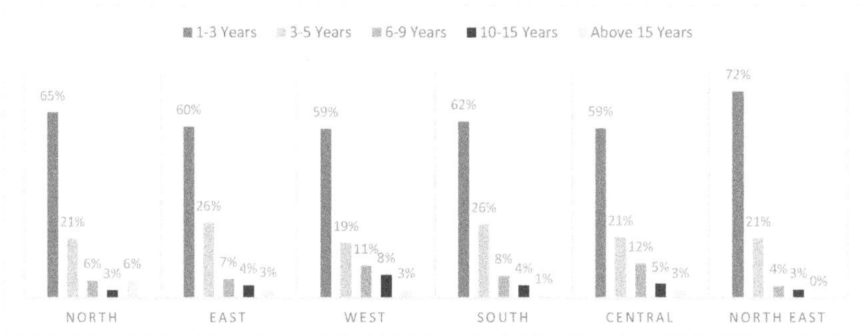

Figure 7.18 Zonal Analysis of Duration of Cases for Trial in Civil Cases

of LACs in the East Zone, and 59% of LACs in the West Zone and Central Zone responded that it takes around one to three years to conclude a trial in a civil case under FLAS.

7.2.9.1.2. THREE TO FIVE YEARS

Another set of LACs opined that it takes around three to five years to conclude a trial in a civil case under FLAS. As shown in Figure 7.18, around 26% of LACs in the East and South Zones, 19% of LACs in the West Zone, and 21% of LACs in the North, Central, and North East Zones responded that it takes around three to five years to conclude a trial in a civil case under FLAS.

7.2.9.1.3. SIX TO NINE YEARS

A few LACs stated that it takes around six to nine years to conclude a trial for a civil case under FLAS. As shown in Figure 7.18, 12% of LACs in the Central Zone, 11% of LACs in the West Zone, 8% of LACs in the South Zone, 7% of LACs in the East Zone, 6% of LACs in the North Zone, and 4% of LACs in the North East Zone said that it takes six to nine years to conclude a trial in a civil case under FLAS.

7.2.9.1.4. TEN TO FIFTEEN YEARS

LACs in almost all zones also responded that it takes ten to fifteen years to conclude trial in a civil case under FLAS. Around 8% of LACs in the West Zone, 5% of LACs in the Central Zone, 4% of LACs in the East and South Zones, and 3% of LACs in the North and North East Zones responded that it takes ten to fifteen years to conclude a trial in a civil case under FLAS.

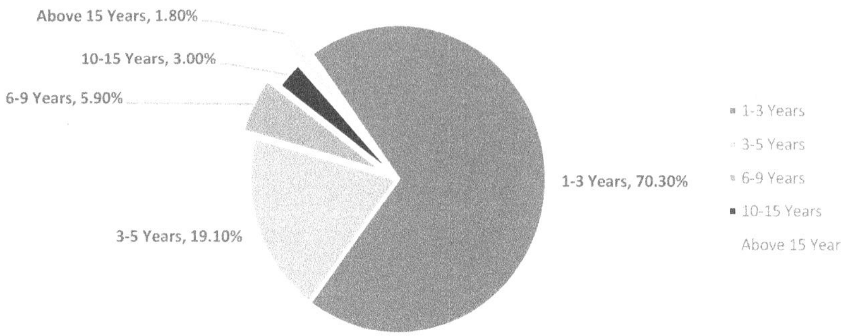

Figure 7.19 Duration of Cases for Trial in Criminal Cases

7.2.9.1.5. ABOVE FIFTEEN YEARS

Surprisingly, around 6% of LACs in the North Zone, 1% of LACs in the South Zone, and 3% of LACs in the East, West, and Central Zones stated that it takes more than fifteen years to conclude a trial in a civil case under FLAS.

7.2.10. Duration of Cases for Trial in Criminal Cases

After asking LACs about the time taken to conclude a trial in a civil case under FLAS, the questionnaire focuses on the average duration of time taken to conclude a trial in a criminal case under FLAS. Figure 7.19 demonstrates the time taken to conclude a trial in a criminal case under FLAS. Around 70.3% of criminal cases concluded in one to three years, 19.1% of criminal cases ended in three to five years, 5.9% of criminal cases took six to nine years to conclude, 3% of criminal cases ended in ten to fifteen years, and 1.8% of criminal cases took more than fifteen years to conclude.

7.2.10.1. Zonal Analysis of Duration of Cases for Trial in Criminal Cases

7.2.10.1.1. ONE TO THREE YEARS

LACs in almost every zone responded that it takes around one to three years to conclude a criminal case under FLAS. As shown in Figure 7.20, 79% of LACs in the South Zone, 74% of LACs in the East Zone, 68% of LACs in the Central Zone, 65% of LACs in the West Zone and North Zone, and 60% of LACs in the North East Zone responded that it takes one to three years to conclude a criminal case under FLAS.

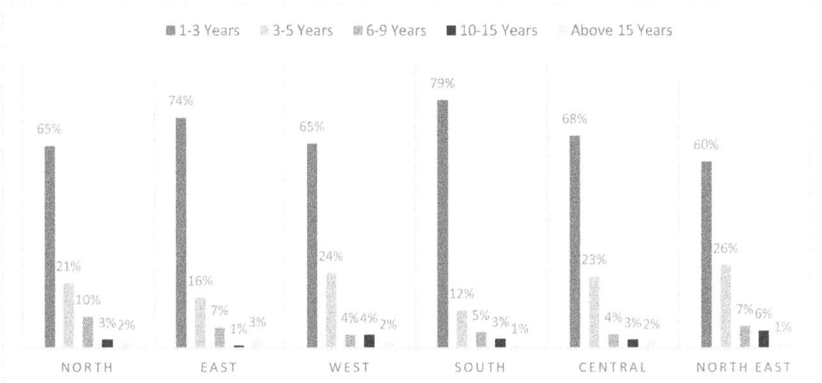

Figure 7.20 Zonal Analysis of Duration of Cases for Trial in Criminal Cases

7.2.10.1.2. THREE TO FIVE YEARS

Few LACs opined that it takes around three to five years to conclude a criminal case under FLAS. As shown in Figure 7.20, 26% of LACs in the North East Zone, 24% of LACs in the West Zone, and 23% of LACs in the South Zone responded that it takes around three to five years to conclude a criminal case under FLAS.

7.2.10.1.3. SIX TO NINE YEARS

In Figure 7.20, we see that around 10% of LACs in the North Zone, 7% of LACs in the East Zone and North East Zone, 5% of LACs in the South Zone, and 4% of LACs in the West Zone and Central Zone told that it takes around six to nine years to conclude a criminal case under FLAS.

7.2.10.1.4. TEN TO FIFTEEN YEARS

As shown in Figure 7.20, some LACs in the North East Zone (6%), West Zone (4%), North Zone (3%), South Zone (3%), Central Zone (3%), and East Zone (1%) opined that it takes around ten to fifteen years to conclude a trial in a criminal case under FLAS.

7.2.10.1.5. ABOVE FIFTEEN YEARS

Around 3% of LACs in the East Zone and 2% of LACs in the North Zone, West Zone, and Central Zone responded that it takes more than fifteen years to conclude a criminal case under FLAS. Similarly, 1% of LACs in the South Zone and North East Zone also affirmed that it takes more than fifteen years to conclude a trial in a criminal case under FLAS.

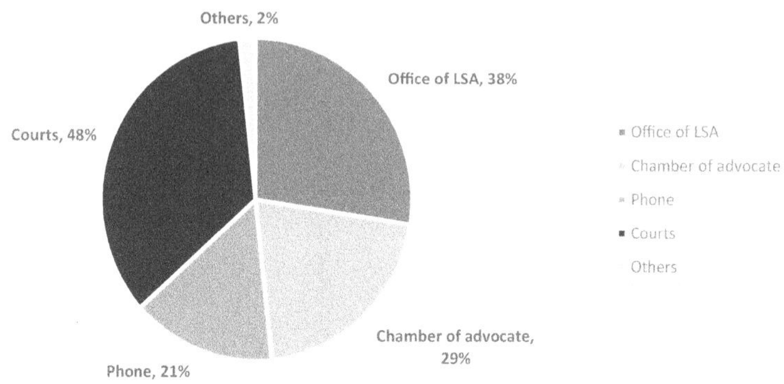

Figure 7.21 Place of LACs' Interaction With Beneficiaries*

*Multiple-response question. Percentages are based on respondents.

7.2.11. Place of LACs' Interaction with Beneficiaries

The places of LACs' interaction with their beneficiaries play a significant role in the proper delivery of services under FLAS. Often beneficiaries have complained about LACs not interacting with them properly. One of the reasons for not having quality interaction with LACs might be the lack of a proper place to interact. This section focuses on the places where the beneficiaries and LACs usually meet to discuss the cases. One can decipher that most meetings take place in the court premises or the chamber of the advocate. Figure 7.21 records the places of interaction between LACs and the beneficiaries to discuss FLAS cases. Of the total respondents in the universe, 38% of LACs interacted with the beneficiaries at the office of the LSA, 29% of LACs interacted in the chambers of the advocates, 21% of LACs interacted over the phone, 48% of LACs interacted in the court premises, and 2% of LACs used other places for interaction.

7.2.11.1. Zonal Analysis of Place of LACs' Interaction with Beneficiaries

7.2.11.1.1. OFFICE OF THE LSA

LACs, in general, do not have their own places where they can interact with legal aid beneficiaries. It is because, in most cases, LACs are early-career legal practitioners with a minimum of three years of experience. It is difficult for them to get their own chambers or place due to a lack of infrastructure. As shown in Figure 7.22, 55% of LACs in the South Zone, 52% of LACs in the East Zone, and 40% of LACs in the West Zone responded that they interacted with their legal aid beneficiaries at the office of the DLSA.

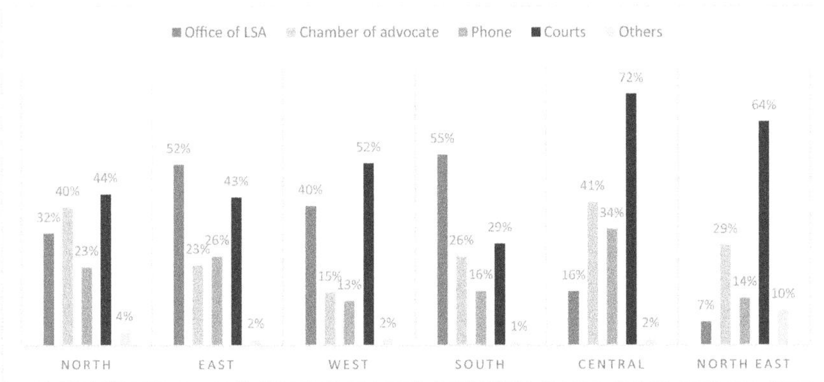

Figure 7.22 Zonal Analysis of Place of LACs' Interaction With Beneficiaries*
*Multiple-response question. Percentages are based on respondents.

Similarly, 32% of LACs in the North Zone, 16% of LACs in the Central Zone, and 7% of LACs in the North East Zone also stated that they interacted with their legal aid beneficiaries at the office of the DLSA.

7.2.11.1.2. CHAMBER OF ADVOCATES

LACs in a few zones agreed that they interacted with their legal aid beneficiaries at the chamber of the advocate. As shown in Figure 7.22, 41% of LACs in the Central Zone, 40% of LACs in the North Zone, 29% of LACs in the North East Zone, 26% of LACs in the South Zone, 23% of LACs in the East Zone, and 15% of LACs in the West Zone responded that interaction between them and legal aid beneficiaries often takes place at the chamber of the advocate.

7.2.11.1.3. PHONE

Since LACs are too preoccupied with their private practice or it is not possible for legal aid beneficiaries to attend court proceedings every time, LACs rely on telephonic conversation to interact with their legal aid beneficiaries. As shown in Figure 7.22, 34% of LACs in the Central Zone, 26% of LACs in the East Zone, 24% of LACs in the North Zone, 16% of LACs in the South Zone, 14% of LACs in the North East Zone, and 13% of LACs in the West Zone responded that they often interact with their LACs over the telephone.

7.2.11.1.4. COURTS

Most of the LACs interacted with their legal aid beneficiaries near the court premises. Since LACs are preoccupied with their private practice, it becomes

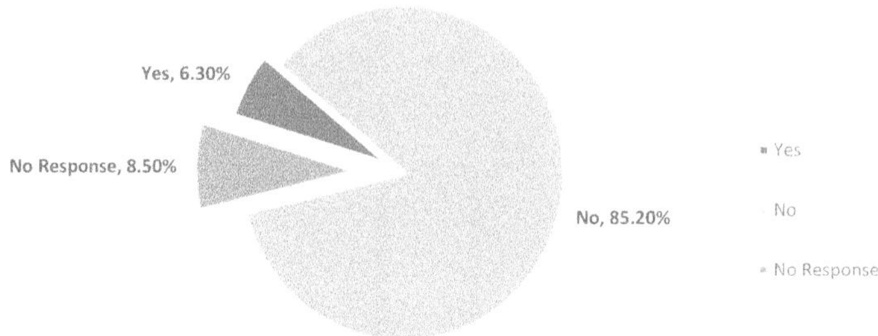

Figure 7.23 LACs Demanding Money From the Beneficiaries Under the LSA

hard for them to always interact with LACs in places like the office of the DLSA or chamber of advocates. LACs choose to interact with their clients near the court premises. As shown in Figure 7.22, 72% of LACs in the Central Zone, 62% of LACs in the North East Zone, 55% of LACs in the South and East Zones, 52% of LACs in the West Zone, and 44% of LACs in the North Zone responded that they interact with their beneficiaries near the court premises.

7.2.12. LACs Demanding Money From the Beneficiaries Under the LSA

There has always been blaming against LACs that to gain any sort of monetary benefits from the legal aid beneficiaries, they often demand money from them after or before the hearing of a legal aid case. This section focuses on a direct question asked to LACs on whether they demand money from legal aid beneficiaries or not. NALSA (Free and Competent Legal Services) Regulations, 2010, mandates that panel lawyers who have rendered their legal services to any beneficiary should not ask for any form of fee or remuneration.

As shown in Figure 7.23, 85.2% of LACs responded that they did not demand money from the beneficiaries under FLAS. Only 6.3% of LACs were honest enough to say that they did ask for money from legal aid beneficiaries, whereas 8.5% of LACs of refrained from responding to this question.

7.2.12.1. Zonal Analysis of LACs Demanding Money From the Beneficiaries Under the LSA

7.2.12.1.1. YES

As shown in Figure 7.24, around 9% of LACs in the South Zone, 7% of LACs in the West Zone and Central Zone, 6% of LACs in the North East

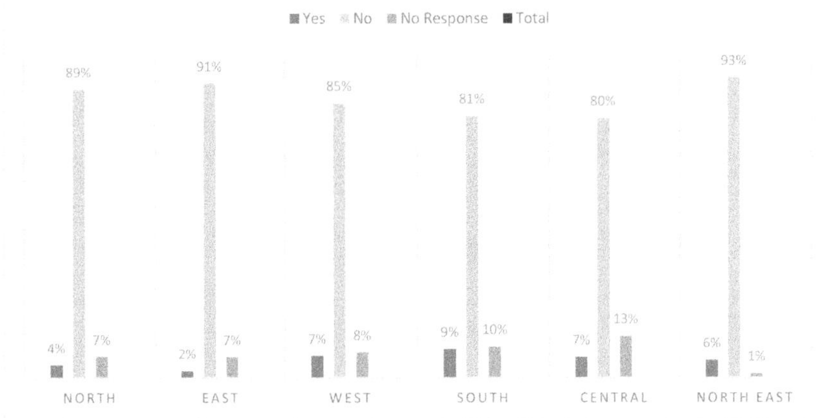

Figure 7.24 Zonal Analysis of LACs Demanding Money From the Beneficiaries Under the LSA

Zone, 4% of LACs in the North Zone, and 2% of LACs in the East Zone affirmed that they did demand money from their legal aid beneficiaries.

7.2.12.1.2. NO

Around 93% of LACs in the North East Zone, 91% of LACs in the East Zone, 89% of LACs in the North Zone, 85% of LACs in the West Zone, 81% of LACs in the South Zone, and 80% of LACs in the Central Zone denied that they demanded money from beneficiaries at any instant while rendering their legal services.

7.2.13. Difficulties Faced by LACs With Beneficiaries

LACs under the LAS of India also face difficulties while providing their services to beneficiaries of legal aid. In some cases, they do not receive their entitled honorarium on time, or they face issues pertaining to lack of infrastructure. Figure 7.25 covers all these difficulties faced by LACs in the six zones. The data shows that 19.7% of LACs responded that lack of infrastructure is one of the difficulties they face while interacting with beneficiaries. On the other hand, 23% of LACs responded that the quantum of honorarium was the problem, 5.8% of LACs of responded they are preoccupied with their private practices, 23.9% of LACs responded that the attitude of beneficiaries was the problem, 23.1% of LACs responded that absence of effective communication is one of the greatest difficulties, 7.3% of LACs responded that the attitude of the DLSA is the greatest difficulty, and 32.3% of LACs did not respond.

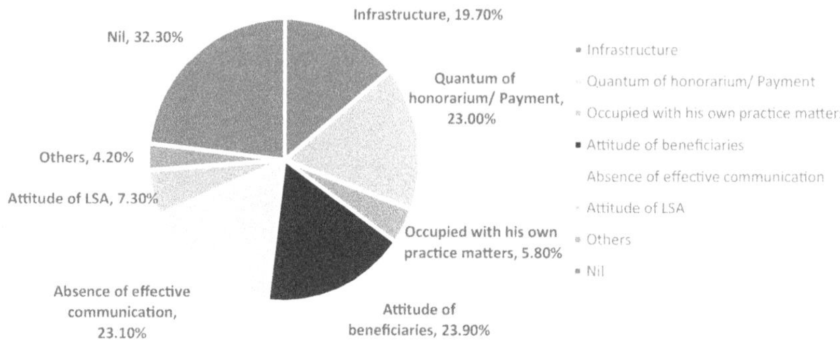

Figure 7.25 Difficulties Faced by LACs With Beneficiaries*

*Multiple-response question. Percentages are based on respondents.

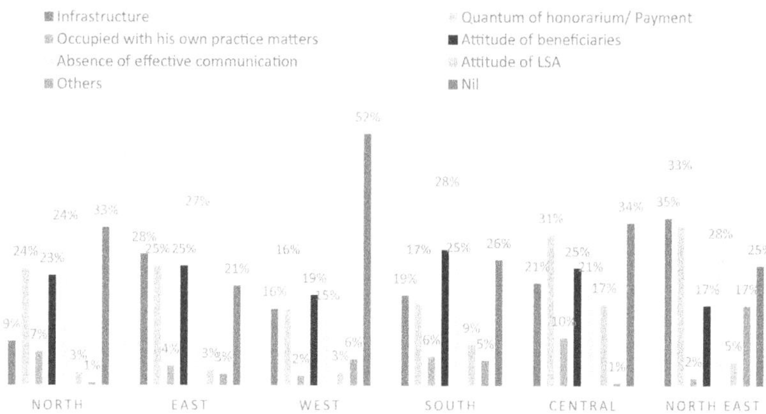

Figure 7.26 Zonal Analysis of Difficulties Faced by LACs With Beneficiaries*

*Multiple-response question. Percentages are based on respondents.

7.2.13.1. *Zonal Analysis of Difficulties Faced by LACs With Beneficiaries*

7.2.13.1.1. INFRASTRUCTURE

LACs in almost every zone faced difficulties due to a lack of infrastructure. These difficulties range from the unavailability of proper space at the DLSA to interact with the LACs to a lack of IT equipment to meet the daily photocopying or paper works. As shown in Figure 7.26, 35% of LACs in the North East Zone, 28% of LACs in the East Zone, 21% of LACs in the Central Zone, 19% of LACs in the South Zone, 16% of LACs in the West Zone, and 9% of LACs in the North Zone responded that lack of proper infrastructure is one of the difficulties faced by them while interacting beneficiaries.

7.2.13.1.2. QUANTUM OF HONORARIUM

LACs also face difficulties because of the low quantum of honorarium for the legal aid services. Further, a few LACs were even vocal in responding informally that delay in receiving the honorarium is also an issue. As shown in Figure 7.26, 33% of LACs in the North East Zone, 31% of LACs in the Central Zone, 25% of LACs in the East Zone, 24% of LACs the North Zone, 17% of LACs in the South Zone, and 16% of LACs in the West Zone responded that they face difficulties with beneficiaries because of low and delayed honorarium for the legal aid.

7.2.13.1.3. BEING OCCUPIED WITH THEIR OWN PRIVATE PRACTICE

In Figure 7.26, around 10% of LACs in the Central Zone, 7% of LACs in the North Zone, 6% of LACs in the South Zone, 4% of LACs in the East Zone, and 2% of LACs in the West Zone and North East Zone responded that their preoccupation with their own private practice is one of the difficulties they face.

7.2.13.1.4. ATTITUDE OF BENEFICIARIES

LACs also faced difficulties due to the attitude shown by beneficiaries. At times, beneficiaries expect too much in the legal aid services, and they expect LACs to be available at their whim. As shown in Figure 7.26, 28% of LACs in the South Zone, 25% of LACs in the East and Central Zones, 23% of LACs in the North Zone, 19% of LACs in the West Zone, and 17% of LACs in the North East Zone responded that the attitude of beneficiaries is one of the issues faced by them while dealing with beneficiaries under FLAS.

7.2.13.1.5. ABSENCE OF EFFECTIVE COMMUNICATION

LACs suffer due to the absence of communication from beneficiaries. As shown in Figure 7.26, 28% of LACs in the North East Zone, 27% of LACs in the East Zone, 25% of LACs in the South Zone, 24% of LACs in the North Zone, and 21% of LACs in the Central Zone face difficulties due to the absence of effective communication with their beneficiaries.

7.2.13.1.6. ATTITUDE OF THE LSA

Some LACs often face difficulties from the office of the DLSA also. These difficulties revolve around not getting desired legal aid cases or delays in getting the honorarium. In Figure 7.26, around 17% of LACs in the Central Zone, 9% of LACs in the South Zone, 5% of LACs in the North East Zone, and 3% of LACs in the North, East, and West Zones responded that the attitude of beneficiaries is one of the difficulties they face while interacting with beneficiaries.

7.2.14. Level of Satisfaction With the Process of Payment of Honorarium by the LSA

As pointed out in the previous section, LACs also face difficulties due to the delay in getting the honorarium. Figure 7.28 consolidates the data collected from LACs regarding their level of satisfaction with the process of payment of honorariums. As shown in Figure 7.27, 34.9% of LACs were satisfied with the process of payment of honorarium by the DLSA. Further, 23.9% of LACs responded that the process of payment of honorarium is unsatisfactory. Around 5.6% of LACs marked the process as highly satisfactory, while another 10.4% of LACs marked the process as highly unsatisfactory. Moreover, 25.2% of LACs did not comment.

7.2.14.1. Zonal Analysis of Level of Satisfaction With the Process of Payment of Honorarium by the LSA

7.2.14.1.1. HIGHLY SATISFACTORY

In Figure 7.28, around 9% of LACs in the South Zone, 7% of LACs in the West Zone, 5% of LACs in the North Zone, and 4% of LACs in the Central

Figure 7.27 Level of Satisfaction With the Process of Payment of Honorarium by the LSA

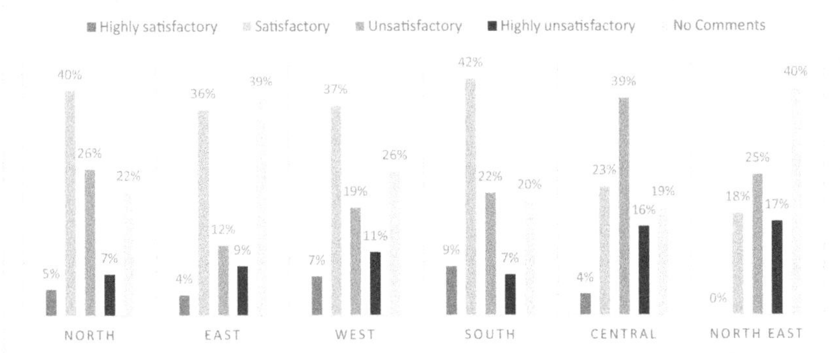

Figure 7.28 Zonal Analysis of Level of Satisfaction With the Process of Payment of Honorarium by the LSA

and East Zones responded that they are highly satisfied with the process of payment of honorarium by the DLSA.

7.2.14.1.2. SATISFACTORY

Most of the LACs marked the process of payment of honorarium by the DLSA as satisfactory. As shown in Figure 7.28, 42% of LACs in the South Zone, 40% of LACs in the North Zone, 37% of LACs in the West Zone, 36% of LACs in the East Zone, 23% of LACs in the Central Zone, and 18% of LACs in the North East Zone marked the process of payment of honorarium by the DLSA as satisfactory.

7.2.14.1.3. UNSATISFACTORY

A significant percentage of LACs were not satisfied with the process of payment of honorarium by the DLSA. As shown in Figure 7.28, 39% of LACs in the Central Zone, 26% of LACs in the North Zone, 25% of LACs in the North East Zone, 22% of LACs in the South Zone, 19% of LACs in the West Zone, and 12% of LACs in the East Zone responded that the process of payment of honorarium by the DLSA is unsatisfactory.

7.2.14.1.4. HIGHLY UNSATISFACTORY

Around 17% of LACs in the North East Zone, 16% of LACs in the Central Zone, 11% of LACs in the West Zone, 9% of LACs in the East Zone, and 7% of LACs in the North and South Zones marked the process of payment of honorarium by the DLSA as highly unsatisfactory.

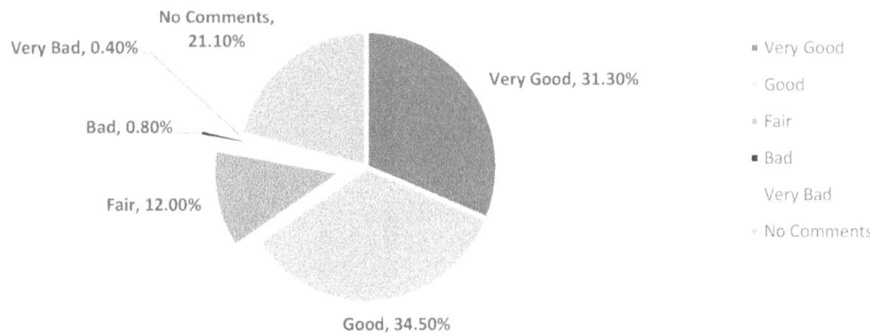

Figure 7.29 Quality of Arguments of LACs

7.2.15. Quality of Arguments of LACs

The questionnaire for LACs focuses on rating the skills that are essential in the profession. As shown in Figure 7.29, around 34.5% of LACs rated their quality of argument as good, whereas 31.3% of LACs rated their quality of arguments as very good. Only 12% of LACs rated their quality of arguments as fair.

7.2.15.1. Zonal Analysis of Quality of Arguments of LACs

7.2.15.1.1. VERY GOOD

In Figure 7.30, around 50% of LACs in the Central Zone, 43% of LACs in the North Zone, 36% of LACs in the East Zone, 25% of LACs in the West Zone and North East Zone, and 16% of LACs in the South Zone rated their quality of argument skills as very good.

7.2.15.1.2. GOOD

LACs rated their quality of arguments skills as good also. As shown in Figure 7.30, around 40% of LACs in the South Zone, 38% of LACs in the East Zone, 35% of LACs in the Central Zone, 33% of LACs in the North East Zone, and 28% of LACs in the North Zone rated their quality of argument skills as good.

7.2.15.1.3. FAIR

A very few LACs also rated their argument skills as fair. As shown in Figure 7.30, 18% of LACs in the North East Zone, 16% of LACs in the South Zone, 11% of LACs in the North Zone, 10% of LACs in the West Zone,

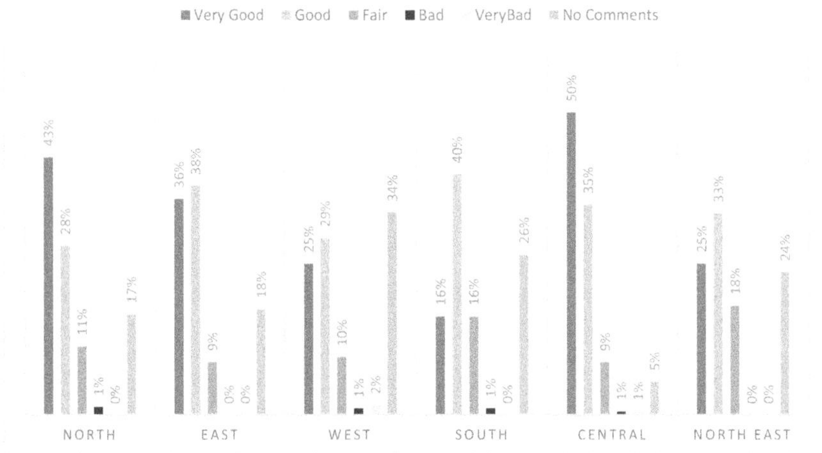

Figure 7.30 Zonal Analysis of Quality of Arguments of LACs

and 9% of LACs in the East Zone and Central Zone responded that they have fair quality of argument skills.

7.2.15.1.4. BAD

A very small percentage of LACs rated their argument skills as bad. As shown in Figure 7.30, only 1% of LACs in the North, West, South, and Central Zones rated the quality of their argument skills as bad.

7.2.15.1.5. VERY BAD

Only 2% of LACs in the West Zone and 1% of LACs in the Central Zone rated the quality of their argument skills as very bad.

7.2.15.1.6. NO COMMENTS

As shown in Figure 7.30, around 34% of LACs in the West Zone, 26% of LACs in the South Zone, 24% of LACs in the North East Zone, 18% of LACs in the East Zone, 17% of LACs in the North Zone refrained from rating their argument skills.

7.2.16. Quality of Presentation/Articulation of LACs

The LACs also rated the quality of their presentation or articulation skills. As shown in Figure 7.31, around 32.4% of LACs rated the quality of their presentation or articulation skills as good, while 29.3% of LACs rated the

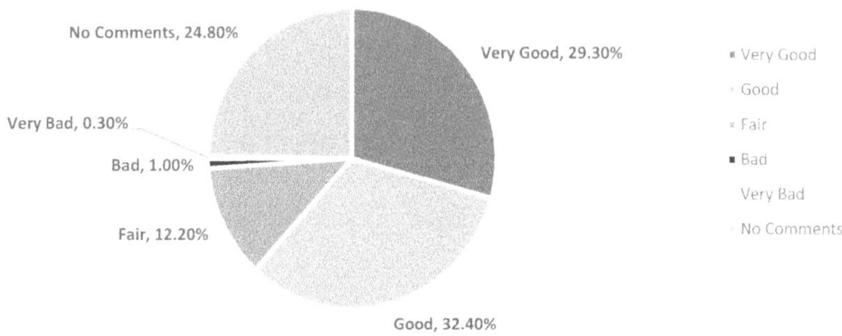

Figure 7.31 Quality of Presentation/Articulation of LACs

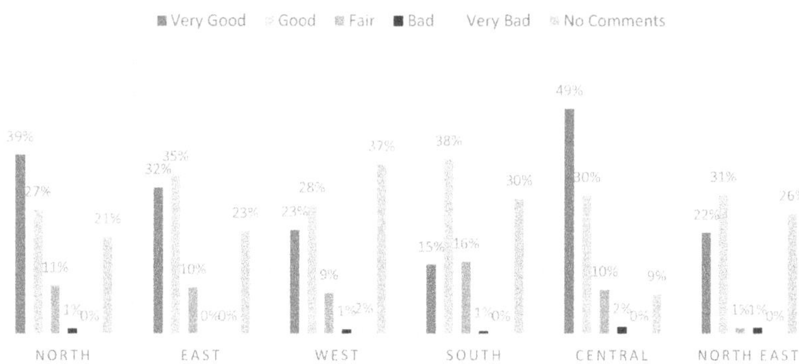

Figure 7.32 Zonal Analysis of Quality of Presentation/Articulation of LACs

quality of their presentation or articulation skills as very good. Further, 12.2% of LACs rated the quality of their articulation or presentation skills as fair. Only 1% of LACs rated the quality of their presentation or articulation skills as bad. Moreover, around 24.8% of LACs did not rate the quality of their presentation or articulation skills.

7.2.16.1. *Zonal Analysis of Quality of Presentation/Articulation of LACs*

7.2.161.1. VERY GOOD

Figure 7.32 demonstrates that 49% of LACs in the Central Zone, 39% of LACs in the North Zone, 32% of LACs in the East Zone, 23% of LACs in the

West Zone, 22% of LACs in the North East Zone, and 15% of LACs in the South Zone rated the quality of their presentation or articulation skills as good.

7.2.16.1.2. GOOD

As shown in Figure 7.32, 38% of LACs in the South Zone, 35% of LACs in the East Zone, 31% of LACs in the North East Zone, 30% of LACs in the Central Zone, 28% of LACs in the West Zone, and 27% of LACs in the North Zone rated the quality of their presentation or articulation skills as good.

7.2.16.1.3. FAIR

A few LACs in every zone rated the quality of their presentation or articulation as fair. As shown in Figure 7.32, 16% of LACs in the South Zone, 11% of LACs in the North Zone, 10% of LACs in the Central Zone and East Zone, and 1% of LACs in the North East Zone rated the quality of their presentation or articulation skills as fair.

7.2.16.1.4. BAD

Only 2% of LACs in the Central Zone and 1% of LACs in the North East Zone, South Zone, West Zone, and North Zone rated the quality of their presentation or articulation skills as bad.

7.2.16.1.5. NO COMMENTS

Around 37% of LACs in the West Zone, 30% of LACs in the South Zone, 26% of LACs in the North East Zone, 23% of LACs in the East Zone, 21% of LACs in the North Zone, and 9% of LACs in the Central Zone refrained from rating the quality of their presentation or articulation skill.

7.2.17. Quality of Drafting Skills of LACs

Figure 7.33 demonstrates the way LACs have rated their drafting skills. As shown, 31.4% of LACs rated the quality of their drafting skills as good, whereas 29.8% of LACs rated the quality of their drafting skills as very good. Another 12.8% of LACs rated the quality of their drafting skills as fair. Only 1.5% of LACs rated the quality of their drafting skills as bad. Further, around 24.3% of LACs did not rate the quality of their drafting skills.

7.2.17.1. Zonal Analysis of Quality of Drafting Skills of LACs

7.2.17.1.1. VERY GOOD

In Figure 7.34, around 47% of LACs in the Central Zone, 39% of LACs in the North Zone, 36% of LACs in the East Zone, 27% of LACs in the West

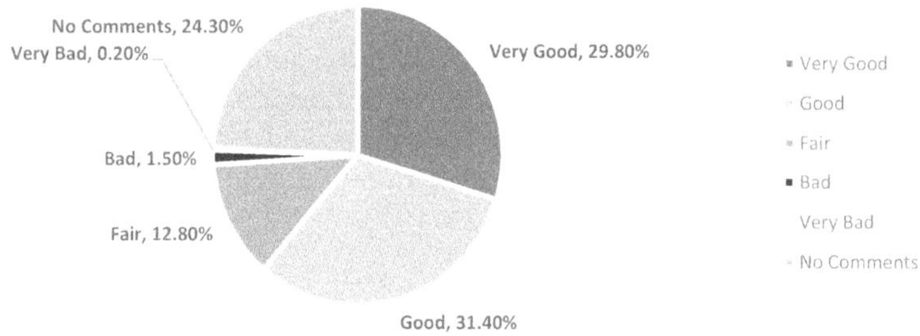

Figure 7.33 Quality of Drafting Skills of LACs

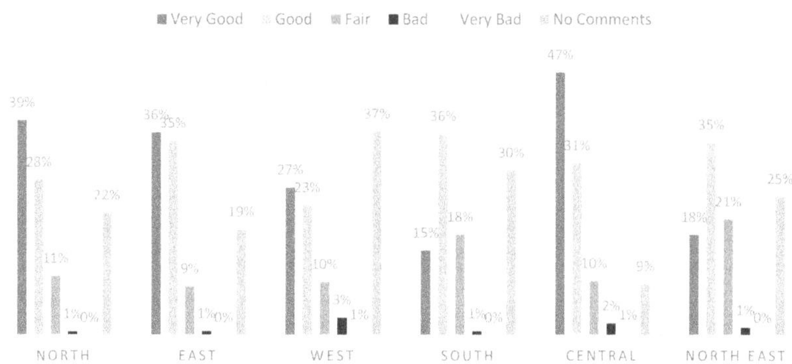

Figure 7.34 Zonal Analysis of Quality of Drafting Skills of LACs

Zone, 18% of LACs in the North East Zone, and 15% of LACs in the South Zone rated the quality of their drafting skills as very good.

7.2.17.1.2. GOOD

Most of the LACs rated the quality of their drafting skills as good. As shown in Figure 7.34, 36% of LACs in the South Zone, 35% of LACs in the East Zone and North East Zone, 31% of LACs in the Central Zone, 28% of LACs in the North Zone, and 23% of LACs in the West Zone rated the quality of their drafting skills as good.

7.2.17.1.3. FAIR

As shown in Figure 7.34, 21% of LACs in the North East Zone, 18% of LACs in the South Zone, 11% of LACs in the North Zone, 10% of LACs in the West Zone and Central Zone, and 9% of LACs in the East Zone rated the quality of their drafting skills as fair.

7.2.17.1.4. BAD

As shown in Figure 7.34, 3% of LACs in the West Zone, 2% of LACs in the Central Zone, and 1% of LACs in the North Zone, East Zone, and North East Zone rated the quality of their drafting skills as bad.

7.2.17.1.5. NO COMMENTS

A significant percentage of LACs did not rate the quality of their drafting skills. As shown in Figure 7.34, 37% of LACs in the West Zone, 30% of LACs in the South Zone, 25% of LACs in the North East Zone, 22% of LACs in the North Zone, 19% of LACs in the East Zone, and 9% of LACs in the Central Zone did not comment on the quality of their drafting skills.

7.2.18. Level of Self-Satisfaction Regarding Professional Skills Among LACs

Figure 7.35 demonstrates the level of self-satisfaction LACs have regarding their professional skills. Around 33.8% of LACs rated their professional skills as good, while 28.4% of LACs rated their professional skills as very good. Another 12.8% of LACs rated their professional skills as fair. Around 23.9% of LACs refrained from marking the quality of their professional skills. Only 0.6% of LACs rated their professional skills as bad, whereas 0.5% of LACs rated their professional skills as very bad.

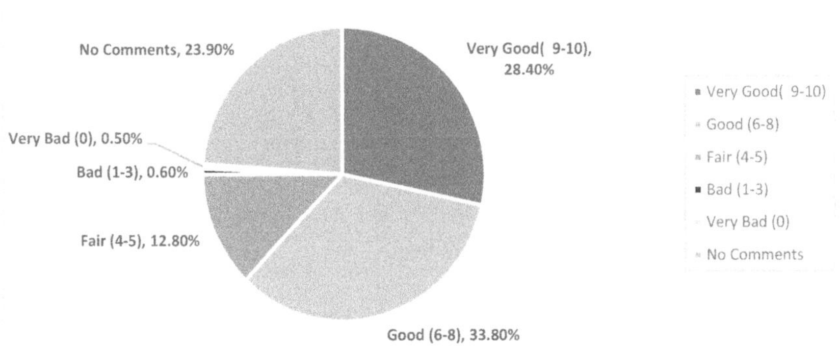

Figure 7.35 Level of Self-Satisfaction Regarding Professional Skills Among LACs

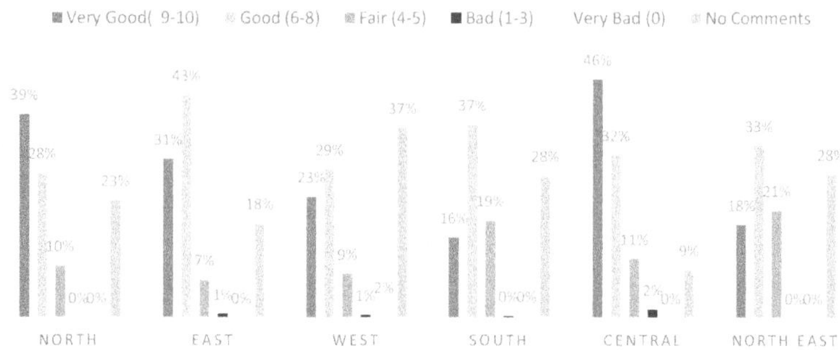

Figure 7.36 Zonal Analysis of Level of Self-Satisfaction Regarding Professional Skills Among LACs

7.2.18.1. *Zonal Analysis of Level of Self-Satisfaction Regarding Professional Skills Among LACs*

7.2.18.1.1. VERY GOOD

In Figure 7.36, 46% of LACs in the Central Zone, 39% of LACs in the North Zone, 31% of LACs in the East Zone, 23% of LACs in the West Zone, 18% of LACs in the North East Zone, and 16% of LACs in the South Zone rated their overall professional skills as very good.

7.2.18.1.2. GOOD

Most of the LACs also rate their overall professional skills as good. As shown in Figure 7.36, 43% of LACs in the East Zone, 37% of LACs in the South Zone, 33% of LACs in the North East Zone, 32% of LACs in the Central Zone, 29% of LACs in the West Zone, and 28% of LACs in the North Zone rated the quality of their professional skills as good.

7.2.18.1.3. FAIR

Around 21% of LACs in the North East Zone, 19% of LACs in the South Zone, 11% of LACs in the Central Zone, 10% of LACs in the North Zone, 9% of LACs in the West Zone, and 7% of LACs in the East Zone rated the quality of their professional skills as fair.

7.2.18.1.4. BAD AND VERY BAD

Only 2% of LACs in the Central Zone and 1% of LACs in the East Zone and West Zone rated their professional skills as bad. Further, only in the

West Zone, 2% of LACs rated the quality of their professional skills as very bad.

7.2.18.1.5. NO COMMENTS

Some LACs in the six zones refrained from rating their professional skills. As shown in Figure 7.36, 37% of LACs in the West Zone, 28% of LACs in the North East Zone and South Zone, 23% of LACs in the North Zone, 18% of LACs in the East Zone, and 9% of LACs in the Central Zone did not rate their professional skills.

7.2.19. Scrutiny/Review/Feedback of LACs' Legal Aid Services by the LSA or Beneficiaries

LACs come under the purview of the LSA Act, 1987, and NALSA (Free and Competent Legal Services) Regulations, 2010. Their performance and work are always under the review of the DLSA. The questionnaire also focused on the scrutinization of their work by the DLSA. In Figure 7.37, around 36.3% of LACs opined that the DLSA did perform peer review scrutiny of their services under legal aid. On the other hand, 41.1% of LACs denied any such scrutiny either by beneficiaries or the DLSA. Further, around 22.5% of LACs did not respond to this section.

7.2.19.1. Scrutiny/Review/Feedback of LACs' Legal Aid Services by the LSA or Beneficiaries

7.2.19.1.1. YES

As shown in Figure 7.38, 49% of LACs in the South Zone, 47% of LACs in the East Zone, 32% of LACs in the North Zone and West Zone, 28%

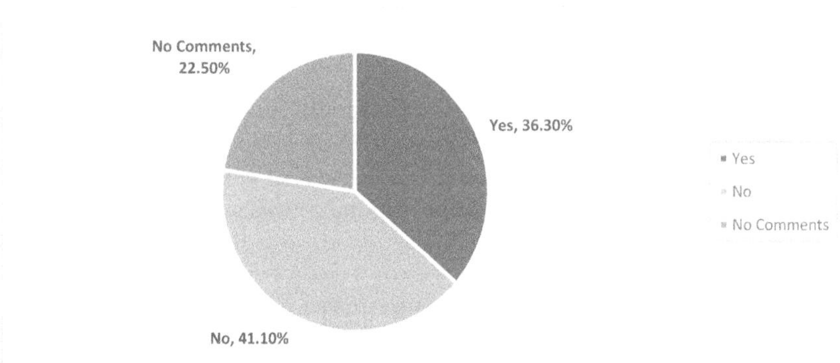

Figure 7.37 Scrutiny/Review/Feedback of LACs' Legal Aid Services by the LSA or Beneficiaries

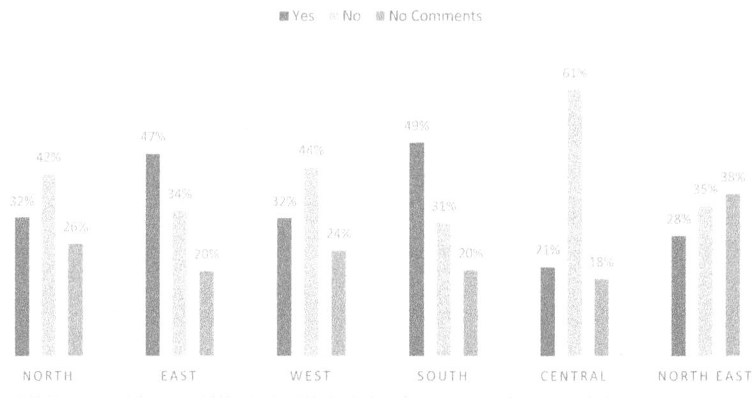

Figure 7.38 Zonal Analysis of Scrutiny/Review/Feedback of LACs' Legal Aid Services by the LSA or Beneficiaries

of LACs in the North East Zone, and 21% of LACs in the Central Zone affirmed that the DLSA or beneficiaries did scrutinize their services under legal aid.

7.2.19.1.2. NO

Around 61% of LACs in the Central Zone, 44% of LACs in the West Zone, 42% of LACs in the North Zone, 35% of LACs in the North East Zone, 34% of LACs in the East Zone, and 31% of LACs in the South Zone denied any such scrutiny on their services under legal aid by the DLSA or beneficiaries.

7.2.19.1.3. NO COMMENTS

A few LACs preferred not to answer this section. As shown in Figure 7.38, 38% of LACs in the North East Zone, 26% of LACs in the North Zone, 24% of LACs in the West, 20% of LACs in the East Zone and South Zone, and 18% of the Central Zone did not respond to this section.

7.2.20. LACs' View on Full-Time Tenure-Based Empanelment in the Legal Aid Services

Figure 7.39 analyzes LACs views on full-time tenure-based empanelment of panel lawyers. As shown, around 42.5% of LACs recommended a full-time tenure-based empanelment in the legal aid services, while 24.4% of LACs

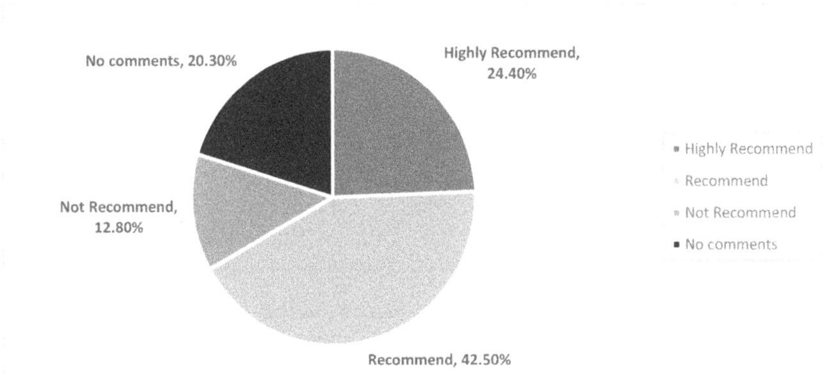

Figure 7.39 LACs' View on Full-Time Tenure-Based Empanelment in the Legal Aid Services

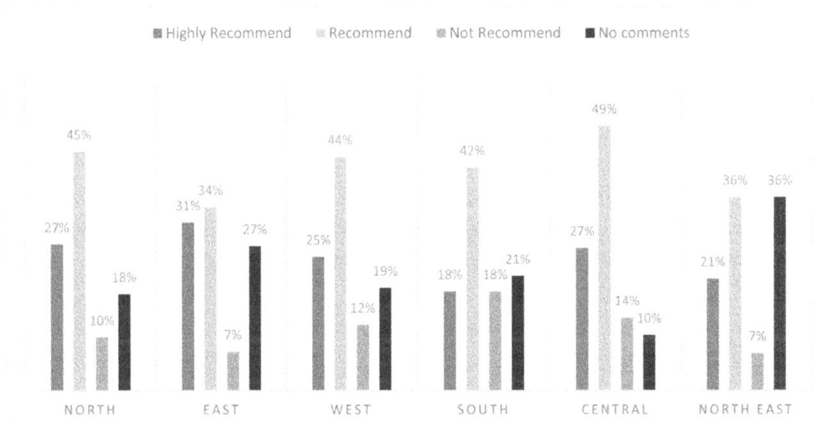

Figure 7.40 Zonal Analysis of LACs' View on Full-Time Tenure-Based Empanelment in the Legal Aid Services

highly recommended such a type of engagement. Further, around 12.8% of LACs did not recommend any such type of engagement.

7.2.20.1. *Zonal Analysis of LACs' View on Full-Time Tenure-Based Empanelment in the Legal Aid Services*

7.2.20.1.1. HIGHLY RECOMMENDED

As shown in Figure 7.40, around 31% of LACs in the East Zone, 27% of LACs in the North Zone and Central Zone, 25% of LACs in the West Zone, 21%

of LACs in the North East Zone, and 18% of LACs in the South Zone highly recommended full-time tenure-based empanelment in the legal aid services.

7.2.20.1.2. RECOMMENDED

LACs in most of the zones were vocal about full-time tenure-based empanelment. As shown in Figure 7.40, around 49% of LACs in the Central Zone, 45% of LACs in the North Zone, 44% of LACs in the West Zone, 42% of LACs in the South Zone, 36% of LACs in the North East Zone, and 34% of LACs in the East Zone recommended a full-time empanelment.

7.2.20.1.3. NOT RECOMMENDED

Only 18% of LACs in the South Zone, 14% of LACs in the Central Zone, 12% of LACs in the West Zone, 10% of LACs in the North Zone, and 7% of LACs in the East Zone and North East Zone did not recommend a full-time tenure-based empanelment in the legal aid services. They were of the view that this type of engagement might hamper the monetary benefits in their private practice.

7.2.20.1.4. NO COMMENTS

A few LACs did not comment on this section of the questionnaire. As shown in Figure 7.40, 36% of LACs in the North East Zone, 27% of LACs in the East Zone, 21% of LACs in the South Zone, 19% of LACs in the West Zone, 18% of LACs in the North Zone, and 10% of LACs in the Central Zone did not comment on this section.

7.2.21. Suggestions to Solve the Problems Faced by LACs

The open-ended question on the suggestions to improve the legal aid services from the perspective of LACs furnishes varied ideas to solve the problems primarily faced by them. It becomes important to mention that in the open-ended question, the frequency of suggestions should not be a parameter. It is the suggestions that matter, not the number of times they were suggested. In Figure 7.41, around 55.2% of LACs did not even complete or respond to the open-ended question. However, a significant number of LACs, around 19.8% of LACs, responded that speedy payment and enhancement of the quantum of honorarium from the DLSA would make services better. Further, 9.1% of LACs opined that there is a need for quality infrastructure at the DLSA office. Another 7.6% of LACs suggested that more campaigns about awareness about the legal aid services should come into place. Around 7% of LACs even suggest that LACs should receive training before joining the legal aid services. A few LACs also suggest that fairness in empanelment and allotment of legal aid cases will improve the legal aid services. Moreover,

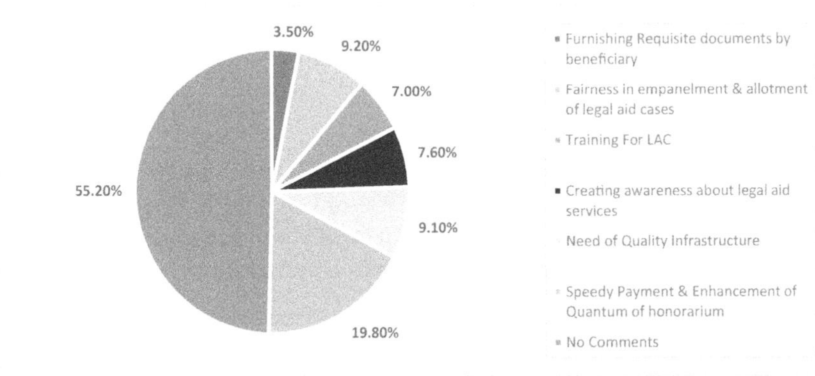

Figure 7.41 Suggestions to Solve the Problems Faced by LACs

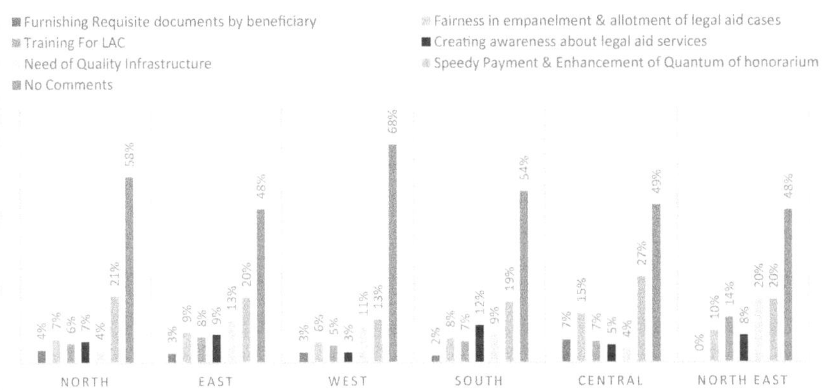

Figure 7.42 Zonal Analysis of Suggestions to Solve the Problems Faced by LACs

3.5% of LACs responded that timely furnishing of requisite documents related to beneficiaries would also improve the services.

7.2.21.1. *Zonal Analysis of Suggestions to Solve the Problems Faced by LACs*

7.2.21.1.1. SPEEDY PAYMENT AND ENHANCEMENT IN QUANTUM OF HONORARIUM

In Figure 7.42, around 27% of LACs in the Central Zone, 21% of LACs in the North Zone, 20% of LACs in the East Zone and North East Zone, 19%

of LACs in the South Zone, and 13% of LACs in the West Zone suggested speedy payment and enhancement in quantum of honorarium to improve the services.

7.2.21.1.2. NEED FOR QUALITY INFRASTRUCTURE

Around 20% of LACs in the North East Zone, 13% of LACs in the East Zone, 11% of LACs in the West Zone, 9% of LACs in the South Zone, and 4% of LACs in the North Zone and Central Zone suggested the need of quality infrastructure to improve the legal aid services.

7.2.21.1.3. CREATING AWARENESS ABOUT THE LEGAL AID SERVICES

Figure 7.42 also demonstrates that 12% of LACs in the South Zone, 9% of LACs in the East Zone, 8% of LACs in the North East Zone, 7% of LACs in the North Zone, 5% of LACs in the Central Zone, and 3% of LACs in the West Zone suggested creating awareness about the legal aid services.

7.2.21.1.4. TRAINING OF LACS

Another 14% of LACs in the North East Zone, 8% of LACs in the East Zone, 7% of LACs in the South Zone and Central Zone, 6% of LACs in the North Zone, and 5% of LACs in the West Zone suggested training LACs before making them join the legal aid services.

7.2.21.1.5. FAIRNESS IN EMPANELMENT AND ALLOTMENT OF LEGAL AID CASES

LACs also suggested fairness in empanelment and allotment of legal aid cases. As shown in Figure 7.42, 15% of LACs in the Central Zone, 10% of LACs in the North East Zone, 9% of LACs in the East Zone, 8% of LACs in the South Zone, 7% of LACs in the North Zone, and 6% of LACs in the West Zone suggested improving the legal aid services fairness in empanelment and allotment of legal aid cases.

7.2.21.1.6. FURNISHING REQUISITE DOCUMENTS BY BENEFICIARIES

As shown in Figure 7.42, a few LACs in the Central Zone (7%), North Zone (4%), East Zone (2%), West Zone (2%), and South Zone (1%) suggested timely furnishing of requisite documents by beneficiaries to improve the legal aid services.

8 Assessment of the Competence and Commitment of LACs

8.1. Introduction

The preceding chapters have discussed the perceptions of all the five stakeholders involved in delivering free legal aid under the ambit of the Legal Services Authorities Act, 1987. This chapter focuses on elaborating the hypothesis of this study. Therefore, this chapter does a zone-wise analysis of variables that play a crucial role in delivering quality legal aid services. To achieve the stated objectives, it is crucial to analyze all the parameters based on the data collected from the beneficiaries, judges, regulators, and LACs.

As stated earlier (see Chapter 1), the study aimed to promote and provide access to justice for the weaker sections of the society by evaluating the ambiguities omnipresent in the LAS in 18 states of India, spread over six geographical zones. Therefore, a comparative assessment to highlight the ambiguities cited and prompted by every stakeholder becomes necessary.

The assessment focuses on the amplitude of the services offered by LACs under the legal aid program. It primarily investigates the factors that might have shattered the trust of legal aid services' potential beneficiaries under the LSA Act, 1987.

8.2. A Comparative Assessment of Level of Professional Competence Skills of LACs

Professional skill set is the first parameter to test the hypothesis, reflecting upon the empaneled lawyers' competency in the legal aid services. This section comparatively analyzes the responses received from various stakeholders on the professional skills of LACs.

8.2.1. Quality of Arguments in Various Zones

Among the first skills that every lawyer should have is the ability to argue in favor of the client. As seen in Figure 8.1, around 44% (cumulative of "fair" [19%], "bad" [19%], and "very bad" [6%]) of the beneficiaries in

DOI: 10.4324/9781003158325-8

Table 8.1 Quality of Argument of LACs as Told by the Stakeholders in the North Zone

Respondents		*Very Good*	*Good*	*Fair*	*Bad*	*Very Bad*	*No Comments*	*Total*
Judicial Officers	Count	4	35	45	7	0	4	95
	% of Total	4%	37%	47%	7%	0%	4%	100%
LACs	Count	64	42	17	2	0	25	150
	% of Total	43%	28%	11%	1%	0%	17%	100%
Regulators	Count	0	4	3	1	0	0	8
	% of Total	0%	50%	38%	13%	0%	0%	100%
Beneficiaries	Count	73	104	106	102	30	130	545
	% of Total	13%	19%	19%	19%	6%	24%	100%

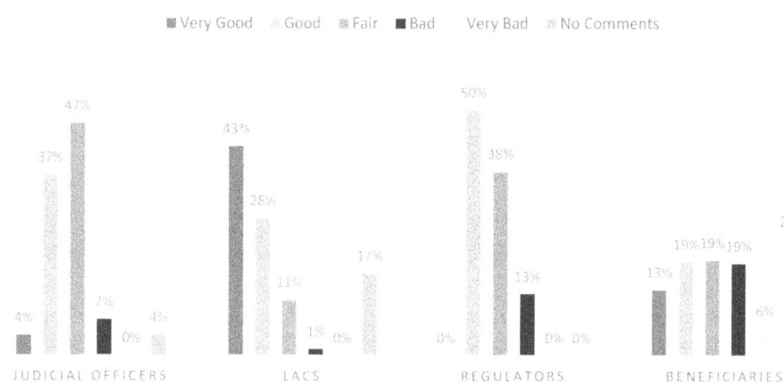

Figure 8.1 Quality of Argument of LACs as Told by the Stakeholders in the North Zone

the North Zone believed that the argument skills of LACs were moderately low level.

The beneficiaries' perception of the low quality of argument skills among LACs resonates with the responses received from the judicial officers: 54% (cumulative of "fair" [47%] and "bad" [7%]) of them responded that LACs have a moderately low level of argument skills.

However, regulators from the North Zone had a somewhat balanced opinion about the argument skills of LACs, as around 51% (cumulative of "fair" [38%] and "bad" [13%]) of them responded that LACs have a moderately low level of these skills, while another 50% believed LACs have

Table 8.2 Quality of Argument of LACs as Told by the Stakeholders in the East Zone

Respondents		*Very Good*	*Good*	*Fair*	*Bad*	*Very Bad*	*No Comments*	*Total*
Judicial Officers	Count	5	39	41	2	1	8	96
	% of Total	5%	41%	43%	2%	1%	8%	100%
LACs	Count	49	52	12	0	0	24	137
	% of Total	36%	38%	9%	0%	0%	18%	100%
Regulators	Count	0	0	3	0	0	2	5
	% of Total	0%	0%	60%	0%	0%	40%	100%
Beneficiaries	Count	76	221	100	62	23	38	520
	% of Total	15%	43%	19%	12%	4%	7%	100%

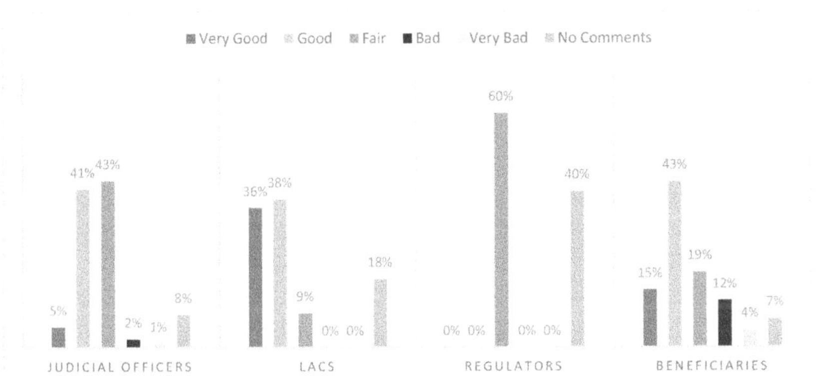

Figure 8.2 Quality of Argument of LACs as Told by the Stakeholders in the East Zone

fairly good argument skills. In congruence with this pattern, more than 70% (cumulative of "very good" [43%] and "good" [28%]) of LACs from the North Zone marked their argument skills as exceptional.

In the East Zone, as shown in Figure 8.2, 60% of regulators responded that LACs have a moderately low level of argument skills, while 40% of regulators refrained from commenting on the quality of this skill set. One of the reasons for not commenting on this skill set might be some hesitation among regulators, as they are too involved in formulating a group of empaneled lawyers. Moreover, in the East Zone, around 58% (cumulative of "very good" (15%) and "good" [43%]) of beneficiaries opined that their respective LACs possess a good quality of argument skills, while around 35% (cumulative of "fair" [19%], "bad" [12%], and "very bad" [4%]) of beneficiaries felt that LACs possess a moderately low level of argument skills.

The response from judicial officers in the East Zone was fairly balanced as around 46% (cumulative of "very good" [5%] and "good" [41%]) of judicial officers believed that LACs have a fair quality of argument skills. In contrast, a similar percentage of judicial officers, 46% (cumulative of "fair" [43%], "bad" [2%], and "very bad" [1%]), claimed that the argument skills of LACs were moderately low level. Therefore, in the East Zone, the quality of LACs' argument skills tends to be satisfactory because the level of argument skills from the perspective of judicial officers, regulators, and beneficiaries was above the moderate level.

As shown in Figure 8.3, 80% of regulators responded that LACs recruited or empaneled by them had fairly good argument skills in the West Zone. Also, 54% (cumulative of "very good" [25%] and "good" [29%]) of the LACs rated their argument skills as fairly good. There seems to be a correlation between LACs and regulators.

Regulators in most states are the secretary of the DLSA and, therefore, part of the empanelment process. Regulators in the West Zone marked the skill set of LACs way above the LACs did themselves.

However, beneficiaries' opinions and responses received from judicial officers do not fare well on the quality of argument skills by LACs. As shown, only 29% (cumulative of "very good" [5%] and "good" [24%]) of beneficiaries responded that the argument skills of LACs as fairly good. The findings indicate that 53% of beneficiaries refrained from commenting on

Table 8.3 Quality of Argument of LACs as Told by the Stakeholders in the West Zone

Respondents		*Very Good*	*Good*	*Fair*	*Bad*	*Very Bad*	*No Comments*	*Total*
Judicial Officers	Count	2	46	57	7	0	14	126
	% of Total	2%	37%	45%	6%	0%	11%	100%
LACs	Count	47	55	18	2	3	63	188
	% of Total	25%	29%	10%	1%	2%	34%	100%
Regulators	Count	0	4	1	0	0	0	5
	% of Total	0%	80%	20%	0%	0%	0%	100%
Beneficiaries	Count	22	106	43	15	20	231	437
	% of Total	5%	24%	10%	3%	5%	53%	100%

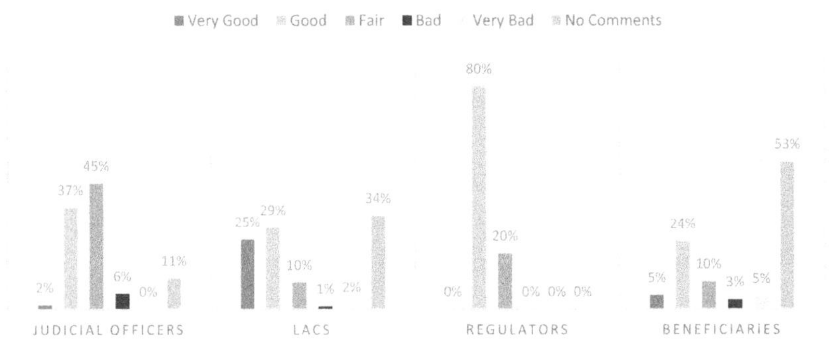

Figure 8.3 Quality of Argument of LACs as Told by the Stakeholders in the West Zone

the quality of argument by their respective LACs. Thus, the distrust among beneficiaries over the skills of LACs in terms of the quality of arguments came through their responses.

Further, around 51% (cumulative of "fair" [45%] and "bad" [6%]) of judicial officers were of the considerate opinion that LACs have a moderately low level of argument skills. Therefore, the evidence in the form of perceptions from all the stakeholders reflects the low quality of argument skills among LACs in the West Zone.

In the South Zone, as shown in Table 8.4, almost 50% of regulators responded that LACs have fairly good argument skills and a similar percentage of regulators (50%) said that LACs have a moderately low level of argument skills. Therefore, no conclusion can be drawn based on the perspectives of regulators.

Moreover, even 58% (cumulative of "very good" [21%] and "good" [37%]) of beneficiaries and 43% (cumulative of "very good" [1%] and "good" [42%]) of judicial officers in the South Zone were also of the opinion that LACs have a fairly good level of argument skills. The stakeholders' perceptions reflect that LACs in the South Zone have a fairly good level of argument skills.

In the Central Zone, as shown in Figure 8.5, 75% of regulators were of the concerned opinion that the quality of argument skills among LACs was moderately low level. Similarly, 58% (cumulative of "fair" [41%], "bad" [14%], and "very bad" [3%]) of judicial officers were also of the opinion that the skill set of LACs related to their argument skills was at a moderately low level.

Although 45% (cumulative of "very good" [13%] and "good" [32%]) of beneficiaries opined that LACs have a fairly good level of argument skills, it should be seen from the perspective of the percentage of beneficiaries

Table 8.4 Quality of Argument of LACs as Told by the Stakeholders in the South Zone

Respondents		*Very Good*	*Good*	*Fair*	*Bad*	*Very Bad*	*No Comments*	*Total*
Judicial Officers	Count	2	68	77	8	2	4	161
	% of Total	1%	42%	48%	5%	1%	2%	100%
LACs	Count	45	110	45	3	0	73	276
	% of Total	16%	40%	16%	1%	0%	26%	100%
Regulators	Count	0	4	4	0	0	0	8
	% of Total	0%	50%	50%	0%	0%	0%	100%
Beneficiaries	Count	181	323	175	50	13	124	866
	% of Total	21%	37%	20%	6%	2%	14%	100%

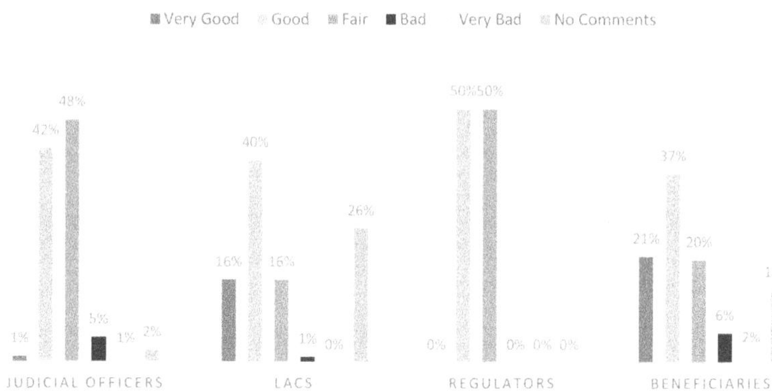

Figure 8.4 Quality of Argument of LACs as Told by the Stakeholders in the South Zone

responding to the quality of argument by LACs as moderately low and not commenting on it. Thus, according to stakeholders, in the Central Zone, LACs have a moderately low level of argument skills.

In a similar pattern, in the North East Zone, as shown in Figure 8.6, around 49% (cumulative of "fair" [36%], "bad" [11%], and "very bad" [2%]) of judicial officers opined that argument skills of LACs were of moderately low level/quality, while 46% (cumulative of "fair" [27%], "bad" [14%], and "very bad" [5%]) of beneficiaries also had the same opinion. Therefore, from judicial officers' and beneficiaries' perspectives, LACs in

Table 8.5 Quality of Argument of LACs as Told by the Stakeholders in the Central Zone

Respondents		*Very Good*	*Good*	*Fair*	*Bad*	*Very Bad*	*No Comments*	*Total*
Judicial officers	Count	4	28	35	12	3	4	86
	% of Total	5%	33%	41%	14%	3%	5%	100%
LACs	Count	92	64	16	1	1	10	184
	% of Total	50%	35%	9%	1%	1%	5%	100%
Regulators	Count	0	1	3	0	0	0	4
	% of Total	0%	25%	75%	0%	0%	0%	100%
Beneficiaries	Count	48	122	89	34	14	73	380
	% of Total	13%	32%	23%	9%	4%	19%	100%

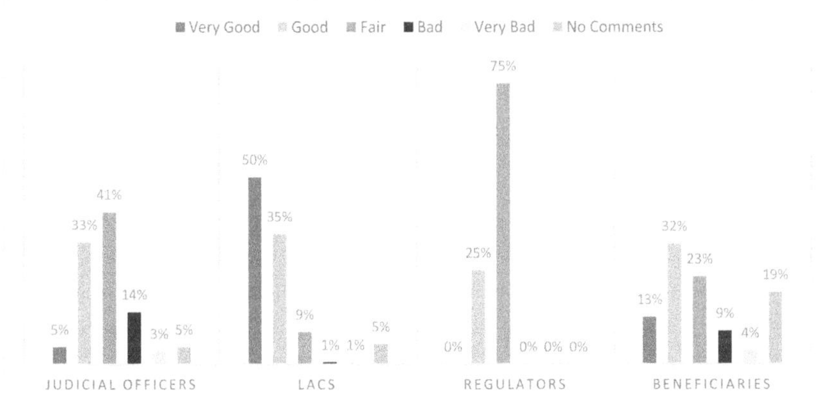

Figure 8.5 Quality of Argument of LACs as Told by the Stakeholders in the Central Zone

the North East Zone were not good in their argument skills. Surprisingly, 67% of regulators refrained from commenting on the argument skills of LACs, and the remaining 33% of regulators responded that LACs have moderately a low level of argument skills.

Contrary to the opinions of judicial officers, beneficiaries, and regulators, 58% (cumulative of "very good" [25%] and "good" [33%]) of LACs rated that they have fairly good argument skills, which does not support the opinion of any other stakeholders. Thus, LACs in the North East Zone also have a moderately low level of argument skills.

Table 8.6 Quality of Argument of LACs as Told by the Stakeholders in the North East Zone

Respondents		*Very Good*	*Good*	*Fair*	*Bad*	*Very Bad*	*No Comments*	*Total*
Judicial Officers	Count	1	16	16	5	1	6	45
	% of Total	2%	36%	36%	11%	2%	13%	100%
LACs	Count	18	24	13	0	0	17	72
	% of Total	25%	33%	18%	0%	0%	24%	100%
Regulators	Count	0	0	1	0	0	2	3
	% of Total	0%	0%	33%	0%	0%	67%	100%
Beneficiaries	Count	17	64	76	39	14	71	281
	% of Total	6%	23%	27%	14%	5%	25%	100%

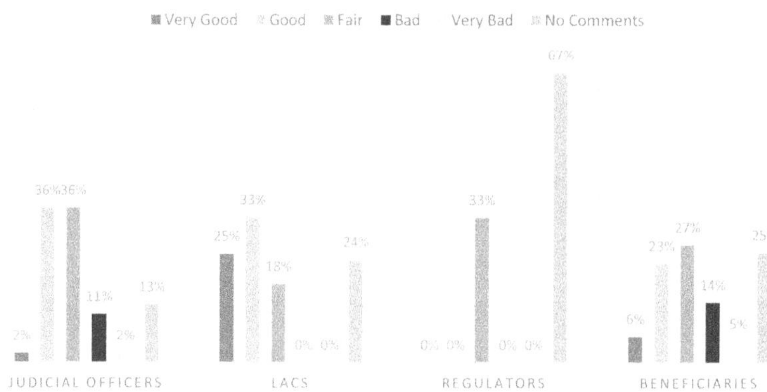

Figure 8.6 Quality of Argument of LACs as Told by the Stakeholders in the North East Zone

Apart from the West and South Zones, the argument skills of LACs were moderately low, as rated by judicial officers, regulators, and beneficiaries. Figure 8.7 shows the opinion of stakeholders from the six zones. It is essential to mention that the field investigators and the research associate, and the director also witnessed the proceedings in civil and criminal cases involving legal aid services. Therefore, the report also considers the quality of arguments raised before the judicial officers and appreciation or non-appreciation of the judicial officers' arguments.

Table 8.7 Quality of Argument of LACs as Told by the Stakeholders in the Six Zones

Respondents		*Very Good*	*Good*	*Fair*	*Bad*	*Very Bad*	*No Comments*	*Total*
Judicial Officers	Count	18	232	271	41	7	40	609
	% of Total	3%	38%	44%	7%	1%	7%	100%
LACs	Count	315	347	121	8	4	212	1007
	% of Total	31%	34%	12%	1%	0%	21%	100%
Regulators	Count	0	13	15	1	0	4	33
	% of Total	0%	39%	45%	3%	0%	12%	100%
Beneficiaries	Count	417	940	589	302	114	667	3,029
	% of Total	14%	31%	19%	10%	4%	22%	100%

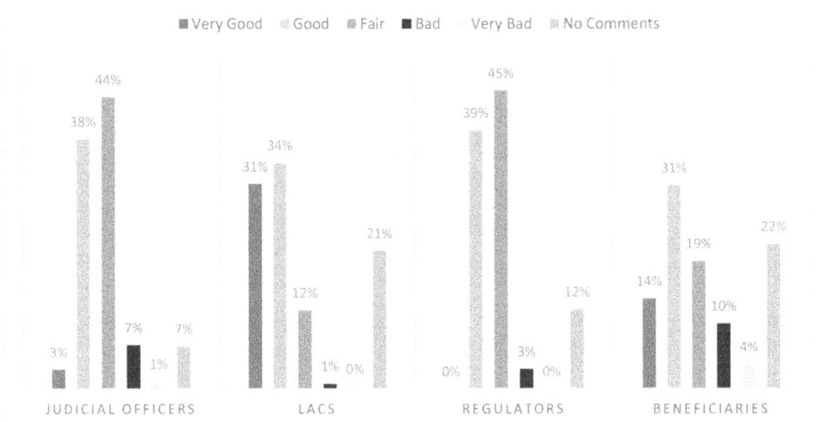

Figure 8.7 Quality of Argument of LACs as Told by the Stakeholders in the Six Zones

In all the six zones, it can be observed that 52% (cumulative of "fair" [44%], "bad" [7%], and "very bad" [1%]) of judicial officers, 48% (cumulative of "fair" [45%] and "bad" [3%]) of regulators, and 33% (cumulative of "fair" [19%], "bad" [10%], and "very bad" [4%]) of beneficiaries believed that argument skills of LACs were not up to the desired level and of moderately low quality. The opinion of fairly good argument skills by LACs stands doubtful as most stakeholders opined that the performance of LACs, in terms of argument skills, is of a moderately low level.

8.2.2. *Quality of Presentation Skills of LACs as Told by the Stakeholders*

Good articulation skills are another essential for an effective lawyer. Knowing when to put forth which argument during the trial can make an immense difference to the nature of the final judgment of any case. Therefore, the questionnaire distributed to the stakeholders also attempted to rate the quality of presentation/articulation skills of LACs.

As shown in Figure 8.8, around 59% (cumulative of "fair" [52%], "bad" [6%], and "very bad" [1%]) of judicial officers and 51% (cumulative of

Table 8.8 Quality of Presentation of LACs as Told by the Stakeholders in the North Zone

Respondents		*Very Good*	*Good*	*Fair*	*Bad*	*Very Bad*	*No Comments*	*Total*
Judicial Officers	Count	4	31	49	6	1	4	95
	% of Total	4%	33%	52%	6%	1%	4%	100%
LACs	Count	59	41	16	2	0	32	150
	% of Total	39%	27%	11%	1%	0%	21%	100%
Regulators	Count	0	3	3	1	0	1	8
	% of Total	0%	38%	38%	13%	0%	13%	100%
Beneficiaries	Count	68	101	107	100	34	135	545
	% of Total	12%	19%	20%	18%	6%	25%	100%

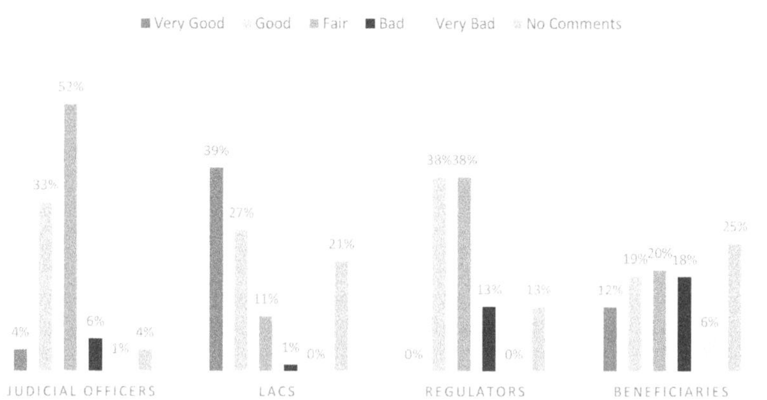

Figure 8.8 Quality of Presentation of LACs as Told by the Stakeholders in the North Zone

"fair" [38%] and "bad" [13%]) of regulators in the North Zone have ranked the quality of articulation skills of LACs as moderately low. On the other hand, 31% of the beneficiaries have rated the articulation skills of LACs as fairly good.

However, 44% (cumulative of "fair" [20%], "bad" [18%], and "very bad" [6%]) of the beneficiaries stated that the articulation ability of their respective LACs was moderately low in nature. A pessimistic assessment of judicial officers and regulators reflects on the quality of articulation of LACs is more relevant as they are the subject matter experts.

In the East Zone, as shown in Figure 8.9, a remarkable 40% of regulators refrained from rating the LACs, while 20% of regulators rated the LACs as

Table 8.9 Quality of Presentation of LACs as Told by the Stakeholders in the East Zone

Respondent		*Very Good*	*Good*	*Fair*	*Bad*	*Very Bad*	*No Comments*	*Total*
Judicial Officers	Count	3	39	45	0	1	8	96
	% of Total	3%	41%	47%	0%	1%	8%	100%
LACs	Count	44	48	14	0	0	31	137
	% of Total	32%	35%	10%	0%	0%	23%	100%
Regulators	Count	1	1	1	0	0	2	5
	% of Total	20%	20%	20%	0%	0%	40%	100%
Beneficiaries	Count	69	201	128	69	22	31	520
	% of Total	13%	39%	25%	13%	4%	6%	100%

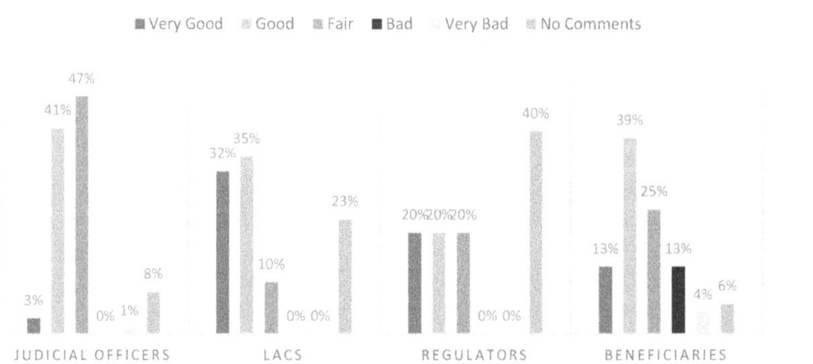

Figure 8.9 Quality of Presentation of LACs as Told by the Stakeholders in the East Zone

having a moderately low level of articulation skills. The perspective from 20% becomes crucial as 44% (cumulative of "very good" [3%] and "good" [41%]) of judicial officers and 42% of beneficiaries also rated the articulation skills of LACs as moderately low.

Although 52% (cumulative of "very good" [13%] and "good" [39%]) of beneficiaries rated LACs' articulation skills as fairly good, it does not reflect an accurate picture at as beneficiaries the district level seldom have any idea of standards of presentation and articulation skills. Since judicial officers and regulators have been witnessing the PLPs, their perceptions outweigh those of the beneficiaries. Hence, in the East Zone, the quality of articulation skills of LACs remains moderately low.

In the West Zone, as shown in Figure 8.10, around 54% of beneficiaries refused to rate their LACs. This reflects the kind of distress they go through while availing themselves of FLAS. However, 60% (cumulative of "very good" [20%], "good" [40%], and "fair" [40%]) of regulators in the West Zone rated the presentation and articulation skills of LACs as fairly good quality, yet around 50% (cumulative of "fair" [45%] and "bad" [5%]) of judicial officers rated the quality of presentation and articulation at a moderately low level.

As explained earlier, judges' perception holds greater validity as they weigh the validity of cross-questioning and trials by lawyers daily. Therefore, in the West Zone, the quality of articulation and presentation were done by the LACs remains at a moderately low level.

In the South Zone, as shown in Figure 8.11, around 32% (cumulative of "fair" [24%], "bad" [6%], and "very bad" [2%]) of beneficiaries rated their LACs' presentation and articulation skills as moderately low; 51%

Table 8.10 Quality of Presentation of LACs as Told by the Stakeholders in the West Zone

Respondents		*Very Good*	*Good*	*Fair*	*Bad*	*Very Bad*	*No Comments*	*Total*
Judicial Officers	Count	1	50	57	6	0	12	126
	% of Total	1%	40%	45%	5%	0%	10%	100%
LACs	Count	43	53	17	2	3	70	188
	% of Total	23%	28%	9%	1%	2%	37%	100%
Regulators	Count	1	2	2	0	0	0	5
	% of Total	20%	40%	40%	0%	0%	0%	100%
Beneficiaries	Count	25	88	47	20	22	235	437
	% of Total	6%	20%	11%	5%	5%	54%	100%

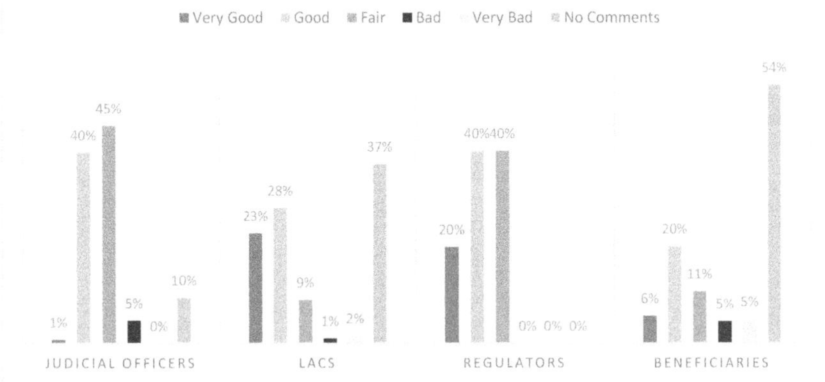

Figure 8.10 Quality of Presentation of LACs as Told by the Stakeholders in the West Zone

(cumulative of "very good" [17%] and "good" [34%]) of beneficiaries in the South Zone seemed to be satisfied with the quality of presentation and articulation skills showed by their LACs. However, judicial officers and regulators presented a grim reality of LACs' professional competence.

Per the judicial officers, 50% (cumulative of "fair" [44%] and "bad" [6%]) of LACs have a moderately low level of articulation and presentation skills. Similarly, 63% of regulators also rated that the LACs have a moderately low level of presentation and articulation skills. Thus, LACs in the South Zone have a moderately low level of articulation and presentation skills.

As shown in the Central Zone, Figure 8.12, LACs' quality of presentation and articulation skills recorded the worst. As shown, 75% of regulators rated the quality of articulation by LACs as moderately low. On the other hand, 62% (cumulative of "fair" [52%], "bad" [7%], and "very bad" [3%]) of judicial officers also rated the quality of presentation and articulation skills of LACs as moderately low.

Unquestionably, LACs in the Central Zone lacked when it came to articulation skills, as even 40% (cumulative of "fair" [24%], "bad" [12%], and "very bad" [4%]) of beneficiaries also rated the articulation skills of their LACs as moderately low. Therefore, LACs in the Central Zone have a moderately low level of articulation skills.

In the North East Zone, as shown in Figure 8.13, 49% (cumulative of "fair" [30%], "bad" [14%], and "very bad" [5%]) of beneficiaries rate the presentation and articulation skills of their respective LACs at a moderately low level, compared to 25% (cumulative of "very good" [5%] and "good"

Table 8.11 Quality of Presentation of LACs as Told by the Stakeholders in the South Zone

Respondents		*Very Good*	*Good*	*Fair*	*Bad*	*Very Bad*	*No Comments*	*Total*
Judicial Officers	Count	2	72	71	10	0	6	161
	% of Total	1%	45%	44%	6%	0%	4%	100%
LACs	Count	42	106	44	2	0	82	276
	% of Total	15%	38%	16%	1%	0%	30%	100%
Regulators	Count	0	2	5	0	0	1	8
	% of Total	0%	25%	63%	0%	0%	13%	100%
Beneficiaries	Count	145	293	211	55	16	146	866
	% of Total	17%	34%	24%	6%	2%	17%	100%

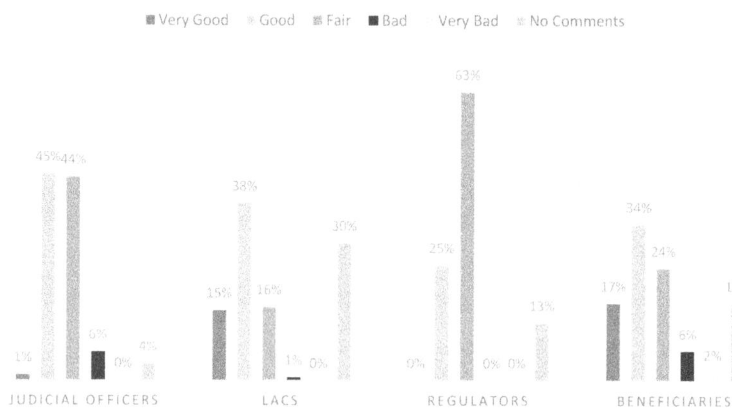

Figure 8.11 Quality of Presentation of LACs as Told by the Stakeholders in the South Zone

[20%]) who rated them as fairly good. Although 53% (cumulative of "very good" [22%] and "good" [31%]) of LACs did mark their articulation and presentation skills as fairly good quality, their assessment does not match with that of regulators and judicial officers who usually interact with LACs regularly.

As shown in Figure 8.13, 67% of regulators refrained from rating the skills of LACs as they cited that they were involved in the selection process

Table 8.12 Quality of Presentation of LACs as Told by the Stakeholders in the Central Zone

Respondents		*Very Good*	*Good*	*Fair*	*Bad*	*Very Bad*	*No Comments*	*Total*
Judicial Officers	Count	2	26	45	6	3	4	86
	% of Total	2%	30%	52%	7%	3%	5%	100%
LACs	Count	91	56	18	3	0	16	184
	% of Total	49%	30%	10%	2%	0%	9%	100%
Regulators	Count	0	1	3	0	0	0	4
	% of Total	0%	25%	75%	0%	0%	0%	100%
Beneficiaries	Count	48	101	91	47	16	77	380
	% of Total	13%	27%	24%	12%	4%	20%	100%

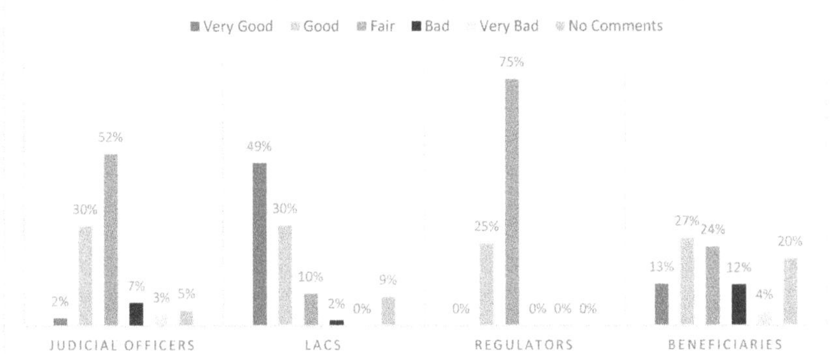

Figure 8.12 Quality of Presentation of LACs as Told by the Stakeholders in the Central Zone

of these LACs, while the remaining 33% of regulators rated the articulation and presentation skills of LACs as moderately low level. The judicial officers of the North East Zone resonate with a similar opinion, as 47% (cumulative of "fair" [36%] and "bad" [11%]) of them rated the presentation and articulation skills of LACs at a moderately low level.

In all the zones, the quality of presentation and articulation skills rated by various stakeholders was moderately low. The following section elaborates on the responses received from all the six zones regarding the quality of presentation and articulation skills of LACs.

Table 8.13 Quality of Presentation of LACs as Told by the Stakeholders in the North East Zone

Respondents		*Very Good*	*Good*	*Fair*	*Bad*	*Very Bad*	*No Comments*	*Total*
Judicial Officers	Count	1	16	16	5	0	7	45
	% of Total	2%	36%	36%	11%	0%	16%	100%
LACs	Count	16	22	14	1	0	19	72
	% of Total	22%	31%	19%	1%	0%	26%	100%
Regulators	Count	0	0	1	0	0	2	3
	% of Total	0%	0%	33%	0%	0%	67%	100%
Beneficiaries	Count	14	56	85	40	15	71	281
	% of Total	5%	20%	30%	14%	5%	25%	100%

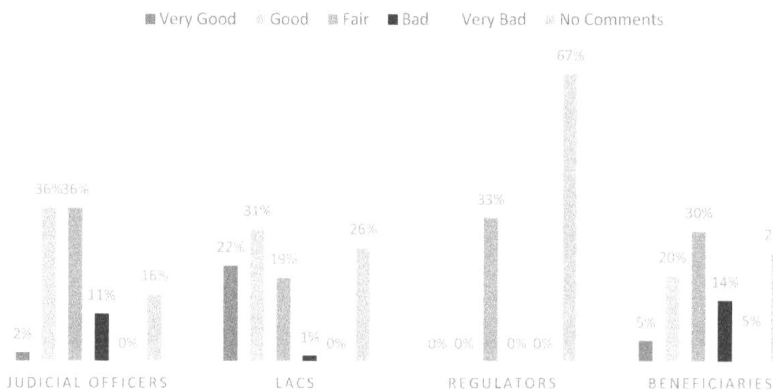

Figure 8.13 Quality of Presentation of LACs as Told by the Stakeholders in the North East Zone

As shown in Figure 8.14, around 49% (cumulative of "fair" [46%] and "bad" [3%]) of regulators rated the quality of articulation and presentation skills of LACs at a moderately low level. This consistent rating of moderately low level of presentation and articulations skills resonates with the opinion of judicial officers. Around 53% (cumulative of "fair" [47%], "bad" [5%], and "very bad" [1%]) of judicial officers of the research universe rated the presentation and articulation skills of LACs at a moderately low level. Therefore, LACs lack terms of presentation and articulation skills significantly.

Table 8.14 Quality of Presentation of LACs as Told by the Stakeholders in the Six Zones

Respondents		*Very Good*	*Good*	*Fair*	*Bad*	*Very Bad*	*No Comments*	*Total*
Judicial Officers	Count	13	234	283	33	5	41	609
	% of Total	2%	38%	47%	5%	1%	7%	100%
LACs	Count	295	326	123	10	3	250	1007
	% of Total	29%	32%	12%	1%	0%	25%	100%
Regulators	Count	2	9	15	1	0	6	33
	% of Total	6%	27%	46%	3%	0%	18%	100%
Beneficiaries	Count	369	840	669	331	125	695	3,029
	% of Total	12%	28%	22%	11%	4%	23%	100%

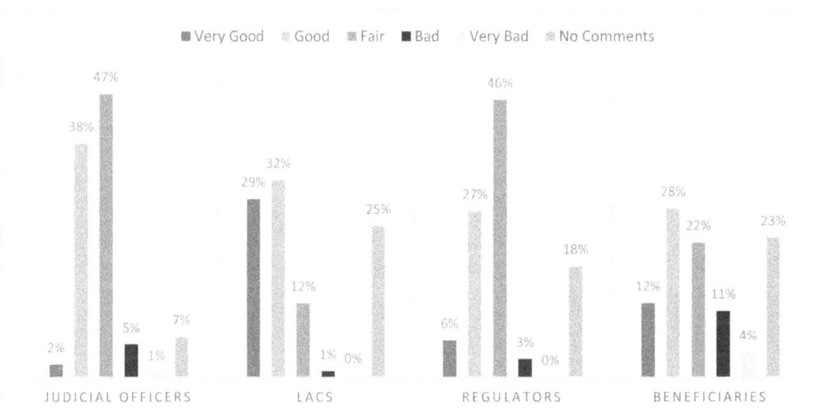

Figure 8.14 Quality of Presentation of LACs as Told by the Stakeholders in the Six Zones

8.2.3. *Quality of Drafting of LACs as Told by the Stakeholders*

Verba volant, scripta manent – words fly away, written words remain! Hence, an effective lawyer must have good drafting skills. To assess the drafting skills of LACs in all the six zones, the questionnaires provided to all the stakeholders consisted of questions related to the same. The rationale for inserting drafting as an essential skill in the questionnaire was that since drafting is the most intellectually demanding of all the lawyers' skills, LACs

Table 8.15 Quality of Drafting of LACs as Told by the Stakeholders in the North Zone

Respondents		*Very Good*	*Good*	*Fair*	*Bad*	*Very Bad*	*No Comments*	*Total*
Judicial Officers	Count	5	30	46	9	1	4	95
	% of Total	5%	32%	48%	9%	1%	4%	100%
LACs	Count	58	42	16	1	0	33	150
	% of Total	39%	28%	11%	1%	0%	22%	100%
Regulators	Count	0	4	2	1	0	1	8
	% of Total	0%	50%	25%	13%	0%	13%	100%
Beneficiaries	Count	71	95	102	96	32	149	545
	% of Total	13%	17%	19%	18%	6%	27%	100%

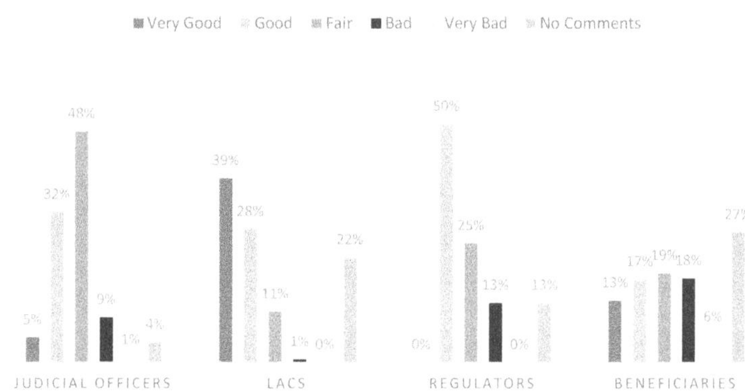

Figure 8.15 Quality of Drafting of LACs as Told by the Stakeholders in the North Zone

must be competent. A well-drafted document is equivalent to strong argument and articulation.

In the North Zone, as shown in Figure 8.15, 50% of regulators were of the concerned opinion that LACs have fairly good drafting skills, further even 67% (cumulative of "very good" [39%] and "good" [28%]) of LACs themselves rated their drafting skills as fairly good quality.

However, a regulator or LAC does not decide on a trial. It is the judicial officers who decide the nature and future of the cases. Around 56% (cumulative of "fair" [46%], "bad" [9%], and "very bad" [1%]) of judicial officers rated the drafting skills of LACs at a moderately low level. Moreover,

Table 8.16 Quality of Drafting of LACs as Told by the Stakeholders in the East Zone

Respondents		*Very Good*	*Good*	*Fair*	*Bad*	*Very Bad*	*No Comments*	*Total*
Judicial Officers	Count	3	35	43	2	1	12	96
	% of Total	3%	36%	45%	2%	1%	13%	100%
LACs	Count	50	48	12	1	0	26	137
	% of Total	36%	35%	9%	1%	0%	19%	100%
Regulators	Count	0	3	0	0	0	2	5
	% of Total	0%	60%	0%	0%	0%	40%	100%
Beneficiaries	Count	76	196	125	65	23	35	520
	% of Total	15%	38%	24%	13%	4%	7%	100%

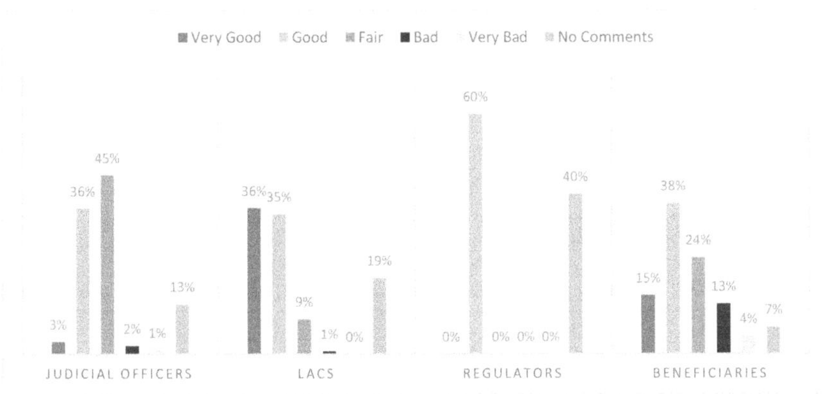

Figure 8.16 Quality of Drafting of LACs as Told by the Stakeholders in the East Zone

43% (cumulative of "fair" [19%], "bad" [18%], and "very bad" [6%]) of beneficiaries in the North Zone also rated the drafting skills of LACs at a moderately low level. Indeed, the drafting skills of LACs in the North Zone are moderately low, and they need to improve further to provide better and more effective services to the beneficiaries.

As shown in Figure 8.16, 60% of regulators rated the LACs as having fairly good drafting skills in the East Zone. Similarly, 71% (cumulative of "very good" [36%] and "good" [35%]) of LACs marked their drafting skills as fairly good. However, a regulator seldom seeks to see the documents drafted by an LAC.

It is the judicial officers who pass the litigation from LACs. Therefore, only the judicial officers' account will give a complete and comprehensive picture of the quality of drafting skills of the LACs in the East Zone. In this research universe, 48% (cumulative of "fair" [45%], "bad" [2%], and "very bad" [1%]) of judicial officers rated the drafting skills of LACs at a moderately low level. Thus, LACs in the East Zone have a moderately low level of drafting skills and need to improve them to provide better services to the beneficiaries.

As shown in Figure 8.17, the West Zone's data, too, narrates a grim reality for the beneficiaries. While responding, 65% of beneficiaries refrained from rating the drafting skills of their LACs. According to field notes, the

Table 8.17 Quality of Drafting of LACs as Told by the Stakeholders in the West Zone

Respondents		*Very Good*	*Good*	*Fair*	*Bad*	*Very Bad*	*No Comments*	*Total*
Judicial Officers	Count	1	41	62	7	0	15	126
	% of Total	1%	33%	49%	6%	0%	12%	100%
LACs	Count	50	44	18	6	1	69	188
	% of Total	27%	23%	10%	3%	1%	37%	100%
Regulators	Count	1	3	1	0	0	0	5
	% of Total	20%	60%	20%	0%	0%	0%	100%
Beneficiaries	Count	34	55	41	13	12	282	437
	% of Total	8%	13%	9%	3%	3%	65%	100%

Figure 8.17 Quality of Drafting of LACs as Told by the Stakeholders in the West Zone

beneficiaries were often hesitant to answer anything related to their respective LACs. They might be under the impression that if they said anything against LACs, they might lose the legal case, or the concerned LAC might desert them.

However, judicial officers' responses reflect an accurate picture of the quality of drafting skills of LACs. Around 55% (cumulative of "fair" [49%] and "bad" [6%]) of judicial officers in the West Zone rated the drafting skills of LACs at a moderately low level. This assessment of judicial officers reveals the poor quality of drafting skills that LACs have in general.

As shown in Figure 8.18, the quality of drafting skills of LACs seems to be moderately low in the South Zone. Around 75% of regulators in the South Zone rated the quality of drafting skills of LACs as moderately low. The

Table 8.18 Quality of Drafting of LACs as Told by the Stakeholders in the South Zone

Respondents		*Very Good*	*Good*	*Fair*	*Bad*	*Very Bad*	*No Comments*	*Total*
Judicial Officers	Count	2	56	80	13	1	9	161
	% of Total	1%	35%	50%	8%	1%	6%	100%
LACs	Count	42	100	50	2	0	82	276
	% of Total	15%	36%	18%	1%	0%	30%	100%
Regulators	Count	0	1	6	0	0	1	8
	% of Total	0%	13%	75%	0%	0%	13%	100%
Beneficiaries	Count	142	301	196	55	14	158	866
	% of Total	16%	35%	23%	6%	2%	18%	100%

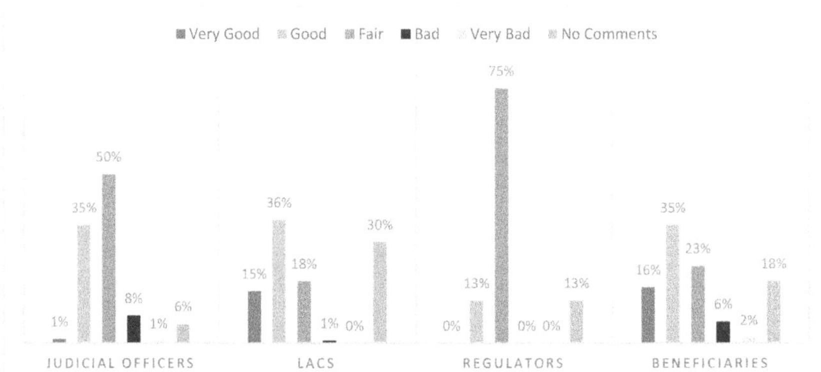

Figure 8.18 Quality of Drafting of LACs as Told by the Stakeholders in the South Zone

responses received from judicial officers also support this trend, as 59% of judicial officers (cumulative of "fair" [50%], "bad" [8%], and "very bad" [1%]) rated the drafting skills of LACs in the South Zone as moderately low.

Although 51% (cumulative of "very good" [16%] and "good" [35%]) of beneficiaries rated the quality of drafting skills of LACs as fairly good, one should not consider their experience and rating of drafting at par beneficiaries are often not aware of the legal terminology used in litigation. Therefore, LACs in the South Zone also have a moderately low level of drafting skills.

In the Central Zone, as shown in Figure 8.19, 50% (cumulative of "fair" [25%] and "bad" [25%]) of regulators rated the drafting skills of LACs as moderately low, while another 50% of regulators rated the drafting skills as

Table 8.19 Quality of Drafting of LACs as Told by the Stakeholders in the Central Zone

Respondents		*Very Good*	*Good*	*Fair*	*Bad*	*Very Bad*	*No Comments*	*Total*
Judicial Officers	Count	1	28	34	14	4	5	86
	% of Total	1%	33%	40%	16%	5%	6%	100%
LACs	Count	87	57	18	4	1	17	184
	% of Total	47%	31%	10%	2%	1%	9%	100%
Regulators	Count	0	2	1	1	0	0	4
	% of Total	0%	50%	25%	25%	0%	0%	100%
Beneficiaries	Count	56	105	85	37	18	79	380
	% of Total	15%	28%	22%	10%	5%	21%	100%

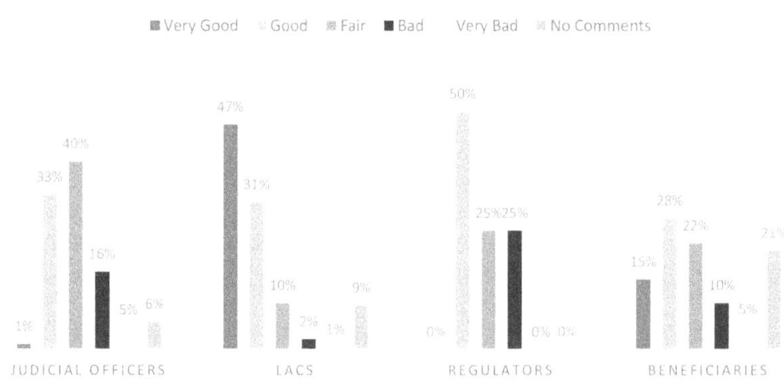

Figure 8.19 Quality of Drafting of LACs as Told by the Stakeholders in the Central Zone

reasonably good quality. Although 37% (cumulative of "fair" [22%], "bad" [10%], and "very bad" [5%]) of beneficiaries rated the drafting skills of LACs at a moderately low level, 43% (cumulative of "very good" [15%] and "good" [28%]) of beneficiaries rated the drafting skills of LACs as reasonably good. Therefore, responses received from regulators give no conclusive results.

However, ratings from 61% of the judicial officers (cumulative of "fair" [40%], "bad" [16%], and "very bad" [5%]) confirm that the drafting skills of most LACs in the Central Zone are of moderately low level, which affects the quality of legal aid services.

In the North East Zone, as shown in Figure 8.20, most regulators refrained from rating the LACs, and those who did rate the drafting ability

Table 8.20 Quality of Drafting of LACs as Told by the Stakeholders in the North East Zone

Respondents		*Very Good*	*Good*	*Fair*	*Bad*	*Very Bad*	*No Comments*	*Total*
Judicial Officers	Count	0	13	19	6	0	7	45
	% of Total	0%	29%	42%	13%	0%	16%	100%
LACs	Count	13	25	15	1	0	18	72
	% of Total	18%	35%	21%	1%	0%	25%	100%
Regulators	Count	0	1	0	0	0	2	3
	% of Total	0%	33%	0%	0%	0%	67%	100%
Beneficiaries	Count	15	55	83	40	13	75	281
	% of Total	5%	20%	30%	14%	5%	27%	100%

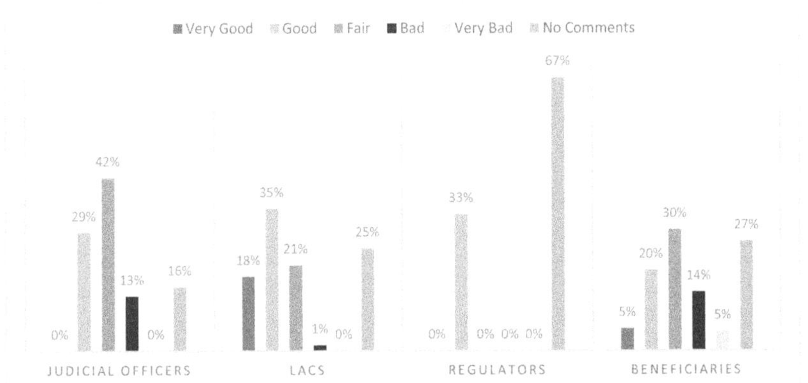

Figure 8.20 Quality of Drafting of LACs as Told by the Stakeholders in the North East Zone

of LACs did it as fairly good. However, most of the beneficiaries (around 49%, cumulative of "fair" [30%], "bad" [14%], and "very bad" [5%]) rated the drafting skills of LACs as moderately low. The beneficiaries' narrative finds its support from the ratings of judicial officers.

Further, 55% (cumulative of "fair" [42%] and "bad" [13%]) of judicial officers rated the quality of drafting skills of LACs as at a moderately low level. Thus, LACs have a moderately low level of drafting skills per the majority of stakeholders.

The previous sections focus on the zone-wise assessment of the quality of drafting skills of LACs. As Figure 8.21 shows, the data collected from the

Table 8.21 Quality of Drafting of LACs as Told by the Stakeholders in the Six Zones

Respondents		*Very Good*	*Good*	*Fair*	*Bad*	*Very Bad*	*No Comments*	*Total*
Judicial Officers	Count	12	203	284	51	7	52	609
	% of Total	2%	33%	47%	8%	1%	9%	100%
LACs	Count	300	316	129	15	2	245	1007
	% of Total	30%	31%	13%	2%	0%	24%	100%
Regulators	Count	1	14	10	2	0%	6	33
	% of Total	3%	42%	30%	6%	0%	18%	100%
Beneficiaries	Count	394	807	632	306	112	778	3,029
	% of Total	13%	27%	21%	10%	4%	26%	100%

Figure 8.21 Quality of Drafting of LACs as Told by the Stakeholders in the Six Zones

six zones from all the five stakeholders in the LAS. Regulators have supported and rated the drafting skills of LACs as fairly good (45%, cumulative of "very good" [42%] and "good" [3%]). However, one must consider that it is not the regulator who deals with the LACs regularly but a judicial officer.

Therefore, judicial officers' assessment holds more validity than that of other stakeholders regarding the quality of drafting skills of LACs. In the six zones, 56% (cumulative of "fair" [47%], "bad" [8%], and "very bad" [1%]) of judicial officers rated the quality of drafting skills of LACs at a moderately low level, compared to 35% (cumulative of "very good" [2%] and "good" [33%]) of judicial officers who rated the drafting quality of LACs as fairly good. Thus, in the research universe, in all the six zones, the quality of drafting skills of LACs happens to be of a moderately low quality, which directly affects the quality of legal aid services offered to legal aid beneficiaries.

Table 8.22 highlights the overall quality of LACs from the perspective of judicial officers, LACs, regulators, and beneficiaries. The field investigators informed respondents that while answering this question, they must emphasize the holistic professional skills of LACs. Most judicial officers, around 54% (cumulative of "fair" [46%], "bad" [7%], and "very bad" [1%]), said that LACs have a moderately average overall professional skill. In contrast, 52% (cumulative of "very good" [3%] and "good" [49%]) of regulators from the six zones responded that LACs have fairly good overall professional skills.

Similarly, most LACs, around 62% (cumulative of "very good: [28%] and "good" [34%]), also responded that their overall professional skills are of fairly good quality. However, since LACs and regulators both have a stake in the selection and dereliction of legal aid services, their responses regarding the quality of professional skills cannot represent an accurate picture. The beneficiaries' perspective must validate their views, but beneficiaries are usually not adept with legal terminology and topology. Consequently, judicial officers' perspectives hold much sanctity as the judicial officers deal with competent and incompetent legal practitioners. Hence, in terms of the overall quality of professional skills, LACs have moderately average professional skills.

8.2.4. *Comparative Analysis of PLPs and LACs: Quality of Professional Skills (by Judicial Officers)*

This section focuses on the comparative analysis of the professional qualities of LACs and those of PLPs from judicial officers' perspective. This comparative analysis becomes necessary as it narrates the disparity between an LAC and a PLP. Judicial officers' perspective is considered as they interact with PLPs and LACs regularly and can weigh on the professional competence of advocates in general.

Table 8.22 Overall Quality of Professional Skills of LACs per the Respondents in the Six Zones

Respondents		*Very Good*	*Good*	*Fair*	*Bad*	*Very Bad*	*No Comments*	*Total*
Judicial Officers	Count	19	207	278	44	6	55	609
	% of Total	3%	34%	46%	7%	1%	9%	100%
LACs	Count	286	340	129	6	5	241	1007
	% of Total	28%	34%	13%	1%	1%	24%	100%
Regulators	Count	1	16	8	2	0	6	33
	% of Total	3%	49%	24%	6%	0%	18%	100%
Beneficiaries	Count	443	843	649	351	167	576	3,029
	% of Total	15%	28%	21%	12%	6%	19%	100%

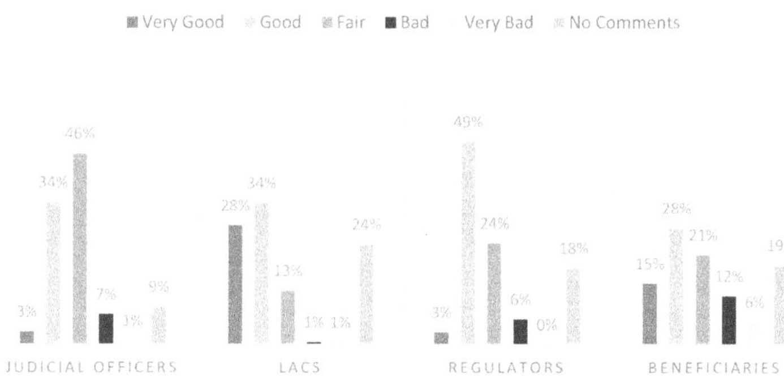

Figure 8.22 Overall Quality of Professional Skills of LACs per the Respondents in the Six Zones

In the North Zone, as shown in Figure 8.23, 64% of judicial officers were of the considerate opinion that PLPs have fairly good argument skills, while in the case of LACs, a meager 37% of judicial officers were convinced that LACs have fairly good argument skills. LACs, per the judicial officers (47%), have a moderately low level of argument skills.

In terms of presentation and articulation skills, the North Zone's judicial officers rated the PLPs way ahead of LACs, as for the majority of judicial officers' (61%), PLPs have fairly good articulation and presentation skills compared to LACs. Meanwhile, according to judicial officers, the majority of LACs (52%) have a moderately low level of articulation skills.

Further, judicial officers rated the drafting skills of PLPs ahead of those of LACs. Around 61% of judicial officers rated PLPs to have fairly good drafting skills, while most LACs, 48%, have a moderately low level of drafting skills.

Therefore, it is worth mentioning that in all three professional skills, LACs lack significantly from PLPs. As shown in Figure 8.23, most judicial officers rated the level of overall satisfaction with PLPs as fairly good, whereas, for the LACs, the majority of judicial officers rated the overall satisfaction as moderately low quality. The data reflects that the professional skills of PLPs are higher than those of most LACs. It also substantiates the lack of competent LACs in the LAS.

In the East Zone, as shown in Table 8.24, per the opinion of 54% of judicial officers, a majority of PLPs have fairly good argument skills compared to that of LACs, where 43% of judicial officers rated that most LACs have a moderately low level of argument skills. However, compared to the North Zone, the disparity between PLPs and LACs seems negligible in the East Zone.

Similarly, in terms of presentation and articulation skills, 54% of judicial officers responded that PLPs had a relatively good level of articulation and presentation skills compared to LACs, where a majority of judicial officers (47%) opined that LACs had a moderately low level of presentation and articulation skills.

In the case of drafting skills, the majority of judicial officers were of the considerate opinion that PLPs had a pretty good level of drafting skills (47%), while LACs had a moderately low level of drafting skills (45%).

Comparatively, as demonstrated in Figure 8.24, 55% of judicial officers rated the level of overall satisfaction with PLPs as fairly good, whereas most judicial officers rated the level of overall satisfaction with LACs at a moderately low level (49%). The disparity between PLPs and LACs is evidence that in the East Zone also, LACs lack significantly in terms of professional skills. This deficiency often translates into a lack of competence when these LACs provide FLAS to a legal aid beneficiary.

In the West Zone, as shown in Figure 8.25, the majority of judicial officers responded that PLPs have a fairly good level of argument skills (54%), whereas LACs in most of the cases have a moderately low level of argument skills (45%). In the West Zone, the disparity in argument skills between PLPs and LACs happens to be wider than in the East Zone.

In terms of articulation and presentation skills, 52% of judicial officers opined that PLPs have fairly good presentation and articulation skills. According to PLPs, most LACs have a moderately low level of articulation and presentation skills (45%). Additionally, some of the judicial officers even rated the articulation and presentation skills of LACs as bad at times.

Table 8.23 Comparative Analysis of PLPs and LACs: Quality of Professional Skills (by Judicial Officers) in the North Zone

ARGUMENTS								
Respondents		*Very Good*	*Good*	*Fair*	*Bad*	*Very Bad*	*No Comments*	*Total*
PLPs	Count	9	61	16	3	0	6	95
	% of Total	9%	64%	17%	3%	0%	6%	100%
LACs	Count	4	35	45	7	0	4	95
	% of Total	4%	37%	47%	7%	0%	4%	100%
PRESENTATION								
Respondents		*Very Good*	*Good*	*Fair*	*Bad*	*Very Bad*	*No Comments*	*Total*
PLPs	Count	7	58	24	2	0	4	95
	% of Total	7%	61%	25%	2%	0%	4%	100%
LACs	Count	4	31	49	6	1	4	95
	% of Total	4%	33%	52%	6%	1%	4%	100%
DRAFTING								
Respondents		*Very Good*	*Good*	*Fair*	*Bad*	*Very Bad*	*No Comments*	*Total*
PLPs	Count	6	58	23	2	1	5	95
	% of Total	6%	61%	24%	2%	1%	5%	100%
LACs	Count	5	30	46	9	1	4	95
	% of Total	5%	32%	48%	9%	1%	4%	100%
OVERALL								
Respondents		*Very Good*	*Good*	*Fair*	*Bad*	*Very Bad*	*No Comments*	*Total*
PLPs	Count	7	60	21	2	0	5	95
	% of Total	7%	63%	22%	2%	0%	5%	100%
LACs	Count	6	27	48	8	0	6	95
	% of Total	6%	28%	51%	8%	0%	6%	100%

Drafting skills of LACs happen to be of moderately low level when compared to those of PLPs. As shown in Figure 8.24, 52% of judicial officers opined that PLPs had a fairly good level of drafting skills, while most judicial officers rated the drafting skills of LACs as moderately low (49%).

Figure 8.23 Comparative Analysis of PLPs and LACs: Quality of Professional Skills in the North Zone

Certainly, the disparity among LACs and PLPs is noticeable even by beneficiaries in the West Zone in terms of drafting skills.

Finally, in the West Zone, most judicial officers rated the level of overall satisfaction with PLPs (49%) as way higher and of fairly good quality when compared to LACs (48%). In terms of LACs, most judicial officers opined that a beneficiary's overall satisfaction with LACs happens to be moderately low.

In the South Zone, as shown in Figure 8.26, 49% of judicial officers responded that the argument skills of PLPs were of fairly good quality, whereas in the case of LACs, most of the judicial officers (48%) felt the skills were of moderately low quality. However, the disparity between fairly good levels of argument skills in LACs and PLPs is minuscule (6%). Therefore, in the South Zone, it can be observed that the argument skills of LACs are somewhat in parity with PLPs.

In terms of articulation and presentation skills, most judicial officers rated that PLPs have fairly good presentation and articulation skills (47%), whereas most judicial officers rated the articulation and presentation skills

Table 8.24 Comparative Analysis of PLPs and LACs: Quality of Professional Skills (by Judicial Officers) in the East Zone

Respondents		*Very Good*	*Good*	*Fair*	*Bad*	*Very Bad*	*No Comments*	*Total*
ARGUMENTS								
PLPs	Count	9	52	24	0	0	11	96
	% of Total	9%	54%	25%	0%	0%	11%	100%
LACs	Count	5	39	41	2	1	8	96
	% of Total	5%	41%	43%	2%	1%	8%	100%
PRESENTATION								
Respondents		*Very Good*	*Good*	*Fair*	*Bad*	*Very Bad*	*No Comments*	*Total*
PLPs	Count	5	52	24	2	0	13	96
	% of Total	5%	54%	25%	2%	0%	14%	100%
LACs	Count	3	39	45	0	1	8	96
	% of Total	3%	41%	47%	0%	1%	8%	100%
DRAFTING								
Respondents		*Very Good*	*Good*	*Fair*	*Bad*	*Very Bad*	*No Comments*	*Total*
PLPs	Count	5	45	27	4	0	15	96
	% of Total	5%	47%	28%	4%	0%	16%	100%
LACs	Count	3	35	43	2	1	12	96
	% of Total	3%	36%	45%	2%	1%	13%	100%
OVERALL								
Respondents		*Very Good*	*Good*	*Fair*	*Bad*	*Very Bad*	*No Comments*	*Total*
PLPs	Count	5	53	23	2	0	13	96
	% of Total	5%	55%	24%	2%	0%	14%	100%
LACs	Count	4	32	47	0	1	12	96
	% of Total	4%	33%	49%	0%	1%	13%	100%

of LACs as moderately low (44%). As shown in Figure 8.26, it is pertinent to notice that the difference between the rating of LACs and PLPs is not that large, as almost 45% of judicial officers responded that LACs have fairly good articulation and presentation skills.

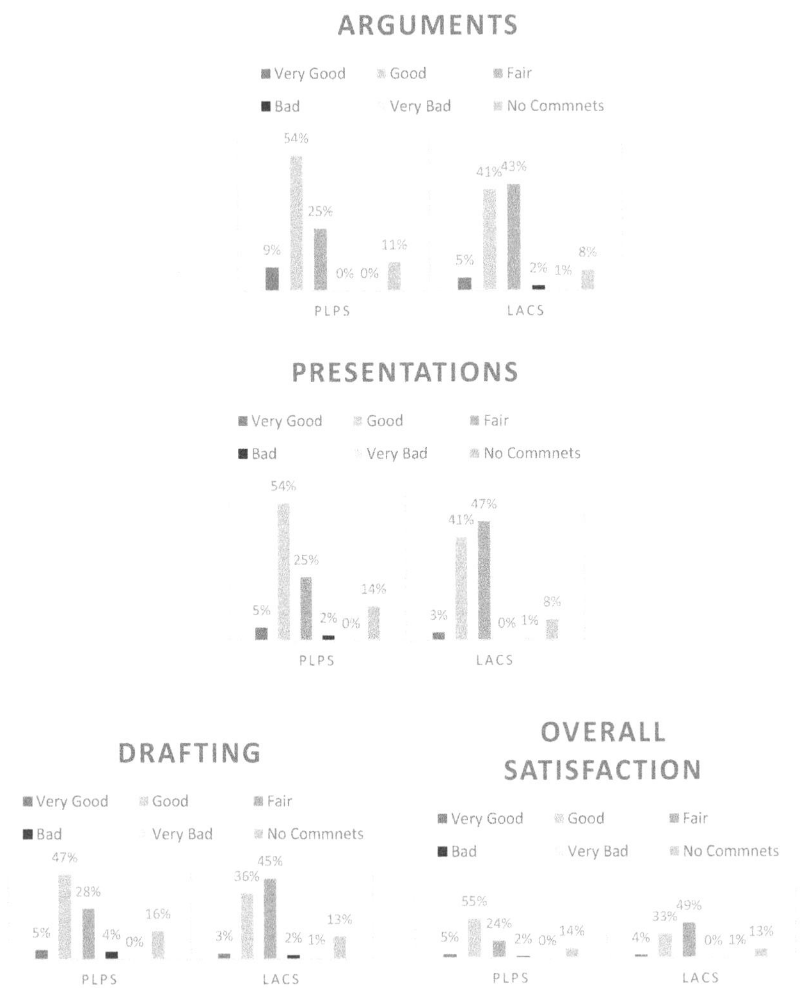

Figure 8.24 Comparative Analysis of PLPs and LACs: Quality of Professional Skills in the East Zone

Further, most judicial officers rated that PLPs have fairly good drafting skills compared to LACs (43%), as around 50% of judicial officers opined that LACs have a moderately low level of drafting skills. Indeed, in terms of drafting skills also, PLPs are more competent than LACs.

In the South Zone, PLPs' competence in argument, presentation, and drafting skills is way ahead. Moreover, the degree of overall satisfaction rated by judicial officers reflects the same trend. Around 46% of judicial officers rated that the level of overall satisfaction with PLPs is of fairly good

Table 8.25 Comparative Analysis of PLPs and LACs: Quality of Professional Skills (by Judicial Officers) in the West Zone

ARGUMENTS									
Respondents		*Very Good*	*Good*	*Fair*	*Bad*	*Very Bad*	*No Comments*	*Total*
PLPs	Count	4	68	31	0	0	23	126
	% of Total	3%	54%	25%	0%	0%	18%	100%
LACs	Count	2	46	57	7	0	14	126
	% of Total	2%	37%	45%	6%	0%	11%	21%
PRESENTATION								
Respondents		*Very Good*	*Good*	*Fair*	*Bad*	*Very Bad*	*No Comments*	*Total*
PLPs	Count	1	66	37	0	0	22	126
	% of Total	1%	52%	29%	0%	0%	17%	100%
LACs	Count	1	50	57	6	0	12	126
	% of Total	1%	40%	45%	5%	0%	10%	100%
DRAFTING								
Respondents		*Very Good*	*Good*	*Fair*	*Bad*	*Very Bad*	*No Comments*	*Total*
PLPs	Count	4	66	34	0	0	22	126
	% of Total	3%	52%	27%	0%	0%	17%	100%
LACs	Count	1	41	62	7	0	15	126
	% of Total	1%	33%	49%	6%	0%	12%	100%
OVERALL								
Respondents		*Very Good*	*Good*	*Fair*	*Bad*	*Very Bad*	*No Comments*	*Total*
PLPs	Count	4	62	35	1	0	24	126
	% of Total	3%	49%	28%	1%	0%	19%	100%
LACs	Count	3	38	60	7	0	18	126
	% of Total	2%	30%	48%	6%	0%	14%	100%

quality. On the contrary, most judicial officers rated the overall satisfaction with LACs at a moderately low level.

In the Central Zone, as shown in Figure 8.27, most of the judicial officers (44%) responded that PLPs have a fairly good quality of argument skills,

Figure 8.25 Comparative Analysis of PLPs and LACs: Quality of Professional Skills in the West Zone

whereas the majority of judicial officers (41%) opined that LACs have a moderately low level of argument skills. Certainly, PLPs stand above in terms of skills related to arguments during a trial or hearing.

In terms of presentation and articulation skills, most judicial officers also responded that PLPs have a fairly good quality of articulation and presentation skills (44%). On the contrary, 52% of judicial officers opined that LACs have a moderately low level of articulation and presentation skills. Therefore, in terms of articulation and presentation skills, PLPs have a higher competence level per the judicial officers in the Central Zone.

Further, around 44% of judicial officers even stated that PLPs have fairly good drafting skills, contrary to the majority of judicial officers (40%) who rated that LACs have a moderately low level of drafting skills. Indeed, in the Central Zone, per the perceptions of judicial officers, PLPs have a higher quality of drafting skills than LACs.

In the Central Zone, in terms of the argument, presentation, and drafting skills, PLPs are way ahead in terms of quality and competence per the opinion of judicial officers, but does it affect the overall satisfaction level? Per judicial officers' opinion, most of them rated PLPs' (48%) overall professional skills as fairly good quality than LACs (42%), where judicial officers'

Table 8.26 Comparative Analysis of PLPs and LACs: Quality of Professional Skills (by Judicial Officers) in the South Zone

ARGUMENTS								
Respondents		*Very Good*	*Good*	*Fair*	*Bad*	*Very Bad*	*No Comments*	*Total*
PLPs	Count	8	79	58	0	1	15	161
	% of Total	5%	49%	36%	0%	1%	9%	100%
LACs	Count	2	68	77	8	2	4	161
	% of Total	1%	42%	48%	5%	1%	2%	100%
PRESENTATION								
Respondents		*Very Good*	*Good*	*Fair*	*Bad*	*Very Bad*	*No comments*	*Total*
PLPs	Count	7	76	58	0	1	19	161
	% of Total	4%	47%	36%	0%	1%	12%	100%
LACs	Count	2	72	71	10	0	6	161
	% of Total	1%	45%	44%	6%	0%	4%	100%
DRAFTING								
Respondents		*Very Good*	*Good*	*Fair*	*Bad*	*Very Bad*	*No comments*	*Total*
PLPs	Count	9	69	64	1	0	18	161
	% of Total	6%	43%	40%	1%	0%	11%	100%
LACs	Count	2	56	80	13	1	9	161
	% of Total	1%	35%	50%	8%	1%	6%	100%
OVERALL								
Respondents		*Very Good*	*Good*	*Fair*	*Bad*	*Very Bad*	*No comments*	*Total*
PLPs	Count	10	74	57	1	0	19	161
	% of Total	6%	46%	35%	1%	0%	12%	100%
LACs	Count	4	66	70	11	2	8	161
	% of Total	2%	41%	43%	7%	1%	5%	100%

overall satisfaction level with respect to the skills of the LACs was moderately low quality. Indeed, the disparity is glaring between the low level of professional skills of LACs and the comparatively high level of professional skills of PLPs in the Central Zone.

Figure 8.26 Comparative Analysis of PLPs and LACs: Quality of Professional Skills in the South Zone

In the North East Zone, as shown in Figure 8.28, the majority of judicial officers (62%) opined that PLPs have a fair quality of argument skills, while most judicial officers responded that LACs have a moderately low level of argument skills (36%). Certainly, the argument skills of LACs must have been low quality to such an extent that 11% of judicial officers even rated them bad.

Similarly, most judicial officers (64%) opined that the articulation and presentation skills of PLPs were of fairly good quality. On the other hand, most judicial officers also rated the articulation and presentation skills of LACs (36%) as moderately low level. Indeed, the level of articulation and presentation skills of LACs must have been declining as around 11% of judicial officers even rated them as bad.

Further, the PLPs (62%) in the North East Zone rated as fairly good in terms of their drafting skills. Most judicial officers (42%) rated the drafting skills of LACs (42%) as moderately low. Surprisingly, 13% of judicial officers rated the drafting skills of LACs as bad, which reflects the lack of quality professional skills among the LACs in the North East Zone.

Table 8.27 Comparative Analysis of PLPs and LACs: Quality of Professional Skills (by Judicial Officers) in the Central Zone

ARGUMENTS								
Respondents		*Very Good*	*Good*	*Fair*	*Bad*	*Very Bad*	*No Comments*	*Total*
PLPs	Count	15	38	24	1	0	8	86
	% of Total	17%	44%	28%	1%	0%	9%	100%
LACs	Count	4	28	35	12	3	4	86
	% of Total	5%	33%	41%	14%	3%	5%	100%
PRESENTATION								
Respondents		*Very Good*	*Good*	*Fair*	*Bad*	*Very Bad*	*No Comments*	*Total*
PLPs	Count	12	38	26	2	0	8	86
	% of Total	14%	44%	30%	2%	0%	9%	100%
LACs	Count	2	26	45	6	3	4	86
	% of Total	2%	30%	52%	7%	3%	5%	100%
DRAFTING								
Respondents		*Very Good*	*Good*	*Fair*	*Bad*	*Very Bad*	*No Comments*	*Total*
PLPs	Count	9	38	29	2	0	8	86
	% of Total	10%	44%	34%	2%	0%	9%	100%
LACs	Count	1	28	34	14	4	5	86
	% of Total	1%	33%	40%	16%	5%	6%	100%
OVERALL								
Respondents		*Very Good*	*Good*	*Fair*	*Bad*	*Very Bad*	*No Comments*	*Total*
PLPs	Count	9	41	24	2	0	10	86
	% of Total	10%	48%	28%	2%	0%	12%	100%
LACs	Count	2	28	36	13	3	4	86
	% of Total	2%	33%	42%	15%	3%	5%	100%

To sum up, in terms of overall satisfaction, around 62% of judicial officers responded that the level of satisfaction with the services offered by PLPs is fairly good. The narrative of LACs seemed to be rather grim, as most judicial officers rated the satisfaction level as moderately low level. Also,

Figure 8.27 Comparative Analysis of PLPs and LACs: Quality of Professional Skills in the Central Zone

11% of judicial officers even rated the overall satisfaction level of LACs as bad. Therefore, in the North East Zone also, the professional skills of PLPs are way better than those of the LACs.

8.2.4.1. Comparative Analysis of PLPs and LACs: Quality of Professional Skills (by Judicial Officers) in the Six Zones

In almost every zone, judicial officers from every zone rated the professional skills of PLPs as fairly good quality. On the contrary, LACs were rated too low in terms of their professional skills vis-à-vis services to legal aid beneficiaries. In total, as shown in Figure 8.29, 54% of judicial officers rated that the argument skills of PLPs were fairly good quality. The reflection of judicial officers from the six zones on the argument skills of LACs was a somewhat discouraging one, as a majority of judicial officers opined that LACs (44%) had a moderately low level of argument skills.

In terms of articulation and presentation skills, the data from the six zones reflects that the majority of judicial officers rated that PLPs (52%) have fairly good articulation and presentation skills. On the other hand,

Table 8.28 Comparative Analysis of PLPs and LACs: Quality of Professional Skills (by Judicial Officers) in the North East Zone

ARGUMENTS								
Respondents		*Very Good*	*Good*	*Fair*	*Bad*	*Very Bad*	*No Comments*	*Total*
PLPs	Count	4	28	8	0	0	5	45
	% of Total	9%	62%	18%	0%	0%	11%	100%
LACs	Count	1	16	16	5	1	6	45
	% of Total	2%	36%	36%	11%	2%	13%	100%
PRESENTATION								
Respondents		*Very Good*	*Good*	*Fair*	*Bad*	*Very Bad*	*No Comments*	*Total*
PLPs	Count	2	29	9	0	0	5	45
	% of Total	4%	64%	20%	0%	0%	11%	100%
LACs	Count	1	16	16	5	0	7	45
	% of Total	2%	36%	36%	11%	0%	16%	100%
DRAFTING								
Respondents		*Very Good*	*Good*	*Fair*	*Bad*	*Very Bad*	*No Comments*	*Total*
PLPs	Count	3	28	10	0	0	4	45
	% of Total	7%	62%	22%	0%	0%	9%	100%
LACs	Count	0	13	19	6	0	7	45
	% of Total	0%	29%	42%	13%	0%	16%	100%
OVERALL								
Respondents		*Very Good*	*Good*	*Fair*	*Bad*	*Very Bad*	*No Comments*	*Total*
PLPs	Count	1	28	12	0	0	4	45
	% of Total	2%	62%	27%	0%	0%	9%	100%
LACs	Count	0	16	17	5	0	7	45
	% of Total	0%	36%	38%	11%	0%	16%	100%

the majority of judicial officers responded that LACs (47%) had a moderately low level of articulation and presentation skills. Indeed, the data reflects the disparity in terms of articulation and presentation skills of PLPs and LACs.

Figure 8.28 Comparative Analysis of PLPs and LACs: Quality of Professional Skills in the North East Zone

Further, the data from the six zones also reflects that the drafting skills of PLPs (50%) are fairly good compared to LACs, as a majority of judicial officers rated the drafting skills of PLPs as fairly good quality while those of LACs (47%) as moderately low quality. The disparity in terms of drafting skills is the reflection of incompetent LACs as compared to PLPs.

Therefore, the question arises whether this disparity reflects in terms of overall satisfaction too. Per data from the six zones, the disparity is visible in terms of overall satisfaction. As shown in Figure 8.28, 52% of judicial officers believe that the overall satisfaction with PLPs is fairly good, while 46% of judicial officers opined that the overall satisfaction with LACs is moderately low level. Therefore, we tend to see a pattern in judicial officers' opinions from all the zones that LACs lack some level of competence at every essential skill compared to PLPs.

8.2.5. *Reasons for Not Opting/Discontinuing the Services of LACs Under FLAS in the Six Zones (Aware Women)*

The previous section delved into a comparison of the disparity between the level of professional skills of LACs and PLPs. The assessment has

Table 8.29 Comparative Analysis of PLPs and LACs: Quality of Professional Skills (by Judicial Officers) in the Six Zones

ARGUMENTS								
Respondents		*Very Good*	*Good*	*Fair*	*Bad*	*Very Bad*	*No Comments*	*Total*
PLPs	Count	49	326	161	4	1	68	609
	% of Total	8%	54%	26%	1%	0%	11%	100%
LACs	Count	18	232	271	41	7	40	609
	% of Total	3%	38%	44%	7%	1%	7%	100%
PRESENTATION								
Respondents		*Very Good*	*Good*	*Fair*	*Bad*	*Very Bad*	*No Comments*	*Total*
PLPs	Count	34	319	178	6	1	71	609
	% of Total	6%	52%	29%	1%	0%	12%	100%
LACs	Count	13	234	283	33	5	41	609
	% of Total	2%	38%	47%	5%	1%	7%	100%
DRAFTING								
Respondents		*Very Good*	*Good*	*Fair*	*Bad*	*Very Bad*	*No Comments*	*Total*
PLPs	Count	36	304	187	9	1	72	609
	% of Total	6%	50%	31%	2%	0%	12%	100%
LACs	Count	13	234	283	33	5	41	609
	% of Total	2%	38%	47%	5%	1%	7%	100%
OVERALL								
Respondents		*Very Good*	*Good*	*Fair*	*Bad*	*Very Bad*	*No Comments*	*Total*
PLPs	Count	36	318	172	8	0	75	609
	% of Total	6%	52%	28%	1%	0%	12%	100%
LACs	Count	19	207	278	44	6	55	609
	% of Total	3%	34%	46%	7%	1%	9%	100%

Figure 8.29 Comparative Analysis of PLPs and LACs: Quality of Professional Skills in the Six Zones

raised serious questions about the level of competency of LACs. Even though the assessment rests on judicial officers' perspectives only, it endorses the views of entitled women beneficiaries who willingly did not avail of the benefits of FLAS. Table 8.30 demonstrates the zone-wise rationale of these women for not choosing FLAS. In total, lack of competence as the reason to not opt for legal aid services amounts to 28% of the total respondents.

Further, in the six zones, more than 505 women respondents from the North (63%), West (51%), and South Zones (51%) had no faith in the quality of services and operations of the LACs and legal system. Additionally, women respondents of this category in the Central (46%), North East (44%), and East Zones (43%) also had no faith in the LAS too.

Therefore, there is a perception among entitled women beneficiaries who willingly did not avail of the benefits of FLAS due to a lack of competent professional skills. This very rationale resonates with judicial officers' opinion on the quality of professional skills of LACs, where they have rated the overall competence of LACs below PLPs and moderately low quality.

Table 8.30 Reasons for Not Opting/Discontinuing the Services of LACs Under FLAS in the Six Zones (Aware Women)

Region		*Lack of Competence*	*Lack of Experience*	*Lack of Faith in the LAS*	*Non-Availability of Counsel*	*No Commitment and Sincerity Towards LAS*	*Complex Process for Getting Benefits*	*No Accountability of LACs for Dereliction of Duty*	*Demanded Money*	*Others*	*Total*
North	Count	114	44	290	87	70	56	29	31	4	458
	% of Total	25%	10%	63%	19%	15%	12%	6%	7%	1%	100%
East	Count	153	29	194	30	77	45	24	48	8	455
	% of Total	34%	6%	43%	7%	17%	10%	5%	11%	2%	100%
West	Count	114	51	176	40	58	45	25	25	5	343
	% of Total	33%	15%	51%	12%	17%	13%	7%	7%	2%	100%
South	Count	227	186	352	93	117	118	39	53	30	868
	% of Total	33%	15%	51%	12%	17%	13%	7%	7%	2%	100%
Central	Count	72	88	161	33	27	48	38	36	7	347
	% of Total	21%	25%	46%	10%	8%	14%	11%	10%	2%	100%
North East	Count	46	13	62	13	22	31	6	8	1	141
	% of Total	33%	9%	44%	9%	16%	22%	4%	6%	1%	100%
Total	Count	726	411	1235	296	371	343	161	201	55	2612
	%of Total	28%	16%	47%	11%	14%	13%	6%	8%	2%	100%

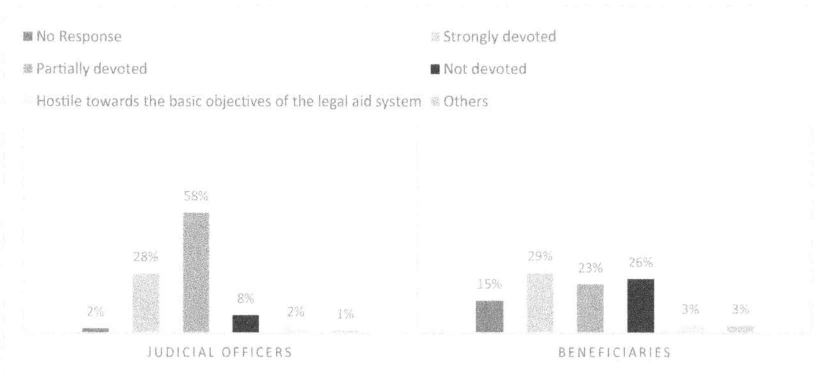

Figure 8.30 Evaluation of the Commitment and Devotion of LACs in the North Zone

Similarly, Table 8.31 shows the response of entitled women beneficiaries who willingly did not avail of the benefits of FLAS in terms of appointing PLPs over LACs. We see three major factors responsible for appointing a PLP over an LAC in almost all the six zones. Accountability in dereliction of duty is the single most prominent issue, found in more than 90% of respondents in every zone. The table also shows that commitment and competence (31%) were among the significant factors in choosing or appointing a PLP over an LAC. Therefore, the women respondents of this category do not have any trust in the quality of services offered by LACs in their respective zones, and the lack of faith in LACs is so deep that they are even ready to pay for a quality PLP.

8.2.5.1. Hypotheses Connected With the Commitment of the LACs

The first section discussed the elements that gauged the competence level of LACs and the LAS in the six zones. The second section of the chapter deals with the hypotheses and research questions related to the level of commitment LACs have towards FLAS in the research universe. As stated in Chapter 1, the data collected for these issues has already been highlighted in the preceding chapters, which deal with stakeholders – namely, legal aid beneficiaries, judicial officers, and LACs. This section draws variables that assess the commitment in the realm of the following hypotheses:

a. A dearth of committed LACs has negatively affected the quality of legal aid services.
b. Beneficiaries of the legal aid services have lost faith in the LAS.
c. People prefer PLPs instead of LACs engaged under FLAS.

Table 8.31 Rationale for Choosing/Appointing PLPs Over LACs in the Six Zones*

Region		*Commitment and Competence*	*Accountability for Dereliction of Duty*	*Proper Control Is Possible over Private Lawyer*	*Others*	*Total*
North	Count	110	467	275	89	484
	% of Total	22.7%	96.5%	56.8%	18.4%	100.0%
East	Count	168	512	364	89	534
	% of Total	31.5%	95.9%	68.2%	16.7%	100.0%
West	Count	89	349	206	93	360
	% of Total	24.7%	96.9%	57.2%	25.8%	100.0%
South	Count	363	920	628	262	1022
	% of Total	35.5%	90.0%	61.4%	25.6%	100.0%
Central	Count	119	395	201	142	411
	% of Total	29.0%	96.1%	48.9%	34.5%	100.0%
North East	Count	85	174	112	44	192
	% of Total	44.3%	90.6%	58.3%	22.9%	100.0%
Total	Count	934	2817	1786	719	3003
	% of Total	31%	94%	59%	24%	100%

*Multiple-response question. Percentages are based on respondents.

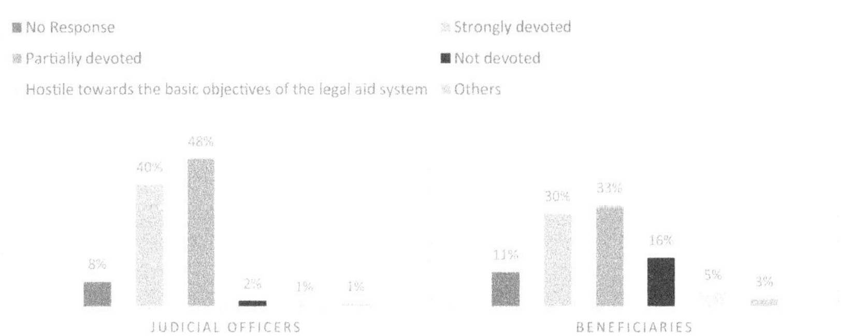

Figure 8.31 Evaluation of the Commitment and Devotion of LACs in the East Zone

The first assessment is based on the legal aid beneficiaries' opinions and judicial officers' opinions to analyze the level of commitment and devotion of LACs towards the mandate of legal aid services prescribed in the LSA Act, 1987. As shown in Figure 8.30, most judicial officers (58% "partially

Table 8.32 Evaluation of the Commitment and Devotion of LACs in the North Zone

Respondents		*No Response*	*Strongly Devoted*	*Partially Devoted*	*Not Devoted*	*Hostile Towards the Basic Objectives of the LAS*	*Others*	*Total*
Judicial Officers	Count	2	27	55	8	2	1	95
	% of Total	2%	28%	58%	8%	2%	1%	100%
Beneficiaries	Count	84	157	127	141	18	18	545
	% of Total	15%	29%	23%	26%	3%	3%	100%

Table 8.33 Evaluation of the Commitment and Devotion of LACs in the East Zone

Respondents		*No Response*	*Strongly Devoted*	*Partially Devoted*	*Not Devoted*	*Hostile Towards the Basic Objectives of the LAS*	*Others*	*Total*
Judicial Officers	Count	8	38	46	2	1	1	96
	% of Total	8%	40%	48%	2%	1%	1%	100%
Beneficiaries	Count	59	157	171	83	25	14	520
	% of Total	11%	30%	33%	16%	5%	3%	100%

devoted" and 8% "hostile") and a majority of beneficiaries in the North Zone responded that LACs are "partially devoted" to the mandate of FLAS.

Even if around 28% of judicial officers and 29% of beneficiaries felt that LACs are "strongly devoted" towards the mandate, it does not affect the overall narrative of LACs devoted partially to the mandate in the North Zone owing to its minute share.

In the East Zone, as shown in Table 8.33, most judicial officers (48% "partially devoted") and most of the beneficiaries (33%) opined that LACs' devotion towards the cause of legal aid services is partial.

Indeed, Figure 8.31 comprehends that more judicial officers and beneficiaries in the East Zone responded that LACs' devotion towards legal aid services is strong compared to the North Zone.

Similarly, in the West Zone, as shown in Figure 8.32, most judicial officers (63% "partially devoted" and 10% "not devoted") and a majority of beneficiaries responded that LACs are usually partially devoted (35%) towards the mandate of FLAS.

Table 8.34 Evaluation of the Commitment and Devotion of LACs in the West Zone

Respondents		*No Response*	*Strongly Devoted*	*Partially Devoted*	*Not Devoted*	*Hostile Towards the Basic Objectives of the LAS*	*Others*	*Total*
Judicial Officers	Count	12	20	80	12	1	1	126
	% of Total	10%	16%	63%	10%	1%	1%	100%
Beneficiaries	Count	83	157	154	63	9	4	437
	% of Total	19%	36%	35%	14%	2%	1%	100%

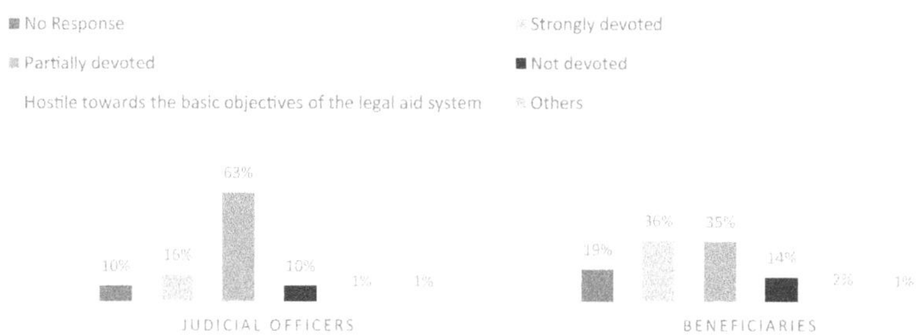

Figure 8.32 Evaluation of the Commitment and Devotion of LACs in the West Zone

Compared to the North and East Zones, the devotion or commitment of LACs, according to the judicial officers' perspective, was low in the West Zone. This highlights the absence of commitment among the LACs in the West Zone.

In the South Zone, as shown in Figure 8.33, more than half of the judicial officers (53%) and most beneficiaries opined that LACs' devotion to their zone is partially towards the mandate of FLAS.

It is pertinent to mention here that the lack of faith in the legal aid services by a potential woman beneficiary in the South Zone is one of the major reasons not to opt for FLAS. Indeed, the low level or partial devotion by the LACs towards the mandate of FLAS plays a vital role in the lack of faith among potential women beneficiaries.

In the Central Zone, as shown in Figure 8.34, interestingly, most of the beneficiaries responded that LACs are strongly devoted. Contrary to most judicial officers who were of the concerned opinion, LACs are only partially

Table 8.35 Evaluation of the Commitment and Devotion of LACs in the South Zone

Respondents		*No Response*	*Strongly Devoted*	*Partially Devoted*	*Not Devoted*	*Hostile Towards the Basic Objectives of the LAS*	*Others*	*Total*
Judicial Officers	Count	9	44	85	16	4	3	161
	% of Total	6%	27%	53%	10%	2%	2%	100%
Beneficiaries	Count	101	157	267	90	37	3	866
	% of Total	12%	18%	31%	10%	4%	0%	100%

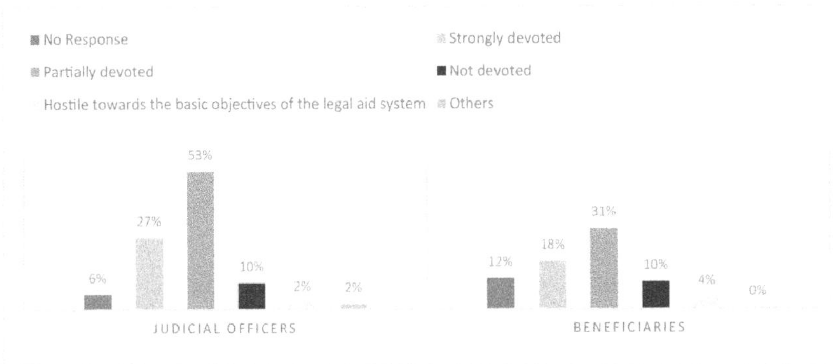

Figure 8.33 Evaluation of the Commitment and Devotion of LACs in the South Zone

devoted (51%). However, the opinion of beneficiaries should be taken holistically.

Therefore, the true nature of beneficiaries' opinions vis-a-vis the commitment and devotion of LACs should combine all the options. Most beneficiaries (37% "partial devoted," 13% "not devoted," 8% "hostile") have rated the level of commitment and devotion as comparatively too low than that of judicial officers.

In the North East Zone, as shown in Figure 8.35, like in the Central Zone, 56% of beneficiaries responded that LACs' devotion towards the mandate of FLAS was strong. As compared to judicial officers, it is indeed quite the opposite. The majority of judicial officers rated the devotion and commitment of LACs (49%) as partial.

Table 8.36 Evaluation of the Commitment and Devotion of LACs in the Central Zone

Respondents		*No Response*	*Strongly Devoted*	*Partially Devoted*	*Not Devoted*	*Hostile Towards the Basic Objectives of the LAS*	*Others*	*Total*
Judicial Officers	Count	10	14	44	12	5	1	86
	% of Total	12%	16%	51%	14%	6%	1%	100%
Beneficiaries	Count	65	157	139	51	31	6	380
	% of Total	17%	41%	37%	13%	8%	2%	100%

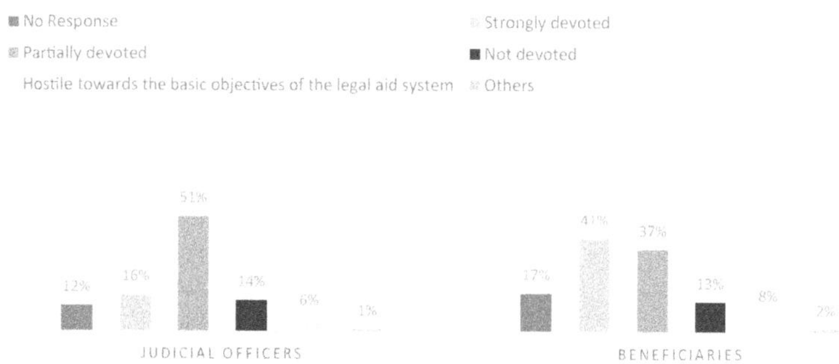

Figure 8.34 Evaluation of the Commitment and Devotion of LACs in the Central Zone

The difference in judicial officers' opinions and legal aid beneficiaries might be due to the legal knowledge level. As judicial officers deal with PLPs and LACs regularly, they are most suited to judge the level of devotion, while the beneficiaries seldom come and talk to lawyers (i.e., they meet the advocates only in a court hearing).

Table 8.38 demonstrates the zone-wise comparative analysis of judicial officers' opinions and beneficiaries from the North, East, West, South, Central, and North East Zones. Apart from the Central and North East Zones, commitment and devotion levels in almost all the zones happened to be partial from judicial officers' and beneficiaries' perspectives. Figure 8.36 shows a complete narrative of the level of commitment and devotion in the six zones. Most judicial officers were of the concerned opinion that LACs (55%) were partially devoted to the mandate of FLAS.

On the other hand, the majority of beneficiaries (32%) also opined that LACs were usually partially devoted. Remarkably, almost half of the

Table 8.37 Evaluation of the Commitment and Devotion of LACs in the North East Zone

Respondents		*No Response*	*Strongly Devoted*	*Partially Devoted*	*Not Devoted*	*Hostile Towards the Basic Objectives of the LAS*	*Others*	*Total*
Judicial Officers	Count	4	14	22	2	1	2	45
	% of Total	9%	31%	49%	4%	2%	4%	100%
Beneficiaries	Count	56	157	99	59	16	6	281
	% of Total	20%	56%	35%	21%	6%	2%	100%

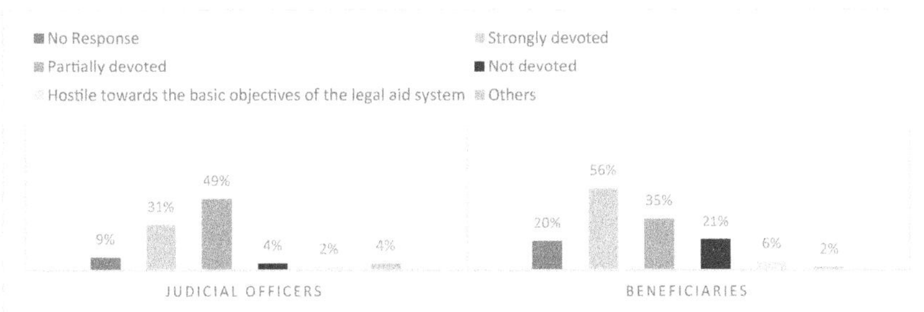

Figure 8.35 Evaluation of the Commitment and Devotion of LACs in the North East Zone

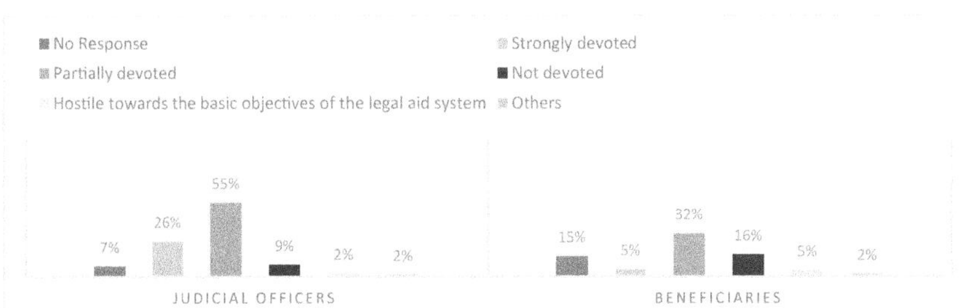

Figure 8.36 Evaluation of the Commitment and Devotion of LACs in the Six Zones

percentage share of beneficiaries, who rated the devotion of LACs as partially devoted, opined LACs were not at all devoted (16%) to the mandate of the legal aid services. Hence, LACs from all the six zones were partially devoted to the mandate of the legal aid services.

Table 8.38 Evaluation of the Commitment and Devotion of LACs in All the Six Zones

Respondents		*No Response*	*Strongly Devoted*	*Partially Devoted*	*Not Devoted*	*Hostile Towards the Basic Objectives of the LAS*	*Others*	*Total*
Judicial Officers	Count	45	157	332	52	14	9	609
	% of Total	7%	26%	55%	9%	2%	2%	100%
Beneficiaries	Count	448	157	957	487	136	51	3,029
	% of Total	15%	5%	32%	16%	5%	2%	100%

8.2.6. Places of Interaction Between LACs and Beneficiaries

This lack of devotion and commitment finds its roots in the very nature of engagement of LACs. Additionally, the low quantum of honorarium offered to LACs in lieu of FLAS also discourages the LACs towards the cause, as they can get a better honorarium in private practice. The data displayed in the earlier tables and oral feedback from the field suggest that LACs were also preoccupied with their private practices. Hence, it results in a low rate of interaction between LACs and beneficiaries.

The places at which LACs interact with their private clients and legal aid beneficiaries also display their commitment to each other. The commitment towards beneficiaries explicitly rests upon the ambiance in which the communication takes place. As shown in Chapter 4, one of the issues that beneficiaries face is a lack of communication with their respective LACs. This section will focus on the various places of interaction between LACs and beneficiaries in the six zones.

As shown in Figure 8.37, the majority of stakeholders in the North Zone responded that interaction between LACs and beneficiaries takes place on court premises, as 44% of LACs, 63% of regulators, and 55% of beneficiaries usually interact on court premises, followed by either the chambers of the advocate per the LACs and beneficiaries and over the phone per regulators.

District courts in the North Zone lack infrastructure, and since most LACs are not senior enough to have a chamber of their own, they certainly choose the court premises for interaction. Since LACs also see their private clients, they tend to spend more time with them. This results in low communication quality between the LACs and beneficiaries as the concerned LACs might be seeing other private clients. Therefore, proper concentration and commitment towards a legal aid beneficiary are hard to attain.

Table 8.39 Places of Interaction Between LACs and Beneficiaries in the North Zone*

Respondents		*Office of the LSA*	*Chamber of Advocates*	*Phone*	*Courts*	*Jail*	*Others*	*Total*
LACs	Count	43	53	30	58	0	5	133
	% of Total	32%	40%	23%	44%	0%	4%	100%
Regulators	Count	4	4	6	5	0	0	8
	% of Total	50%	50%	75%	63%	0%	0%	100%
Beneficiaries	Count	35	139	67	255	36	36	462
	% of Total	8%	30%	15%	55%	8%	8%	100%

*Multiple-response question. Percentages are based on respondents.

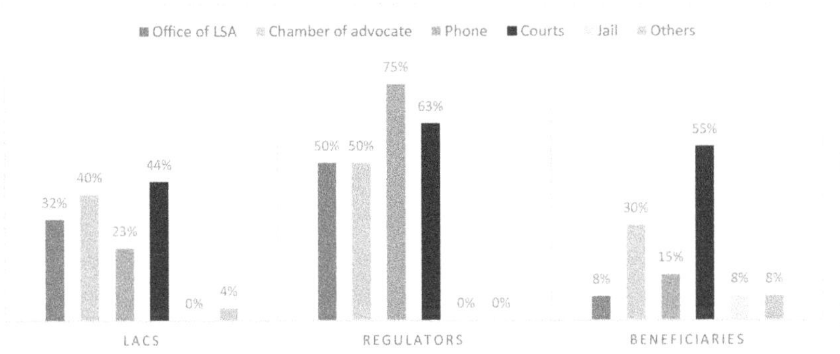

Figure 8.37 Places of Interaction Between LACs and Beneficiaries in the North Zone

Another noticeable aspect is that almost 50% of regulators responded that LACs and beneficiaries interact at the office of the LSA. The claims recorded from regulators do not corroborate the responses given by either LACs or beneficiaries.

In the East Zone, as shown in Figure 8.38, the majority of stakeholders responded that the LACs and beneficiaries often talk in the office of the LSA, followed by the court premises, as 43% of LACs and 41% of beneficiaries coordinated with each other.

It is pertinent to note that per the field notes, the office of the DLSA is overburdened with daily cause listing, administrative work, and spaces for pre-negotiations. Therefore, indirectly, a lack of communication between the LACs and beneficiaries is bound to occur as beneficiaries do not have any specific place for discussion of their case.

Table 8.40 Places of Interaction Between LACs and Beneficiaries in the East Zone*

Respondents		*Office of the LSA*	*Chamber of Advocates*	*Phone*	*Courts*	*Jail*	*Others*	*Total*
LACs	Count	61	27	30	50	0	2	117
	% of Total	52%	23%	26%	43%	0%	2%	100%
Regulators	Count	3	0	0	0	0	0	3
	% of Total	100%	0%	0%	0%	0%	0%	100%
Beneficiaries	Count	144	130	87	199	3	31	481
	% of Total	30%	27%	18%	41%	1%	6%	100%

*Multiple-response question. Percentages are based on respondents.

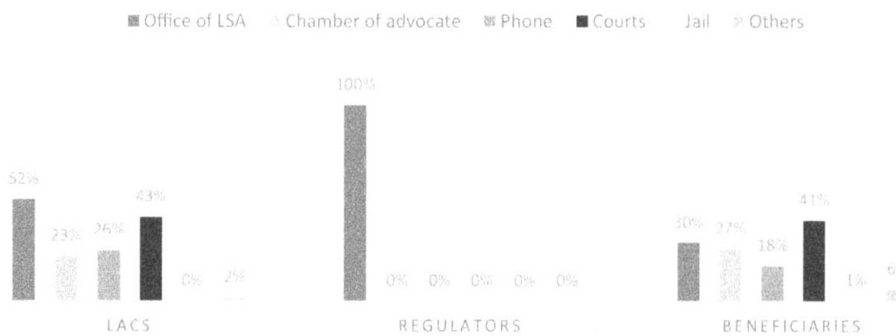

Figure 8.38 Places of Interaction Between LACs and Beneficiaries in the East Zone

In the West Zone, as shown in Figure 8.39, the majority of LACs (52%), regulators (60%), and beneficiaries (61%) opined that interaction between LACs and beneficiaries takes place on the court premises. Further, the interaction also takes place at the office of the LSA. Compared to the North and East Zones, beneficiaries interact less over the phone in the West Zone.

In the West Zone, the possibility of having quality communication with beneficiaries is implausible as the interaction takes place in heavily crowded places with no or very basic infrastructure. This results in the LACs often skipping the interaction with the beneficiaries as it becomes a cumbersome task.

In the South Zone, as shown in Figure 8.40, per the opinion of LACs (55%), regulators (88%), and beneficiaries (47%), most of the interaction between LACs and beneficiaries takes place at the office of LAS, followed by the court premises.

Therefore, in the South Zone, the interaction between LACs and beneficiaries occurs in the office of the LSA and near the court premises. However, per the observations made by the research associate and field investigators,

Table 8.41 Places of Interaction Between LACs and Beneficiaries in the West Zone*

Respondents		*Office of the LSA*	*Chamber of Advocates*	*Phone*	*Courts*	*Jail*	*Others*	*Total*
LACs	Count	66	25	21	86	0	3	164
	% of Total	40%	15%	13%	52%	0%	2%	100%
Regulators	Count	2	2	0	3	0	0	5
	% of Total	40%	40%	0%	60%	0%	0%	100%
Beneficiaries	Count	**116**	80	58	242	5	18	398
	% of Total	**29%**	20%	15%	61%	1%	5%	100%

*Multiple-response question. Percentages are based on respondents.

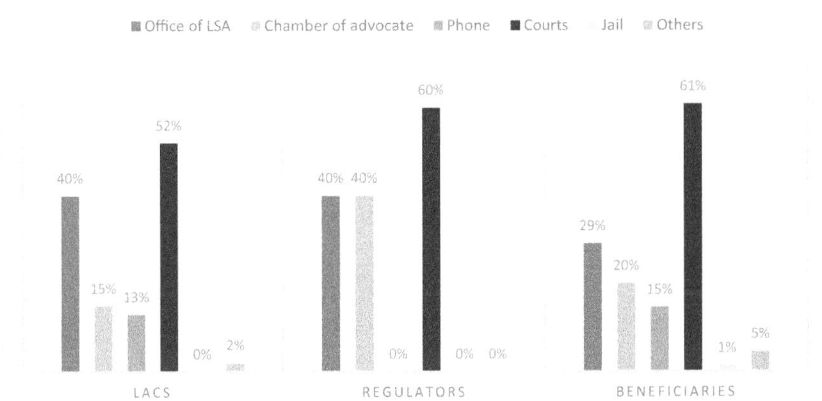

Figure 8.39 Places of Interaction Between LACs and Beneficiaries in the West Zone

in the South Zone, only the first interaction takes place in the office of the LSA; the rest of all the subsequent interactions between the LACs and beneficiaries take place in or near the court premises.

Per the opinions of most LACs (72%), regulators (100%), and beneficiaries (72%), the interaction between LACs and beneficiaries in the Central Zone usually takes place on the court premises. This is followed by the chamber of advocates as the place of interactions with LACs. Per the researchers' field observations, most of the LACs do not have any chambers as they are not that senior enough.

Thus, most of the interaction is bound to occur outside or in crowded places, which affects the discussion or conversation between a beneficiary and LACs and demotivates LACs to interact at length.

Table 8.42 Places of Interaction Between LACs and Beneficiaries in the South Zone*

Respondents		*Office of the LSA*	*Chamber of Advocates*	*Phone*	*Courts*	*Jail*	*Others*	*Total*
LACs	Count	133	62	38	71	0	2	242
	% of Total	55%	26%	16%	29%	0%	1%	100%
Regulators	Count	7	2	2	0	0	5	8
	% of Total	88%	25%	25%	0%	0%	63%	100%
Beneficiaries	Count	374	184	186	273	10	4	799
	% of Total	47%	23%	23%	34%	1%	1%	100%

*Multiple-response question. Percentages are based on respondents.

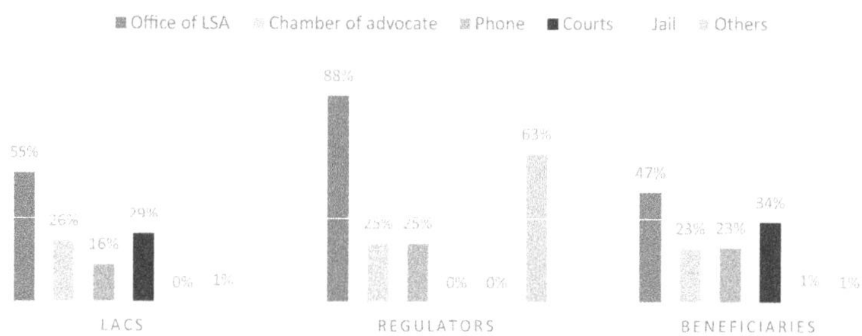

Figure 8.40 Places of Interaction Between LACs and Beneficiaries in the South Zone

*Multiple-response question. Percentages are based on respondents.

In the North East Zone, as shown in Figure 8.42, the majority of LACs (64%) and beneficiaries (46%) responded that they usually interact with each other in or near the court premises. The second most preferable place for them to interact is the chamber of the LACs.

Interestingly, the regulators (50%) in the North East Zone were of the impression that the interaction between LACs and beneficiaries often takes place in the office of the LSA. However, a minute 7% of LACs and 11% of beneficiaries said that they interact with LACs in the office of the LSA.

Figure 8.43 highlights the responses from all the six zones regarding places where the interaction between LACs and beneficiaries happens. Around 48% of LACs, 63% of regulators, and 49% of beneficiaries responded that the interaction between a beneficiary and an LAC occurs near or on the court premises.

Per the empirical study, the second-best place where LACs and beneficiaries often interact is the office of the LSA, followed by the chamber of

Table 8.43 Places of Interaction Between LACs and Beneficiaries in the Central Zone*

Respondents		*Office of the LSA*	*Chamber of Advocates*	*Phone*	*Courts*	*Jail*	*Others*	*Total*
LACs	Count	26	69	56	121	0	3	167
	% of Total	16%	41%	34%	72%	0%	2%	100%
Regulators	Count	3	2	3	4	0	0	4
	% of Total	75%	50%	75%	100%	0%	0%	100%
Beneficiaries	Count	49	92	84	247	2	7	344
	% of Total	14%	27%	24%	72%	1%	2%	100%

*Multiple-response question. Percentages are based on respondents.

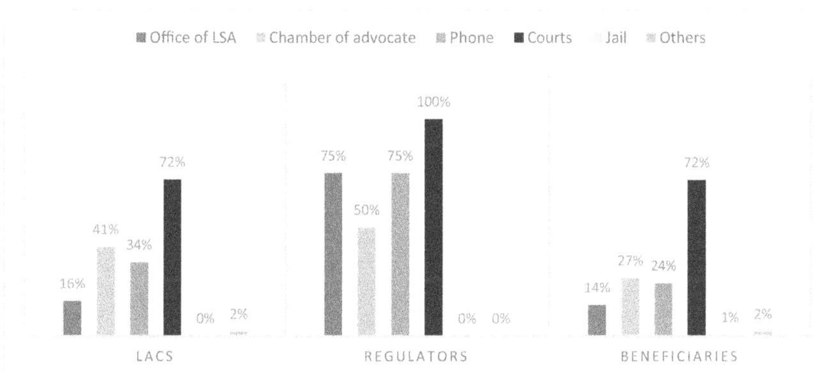

Figure 8.41 Places of Interaction Between LACs and Beneficiaries in the Central Zone

advocates and a few interactions over the phone. Per the field observations, the higher rate of interaction with LACs at the office of the LSA might be due to the acquaintance of a beneficiary with the front office and the office of the LSA. Similarly, LACs often interact with beneficiaries over the phone to skip long in-person conversations. Since empaneled lawyers are often not the most senior, they seldom have any chambers. Instead, the beneficiary's chambers are the common advocates' room present at every district court.

Hence, the interaction between LACs and beneficiaries often takes place in crowded places, like court premises and the office of the LSA. Given that LACs have their private cases, the quality of discussion at these places is bound to be of low quality and considerably minimum period.

Table 8.44 Places of Interaction Between LACs and Beneficiaries in the North East Zone*

Respondents		*Office of the LSA*	*Chamber of Advocates*	*Phone*	*Courts*	*Jail*	*Others*	*Total*
LACs	Count	4	17	8	38	0	6	59
	% of Total	7%	29%	14%	64%	0%	10%	100%
Regulators	Count	1	0	1	0	0	2	2
	% of Total	50%	0%	50%	0	0	100%	100%
Beneficiaries	Count	29	59	34	126	13	15	276
	% of Total	11%	21%	12%	46%	5%	5%	100%

*Multiple-response question. Percentages are based on respondents.

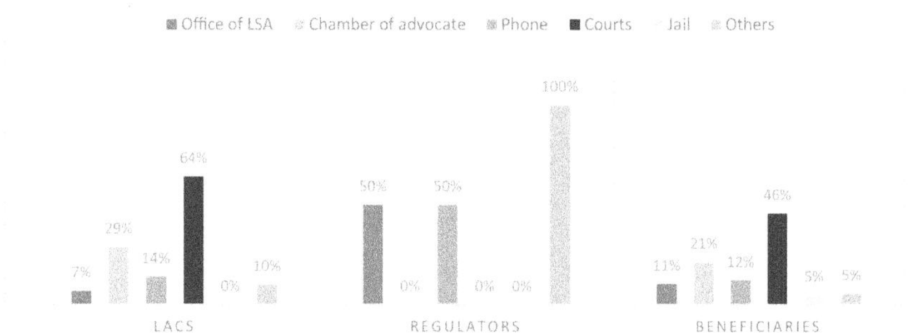

Figure 8.42 Places of Interaction Between LACs and Beneficiaries in the North East Zone

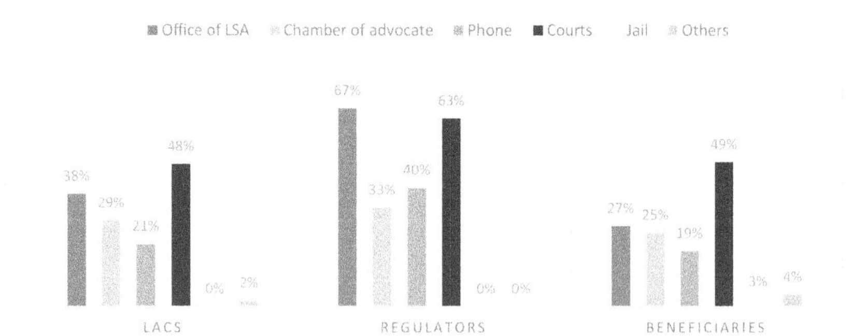

Figure 8.43 Places of Interaction Between LACs and Beneficiaries in the Six Zones*

Table 8.45 Places of Interaction Between LACs and Beneficiaries in All the Six Zones*

Respondents		*Office of the LSA*	*Chamber of Advocates*	*Phone*	*Courts*	*Jail*	*Others*	*Total*
LACs	Count	333	253	183	424	0	21	882
	% of Total	38%	29%	21%	48%	0%	2%	100%
Regulators	Count	20	10	12	19	0	0	30
	% of Total	67%	33%	40%	63%	0%	0%	100%
Beneficiaries	Count	747	684	516	1342	69	111	2696
	% of Total	27%	25%	19%	49%	3%	4%	100%

*Multiple-response question. Percentages are based on respondents.

8.2.7. *Time Spent by LACs in a Week on LAS and Private Cases*

As seen in Chapter 3, most beneficiaries faced difficulties in communication and interaction with their LACs. It might be that quality interaction rests on the place of interaction and where an LAC remains focused and committed to their beneficiaries.

Further, in the previous section, since most times the interaction between LACs and beneficiaries takes place in a highly crowded vicinity, often LACs escape from the conversations to focus on their private clients. This section compares and aims to justify the assertion that LACs spend far less time on legal aid cases than on private ones.

As shown in Figure 8.44, in the North Zone, most LACs (56%) opined that they spend 20 hours and above per week on their private cases. Compared to the legal aid cases, around 70% of LACs responded that they spend less than 10 hours per week on legal aid cases.

The disparity in terms of commitment of time is an explanation of the lack of commitment by LACs on the cases under free legal aid. Therefore, often LACs skip communication with legal aid beneficiaries and devote less time to legal aid services in the North Zone.

In the East Zone, as shown in Figure 8.45, most LACs devote either less than 10 hours (44%) or around 11 to 20 hours (50%) to LAS cases, whereas most LACs devote more than 20 hours to their respective private cases (59%).

Compared to the North Zone, the LACs devoted more time to legal aid services. However, the time spent on private clients remains too high. Therefore, in the East Zone, the time committed to legal aid services remains lower than that spent in private cases of LACs.

In the West Zone, as shown in Figure 8.46, there is a complete distinction between the average times spent by LACs in a private case and in legal aid services. Per the opinions of the LACs, the majority of LACs (around 60%)

Table 8.46 Time Spent by LACs in a Week on LAS and Private Cases in the North Zone

Type of Cases		*1 to 10 Hours*	*11 to 20 Hours*	*20 Hours and Above*	*Nil/No Comments*	*Total*
Legal Aid Cases	Count	105	32	0	13	150
	% Total	70%	21%	0%	9%	100%
Private Cases	Count	35	21	84	10	150
	%Total	23%	14%	56%	7%	100%

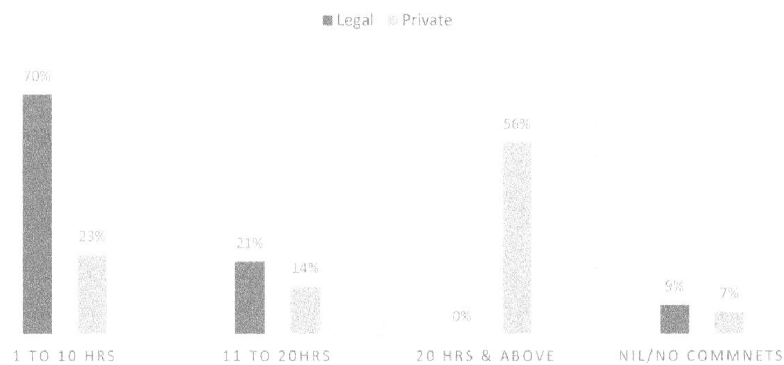

Figure 8.44 Time spent in a week by LAC on LAS and Private Cases in the North Zone

spend less than 10 hours per week on legal aid services. On the other hand, the majority of LACs responded that they spend more than 20 hours per week on their private cases (65%).

Indeed, this variation between legal aid services and private cases reflects the lack of commitment of LACs for the legal aid services in the West Zone. Hence, in the West Zone, the average time spent by LACs on legal aid services stands far too less than on private cases.

In the South Zone, as shown in Figure 8.47, the majority of LACs opined that they devote more than 20 hours on an average towards their private cases (60%) per week, while, for the legal aid cases, they devote less than 10 hours per week (53%).

The disparity between the hours is almost double, reflecting the degree of commitment of LACs towards the legal aid services. However, 37% of LACs responded that they devote around 11 to 20 hours on average to LAS cases per week. But this stands nowhere near in terms of commitment and

Table 8.47 Time Spent by LACs in a Week on LAS and Private Cases in the East Zone

Type of Cases		*1 to 10 Hours*	*11 to 20 Hours*	*20 Hours and Above*	*Nil/No Comments*	*Total*
Legal Aid Cases	Count	60	68	0	9	137
	% Total	44%	50%	0%	7%	100%
Private Cases	Count	21	27	80	9	137
	%Total	15%	20%	58%	7%	100%

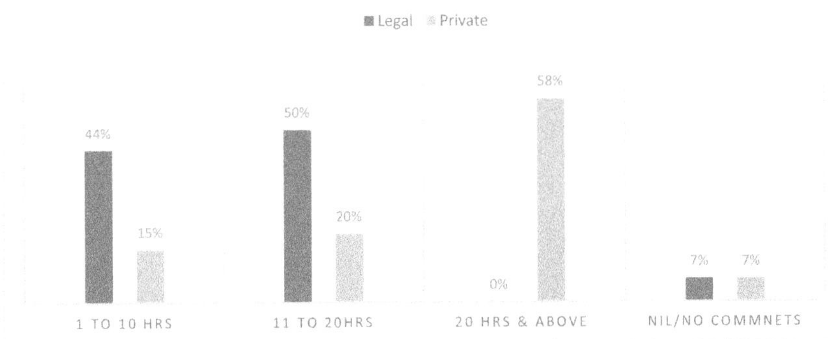

Figure 8.45 Time Spent by LACs in a Week on LAS and Private Cases in the East Zone

devotion towards private cases. Thus, in the South Zone, the average time spent on LAS cases remains far too less than time spent on private cases.

The disparity between the average time spent on legal aid services and private cases also remains significantly high in the Central Zone. As shown in Figure 8.48, most LACs (52%) responded that the average time spent on legal aid services in a week is less than 10 hours. Further, the same LACs responded that their average time spent on private cases (59%) in a week stands above 20 hours a week.

Indeed, there is much disparity in the devotion and commitment of LACs in time devoted per week. Thus, in the Central Zone, the lack of commitment in terms of time spent on legal aid services is evident enough.

The North East Zone, as shown in Figure 8.49, remains the most balanced in terms of LACs spending time with their beneficiaries and private clients. The majority of LACs (61%) replied that the average time spent on legal aid services is less than 10 hours. On the other hand, 39% of LACs responded that they spend around 1 to 10 hours (20%) and more than 20 hours (59%) over a week on private cases.

Table 8.48 Time Spent by LACs in a Week on LAS and Private Cases in the West Zone

Type of Cases		*1 to 10 Hours*	*11 to 20 Hours*	*20 Hours and Above*	*Nil/No Comments*	*Total*
Legal Aid Cases	Count	112	66	0	10	188
	% Total	60%	35%	0%	5%	100%
Private Cases	Count	35	24	122	7	188
	%Total	19%	13%	65%	4%	100%

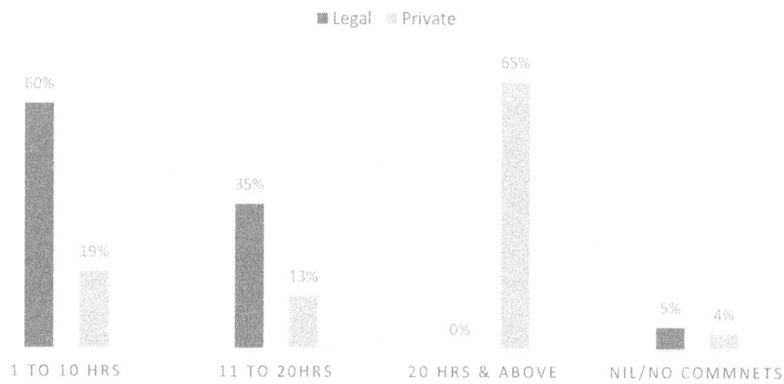

Figure 8.46 Time Spent by LACs in a Week on LAS and Private Cases in the West Zone

Undoubtedly, LACs prefer to devote more time to private cases than LAS cases. Therefore, in the North East Zone, LACs spend more time on private cases than cases under FLAS.

The zone-wise analysis showed that in almost every zone, LACs devoted and committed more time to private cases as compared to the legal aid services. Figure 8.50 shows the collective response from LACs over all the six zones. As it is evident, a stark disparity exists between LACs spending their time on legal aid services and LACs spending their time on private cases.

Around 56% of LACs responded that the time spent by them on the LAS cases throughout the week was less than or equal to 10 hours. On the contrary, 58% of the same LACs responded that they spend 20 hours and above on private cases.

Table 8.49 Time Spent by LACs in a Week on LAS and Private Cases in the South Zone

Type of Cases		*1 to 10 Hours*	*11 to 20 Hours*	*20 Hours and Above*	*Nil/No Comments*	*Total*
Legal Aid Cases	Count	146	101	0	29	276
	% Total	53%	37%	0%	11%	100%
Private Cases	Count	52	29	165	30	276
	%Total	19%	11%	60%	11%	100%

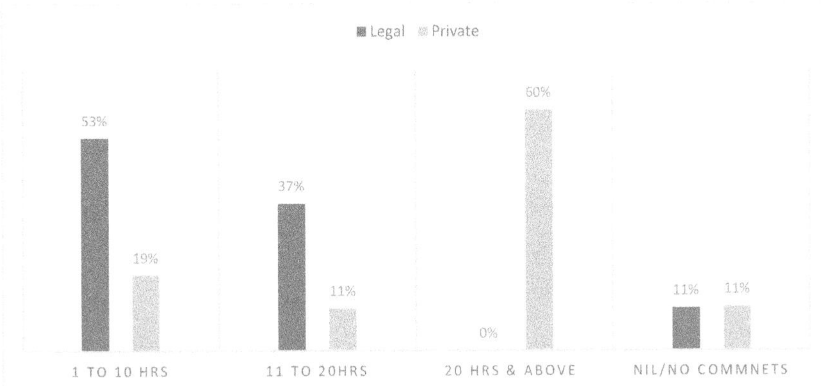

Figure 8.47 Time Spent by LACs in a Week on LAS and Private Cases in the South Zone

8.2.8. *Difficulties/Issues Faced While Interacting With LACs in the Six Zones*

One can easily comprehend why LACs are often absent or underprepared during a legal aid case hearing or briefing, as they devote a large chunk of their time to private cases. Therefore, the lack of devotion in terms of time and commitment is evident from the data.

The factors that contribute to the less interaction between LACs and beneficiaries are also related to lack of infrastructure, as explained earlier in the section, and how most of the time, beneficiaries and LACs interact in crowded places. Another factor is related to the low honorarium involved with legal aid services. LACs focus more on private clients as they get comparatively higher income from them than cases under free legal aid.

Table 8.50 Time Spent by LACs in a Week on LAS and Private Cases in the Central Zone

Type of Cases		*1 to 10 Hours*	*11 to 20 Hours*	*20 Hours and Above*	*Nil/No Comments*	*Total*
Legal Aid Cases	Count	96	77	0	11	184
	% Total	52%	42%	0%	6%	100%
Private Cases	Count	37	32	109	6	184
	%Total	20%	17%	59%	3%	100%

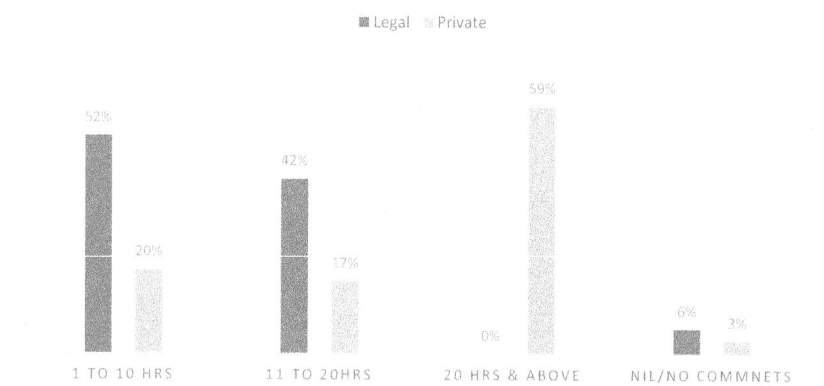

Figure 8.48 Time Spent by LACs in a Week on LAS and Private Cases in the Central Zone

In the previous section, the focus was on assessing the constraints faced by beneficiaries while interacting with their respective LACs. Researchers also asked beneficiaries and judicial officers about the difficulties they faced while interacting with LACs. Responses from legal aid beneficiaries and judicial officers were considered because, among the stakeholders, these two categories interact with LACs the most. In total, 1,815 beneficiaries attempted to answer the question, out of which around 76% (see Figure 8.51) were hesitant to communicate about any difficulties they faced.

Similarly, 350 out of 609 judicial officers either did not comment on the specific question or did not face any difficulties. However, it is important to note the difficulties flagged out by judicial officers and legal aid beneficiaries. As shown in Figure 8.51, LACs occupied with their private practice was one of the major issues flagged by judicial officers and beneficiaries.

Table 8.51 Time Spent by LACs in a Week on LAS and Private Cases in the North East Zone

Type of Cases		*1 to 10 Hours*	*11 to 20 Hours*	*20 Hours and Above*	*Nil/No Comments*	*Total*
Legal Aid Cases	Count	96	77	0	11	184
	% Total	52%	42%	0%	6%	100%
Private Cases	Count	37	32	109	6	184
	%Total	20%	17%	59%	3%	100%

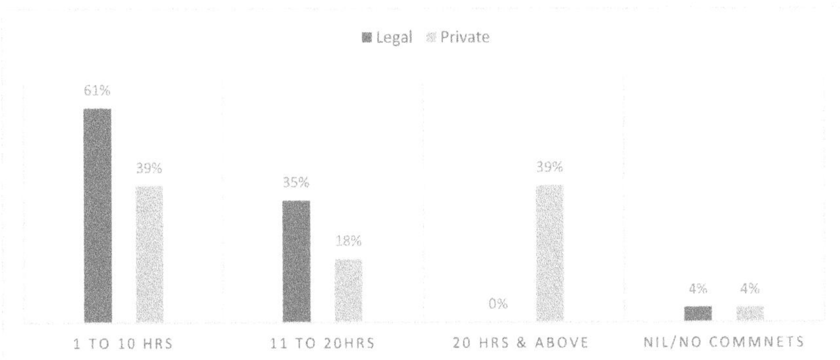

Figure 8.49 Time Spent by LACs in a Week on LAS and Private Cases in the North East Zone

Indeed, beneficiaries even stated that LACs showed no keen interest, as 273 out of 1,815 voiced this issue. Per the researchers' field observations, most of the time, judicial officers often call LACs from some other courts or cases to attend the legal aid hearing case. The concern voiced by judicial officers and beneficiaries across the six zones transpires to fall under the garb of the lack of commitment shown by LACs concerning cases related to legal aid services.

The beneficiaries and judicial officers responded about the nature of complaints, formal or informal, made by them. Per the field observations, judicial officers or regulators do not lodge any formal/written complaint records. Nevertheless, regulators and judicial officers receive complaints about the services offered by LACs under FLAS.

As shown in Table 8.54, most regulators (27%) received complaints from beneficiaries about the LACs not interacting and attending the courts late in the North Zone. Similarly, as shown in Table 8.55, around 50% of judicial officers in the North Zone received complaints from the beneficiaries about LACs being unavailable for arguments, and 44% of judicial officers also

Table 8.52 Time Spent by LACs in a Week on LAS and Private Cases in All the Six Zones

Type of Cases		*1 to 10 Hours*	*11 to 20 Hours*	*20 Hours and Above*	*Nil/No Comments*	*Total*
Legal Aid Cases	Count	563	369	0	75	1007
	% Total	56%	37%	0%	7%	100%
Private Cases	Count	208	146	588	65	1007
	%Total	21%	14%	58%	6%	100%

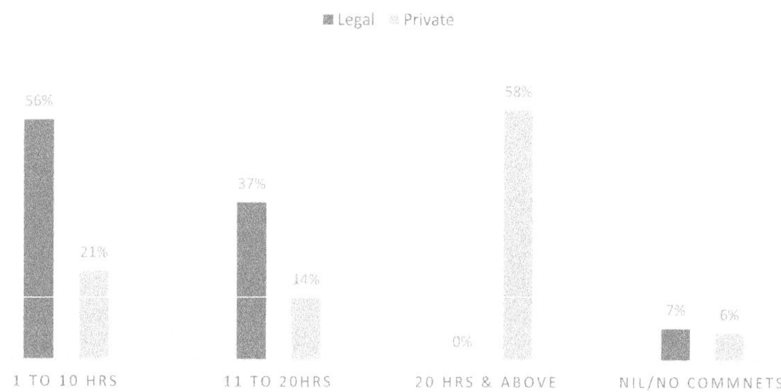

Figure 8.50 Time Spent by LACs in a Week on LAS and Private Cases in the Six Zones

received complaints about LACs not interacting with the beneficiaries. One of the issues that beneficiaries pointed out in front of regulators and judicial officers was LACs not raising quality arguments.

However, as shown in Table 8.56, most judicial officers, 40% in the North Zone, criticized LACs for the low quality of arguments presented by LACs and LACs attending the court late. Certainly, in the North Zone, complaints received against LACs are their failure to interact with beneficiaries or often being late for attending the hearing. Therefore, the data reflects the lack of commitment among the LACs.

As shown in Table 8.54, 50% of regulators received complaints from beneficiaries pertaining to LACs not interacting with their respective beneficiaries in the East Zone. Further, 50% of regulators also received complaints about LACs not protecting their beneficiaries' interests. Similarly, as shown in Table 8.54, 33% of the judicial officers in the East Zone received complaints from beneficiaries that LACs often demanded money and were also not available for arguments at the time of the hearing.

Similarly, in the West Zone, as shown in Table 8.54, 50% of regulators received complaints about the LACs attending the court late and not being prepared for the argument. The beneficiaries highlight the same concerns in their complaints to judicial officers in the West Zone. As shown in Table 8.55, 40% of judicial officers received complaints from beneficiaries related to LACs seeking frequent adjournments, 30% related to demanding money for services, 20% related to not being ready for arguments, and 20% related to not interacting with legal aid beneficiaries. Regulators in the West Zone, as shown in Table 8.54, received complaints from the only judicial officer pertaining to LACs being unprepared for arguments at the time of the hearing. Thus, per the complaints made by either beneficiaries or judicial officers to the regulators, LACs are not prepared for arguments, do not interact with the beneficiaries, do not attend the court, and even seek frequent adjournments. The data reflects the lack of commitment among the LACs in the West Zone.

As shown in Table 8.54, 40% of regulators received complaints from beneficiaries regarding LACs not interacting with beneficiaries, followed by 20% of regulators receiving complaints from beneficiaries regarding LACs attending the court late, not being prepared for arguments, and not raising quality arguments. Similarly, as shown in Table 8.55, around 38% of judicial officers responded beneficiaries complained about both LACs not cooperating with them and not raising good arguments. Further, 19% of judicial officers in the South Zone also received complaints from beneficiaries that LACs are neither attending the courts on time nor interacting with beneficiaries.

Moreover, per the judicial officers, 13% of beneficiaries also complained about LACs taking frequent adjournments, 13% of them complained about LACs being unprepared for arguments, and 25% of them complained about LACs demanding money. Similarly, judicial officers in the South Zone were also vocal in complaining about LACs. As shown in Table 8.56, 33% of regulators received complaints about LACs frequently attending the courts late, seeking many adjournments, and not making quality arguments. Therefore, the responses received from regulators and judicial officers about the complaints they often receive from either beneficiaries or judicial officers echo the lack of commitment among LACs in the South Zone.

Similarly, in the Central Zone, as shown in Table 8.54, 33% of regulators received complaints from beneficiaries concerning LACs being late to attend the court and not interacting with beneficiaries. Further, 17% of regulators received complaints from beneficiaries related to LACs seeking many adjournments and not protecting beneficiaries' interests. Similarly, as shown in Table 8.55, 54% of judicial officers received complaints from beneficiaries in the Central Zone that LACs are not interacting with beneficiaries at all.

Furthermore, around 23% of judicial officers also received complaints from beneficiaries pertaining to LACs deputing others or juniors for the court cases under free legal aid. Apart from these, judicial officers also

Table 8.53 Difficulties/Issues Faced While Interacting With LACs in the Six Zones

Respondents		*Low Rates of Honorarium for Services of the LAC*	*No Keen Interest to Interact*	*Occupied With his Private Practice Matters*	*Non-Commitment Towards the Legal Aid Services*	*Money Demanded* **on Every Hearing/Listing**	*Others*	*No Comments*	*Total*
Beneficiaries	Count	168	273	176	195	134	7	1376	1,815
	% of Total	9%	15%	10%	11%	7%	0%	76%	100%
Respondents		**No Response**	**LAC Occupied With his Private Practice Matters**	**Attitude of Beneficiaries**	**Attitude of LAC**	**Others**	**Nil**	**Total**	
Judicial Officers	Count	67	170	38	29	22	283	609	
	% of Total	11%	28%	6%	5%	4%	47%	100%	

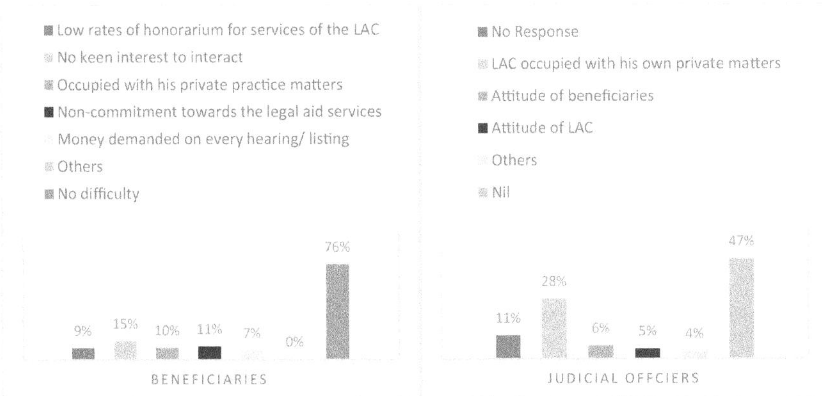

Figure 8.51 Difficulties/Issues Faced While Interacting With LACs in the Six Zones

received complaints related to LACs being absent, not being prepared for arguments (15%), and seeking many adjournments (8%). On the other hand, 50% of judicial officers in the Central Zone, as shown in Table 8.56, complained to regulators about LACs not being prepared for arguments and LACs not interacting with their respective beneficiaries. Thus, these complaints from either beneficiaries or judicial officers to the regulators in the Central Zone sum up that the LACs' lack devotion and commitment towards their beneficiaries.

In each zone, the nature of complaints against LACs revolved around themes of lacking commitment to LACs. In terms of all the six zones, as shown in Figure 8.52, most of the complaints received from beneficiaries to regulators are either LACs not interacting with clients or LACs attending the court late. In the case of complaints received from beneficiaries to judicial officers, the majority are related to LACs having no time to interact with their clients, LACs not being present for arguments, and deputing a junior or another person for arguments. Further, even the complaints filed by judicial officers to regulators in all the six zones show a homogeneity, as complaints share a similar nature – LACs not attending the courts on time and LACs not being prepared for arguments. Additionally, seeking too many adjournments seems to be a common complaint by beneficiaries and judicial officers. Hence, the lack of commitment among the LACs in the six zones is evident, which affects the quality of legal aid services negatively.

8.2.8.1. Hypothesis: Beneficiaries Have No Faith in the LAS and Opt for Free Legal Aid Out of Compulsion

One of the hypotheses proposed revolves around the faith of beneficiaries in the present LAS. Many potential beneficiaries do not have faith in the LAS

Table 8.54 Nature of Complaints by Beneficiaries to Regulators in the Five Zones

Region		*Not Being Prepared for the Arguments*	*Being Late for Attending Courts*	*Seeking Many Adjournments*	*Not Protecting the Interests of Beneficiaries*	*Quality of Arguments*	*Not Interacting With Clients*	*Total*
North	Count	0	3	2	1	2	3	11
	% of Total	0%	27%	18%	9%	18%	27%	100%
East	Count	0	0	0	1	0	1	2
	% of Total	0%	0%	0%	50%	0%	50%	100%
West	Count	1	1	0	0	0	0	2
	% of Total	50%	50%	0%	0%	0%	0%	100%
South	Count	1	1	0	0	1	2	5
	% of Total	20%	20%	0%	0%	20%	40%	100%
Central	Count	0	2	1	1	0	2	6
	% of Total	0%	33%	17%	17%	0%	33%	100%
Total	Count	2	7	3	3	3	8	26
	% of Total	8%	27%	12%	12%	12%	31%	100%

Figure 8.52 Nature of Complaints by Beneficiaries to Judicial Officers and Regulators and by Regulators to Judicial Officers

and prefer a PLP over an LAC. Those who opt for legal aid services believe they do not have enough resources to engage PLPs. To get a complete and balanced picture, the researchers collected data in the form of questionnaires from three distinct respondents. These respondents were potential legal aid beneficiaries, the aware entitled women, yet they did not opt for the free legal aid and were unaware entitled women respondents. The field investigator first informed the unaware entitled women respondents about their eligibility to get free legal aid and subsequently requested their willingness and unwillingness to opt for FLAS.

Table 8.55 Nature of Complaints by Beneficiaries to Judicial Officers in the Six Zones

Regions		*Not Raising Good Arguments*	*Not Being Available for Arguments*	*Seeking Frequent Adjournments*	*Not Being Ready for Arguments*	*Deputing Juniors or Another Person*	*No Time to Interact With Clients*	*No Cooperation From the LAC*	*Demanding Money for the Legal Services*	*Others*	*Total*
North	Count	3	8	1	5	0	7	3	9	0	16
	% of Total	19%	50%	6%	31%	0%	44%	19%	56%	0%	100%
East	Count	0	1	0	0	0	0	0	1	1	3
	% of Total	0%	33%	0%	0%	0%	0%	0%	33%	33%	100%
West	Count	1	1	4	2	0	2	0	3	1	10
	% of Total	10%	10%	40%	20%	0%	20%	0%	30%	10%	100%
South	Count	6	3	2	2	2	3	6	4	0	16
	% of Total	38%	19%	13%	13%	13%	19%	38%	25%	0%	100%
Central	Count	2	2	1	2	3	7	0	3	0	13
	% of Total	15%	15%	8%	15%	23%	54%	0%	23%	0%	100%
North East	Count	0	0	1	0	0	0	1	0	0	2
	% of Total	0%	0%	50%	0%	0%	0%	50%	0%	0%	100%
Total	Count	12	15	9	11	5	19	10	20	2	60
	% of Total	20%	25%	15%	18%	8%	32%	17%	33%	3%	100%

Table 8.56 Nature of Complaints by Judicial Officers to Regulators in All the Six Zones

Region		*Not Being Prepared for the Arguments*	*Being Late for Attending the Courts*	*Seeking Many Adjournments*	*Not Protecting the Interests of Beneficiaries*	*Quality of Arguments*	*Not Interacting With Clients*	*Total*
North	Count	0	1	1	1	2	0	5
	% of Total	0%	20%	20%	20%	40%	0%	100%
West	Count	1	0	0	0	0	0	1
	% of Total	100%	0%	0%	0%	0%	0%	100%
South	Count	0	1	1	0	1	0	3
	% of Total	0%	33%	33%	0%	33%	0%	100%
Central	Count	1	0	0	0	0	1	2
	% of Total	50%	0%	0%	0%	0%	50%	100%
Total	Count	2	2	2	1	3	1	11
	% of Total	18%	18%	18%	9%	27%	9%	100%

8.2.9. Beneficiaries' Rationale for Opting for Free Legal Aid

As shown in Table 8.57, in each zone, more than 70% (77%) of beneficiaries responded they had opted for FLAS because they did not have enough resources to engage a PLP for their cases. Per data collected, in total, 2,284 out of 3,029 beneficiaries (i.e., around 75% of beneficiaries) responded that they did not have ample resources to get a PLP for their respective cases. Indeed, as shown in Figure 8.53, beneficiaries were clear about their rationale for taking up legal aid.

To weigh in the rationale of opting for legal aid services, respondents were asked a similar question about the willingness or unwillingness to opt for the legal aid services. As seen in Table 8.57, around 70% (67%) of unaware women were willing to opt for FLAS only because they did not have proper resources in the North Zone. Similarly, unaware women from the North Zone (72%), East Zone (66%), West Zone (61%), South Zone (65%), Central Zone (74%), and North East Zone (73%) were willing to opt for FLAS

Table 8.57 Beneficiaries' Rationale for Opting for Free Legal Aid

		North	*East*	*West*	*South*	*Central*	*North East*	*India*
No Resource to Engage a Private Lawyer	Count	421 / 545	418 / 520	321 / 437	622 / 866	266 / 380	236 / 281	2,284 / 3,029
	% of Total	77%	80%	73%	72%	70%	84%	75%

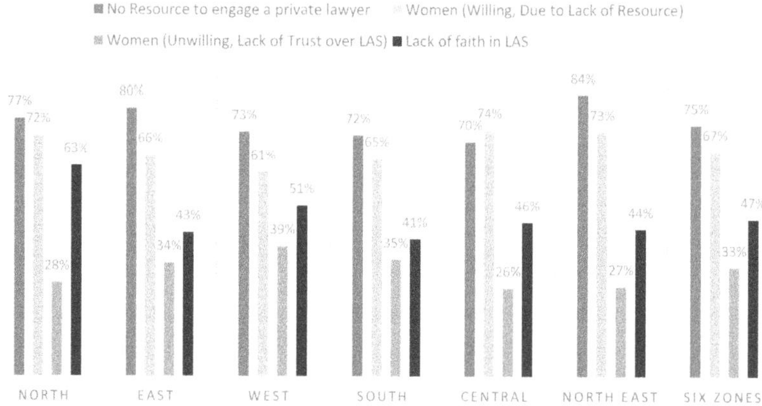

Figure 8.53 Comparative Assessment of Rationale for Opting and Not Opting for Legal Aid in the Six Zones

Table 8.58 Unaware Women's Opinion About Opting for Free Legal Aid

Opinions		*North*	*East*	*West*	*South*	*Central*	*North East*	*India*
Women (Willing, due to Lack of Resources)	Count	661	1,083	817	1,757	1,064	360	5,742
	% of Total	72%	66%	61%	65%	74%	73%	67%
Women (Unwilling, due to Lack of Trust in the LAS)	Count	258	558	520	945	383	133	2,797
	% of Total	28%	34%	39%	35%	26%	27%	33%

Table 8.59 Lack of Faith as Reason for Not Opting for Free Legal Aid

		North	*East*	*West*	*South*	*Central*	*North East*	*India*
Lack of Faith in the LAS	Count	290	194	176	352	161	62	1,235
	% of Total	63%	43%	51%	41%	46%	44%	47%

due to lack of resources. As a result, in Figure 8.53, around 67% of unaware women from all the six zones were willing to opt for free legal aid because of lack of resources.

Table 8.58 also reflects the other part of the hypothesis. Lack of trust and faith in the LAS was one of the main reasons for not opting for legal aid among the unaware women. Therefore, in each zone, the unaware women were also unwilling to opt for free legal aid. The reason these unaware women gave was broadly related to a lack of trust and faith in the LAS.

This empirical study also asked the same questions from aware entitled women respondents for free legal aid and yet opted out of it to support the unaware, unwilling women's response. As shown in Table 8.59, in the North Zone, 63% of women respondents responded they did not opt for free legal aid because they did not have any trust or faith in the

LAS. Similarly, most aware women respondents in the East Zone (43%), West Zone (51%), South Zone (41%), Central Zone (46%), and North East Zone (44%) opined they did not opt for free legal aid as they did not have any trust or faith in the LAS.

Undoubtedly, as shown in Figure 8.53, the inputs from the beneficiaries and unaware women respondents and aware women respondents (who did not opt for legal aid services) elucidated that people or potential beneficiaries had no faith in the LAS; thus, they opted for free legal aid out of compulsion.

8.2.9.1. Hypothesis: Ineffective Control and Monitoring of LACs Has Degraded the Quality of Legal Aid Services

In any system, the institution of a mechanism related to checks and balances makes the system more efficient and accountable. In India's case of FLAS, the LACs can get a warning, they can also get removed, or they can even get replaced in exceptional cases, although the mechanism seems to be ineffective. For instance, the SLSAs or the respective bar councils of the states and in India have hardly penalized any LACs for demanding money from the beneficiaries. Further, to remove any LAC from the case, prior permission from the DLSAs under the SLSA is mandatory.

Additionally, LACs can also resign or refuse to even consider allotted cases or can easily withdraw from the cases under legal aid at any time. In such instances, the legal aid services regulators do not have adequate mechanisms to regulate the services. As a result, beneficiaries suffer the most.

The NALSA Regulations, 2010, mandates that legal aid authorities and committees be bound to constitute a committee to monitor the conduct and progress of the cases allotted under the legal aid. However, during the field observations, no such monitoring committee was functional in the DLSAs of 36 districts. Further, the DLSAs do not even maintain a proper cause list to track the progress of cases under the legal aid program.

Certainly, the lack of accountability and ineffective monitoring of the LACs have encouraged them to be causal in their approach and often not control their respective beneficiaries. As shown in Table 8.60, more than

Table 8.60 Aware Women's Reason for Opting for a PLP Instead of an LAC

		North	*East*	*West*	*South*	*Central*	*North East*	*Six Zones*
Proper Control Is Possible over Private Lawyer	Count	275/484	364/534	206/360	628/1012	201/411	112/192	1,786/3,003
	% of Total	57%	68%	57%	61%	49%	58%	60%

50% of women were aware of FLAS in every zone and yet opted for a PLP because they could have proper control over their respective PLPs. Certainly, LACs' lack of commitment and failure to listen and interact with their clients have made many potential beneficiaries averse to the very idea of opting for FLAS, even though they are eligible for it.

On the administrative aspects of the accountability in the LAS, the researchers often observed that the front offices of the DLSAs were hard to locate. The DLSA offices did not maintain any record of pending cases and the duration of legal aid cases. At times this research showed that both beneficiaries and judicial officers raise frequent or many adjournments. The inability to maintain pending case lists and their durations demonstrates a lack of accountability and a lack of proper monitoring system in the LAS.

The report also showed homogeneity in terms of complaints registered by beneficiaries to regulators and judicial officers, but these complaints were often verbal or informal.

Per the discussions with the regulators from 36 DLSA offices, not a single regulator admitted that no provisions of written complaints against LACs are in practice. To add to the loopholes, the front offices of the DLSAs did not provide the feedback forms to the beneficiaries.

Thus, no stakeholders, be it beneficiaries, regulators, or judicial officers, were able to regulate LACs to provide quality legal aid services. Further, to acquire the ground realities of India's LAS, the questionnaire consisted of an open-ended question regarding the issues they faced and recommendations to improve the LAS's governance aspect and the non-performance of LACs. The majority of issues related to the LAS were related to LACs not being committed, LACs demanding money, DLSAs not being supportive, and almost no accountability towards beneficiaries, as discussed in previous chapters. In terms of suggestions, judicial officers and beneficiaries broadly endorsed monitoring of LACs, which looks towards the accountability aspects of LACs. Further, they also suggested the need for committed and devoted LACs.

Although there is no dearth of resources in the LAS system, the absence of quality lawyers in legal aid services is the most pressing concern. To add to this problem, the existing regulatory framework also seems inefficient and ineffective in assuring the accountability of the LACs. Hence, a lack of commitment of LACs and the impaired monitoring system have eventually decreased the quality of legal services.

Bibliography

List of Cases

Asmaniya Bai v. State of Madhya Pradesh, Criminal Appeal No. 661 of 1993.
Bal Bahadur v. Customs Air Customs Officer IGI Airport, New Delhi, CRL.A. 12/2009 & CRL.M (B) No. 23/2009.
Bandhua Mukti Morcha v. Union of India, (1984) 3 SCC 161.
Francis Coralie Mullin v. Administrator, Union Territory of Delhi, (1981) 2 SCR 516.
Hussainara Khatoon v. Home Secretary, State of Bihar, AIR 1979 SC 1369.
Imtiyaz Ramzan Khan v. State of Maharashtra, 2018 (9) SCC 160.
Janardhan Reddy v. State of Hyderabad and Ors., AIR 1951 SC 217.
Joydeep Mukharjee v. State of West Bengal & Others, AIR 2011 SC 1169.
Khatri and Ors. (II) v. State of Bihar, (1981) 1 SCC 635.
Madhav Hayawadanrao Hoskot v. State of Maharashtra, (1978) 3 SCC 544.
M. C. Mehta v. Union of India, (1986) 2 SCC 176.
Mumbai Kamgar Sabha v. M/s Abdulbhai Faizullabhai and Others, AIR 1976 SC 1455.
Olga Tellis v. Bombay Municipal Corporation, (1985) 3 SCC 545.
People's Union for Democratic Rights v. Union of India, AIR 1982 SC 1473.
Ram Awadh v. State of Uttar Pradesh, 1999 CriLJ 4083.
Ramchandra Nivrutti Mulak v. State of Maharashtra, Criminal Appeal No. 487 of 2008.
Rural Litigation and Entitlement Kendra Dehradun & Ors. v. State of UP & Ors., 1985 SCR (3) 169.
Sheela Barse v. Union of India, AIR 1983 SC 378.
State of Gujarat v. Manjuben D/O Kasturbhai, R/Criminal Confirmation Case No. 1 of 2018.
Sudhakar Tiwari v. State, Criminal Appeal No. 875 of 2011.
Suk Das v. Union Territory of Arunachal Pradesh, (1986) 4 SCC 401.
Sunil Batra v. Delhi Administration, AIR 1978 SC 1675.
Sunil Damodar Gaikwad v. State of Maharashtra, Criminal Appeal Nos. 165–166 of 2011.
Tara Singh v. State of Punjab, AIR 1951 SC 411.
Upendra Baxi v. State of Uttar Pradesh, (1983) 2 SCC 308.

Books

Krishnaswami, P.; *VR Krishna Iyer – A Living Legend*, Universal Law Publishing, 2008.
Mittal, Raman; Sreemithun, K. V.; *Legal Aid: Catalyst for Social Change*, Satyam Law International, 2012.

Mukherjee, Roma; *Women, Law and Free Legal Aid in India*, Deep & Deep, 2000.
Murlidhar, S.; *Law, Poverty and Legal Aid*, LexisNexis Butterworths, 2004.
Narayan, P. S.; *Law Relating to Lok Adalats and Legal Aid*, Orientation Publication, 2008.
Paranjape, N. V.; *PIL, Legal Aid and Services, Lok Adalats and Para Legal Services*, Central Law Agency, 2010.
Patel, Bimal N.; *A Comprehensive Guide of Laws of Human Rights in Commonwealth Countries*, Wadhwa Publications, 2007.
Rai, Kailash; *PIL Lawyering, Legal Aid and Para Legal Service*, Central Law Agency, 2005.
Rao, Mamta; *Public Interest Litigation – Legal Aid and Lok Adalats*, Eastern Book Company, 2015.
Regan, Francis, Paterson, Alan; Fleming, Donald; Goriely, Tamara; *The Transformation of Legal Aid: Comparative and Historical Studies*, Oxford University Press, 1999.
Sarkar, S. K.; *Law Relating to Lok Adalats and Legal Aid*, Orient Publishing Company, 2010.
Sehgal, Justice Sangita Dhingra; *Commentary on the Legal Services Authorities Act*, Universal Publishing Co., 2012.
Sharma, S. S.; *Legal Services, Public Interest Litigations & Para-Legal Services*, Central Law Agency, 2007.
Singh, Sujan; *Legal Aid Human Right to Equality*, Deep & Deep Publications, 1996.
Swaroop, R.; *Law Relating to Legal Aid and Lok Adalat*, Asia Law House, 2003.

Articles

Desai, A. H.; Role and Structure of Legal Profession, *Journal of Bar Council of India*, 112, 1981.
Fleming, Don; *Legal Aid and Human Rights*, Paper presented to the International Legal Aid Group Conference, Antwerp, June 2007.
Gordon, Richard K.; & Lindsay, Jonathan M.; Law and the Poor in Rural India: The Prospects for Legal Aid, *American University International Law Review*, 5(3), Paper 1, 1990.
Granfield, Robert; The Meaning of Pro Bono: Institutional Variations in Professional Obligations among Lawyers, *Law & Society Review*, 41(1), 2007.
Houseman, Alan W.; Civil Legal Assistance for Low-Income Persons: Looking Back and Looking Forward, *Fordham Urban Law Journal*, 29(3), 2002.
Justice Mathivanan, T.; *Legal Aid Issues, Challenges and Solutions on Empirical Study*, Madras High Court Publication, 2013.
Mallikarjun, G.; Legal Aid in India and the Judicial Contribution, *NALSAR Law Review*, 7, 234, 2013.
Mann, J. S.; Restoring the Trust and Faith of the Beneficiaries over the Legal aid Services in India, *International Journal of Law and Policy*, 2, July 2012, 2015.
Menon, N. R. Madhava; Pal, A. C.; & Mehta, Rupa; Social Justice and the Indian Legal System, *Civil and Military Law Journal*, 41, 2005.
Mukherjee, D. V.; Legal Education for Service to the Poor, *AIR*, 27, 1982.
Pelletier, George A.; Legal Aid in France, *Notre Dame Law Review*, 42, 627, 1967.
Sidhva, Persis; Legal Aid in India: The Need for Strong Laws and High Minds, *Oxford Human Rights Hub Blog*, November 18, 2012.
Singh, Abhay; NALSA Chairman Bats for Giving Institutional Form to Legal Aid Services, *Times News Network*, March 4, 2012.

Singh, J. S., Dr.; Right to Legal Aid: A Human Right Perspective; *Nyaya Deep*, 8(3), 2007.
Times News Network; Sack Lawyers Who Don't Show Up for Poor Clients, *Times News Network*, September 14, 2010.
Times News Network; Top Judges Moot an Idea: Free Legal Aid Could Give Lawyers a Leg Up, *Times News Network*, April 21, 2013.
Tushaus, David W., Gupta, Shailendra Kr. & Kapoor, Sumit; India Legal Aid Clinics: Creating Service Learning Research Projects to Study Social Justice, *Asian Journal of Legal Education*, 2(2), 2015.
Zainulbhai, Tameem; Justice for All: Improving the Lok Adalat System in India, *Fordham International Law Journal*, 34, 248, 2011.

Reports of Committees/Commissions/Other Organisations

14th Report of the First Law Commission 1958, Report 14 Volume-1.
Annual Report 2018 National Legal Services Authority (NALSA).
CHRI; Hope Behind Bars? Status Report on Legal Aid for Persons in Custody, 2018, The Commonwealth Human Rights Initiative (CHRI) 2018.
Client Satisfaction Survey 2007–2013 Australia and Scotland.
Delivering Legal Aid Efficiently and Effectively as part of the Justice system; Business Plan 2014/15, Legal Aid Agency, UK.
Government of India and UNDP-Empirical Research on Access to Justice for Marginalized People, 2011, *A Study of Law School Based Legal Services Clinics*, 2011.
Government of India: *Report of the Expert Committee on Legal Aid, Processual Justice to the People*, May 1993.
Harish Narasappa, Kavya etl. *Access to Justice Survey, Introduction, Methodology and Findings*, DAKSH India 2015–16.
International Conference on Equitable Access to Justice: Legal Aid and Legal Empowerment; Conference Report; 17–18 November 2012, organized by Department of Justice, Government of India and the United Nations Development Programme, New Delhi, India, 2012.
Mann JS, *Final Report of the Research Project on Impact Analysis of the Legal Aid Services Provided by the Empanelled Legal Practitioners on the Legal Aid System in City of Delhi*, Under The University Grants Commission Research Award 2012–14.
Mann JS, *Report of the ICSSR Sponsored Research Project Titled* An Empirical Study to Examine the Impact of the Legal Aid Services Provided by the Legal Aid Counsels on the Quality of the Legal Aid System in India *June 2019*.
MARG, New Delhi Empirical Research Conducted on "*Needs Assessment Study of Selected Legal Services Authorities*" for the UNDP, India, 2012.
Report of *Expert Committee on Legal Aid, Processual Justice to the People*, May (1973) 43.
Report of Expert Committee on Legal Aid, Processual Justice to the People. New Delhi, India, May 1973.
Report of National Legal Services Authority submitted to the Hon'ble Supreme Court of India in the Writ Petition (C) No. 56/2004 titled Prajwala v. Union of India and Others 2015.

Report of the First Law Commission, "Reform on Judicial Administration. India, 1958.

Report on Making Legal Empowerment and Legal Aid More Effective: Interventions through the Project on Access to Justice for Marginalized People, A Workshop organized by Department of Justice (Ministry of Law and Justice, Government of India) and United Nations Development Programme in collaboration with National Legal Services Authority; 14 December 2009, at Indian Law Institute, New Delhi, 2009.

Report on *National Juridicare: Equal Justice- Social Justice*, Government of India, 1977.

The Annual Report 2012–13, Western Australia, for Legal Aid Commission Act 1976.

The Council for Social Development (CSD) -*Legal Awareness and Access to Justice for the Marginalised Sections*, March 2017.

Conventions/Bare Acts/Rules/Regulations

Act on Advisory Assistance and Representation for Citizens with a Low Income, Denmark, 1980.

African Charter on the Rights and Welfare of the Child, 1990.

Canadian Charter of Rights and Freedom, Constitution Act 1982.

Civil Procedure Act, Republic of Korea, 2016.

Code of Civil Procedure, Germany, 2005.

Complementary Law No.80/1994, Brazil.

Comprehensive Legal Support Act, Japan, 2004.

Convention against Torture and Other Cruel, Inhuman or Degrading Treatment or Punishment, 1984.

Convention on International Access to Justice, 1980.

Criminal Procedure Law of the People's Republic of China 2018.

Disabilities (Equal Opportunities, Protection of Right and full participation) Act, 1995.

District Legal Services Authority Regulations, 1998.

German Code of Criminal Procedure,1987.

Immoral Traffic (Prevention) Act, 1956.

Implementation of Comprehensive Legal Support by the Japan Legal Support Centre. 2004.

International Convention on the Protection of the Rights of All Migrant Workers and Members of Their Families, 1999.

International Covenant on Civil and Political Rights, 1966.

Juvenile Justice Act, 1986.

Lawyers Law of the People's Republic of China 2017.

Legal Aid Act 1986, Scotland.

Legal Aid Act 1989, Nova Scotia. Canada.

Legal Aid Act, 2011 Federal Republic of Nigeria.

Legal Aid Act, 2054, Nepal.

Legal Aid Act, Republic of Korea, 2008.

Legal Aid, Advice and Assistance (Northern Ireland) Order 1981.

Legal Aid Manual. Legal Aid Council South Africa, 2017.

Legal Aid Services Act, 1998, SO 1998. Canada.
Legal Aid Services Act, 2000, Bangladesh.
Legal Profession Act 1998, British Columbia.
Legal Services Authorities Act, 1987.
Legal Services Corporation Act, 1974, the US.
Legal Services Society Act, British Columbia, 2002.
Legal Services Society Act, Yukon. Canada, 2002.
Mental Health Act, 1987.
National Legal Services Authority (Legal Aid Clinics) Regulations, 2011.
New Brunswick Legal Aid Act. 2014, Canada.
New Brunswick Regulation 2017. Canada
Northwest Territories Legal Aid Act. Canada.
People's Republic of China. Legal Aid Regulations 2003.
Public-Service Advocates Act, Republic of Korea, 1994.
The Act on Special Cases Concerning the Punishment, etc. of Sexual Crimes, Republic of Korea, 2010.
The Act Respecting Legal Aid and the Provision of Certain Other Legal Services. Canada, 2010.
The African Commission on Human and People's Rights, 1990.
The American Convention on Human Rights 1969.
The Board, Legal Aid (Scotland) Act 1986.
The Code of Civil Procedure 1908.
The Code of Criminal Procedure, 1973.
The Constitution of India, 1950.
The Constitution of Kenya, 2010.
The Constitution of Nepal, 2015.
The Constitution of People's Republic of China, 1982.
The Constitution of Socialist Republic of Sri Lanka, 1972.
The Constitution of the Federal Republic of Nigeria, 1999.
The Constitution of the Federative Republic of Brazil, 1988.
The Constitution of the Republic of Korea, 1987.
The Constitutional Court Act, Republic Korea, 1988.
The European Convention of Human Rights 1950.
The Legal Aid Act 2016, Kenya.
The Legal Aid Law No. 27 of 1978. Sri Lanka.
The Legal Aid Manitoba Act. Canada, 1990.
The Legal Services Authorities Act, 1987.
The National Legal Services Authority (Free And Competent Legal Services) Regulations, 2010.
The National Legal Services Authority (NALSA) Child Friendly Legal Services to Children and Their Protection Scheme, 2015.
The National Legal Services Authority (NALSA) Effective Implementation of Poverty Alleviation Schemes Scheme, 2015.
The National Legal Services Authority (NALSA) (Free and Competent Legal Services), 2010.
The National Legal Services Authority (NALSA) Legal Services to Senior Citizens Scheme, 2016.
The National Legal Services Authority (NALSA) Legal Services to the Mentally Ill and Mentally Disabled Persons Scheme, 2015.

The National Legal Services Authority (NALSA) Legal Services to the Victims of Drug Abuse and Eradication of Drug Menace Scheme, 2015.
The National Legal Services Authority (NALSA) Legal Services to the Workers in the Unorganized Sector Scheme, 2015.
The National Legal Services Authority (NALSA) Legal Services to Victims of Acid Attacks Scheme, 2016.
The National Legal Services Authority (NALSA) Protection and Enforcement of Tribal Rights Scheme, 2015.
The National Legal Services Authority (NALSA) Victims of Trafficking and Commercial Sexual Exploitation Scheme, 2015.
The Newfoundland and Labrador Legal Aid Commission. "Legal Aid Act."
The Protection of Persons with Mental Illness and the Improvement of Mental Health Care. General Assembly, United Nations, 1991.
The Protection of Persons with Mental Illness and the Improvement of Mental Health Care, 1991.
The SCLSC Regulations, 1996.
The UK Civil Legal Aid, Legal Aid, Sentencing and Punishment of Offenders Act 2012.
The UN Principles and Guidelines on Access to Legal Aid in Criminal Justice Systems, December 2012.
The Youth Criminal Justice Act, Canada, 2002.

Internet Sources Including Official Websites

Common Cause.
Commonwealth Human Rights Initiative.
Department of Justice, Canada. "Legal Aid Program."
Human Rights Law Network.
Japan Legal Support Centre. "Civil Legal Aid."
Korea Legal Aid Corporation.
Legal Aid Commission of Sri Lanka.
Ministry of Law and Justice, Government of India
National Legal Services Authority
Office of the High Commissioner for Human Rights
State Legal Services Authorities.

Index

For Product Safety Concerns and Information please contact our EU representative GPSR@taylorandfrancis.com
Taylor & Francis Verlag GmbH, Kaufingerstraße 24, 80331 München, Germany

www.ingramcontent.com/pod-product-compliance
Ingram Content Group UK Ltd.
Pitfield, Milton Keynes, MK11 3LW, UK
UKHW020146200926
475702UK00005B/938
* 9 7 8 0 3 6 7 7 0 3 3 8 7 *